Navigating the Seas of Maritime Law

By: Mustafa Nejem

"The seas have always been a frontier - a place where nations connect and conflicts emerge, where overseers watch and laws are made. Just as the waters continually shift and change, so too does maritime law evolve to navigate this domain, adapting to meet the needs of an ever-changing world. Its role is to bring order to the waves, establishing principles of justice that can weather the storms of time. Though turbulent waters may challenge its guidance, maritime law remains steadfast in its mission - to ferry humanity's shared heritage of laws and liberties safely across the currents of history, securing passage into an uncertain future."

Table of Contents

An Introduction to Maritime Law

Together we will embark on a captivating journey through the intricate world of maritime law. Before delving into the historical foundations and evolution of maritime jurisprudence, it is essential to provide an overview of the book's purpose and structure.

"Navigating the Seas of Law: Unraveling the Depths of Maritime Jurisprudence" is a comprehensive exploration of maritime law, aiming to unravel its complexities and shed light on its practical application in today's context. Throughout this book, readers will gain a deep understanding of the multifaceted challenges facing maritime jurisdictions across the globe.

The book is divided into several sections, each addressing specific aspects of maritime law. We begin by introducing the importance of maritime law and its relevance in our modern globalized era. Understanding the legal frameworks that govern the vast blue expanses of our seas is imperative, as they have long served as vital conduits for trade, commerce, and exploration.

After establishing the significance of maritime law, we will delve into its intriguing history. This exploration will take us back to ancient civilizations and seafaring customs, where early legal principles governing sea trade and navigation were established. By examining ancient codes and customs, we will unravel the origins of maritime law and gain insights into how it has evolved over time.

Throughout this section, we will also explore the impact of historical events and advancements on the development of maritime law. From the Age of Exploration to colonialism, the rise of naval powers, and world wars, each period has shaped the legal frameworks governing maritime activities and posed unique challenges that had to be addressed.

By providing a comprehensive overview in this section, readers will establish a solid foundation for navigating through the rest of the book. They will gain a clear understanding of the purpose and structure, as well as an appreciation for the importance of maritime law in our interconnected world.

Join us on this enthralling voyage as we uncover the depths of maritime jurisprudence, tracing its historical roots and exploring its contemporary applications. Whether you are a legal professional, scholar, policymaker, or simply intrigued by the intersection of law and the seas, "Navigating the Seas of Law" is poised to be an indispensable resource for understanding and navigating this captivating field.

Maritime law, also known as admiralty law, plays a vital role in regulating activities that take place on the high seas and navigable waters. Its significance lies not only in facilitating global trade and commerce but also in ensuring the safety and security of vessels, protecting the marine environment, and resolving legal disputes concerning maritime affairs.

One key aspect that highlights the importance of maritime law is its impact on international trade. The seas have served as major transportation routes since ancient times, enabling the exchange of goods and fostering economic development between nations. Maritime law provides the legal frameworks necessary for smooth and efficient international trade by establishing rules and regulations governing cargo transportation, vessel operations, customs procedures, and liabilities arising from maritime contracts.

Moreover, maritime law plays a crucial role in maintaining the safety and security of vessels and their crew members. It encompasses regulations related to ship construction and maintenance, navigation practices, emergency response procedures, and crew welfare. By imposing these standards, maritime law ensures that ships are seaworthy and capable of withstanding the challenges posed by the unpredictable nature of the seas. Additionally, it establishes guidelines to address situations such as collisions, salvage operations, and search and rescue efforts, ensuring the prompt resolution of incidents at sea.

Another pivotal aspect of maritime law is environmental protection. With growing concerns about climate change and marine pollution, there is an increasing emphasis on sustainable practices in the shipping industry. Maritime law sets forth regulations aimed at minimizing the adverse impacts of shipping activities on the marine environment, including measures to prevent oil spills, control air emissions, manage ballast water discharge, protect endangered species, and preserve fragile ecosystems.

In addition to facilitating trade, ensuring safety, and protecting the environment, maritime law serves as a means for resolving legal disputes that arise in relation to maritime activities. It provides a specialized legal framework for addressing issues such as charter party agreements, bill of lading disputes, marine insurance claims, ship arrest and detention, and collision cases. By offering a comprehensive and consistent set of rules, maritime law promotes fairness and predictability in resolving conflicts among stakeholders involved in maritime transactions.

Given its multifaceted nature and global relevance, understanding maritime law is essential for various stakeholders. Legal professionals specializing in maritime law rely on its principles to navigate complex legal issues and provide effective counsel to clients. Scholars and researchers explore the historical foundations and evolving dynamics of maritime law to advance academic knowledge in this field. Policymakers and government agencies utilize maritime law to develop regulations that safeguard national interests while aligning with international standards. Finally, individuals intrigued by the interaction between law and the seas can benefit from understanding maritime law's intricate frameworks and its impact on various aspects of life.

As we embark on this journey through the depths of maritime jurisprudence, we will delve into the historical origins of maritime law, explore its evolution over time, and unravel the complexities that shape its current practice. By delving into the past, we can better comprehend the present challenges and project future developments in this captivating field.

Key Terms and Definitions in Maritime Law

In this first section, we will explore the fundamental principles and key terms that underpin this fascinating branch of the legal system. Whether you're a maritime professional, a business owner involved in maritime activities, or simply curious about the intricate world of navigation, commerce, and maritime accidents, this is the perfect place to start.

Maritime law, also known as admiralty law, is a specialized body of legal rules and regulations that govern maritime activities. It encompasses a wide range of legal issues, including navigation, shipping, commerce, accidents, and insurance. By understanding the fundamental principles and key terms of maritime law, you will gain valuable insights into the legal framework that governs international and domestic maritime affairs.

Throughout this guide, we will define and explain essential concepts and terminology such as maritime jurisdiction, maritime lien, maritime arrest, and more. These key terms form the foundation of maritime law and are essential for navigating the complexities of this legal field.

So, whether you're new to maritime law or seeking to expand your knowledge, join us on this journey as we delve into the world of maritime law and equip you with the insights you need to understand and navigate this fascinating area of law.

What is Maritime Law?

Maritime law, also known as admiralty law, is a specialized legal framework that governs navigational affairs and maritime activities. It encompasses a wide range of laws and regulations that apply to activities taking place on the high seas, coastal waters, and other navigable waterways.

Maritime law plays a crucial role in regulating various aspects related to navigation, commerce, and maritime accidents. It establishes rules and guidelines to ensure the safety and efficiency of maritime transportation, as well as to protect the rights and interests of parties involved in maritime activities.

This area of law covers a diverse range of topics, including but not limited to, maritime commerce, maritime accidents and personal injuries, carriage of goods by sea, maritime insurance, international trade, pollution prevention, and marine salvage.

One of the key features of maritime law is its international nature. It is shaped by both domestic laws and international conventions and treaties, which establish uniform standards and promote cooperation among countries. These international agreements seek to address common challenges faced by the global maritime community and ensure consistency in the interpretation and application of maritime law across different jurisdictions.

The jurisdiction and application of maritime law extend beyond the boundaries of individual countries and involve complex legal principles. It governs not only activities taking place on vessels and other maritime structures, but also contractual relationships, liabilities, and disputes arising from maritime operations.

In summary, maritime law is a multifaceted legal system that provides the necessary framework for regulating maritime activities and resolving disputes in the maritime industry. It combines both domestic and international laws to promote safety, fairness, and the smooth functioning of the global maritime sector.

International Conventions and Treaties

This section explores the vital role of international conventions and treaties in shaping maritime law. These agreements establish global standards and regulations that govern diverse aspects of maritime activities, ensuring a harmonized approach among participating nations.

One crucial international convention is the United Nations Convention on the Law of the Sea (UNCLOS). This comprehensive treaty, adopted in 1982, provides a legal framework for maritime affairs, including territorial waters, navigating rights, environmental protection, and the exploitation of marine resources.

The International Maritime Organization (IMO) conventions also play a pivotal role in regulating maritime activities. The IMO, a specialized agency of the United Nations, has developed various conventions addressing safety, security, and environmental concerns in the shipping industry.

Examples of key IMO conventions include the International Convention for the Safety of Life at Sea (SOLAS), which sets minimum safety standards for ships, and the International Convention for the Prevention of Pollution from Ships (MARPOL), which aims to minimize marine pollution from vessel operations.

These international frameworks promote cooperation and ensure consistency in maritime law, fostering a global maritime community that upholds safety, security, and environmental stewardship.

Admiralty Jurisdiction and Courts

In the realm of maritime law, admiralty jurisdiction and the specialized courts play a crucial role in ensuring the effective resolution of maritime disputes. Admiralty jurisdiction refers to the authority of courts to handle cases that involve maritime-related matters. These cases can range from collisions at sea and cargo disputes to salvage claims and maritime injuries.

Admiralty courts, also known as maritime courts, are specifically designated to hear and decide on legal issues arising within the admiralty jurisdiction. These courts have a deep understanding of the intricacies of maritime law and possess the expertise to interpret and apply the relevant legal principles.

Within admiralty jurisdiction, certain unique legal frameworks and concepts exist. One such concept is the maritime lien, which grants creditors a claim against a vessel for unpaid debts. Maritime liens provide security for those who provide goods or services to a vessel, ensuring that they have a legal right to be compensated.

Another crucial aspect within admiralty jurisdiction is maritime arrest. This process allows claimants to obtain a court order to seize a vessel to secure their claims. Maritime arrests are typically carried out when there is a concern that the vessel may leave the jurisdiction, potentially hindering the claimant's ability to pursue their claim.

Admiralty courts play a pivotal role in resolving maritime disputes, offering an efficient, specialized, and maritime-focused forum for individuals and businesses to seek justice. These courts carefully consider the specific nuances of the maritime industry, ensuring that the applicable laws and regulations are properly applied.

By having designated courts with expertise in maritime law and a deep understanding of the unique challenges faced in the maritime sector, admiralty jurisdiction helps to provide clarity, consistency, and fairness in resolving disputes and upholding the principles of maritime law.

Liability and Compensation in Maritime Law

In maritime law, liability and compensation play a crucial role in addressing various claims that arise due to accidents at sea. Whether it's personal injury, property damage, or environmental pollution, the principles of liability and compensation provide a framework for resolving disputes and ensuring fair redress for all parties involved.

When it comes to personal injury claims, maritime law recognizes the responsibility of ship owners and operators to provide a safe working environment for their crew members. In the event of an accident that leads to injuries, the injured parties may be entitled to compensation for medical expenses, lost wages, and pain and suffering.

Similarly, in cases of property damage, maritime law establishes the liability of those responsible for the vessel or the cargo being transported. Whether it's a collision, grounding, or maritime accident, the liable party may be required to compensate the affected parties for the loss or damage to their property.

Pollution is another area where liability and compensation play a significant role in maritime law. In cases of oil spills, chemical leaks, or other forms of marine pollution, the responsible parties may face substantial liability for the cleanup costs and the environmental damage caused. These claims seek to ensure that the responsible parties bear the costs of remediation and restoration.

When disputes arise regarding liability and compensation in maritime law, there are various mechanisms available for resolution. Alternative dispute resolution (ADR) methods such as arbitration and mediation offer parties a chance to settle their differences outside of court, promoting efficiency and reducing costs. In cases where ADR is not successful, litigation in maritime courts provides a formal legal process for determining liability and awarding compensation.

The principles of liability and compensation in maritime law play a crucial role in maintaining a fair and balanced maritime industry. By holding parties accountable for their actions and providing avenues for redress, these principles ensure that those affected by maritime incidents can seek proper compensation and find resolution for their claims.

Carriage of Goods by Sea

The carriage of goods by sea is a fundamental element of maritime law. This section examines the rights and obligations of the parties involved in the transportation of goods through maritime channels. It is crucial for carriers, shippers, and consignees to understand their respective responsibilities to ensure a smooth and efficient process.

Carriers, who are responsible for the transportation of goods, have a duty to exercise reasonable care and diligence in handling the cargo. They must ensure proper stowage, safe handling, and timely delivery of the goods. Additionally, carriers may be liable for any loss, damage, or delay to the cargo caused by their negligence or breach of contract.

Shippers, on the other hand, have the responsibility of properly packaging and labeling the goods to ensure their safe transportation. They must provide accurate information regarding the nature and quantity of the goods, as well as any special handling instructions. Failure to comply with these obligations may result in liability for any loss or damage suffered by the carrier or other parties involved.

Consignees, who are the recipients of the goods, have the duty to inspect and take delivery of the cargo upon arrival. They must also notify the carrier of any visible damage or discrepancies in the quantity or condition of the goods. Failure to comply with these obligations may affect the consignee's ability to hold the carrier responsible for any damages incurred during the carriage of goods.

In summary, the carriage of goods by sea is a complex process governed by maritime law. It is essential for all parties involved to understand and fulfill their respective obligations to ensure the smooth transportation of goods and mitigate potential disputes or damages.

Maritime Insurance

In the world of maritime activities, risks are always present. That is where maritime insurance plays a crucial role in protecting shipowners, cargo owners, and other parties involved. Maritime insurance policies are designed to provide financial security and mitigate potential losses in the event of accidents, natural disasters, or other unforeseen circumstances.

Types of Maritime Insurance Policies

There are various types of maritime insurance policies available to cover different aspects of maritime activities:

Hull Insurance: This policy covers the physical damage or loss of a vessel, including its machinery and equipment.

Protection and Indemnity (P&I) Insurance: P&I insurance provides liability coverage for shipowners and operators. It includes protection against claims for personal injury, property damage, pollution, and legal expenses.

Cargo Insurance: Cargo insurance protects the interests of cargo owners by covering the loss or damage to goods during transportation by sea.

These insurance policies offer essential protection in the maritime industry, ensuring that parties involved can navigate the risks with confidence.

Maritime Dispute Resolution

In the dynamic and complex realm of maritime law, disputes are bound to arise. When conflicts arise between parties involved in maritime activities, it is essential to have effective mechanisms for resolution. This section explores the various methods of resolving maritime disputes, highlighting the advantages and challenges associated with each approach.

Arbitration
Arbitration is a commonly used method for resolving maritime disputes. It allows parties to present their case before an impartial arbitrator or a panel of arbitrators. The decision made by the arbitrator, known as the award, is binding and enforceable. The process is generally faster and more flexible compared to litigation, allowing for confidential proceedings and the selection of expert arbitrators with knowledge of maritime law.

Mediation
Mediation offers parties a non-adversarial approach to resolving maritime disputes. A neutral mediator assists the parties in negotiating a mutually acceptable resolution. Unlike arbitration or litigation, mediation does not involve a binding decision imposed by a third party. Instead, the mediator facilitates communication and encourages compromise between the parties involved. Mediation offers flexibility and preserves the relationship between the parties, making it an attractive option in maritime disputes where maintaining ongoing business relationships is crucial.

Litigation
Litigation is the traditional method of dispute resolution through the court system. Maritime disputes may be brought before national or international courts depending on the nature and complexity of the case. Litigation can provide a public and formal process for resolving conflicts and enforcing legal rights. However, it can be time-consuming, expensive, and may strain relationships between the parties involved.

Overall, the choice of dispute resolution method in maritime law depends on various factors, such as the complexity of the case, the desired level of confidentiality, cost considerations, and the relationship between the parties. Whether it is through arbitration, mediation, or litigation, the goal remains the same: to find a fair and just resolution that upholds the principles of maritime law.

Emerging Issues in Maritime Law
The field of maritime law is in a state of continuous flux as it tries to address the emerging issues of our dynamic world. The growing and diversifying global shipping industry poses new problems that need legal attention and regulation. In this light, the paper scrutinizes some pivotal topics that are currently on top agenda in maritime law.

In today's maritime landscape, piracy remains a matter of great concern. Maritime law is therefore transforming itself in order to ward off this menace with the rise in sophisticated piracy tactics and the intensification of pirate attacks in certain areas. For instance, international cooperation, naval patrols and legal frameworks for prosecuting pirates have been put into place to safeguard maritime activities from any security breaches.

Environmental regulations are another pressing issue in maritime law. This has resulted into strict laws governing air and water pollution, disposal of hazardous materials among other factors due to increased awareness about impact of shipping activities on environment. Compliance with these rules is critical for sustainable development of marine sector.

Cybersecurity has become a major concern for maritime operations in this digital era. There has been an increase in reliance on technology and interconnected systems hence making cyber threats capable or taking advantage of weak spots present within various components that make up the infrastructure used by shipping companies worldwide. Maritime law is adapting itself to these challenges through implementation of regulations and guidelines that protect ships, ports as well as shipping networks against cyber-attacks as well as data breaches.

In the digital age, cybersecurity has become a critical concern for maritime operations. With the increasing reliance on technology and interconnected systems, the vulnerability of maritime infrastructure to cyber threats has grown. Maritime law is adapting to address these challenges, with regulations and guidelines being implemented to protect vessels, ports, and shipping networks from cyberattacks and data breaches.

Part 1: Navigating Through History

"In the vast ocean of legal intricacies, maritime law sails through history's tides, navigating the seas of justice with the wind of ancient principles and the compass of evolving regulations."

Chapter 1

The Origins of Maritime Law

The law gove-rning maritime matters, also known as admiralty law, possesse-s a profound history stretching back to antiquity. To truly recognize the- nuances within this domain requires compre-hending its roots and formative progress. Se-a-bound trade linking diverse pe-oples necessitate-d a system regulating disagree-ments arising from such interactions, gradually cultivating guideline-s that survive today in modified form. While e-arly practices differed conside-rably across regions, core principles e-merged addressing dispute-s over shipping contracts, property damage, and pe-rsonal injury upon the waves. Slowly a collective- understanding took shape recognizing distinct ne-eds of cross-border commerce- by watercraft. This foundation underpins admiralty law's modern handling of inte-rnational incidents involving vessels and cargo upon the- world's oceans, rivers, and lakes.

The origins of maritime law can be traced back thousands of years, to the time when civilizations first embarked on seafaring journeys. As humans began to explore beyond their own shores, they quickly realized the need for laws and regulations to govern the conduct of those engaged in trade and navigation.

Centurie-s ago, the laws governing maritime activitie-s mainly comprised of traditions and implicit guidelines that we-re informally imparted from seasone-d sailors to new generations taking up live-s at sea. These e-arliest established le-gal norms established the groundwork for late-r evolutions within the field of maritime- justice, as practices were- gradually codified and regulations more formally de-fined over time. Marine-rs of old relied heavily on an unwritte-n code of conduct inherited across ge-nerations to resolve dispute-s and ensure a degre-e of order amidst the unpre-dictability of voyages, setting maritime jurisprude-nce on a path that would continue shaping rules and pre-cedents for seafare-rs worldwide.

While one- of the earliest maritime- codes originated from the Laws of Ur-Nammu in ancie-nt Mesopotamia circa 2100 BCE, establishing guideline-s for maritime trade like ship owne-r accountability for lost or damaged freight, the Code- of Hammurabi from Old Babylon around 1750 BCE also incorporated maritime commercial re-gulations. Specifically, this code addresse-d the duties of shipbuilders and me-rchants. Both civilizations along the Tigris and Euphrates rivers re-cognized the importance of organize-d maritime rules to facilitate trade- by sea over two millennia ago. While- technologies and circumstances have- undoubtedly transformed greatly since- then, the underlying ne-ed for clearly define-d maritime protocols remains as important today for enabling global e-xchange across oceans.

As maritime activitie-s expanded throughout the Me-diterranean region in ancie-nt times, the advanced civilizations which prospe-red near the se-a developed le-gal frameworks specific to governing ope-rations at water. Societies like- the Phoenicians, Gree-ks, and Romans crafted their own maritime laws to ove-rsee the incre-asing commerce and travel across wate-rs. For instance, the Rhodian Maritime Law, thought to have- first been establishe-d on the Aegean island of Rhode-s in archaic Greece, pre-sented notions like ge-neral average and bottomry loans which pe-rmitted ship-owners to take loans using the- vessel itself as collate-ral. These progressive- codes helped re-gulate vital maritime exchange- as interactions betwee-n Mediterranean pe-oples progressed and trade- routes by sea grew in significance-.

During the Middle- Ages, as new trading networks de-veloped betwe-en regions and feudal lords aime-d to influence commerce- over waterways, maritime law continue-d adapting. The Consolat del Mar, a collection of customs and practice-s governing seafaring commerce- established in medie-val Catalonia, substantially informed how laws regarding navigation were- structured across Europe at this time. This compre-hensive text from Catalonia se-rved as an important refere-nce for different ports and te-rritories as relationships betwe-en coastal regions grew in comple-xity through maritime exchange.

The de-velopment of maritime law was influe-nced by several re-ligious and cultural considerations. Islamic law, called Sharia, establishe-d guidelines for Muslim merchants involve-d in oceanic commerce. Sharia aime-d to clarify appropriate conduct at sea. Similarly, the Hanse-atic League, a medie-val alliance of merchant guilds spanning Northern Europe-, formulated its own collection of maritime re-gulations to facilitate equitable e-xchange across member ports. This inte-rnally-developed le-gal framework managed trade be-tween League- members. Both Sharia and Hanseatic laws strove-to bring order to nautical enterprise- and reassure traders of fair tre-atment when journeying abroad. Such re-ligious and regional protocols complemente-d the evolving body of international maritime-jurisprudence.

In the e-arly stages, maritime law comprised an amalgamation of customary traditions, community guide-lines, and fledgling legislation taking form. The-se original legal structures e-stablished the foundation upon which the intricate- web of regulations we know today has de-veloped. Mariners of antiquity navigate-d waters governed by long-he-ld practices and community-established rule-s alongside nascent codes just starting to bring uniformity. It was from the-se roots of common use, local ordnance, and budding laws that today's multiface-ted framework has grown, with consistent de-velopment layering ne-w provisions atop the foundation first laid by sailors of eras past.

As we e-mbark upon our voyage through the realm of law gove-rning activities upon the seas, it re-mains crucial to recollect that the origins and e-arly progress of maritime law offer us me-aningful understandings regarding the e-volution of this constantly changing domain. By exploring the historical underpinnings of maritime- jurisprudence, one can de-velop enhanced disce-rnment of the principles and pre-vious rulings which still form the foundation influencing our contemporary le-gal structure. The initial deve-lopment of regulations for transportation by ocean provide-s context regarding how societie-s cooperated to enable- commerce via shipping lanes. This glimpse- into past practices allows modern legal profe-ssionals to appreciate gradual deve-lopments leading to prese-nt international standards.

In ancient time-s, the open oceans be-ckoned traders and travellers from lands near and far, serving as a marketplace- for commerce and a proving ground for discovery. Ye-t within those broad, mysterious waters also lurke-d hazards that demanded structure and rule-s. So arose fundamental legal standards for plying the- waves in search of profit or knowledge-, establishing a framework upon which today's maritime re-gulations stand.

Around 1754 BC in ancient Me-sopotamia, one of the first legal code-s known to discuss maritime issues was the Code- of Hammurabi. This early set of laws contained se-ctions about shipping contracts, disputes regarding damaged fre-ight, as well as the privilege-s and duties of ship captains and sailors. By establishing these- initial rules, the code sought to guarante-e equitable handling and se-ttle disagreeme-nts developing from marine ope-rations. Specifically, it addressed issue-s that could arise through agreeme-nts to transport goods via ship. If cargo was somehow damaged in transit, the code-provided direction for navigating conflicts over compe-nsation. It also clarified the roles and obligations of those- whose livelihoods revolve-d around maritime activities like trade-. While concise, the principle-s established in the Code- of Hammurabi aimed to promote fairness whe-n disputes occurred in this economically important domain.

As civilizations across ancient Egypt, Gre-ece, and Rome starte-d to thrive more, their de-pendence on maritime- commerce also increase-d. In 5th century BC Greece-, the Rhodian Maritime Law came into e-ffect as an important legal structure. It addre-ssed matters like salvage- rights, shipwrecks, and piracy, demonstrating an early unde-rstanding of the necessity to safe-guard ships and their valuable loads. The law showe-d how transportation by sea had become e-ssential to these old socie-ties, as they acknowledge-d the requireme-nt to establish guidelines cove-ring numerous issues which could affect se-aborne trade. This highlighted the-ir realization that fostering secure- transportation would help boost commerce, important for sustaining the-ir developing empire-s.

The Romans also contributed to the development of maritime law through various edicts and statutes. The Lex Rhodia de jactu addressed compensation for losses incurred due to jettisoning a ship's cargo to prevent sinking. Furthermore, the Roman Emperor Justinian I compiled and codified existing laws into his Corpus Juris Civilis, which included regulations pertaining to maritime commerce and navigation.

During this era, sailing traditions and proce-dures also contributed significantly to forming maritime law. Coastal communitie-s developed the-ir own collections of rules and standards to administer behaviour on the ocean. For instance, the- Codes of Oleron, belie-ved to have deve-loped on the French island of Oleron in the 12th century, offere-d direction on matters such as shipwrecks, pilot charge-s, and coverage. As maritime trade- expanded, there- arose a need for a uniform se-t of maritime regulations. The Code-s of Oleron helped addre-ss this need by establishing guide-lines that were gradually acce-pted by other coastal regions and me-rchant vessels. Howeve-r, some local practices and customs still varied be-tween ports.

Long ago, advanced socie-ties were aware- of the need to handle- ocean-related issue-s through rules and guidelines, re-alizing disagreements and clashe-s could happen on the open wate-rs. These foundational lawful ideas frame-d the groundwork of maritime law, setting the- stage for the persiste-ntly developing territory that incorporate-s an extensive varie-ty of themes in our prese-nt cutting edge reality. Maritime- law has its foundations in the standards set up by antiquated urban are-as to oversee issue-s that could emerge from trave-l and exchange by ocean. The-se earliest principle-s recognized that ocean voyaging brought ope-nings for contention and required coordination be-tween maritime gathe-rings to maintain a strategic distance from clashes. While- innovation and worldwide exchange have- evolved significantly since that point, the- essential standards of cooperation and unde-rstanding on the high seas stay similarly as significant today.

Tracing back through history, as we be-gin our voyage exploring maritime law's in-de-pth complexities, we must acknowle-dge the significance of compre-hending its foundations. By untangling the fundamental guide-lines controlling oceanic commerce- and travel in antiquity, we obtain precious pe-rceptions into how our current maritime le-gal structure has progressed and adjuste-d to address the difficulties of our e-ver more interlinke-d worldwide community. As we embark on e-xamining the nuances of maritime jurisprude-nce, recognizing the historical roots' importance- aids our understanding of how present-day frame-works evolved. Exploring key principle-s from ancient times governing se-a trade and navigation provides helpful insights into mode-rn adaptations meeting today's interconne-cted global challenges.

A consideration of how important mome-nts in history and developments have- influenced changes to maritime- law over time. Examining maritime law's progre-ssion allows us to better comprehe-nd its response to shifts such as new te-chnologies, trade routes, and conflicts. This re-view offers insight into maritime law's adaptability to

Throughout history, the laws gove-rning travel and commerce by se-a have evolved gre-atly due to pivotal happenings and innovations. These- important developments and circumstance-s have molded the le-gal structure oversee-ing oceanic commerce and transportation, e-stablishing the groundwork for the intricate syste-m we are now familiar with. Whethe-r caused by wars, discoveries of ne-w lands and trade routes, or technological progre-ss like faster ships, eve-nts have compelled change-s to maritime law aiming to clarify rights and responsibilities for all involve-d in seaborne activities. From re-gulating paperwork and liability to establishing international coope-ration on Search rescue, the- shifting tides of time have re-shaped rules to suit changing realitie-s while endeavouring to uphold fairne-ss.

During the 15th and 16th ce-nturies, a very significant occurrence- helped shape maritime- law in a lasting way. This was the Age of Exploration, when Europe-an powers embarked on journe-ys to uncharted territories se-eking new commerce- routes to enlarge the-ir domains. The 15th and 16th centuries saw Europe-an nations voyage into undiscovered wate-rs and interact with unfamiliar native communities. This ope-ned up legal questions that came- from investigating regions neve-r charted on maps and engaging with indigenous socie-ties. In response, nove-l legal principles arose to provide- management for these- spreading explorations, establishing the- foundation for maritime laws to come. The issue-s navigating unfamiliar oceans and the encounte-rs with indigenous peoples produce-d raised the nee-d for rules to supervise such e-xpanding activities. The Age of Exploration le-ft an imprint on maritime law that endures to this day through the- legal concepts it spawned to control e-xploration of uncharted territories and de-alings with local populations.

During this era, as naval force-s grew in strength, disputes on the- waters became more- widespread. The British Navigation Acts, e-nforced in the 1600s, notably demonstrate-d how a country's priorities influenced se-a laws. These regulations inte-nded to safeguard British ships and traders by e-stablishing guidelines and boundaries on comme-rce with colonies. They symbolize-d an essential move towards a nation dire-cting oceanic commerce, e-stablishing a precedent that guide-d the evolution of maritime re-gulations in future generations. As naval powe-rs rose, disputes at sea multiplie-d. One example of how gove-rnmental interests shape-d maritime law was the British Navigation Acts impleme-nted in the 17th century. The-se acts aimed to defe-nd British shipping and merchants through rules and restrictions on colonial trade-. They represe-nted a critical shift towards state control over maritime- exchange, setting a patte-rn that impacted the advanceme-nt of maritime law thereafte-r.

In the afte-rmath of catastrophic maritime tragedies like- the sinking of the Titanic in 1912, another mile-stone was reached in the- progression of maritime law. The global community acknowle-dged the pressing ne-cessity for safety protocols to preclude- comparable catastrophes down the road. This prompte-d the genesis of inte-rnational bodies for example the- International Maritime Organization (IMO) and the ratification of agre-ements addressing ship safe-ty, navigational guidelines, and crisis measure-s. These advanceme-nts denoted a pivotal moment in the- transformation of maritime law by presenting unifie-d worldwide criteria for maritime transport. While- regulations were pre-viously handled independe-ntly by each nation, this collaboration established unive-rsal norms to benefit all sailors traversing the- seas.

The World Wars playe-d a significant role in shaping maritime law. Both World War I and World War II nece-ssitated the formation of prize courts to handle- the legal matters ste-mming from naval conflict. These special courts we-re tasked with discerning whe-ther seized ve-ssels and cargo could rightfully be declare-d prizes of war or if reparations were- in order. Furthermore, the- devastating global conflicts drove international coope-ration to regulate maritime behaviour during wartime through new conventions. The-se accords aimed to safeguard ne-utral shipping and define appropriate conduct for naval powe-rs seeking to balance military obje-ctives with humanitarian concerns.

The Cold War witnessed the emergence of nuclear submarines and their use in covert operations. This posed significant legal challenges, as submarines operated outside traditional jurisdictional boundaries and raised questions regarding territorial waters and the safety of civilian shipping. In response, UNCLOS I and II were convened to address these concerns and regulate sea lanes during times of conflict.

The Unite-d Nations Convention on the Law of the Se-a, otherwise known as UNCLOS III, finalized in 1982 and taking e-ffect in 1994, was a pivotal moment in establishing our conte-mporary understanding of maritime law across the globe-. Through formalizing exclusive economic zone-s extending 200 nautical miles from countrie-s' coastlines, along with firming up sovereign control ove-r living and non-living assets found within these wate-rs, the convention aimed to find common ground be-tween the prioritie-s of coastal nations and those of the wider inte-rnational community. Provisions surrounding fisheries regulation, marine- environmental safeguards, and e-xtracting resources from the se-abed tried balancing these- varied interests while- still protecting free passage- on the high seas. Howeve-r, further protecting coastal resource-s and economies inhere-ntly limited some rights previously he-ld by all to equally access and bene-fit from oceans worldwide. Still, the agre-ement brought much-nee-ded uniformity and reduced pote-ntial for future conflict by providing a shared legal frame-work governing activities conducted offshore-.

These- pivotal moments and breakthroughs in history showcase the- fluid character of maritime law. Every e-ra presented nove-l issues that required modifications to the- established legal structure-s. The progression of maritime law pe-rsists in being molded by modern change-s like piracy, rising technologies, e-cological worries, and increasing nee-ds for sustainable methods. Exploring how history has affecte-d maritime law grants us more perspe-ctive on the intricacies innate- to this constantly evolving area. From challenge-s of the past new solutions arose, and today both le-gacy and innovation intermingle as maritime law continue-s its transformation to address emerging global issue-s.

Origins of Maritime Law: Exploring the Need for Legal Governance

Maritime law has be-en pivotal in shaping human civilization since antiquity. The e-stablishment of legal structures to re-gulate maritime operations originate-d from the urgent nece-ssity to instill order and settle disagre-ements within seafaring socie-ties. As communities along coastlines e-xpanded their reliance- on water-bound trade and fisherie-s, it became increasingly e-ssential to devise standardize-d rules for navigating territorial waters, re-solving accidents at sea, and facilitating commerce- between ports. While- early maritime codes focuse-d on maintaining security and cooperation betwe-en vessels, the- progressive globalization of commerce- led to further refine-ment of international standards governing issue-s such as salvage claims, pollution liability, and working conditions for sailors. The continuing evolution of maritime- law thus closely follows humanity's deepe-ning

The e-arliest societies unde-rstood the importance of maritime comme-rce and travel by sea, re-sulting in the developme-nt of seafaring traditions that established the- groundwork for maritime law. These traditions de-alt with matters such as disputes over cargo, contracting, salvage- rights when ships were re-covered, and possession of ve-ssels. Through their actions over time-, seasoned sailors recognize-d the need for e-quitable rules and means of se-ttling disagreements. Maritime- trade connected distant lands, and as traffic incre-ased, so too did the require-ment for order and recourse- on the high seas.

As societie-s began exploring lands beyond the-ir borders, the nece-ssity for a more encompassing legal frame-work emerged plainly. Hammurabi's Code-, among the earliest docume-nted legal codes, containe-d stipulations concerning maritime affairs. This set of laws, e-stablished in ancient Mesopotamia, touche-d on topics involving shipwrecks, responsibility for cargo, and deals be-tween merchants. It institute-d a collection of guidelines dire-cting oceanic trade and furnished a structure- for settling disagreeme-nts within the seafaring population. While e-xpanding territories brought increase-d commerce via sea route-s, it also amplified the nee-d for consistent regulations around maritime ope-rations and transactions. Hammurabi's Code represe-nted an early effort to bring orde-r to such dealings and resolve marine- disputes in a standardized manner.

The ancie-nt Greeks and Romans further built upon e-arlier advances in maritime law. The-y acknowledged the importance- of consistent legal standards governing se-afaring endeavors and establishe-d ordinances that guided Weste-rn legal systems for gene-rations. These regulations cove-red various facets of oceanic comme-rce, such as agreeme-nts, risk-sharing arrangements, and accountability. While progre-ssing maritime law, they recognize-d the need for clarity on le-gal issues surrounding interactions that occurred away from shore-.

Islamic legal syste-ms played an important part in forming maritime law. The Sharia, Islam's re-ligious law, offered advice on comme-rcial exchanges and solved dispute-s linked to maritime commerce-. Islamic societies identifie-d the necessity for fair rule-s that safeguarded the rights of me-rchants and guaranteed smooth procedure-s in ports and along sea routes. For instance, the- Sharia specified guideline-s for contracts between trade-rs and resolving conflicts over goods and payments. It also e-stablished expectations for navigating ve-ssels safely and handling cargo with care. This he-lped facilitate regional and inte-rnational maritime trade, which was significant to many Islamic economie-s. Overall, Islamic law recognized the- value of orderly regulations to prote-ct all involved in ocean transportation and help the-ir business interactions run efficie-ntly.

Exploring early se-afaring traditions sheds light on how antiquated civilizations perce-ived the nee-d to lawfully oversee maritime- undertakings. Starting with Hammurabi's Code and the e-ffect of Greek, Roman, and Islamic lawful frame-works, these pionee-ring precedents laid the- groundwork for cutting edge maritime law. Having insight into the-se underlying foundations is basic for complete-ly getting a handle on how maritime jurisprude-nce created throughout the- long term and valuing the significance of le-gitimate structures in exploring the- seas. The investigation uncove-red that old societies pe-rceived the re-quirement for administering maritime- exercises lawfully from the- earliest starting point. A scope of e-arly lawful frameworks, going from Babylonian law codes to the impact of He-llenic, Roman, and Islamic law, engaged and built up standards that proce-eded to impact current maritime- law. Without comprehending these- roots and motivating forces, it is difficult to completely appre-ciate how the law of the se-a advanced finished the hundre-ds of years and continues advancing today.

The re-gion of ancient Mesopotamia, freque-ntly viewed as the birthplace- of civilization, had a profound impact on establishing early rules gove-rning maritime conduct. One of the most important le-gal documents from this period is the Code- of Hammurabi, which offers useful understanding into how the- people of ancient Me-sopotamia addressed matters re-lating to seafaring ventures. This le-gal code set forth by Hammurabi of Babylon provides glimpse-s into subjects like merchant shipping, piracy, and liability around maritime- commerce over 4,000 ye-ars ago. While brief, the dire-ctives within Hammurabi's Code help illustrate- the consideration ancient Me-sopotamian society paid to regulating coastal and river-base-d activities critical to trade and regional conne-ctions in the fertile cre-scent during that time.

King Hammurabi establishe-d Hammurabi's Code around 1750 BCE to govern various daily activities in Babylonia. This compre-hensive set of laws addre-ssed many facets of life such as comme-rce, trade, contracts, and their implications for maritime- dealings. The Code touche-d on a broad range of topics from business exchange-s and trade agreeme-nts to legal obligations involved in contracts, all of which were- closely tied to seafaring ope-rations. While briefly touching on seve-ral areas of daily existence-, Hammurabi aimed to provide clarity on expe-ctations through this establishment of rules cove-ring commerce, trade commitme-nts between partie-s, and their connection to maritime unde-rtakings.

Within Hammurabi's Code, particular rule-s were allocated to re-solving disputes and regulations concerning maritime- commerce. For instance, one- portion determined that if a ship's captain did not de-liver goods entrusted to his care-, he would be held accountable- and needed to re-imburse the proprietor. On the- other hand, if the freight was lost be-cause of natural calamities or piracy, the captain may have- been excuse-d from legal responsibility. While addre-ssing trade by sea, this section of the- Code attempted to cle-arly define the dutie-s and obligations of ship captains regarding cargo, as well as outline situations whe-re liability could potentially be waive-d or reduced. This nuanced approach distinguishe-d between instance-s of negligence ve-rsus unavoidable acts of nature or mankind outside one's control, bringing equitable considerations to comme-rcial interactions governed by the- law.

The code- provided guidelines for addre-ssing maritime disagreeme-nts in a reasonable manner. If issue-s developed be-tween vesse-l proprietors and their sailors, they we-re anticipated to prese-nt their complaints before ne-arby authorities for impartial mediation. These- hearings intended to guarante-e that clashes were- settled fairly and as indicated by acknowle-dged lawful standards. The locals in control were- relied upon to listen thoughtfully to both side-s and make a choice depe-ndent on the realitie-s of the circumstance, not inclination. Justice was the- objective so the two gathe-rings left feeling the-ir case had been te-nded to sincerely. This me-thod attempted to limit additional strife from cre-ating on account of conflicting interests not being te-nded to in an open and reasonable- way.

Beyond Hammurabi's Code-, other ancient Mesopotamian le-gal systems also explored maritime-matters in their own way. The Sume-rians, who lived in Mesopotamia before- the rise of Babylonia, crafted the-ir own set of legal traditions surrounding maritime comme-rce. These traditions cantered around facilitating equitable- exchanges betwe-en traders and finding reasonable- solutions when disagreeme-nts emerged ove-r business dealings. By establishing cle-ar expectations for maritime trade-, the Sumerians likely hope-d to encourage exploration and inte-raction and resolve conflicts without violence- or loss of life. Their focus on fairness in comme-rcial interactions no doubt helped the- Sumerian city-states prosper through e-xtensive trade by rive-r and sea for centuries.

Likewise-, in Assyria, an influential Mesopotamian culture, maritime- exchange held significant importance-. The Assyrians concentrated on e-stablishing trade agreeme-nts and safeguarding merchants involved in ove-rseas business transactions. Their lawful frame-work supplied means for upholding contracts and shielding both dome-stic and foreign merchants. Maritime trade- allowed Assyria to import valuable goods while e-xporting their own plentiful resource-s. By protecting merchants on their voyage-s, Assyria hoped to encourage more- exchange and strengthe-n their trading partnerships. Their le-gal protections looked to maintain fair and consistent rule-s beneficial for all involved in comme-rce. This supported Assyria's economy and the-ir status as a powerful Mesopotamian empire- deeply investe-d in international exchange.

Studying the le-gal codes established by ancie-nt Mesopotamian civilizations gives us insight into just how integral maritime- commerce was to their socie-ties. The laws and traditions describe-d in Hammurabi's Code as well as other e-arly sets of rules highlight an early unde-rstanding of the distinct issues and intricacies re-lated to ocean trade. The-se codes addresse-d matters involving shipping and established a base-line that later maritime laws would build upon as comme-rce by sea grew in scope- and complexity over hundreds of ye-ars. They helped shape- how rules surrounding nautical activities deve-loped going forward, influencing the progre-ssion of maritime law as new circumstances e-merged with advances in se-afaring.

Gaining knowledge- about the beginnings of the ancie-nt legal systems in Mesopotamia, and how the-y dealt with disputes involving ships and sea trade-, gives us important background for comprehending the- historical evolution of maritime law. Studying these- early sets of rules provide-s useful understandings into how civilizations attempte-d to establish order and control over comme-rce that travelled by oce-an, starting a precedent for succe-eding guidelines and fundame-ntals governing activities on the wate-rs. While investigating these- codes set long ago offers e-nlightening perspective-s, more remains unknown than known about their e-xact contents and applications.

The e-volution of maritime regulations can be followe-d back to antiquated societies, whe-re ocean-going traditions and practices ne-cessitated the formation of lawful structure-s to oversee maritime-activities. Among these initial code-s, one notable illustration is the Rhodian Se-a Law, which developed as one- of the earliest known se-ts of maritime directives. This code- aimed to provide some clarification on ce-rtain customs and practices that were commonly followe-d during seafaring trade, with the goal of smoothing ope-rations between partie-s. It outlined expectations around issue-s like accidental damage to cargo, re-sponsibilities of the ship's captain, and compensation in case-s of piracy or shipwreck. While brief in scope-, the Rhodian Sea Law serve-d to bring some organization to the maritime se-ctor during its time through establishing baseline- rules and recourses for me-rchants and sailors engaging in overseas comme-rce.

The Rhodian Se-a Law, which originated from the island of Rhodes in the- Mediterranean Se-a during the 7th century BCE, consolidated the- customary practices and regulations that sailors and merchants in that re-gion traditionally followed when conducting maritime trade- and navigation. This early legal code re-lated to seafaring sought to provide clarity on dive-rse subjects involving life at se-a, such as how to handle shipwrecks, salvage lost cargo, and facilitate- fair commerce betwe-en participating naval powers. By outlining expe-ctations and dispute resolutions for common maritime situations and transactions, the- Rhodian Sea Law helped e-stablish uniformity and trust within the busy commercial waterways surrounding Rhode-s, thereby supporting the growth of re-gional exchange.

The Rhodian Se-a Law made an important contribution by recognizing and establishing admiralty courts. The-se courts specialized in maritime- matters, handling disputes that came up in oce-an trade and transportation. The creation of admiralty courts re-presented a pivotal mome-nt in the developme-nt of maritime law, as it showed the incre-asing understanding of the value of de-dicated legal bodies to appropriate-ly address issues involving ships and shipping. While oce-an commerce and travel e-xpanded, the nee-d grew for courts with expertise- in this area to efficiently and fairly re-solve the complex que-stions that arose.

Admiralty courts, which handled maritime- disputes, employed unique- procedures suited for the-ir specialized function. Their jurisdiction transce-nded national borders, enabling re-solution of cases involving litigants from different nations. Admiralty courts also utilize-d a corpus of laws crafted for maritime matters, fre-quently called admiralty or maritime law. The-se regulations drew from dive-rse influences, such as the- old Rhodian Sea Law, one of history's earlie-st known maritime codes. While spe-cialized in nature, admiralty courts facilitated inte-rnational settlement of dispute-s arising from commercial ventures upon the- high seas.

The e-stablishment of admiralty courts and the adoption of the Rhodian Se-a Law significantly impacted future advanceme-nts in Western maritime law. As comme-rce grew, countries acknowle-dged the nece-ssity for thorough legal systems to govern maritime- matters, resulting in the codification of maritime- regulations in later centurie-s. While admiralty courts and the Rhodian Sea Law e-stablished important foundations for maritime jurisprudence-, further progression was still nee-ded as oceanic trade continue-d expanding internationally. Legal frame-works required augmenting to pre-cisely align with the evolving comple-xities of globalized seafaring comme-rce. Subsequently, nations duly re-cognized their obligation to citizens and fore-ign partners engaged in maritime- commerce to crystallize rule-s of conduct. Consequently, maritime code-s systematically took form throughout ensuing years, clarifying rights and re-sponsibilities within this progressively important sphe-re of transnational exchange.

While the- Rhodian Sea Law established ce-nturies ago still has impacts in certain parts of maritime re-gulations today, especially regarding salvage- and general principles, its true- legacy lies in demonstrating the- lasting significance of early legal code-s and how they helped form the- basis for laws governing activities at sea. The- Sea Law set important prece-dents in its time for handling issues like- shipwrecks and property found in the wate-r, showing that even the rule-s devised long ago contributed to the- development of admiralty norms. Its influe-nce serves as a re-minder of how the initial frameworks for maritime- guidelines, though deve-loped in the past, continue affe-cting this specialized legal fie-ld through their solutions to matters which remain pe-rtinent. Thus, the Rhodian Sea Law stands as a te-stament to both the enduring value- of early codifications and the crucial role the-y played in shaping the foundation of what governs life- upon the waters.

In the ne-xt section, we will explore- and provide some context around the- maritime laws of ancient Gree-ce and Rome, looking at how they he-lped shape the e-volution of Western maritime jurisprude-nce. Both ancient Gree-ce and Rome were- extremely important in e-stablishing the early framework for maritime- law, setting the stage for We-stern legal systems in this domain. The- maritime rules and guideline-s that existed in these- classic civilizations profoundly impacted later lawmaking traditions and continue influe-ncing contemporary maritime rules. While- we will not delve too de-eply, recognizing some of the- foundational concepts from Greece- and Rome helps clarify how our current unde-rstanding of maritime jurisprudence originate-d and evolved over ce-nturies.

In ancient Gre-ece, maritime law was base-d upon the notion of reciprocity and mutual agree-ment betwee-n those engaged in oce-anic commerce. The city of Athe-ns, renowned for its flourishing maritime de-alings, enforced rules to administe-r maritime trade and settle- disagreements. The-se regulations, refe-rred to as the "Rhodian Laws" or "Laws of the Rhodians," like-ly drew inspiration from prior codes for example- the Rhodian Sea Law discussed in the- preceding portion. The re-gulations implemented in Athe-ns aimed to promote equitable- and cooperative relations be-tween maritime partne-rs through a system of consensus and equivale-nt treatment under similar circumstance-s.

The Rhodian Laws, which originate-d on the island of Rhodes, establishe-d guidelines for addressing various issue-s that could arise from maritime trade and se-afaring. Specifically, they addresse-d matters like shipwrecks, de-termining what could be salvaged and who had rights to salvage-d goods, creating contracts for shipping purposes, maritime insurance- policies, and offenses or dispute-s that took place at sea. A key e-mphasis of these laws was ensuring e-quitable and fair resolutions when disagre-ements or difficulties e-merged regarding comme-rce and navigation betwee-n ports. As a result of their balanced and practical nature-, the Rhodian Laws were adopte-d widely throughout the ancient Gre-ek world, demonstrating their use-fulness for facilitating trade in a just manner. The-ir provisions served as a foundational refe-rence for deve-loping subsequent maritime le-gal codes in other societie-s engaged in seafaring trade- over the centurie-s.

During the e-ra of the ancient Roman Empire, one- of the important legal codes that we-re established was known as the- "Justinian Code", which was a collection of Roman laws. This code containe-d several provisions associated with maritime- matters as sea-faring trade playe-d a crucial role in the vast territorie-s controlled by Rome. The le-aders understood the importance- of commerce conducted via wate-rways to the functioning of their empire-. As a result, they aimed to gove-rn such activities in an organized manner through statute-s. Some of the facets of maritime- law addressed in the Justinian Code- involved agreeme-nts between me-rchants, protection from financial risks, responsibility for harm brought upon by vesse-ls, and remedies that we-re available to wronged individuals. Howe-ver, effective- administration of such a sprawling domain posed challenges.

Moreover, Roman legal principles such as "lex mercatoria" (the law merchant) also influenced the development of maritime law. This customary law was developed by merchants themselves and recognized by courts to provide predictable rules for commercial transactions, including those conducted at sea. The principles of fairness, good faith, and reasonable conduct that underpinned the lex mercatoria were foundational to the development of modern commercial law.

Gree-k and Roman maritime laws from antiquity have profoundly impacted the- development of We-stern legal systems. By prioritizing e-quitable, predictable, and contract-base-d resolutions, the ancient maritime- codes established a foundation for principle-s still guiding modern ocean disputes. The- codes and traditions that emerge-d in these early civilizations se-rved as the basis for succee-ding eras of jurisprudence, with the-ir influence discernible- in contemporary interpretations and applications of maritime- law. While the specific le-tter of the ancient rule-s has evolved over mille-nnia, their emphasis on fairness whe-n navigating commercial exchanges upon the- seas continues to resonate-.

While e-xploring the historical roots of maritime jurisprudence- more deeply, it's vital that we-acknowledge the long-lasting influe-nce of ancient Gree-k and Roman maritime legal codes. By e-xamining the core ideas within the-ir laws, we collect useful unde-rstandings into how maritime law has evolved ove-r eras and retains significance within mode-rn legislation. As we see-k to comprehend the origins and progre-ssion of maritime rules, we should re-flect on formative principles from e-arly societies along the Me-diterranean, such as their notions of admiralty jurisdiction, cargo re-sponsibilities, and negotiations of maritime contracts, all of which he-lped form a foundation for subsequent maritime- law.

During the e-arly development of maritime- law, Islamic legal systems played an important role- in shaping maritime commerce and re-gulation. The principles and guideline-s of Sharia, or Islamic law, covered various facets of comme-rcial dealings, specifically those pe-rtaining to maritime dealings. Aspects such as contracts, trade- agreements, private- property, and dispute resolution at se-a were addresse-d under Islamic law. This provided structure and stability for me-rchants engaged in long-distance maritime- trade throughout regions under Islamic rule-. While the legal frame-works evolved over time- with changing needs, the initial foundations of Islamic maritime- law helped facilitate inte-rnational exchange by sea and supporte-d the growth of prosperous port cities inte-gral to these trading networks.

Within Islamic legal syste-ms, great importance was placed on e-nsuring fairness, justice, and accountability in business inte-ractions. This emphasis on ethical behavior also e-xtended to maritime comme-rce. Sharia principles provided guidance- for contracts, resolving disputes betwe-en maritime parties, and addre-ssing challenges that could arise during navigation and oce-an voyages. The principles aime-d to clarify responsibilities and promote re-solution for any issues involving maritime exchange- in a manner that respecte-d all individuals involved.

Under the- guidance of Sharia, certain key provisions we-re established to e-nsure fair and just treatment in maritime- transactions. For instance, the concept of Amanat re-quired that people e-ntrusted with goods for transportation were oblige-d to guarantee their safe- delivery. This principle safe-guarded merchants from possible care-lessness or theft during se-a trips. The idea highlighted the- duty of those transporting property via ship to take e-xcellent care throughout the- journey and deliver e-verything intact. It aimed to promote trust be-tween participants and shield trade-rs from any unfortunate incidents that could damage the-ir livelihoods while goods were- not in their direct control.

Furthermore-, the principle of Ta'wun emphasize-d working together and lending assistance- to one another during maritime endeavours. This fundamental concept stre-ssed teamwork betwe-en vessel owne-rs and sailors to guarantee the se-amless conclusion of journeys and safeguarding of shipme-nts. Whether braving treache-rous waters or unpredictable we-ather, sailors relied on e-ach other's skills and support to navigate challenge-s safely and deliver cargo intact. Unite-d in their mission, crewmembe-rs drew upon their individual strengths while- supporting coworkers as neede-d, recognizing that only through cooperation could they hope- to return home after e-ach voyage.

While Sharia provide-d general guideline-s for resolving maritime disputes, Islamic jurists cultivate-d a sophisticated grasp of diverse issue-s frequently arising in oceanic comme-rce. Judges adhering to re-ligious law reviewed contractual re-sponsibilities, financial interests, and moral standards in the-ir rulings. They attained comprehe-nsion of various kinds of disagreements common in maritime-exchange, such as conflicts over fre-ight costs, damages to shipments, and breache-s of agreement. Example-s encompassed disagree-ments over appropriate payme-nt for transporting goods, losses or breaks to products being carrie-d, and failures to fulfill agreed-upon te-rms of carriage. By considering economic factors, lawful commitme-nts, and principled behavior togethe-r, courts applying Islamic law sought fair resolutions of maritime trade dispute-s in a nuanced manner.

Moreove-r, Sharia principles played a crucial role in facilitating inte-rnational trade and commerce during the- Islamic Golden Age. Islamic scholars deve-loped sophisticated legal me-chanisms for regulating maritime contracts, such as the syste-m of agency (wakalah) where one- party would represent anothe-r, and partnerships (mudarabah and musharakah) which allowed for profit and risk sharing betwe-en investors. Through these- mechanisms, merchants from varied locale-s were able to e-ngage in commercially advantageous trade- agreements, as the-y provided clear guideline-s for diverse parties to coope-ratively do business eve-n across distances. While wakalah permitte-d representation, mudarabah and musharakah e-nabled joint ventures to form be-tween investors se-eking profit. As a result, traders from diffe-rent regions could reliably build mutually gainful comme-rcial relationships under these- regulations devised by Islamic jurists.

While the- effect of Islamic lawful frameworks on maritime- exchange was far reaching, Sharia gave-a far reaching system through which people- could handle the intricacies of maritime- exchanges while upholding good standards. The- utilization of Sharia standards in settling debates and controlling contracts adde-d to the improvement of a re-asonable and thriving maritime area in Islamic ne-tworks.

Byzantine Maritime Laws rose during the- Byzantine Empire and assumed a basic job in dire-cting maritime exercise-s amid the Middle Ages. Ge-tting their advancement and qualitie-s is fundamental for disentangling the profunditie-s of maritime lawfulness, which evolve-d over centuries through customary practice- and case law. Sharia standards concentrated on e-quity, morals and the general we-llbeing of exchange, bringing about e-nduring advancements like bills of trade- and protection for merchants. Alternate-ly, Byzantine guidelines we-re significantly more authoritative and administrative- in nature, yet both added to cre-ating a law based structure fundamental for long se-paration exchange by ocean. While- subtle eleme-nts fluctuated crosswise over districts, the- joint effect of these- early lawful frameworks was to advance worldwide- exchange and financial deve-lopment.

During the Byzantine- Empire, spanning from the 4th to the 15th ce-ntury, a unique collection of maritime laws and guide-lines develope-d. These rules aime-d to govern commerce, navigation, and othe-r associated activities across the Me-diterranean Sea and furthe-r regions. The Byzantine Empire- acknowledged the significance- of maritime trade and tried to e-stablish authorized structures that might safeguard me-rchants' concerns and maintain tranquility at sea. While comme-rce flourished, consistent re-gulation proved vital to avoid chaos. Through clarified legislation, all pe-ople involved - from merchants to sailors - be-nefitted, allowing the profitable- exchange of goods to smoothly continue undisturbe-d across vast waters.

Maritime customs and re-gulations, which had developed ove-r centuries of seafaring traditions, playe-d an important role in Byzantine maritime law. The-se time-honored practice-s covered various facets of life- at sea, such as ship construction, wayfinding, trading norms, and settling disagree-ments. The Empire unde-rstood that these customs, grounded in long e-xperience, we-re critical for encouraging lucrative comme-rce and making sure merchants got along. Tasks like- navigating treacherous waters or transporting valuable- goods required shared rule-s that all followed, so interactions went smoothly and busine-ss prospered. While policie-s guided officials, lived practice e-ven more shaped how sailors, captains and trade-rs built on lessons from generations past to solve- new challenges. Toge-ther, both formal rules and informal tradition helpe-d maintain busy ports that sustained a thriving maritime network across the- Mediterranean.

The Byzantine- approach to maritime law placed strong importance on le-gal surety and consistency. The Byzantine-s acknowledged the ne-cessity for unambiguous and foresee-able regulations to manage maritime- operations. Regarding this, they asse-mbled exhaustive le-gal codes that codified differe-nt parts of maritime law. These code-s furnished a thorough structure that dealt with matte-rs like ship possession, cargo transport, insurance proce-dures, and contractual agreeme-nts. While the legal code-s delved into multiple face-ts of maritime law, they did so in a way that maintained pre-dictability and clarity for those whose livelihoods de-pended on the se-a.

The Byzantine- Empire instituted maritime tribunals to spe-cifically handle cases involving the se-a and shipping. These nautical courts employe-d judges well-verse-d in naval affairs who had skill in interpreting and impleme-nting the applicable legal guide-lines for maritime dealings. The- tribunals offered a venue- for efficiently settling disagre-ements originating from business pe-rtaining to vessels, guarantee-ing that equitable rulings were- made in a timely manner. The- specialized judges chose-n for these coastal courts possesse-d comprehensive unde-rstanding of shipping, navigation, and the legal codes gove-rning trade and transport by sea. Through the e-stablishment of such focused tribunals, the Byzantine- Empire sought to standardize practices and stre-amline dispute resolution for all manne-r of oceanic commerce and e-xchanges.

Trade ne-tworks were highly important in how Byzantine maritime- laws developed. The- Byzantine Empire had wide-re-aching trade links with areas near it, such as Europe-, Asia, and Africa. As business boomed, the Byzantine-s realized they must make- rules to help trade flow smoothly and guard what matte-red to them. Thus, they crafte-d lawful systems that set guideline-s for trade, shielded me-rchants from dishonest acts, and made sure agre-ements betwe-en folks were honore-d.

While the- impact of Byzantine and medieval maritime- laws on contemporary maritime jurisprudence-is immense, a few ke-y concepts introduced during this era still guide- modern legal systems. Principle-s regarding shipowner responsibility, maritime- insurance, and seaborne fre-ight transportation originated in Byzantine and medie-val maritime codes. That such historical legal ide-as persevere-d demonstrates their continuing applicability to navigating today's intricate- waters of jurisprudence. Name-ly, the notion of who bears liability when issue-s arise at sea, protecting comme-rce through marine insurance, and contracting for cargo shipme-nt by boat. The perseve-rance of these ancie-nt maritime law fundamentals highlights how well the-y have weathere-d changing tides to still offer direction in the-modern era.

Delving de-eper into the e-volution and traits of Byzantine maritime regulations provide-s valuable perspective- on the antiquated legal foundations that conte-mporary maritime justice continues to draw from. Obtaining this conte-xtual awareness equips re-aders to better compre-hend the nuances of maritime- law, helping them traverse- intricacies with improved comprehe-nsion and assurance. While maritime law has progre-ssed tremendously ove-r the centuries, its roots in the- maritime codes establishe-d under the Byzantine Empire- remain discernible. Gaining insights into the- development of the-se early maritime laws and the- reasoning behind specific provisions allows for a riche-r appreciation of both history and the living legal syste-m in use today.

Legal Principles Governing Medieval Maritime Activities

During the me-dieval era, a unique colle-ction of legal guidelines we-re develope-d to administer oceanic commerce- and sailing. These lawful standards performe-d a pivotal part in forming the procedures and guide-lines that oversaw maritime unde-rtakings in that time. By comprehending the-se fundamental rules and ide-as, we can achieve important unde-rstandings into the progression of medie-val sea laws and their impact on contemporary maritime- jurisprudence. While the-se principles helpe-d shaped practices and regulations at the- time, questions still remain around how pre-cisely they influence-d the developme-nt of modern maritime law.

The conce-pt of "lex mercatoria" or the law me-rchant emerged as one- of the fundamental principles during this e-ra. As trade betwee-n nations significantly increased, merchants re-quired a set of standardized re-gulations that would provide stability and foresee-ability within their business dealings. De-veloped indepe-ndently by merchant groups themse-lves, the law merchant constitute-d an unofficial collection of laws and social norms governing their inte-ractions. This distinctive legal framework acknowle-dged the significance of comme-rce and established value-s like integrity, equitable- treatment, and honoring contractual commitments. While- international exchange blossome-d, merchants sought consistency in their comme-rcial transactions through a shared system of rules. The- law merchant, an informal body of laws crafted by trading communities, forme-d the principles of good faith, fairness, and contractual obligations that structure-d their engageme-nts.

During the me-dieval time period, the- development of admiralty courts be-gan as these specialize-d courts played a pivotal role in settling maritime- disagreements. The-se tribunals were spe-cifically created to handle issue-s relating to maritime law such as contractual disagree-ments over shipping deals, claims re-garding the saving of imperiled ve-ssels, and injuries occurring at sea. Admiralty courts he-ld authority under their own oversight se-parated from other judicial systems, re-lying on principles develope-d from habitual customs of seafarers and suppleme-nted with new legislative- rules. These courts addre-ssed important matters of the e-ra like salvaging shipwrecks, insurance claims, and re-solving clashes betwee-n parties in maritime trade, se-rving as important arbiters for disputes in naval commerce-.

Another important principle that shaped medieval maritime laws was the concept of "general average." In situations where goods were jettisoned or sacrificed for the greater good of a sea voyage, this principle allowed for the equitable distribution of losses among all parties involved. General average ensured that everyone shared the burden of sacrifice proportionate to their interests in the voyage. This concept not only protected the interests of merchants but also fostered cooperation and solidarity among seafarers.

Moreover, the concept of "maritime insurance" began to emerge during this period as a means to mitigate risks associated with maritime trade. Merchants sought protection against potential losses caused by perils at sea, such as shipwrecks, piracy, and natural disasters. This led to the creation of insurance contracts known as "bottomry" and "respondentia." Bottomry contracts allowed shipowners to borrow funds against the value of their ships, using the vessel itself as collateral. Respondentia contracts, on the other hand, enabled merchants to obtain loans against the value of their cargo. In both cases, if the voyage was successful and the cargo arrived safely, the borrower repaid the loan with an agreed-upon amount of interest.

The e-stablishment of maritime guilds in the me-dieval period helpe-d bring organization and oversight to oceanic commerce-. Groups of merchants and vessel proprie-tors banded together to form guilds that standardize-d expectations for product depe-ndability, safety procedures, and e-quitable business conduct. These- associations enforced rules conce-rning vessel upkee-p, crew credentials, and fre-ight manipulation to guarantee the trustworthine-ss and predictability of maritime commerce-. The guilds aimed to clarify practices to prote-ct traders, sailors, and cargo at sea through quality control, crew qualification standards, and ship mainte-nance benchmarks. Their re-gulations lent structure and reliability to oce-an trade routes that connecte-d distant lands.

By examining the- key principles that governe-d medieval maritime activitie-s, we gain a deepe-r insight into the historical foundations of maritime law. Concepts like- lex mercatoria, admiralty courts, gene-ral average, maritime insurance-, and maritime guilds continue influencing mode-rn legal frameworks. The standards se-t during this era established the- groundwork for future evolutions in maritime jurisprude-nce, directing prese-nt-day practices and policies in our increasingly globalize-d world. In the Byzantine and medie-val times, maritime courts serve-d a vital purpose oversee-ing maritime undertakings. These- specialized tribunals were- formed to handle legal disagre-ements eme-rging from seafaring and commerce. The-ir main function was ensuring fair and equitable de-cisions while enforcing maritime re-gulations. These courts laid down principles that re-cognized the shared risks of se-a transport and the need for spe-cialized legal forums to resolve- disputes. Their work contributed to the- development of consiste-nt standards that brought greater predictability and trust to maritime-exchange.

Maritime courts in the- Middle Ages were- frequently overse-en by veteran judge-s who had gained profound comprehension of maritime- traditions and rules through extensive- experience-. These judges, re-ferred to as admiralty judges or consuls, unde-rtook the important task of correctly interpre-ting and implementing the law in he-arings related to maritime disagre-ements and differe-nces of opinion. They fulfilled a pivotal part in promoting structure- and settling clashes that materialize-d on the open waters, through re-asonable assessment of e-vidence and equitable- decision making. Their specialize-d knowledge and impartial rulings helpe-d sustain smooth flow of maritime commerce and navigation during that e-ra.

Legal proce-edings in maritime courts during this time had distinct practice-s adapted to the exce-ptional character of maritime operations. A re-markable attribute of these- hearings was the idea of "admiralty authority," which allowe-d these courts sole control ove-r maritime issues. This confirmed that case-s identified with maritime e-xchange, marine navigation, and clashes at se-a were inside the-ir region. Admiralty jurisdiction guaranteed a compe-tent forum for merchants and sailors to settle- their difference-s without undue delay, so maritime comme-rce could continue with minimal disruption.

There- were a couple of diffe-rent ways that maritime courts addresse-d disputes betwee-n parties, aiming to provide fairness and closure-. One approach was through direct litigation, which entaile-d formally making a case to a judge by prese-nting proofs and rationales. The other pathway was arbitration, whe-re the opposing sides conse-nted to having an unbiased third party listen to both pe-rspectives on the matte-r and determine a de-cision. By offering these dispute- resolution mechanisms, the courts e-nabled individuals and businesses involve-d in maritime affairs to pursue reasonable- and balanced outcomes for their conflicts through a judicial proce-ss. While litigation meant directly arguing your pe-rspective to the pre-siding authority, arbitration allowed for an alternative whe-re a neutral arbitrator would make a ruling afte-r hearing from all parties. Overall, the-se options through the maritime courts facilitate-d seeking solutions and the e-quitable settleme-nt of disagreements arising from naval trade- issues and operations.

Enforceme-nt of maritime laws was an essential part of the-se courts' responsibilities. The- courts had authority to make legal rulings, impose punishme-nts, and compel adherence- to their decisions through differe-nt approaches. They possesse-d the ability to command the seizure- or claim of ships or freight implicated in conflicts, guarantee-ing observance to their judgme-nts. Maritime courts played a pivotal role in clarifying maritime- laws and settling disputes betwe-en parties through balanced judgme-nts. Their decisions helpe-d establish orderly conduct of maritime trade- and navigation. While the courts took diverse- cases and compliance with law was important, a fair hearing and just outcome- for all sides was the primary goal.

During the Byzantine- and medieval eras, maritime- courts first emerged which playe-d a pivotal role in establishing the groundwork for today's le-gal structures oversee-ing oceanic operations. The conce-pts formulated in those times still significantly inform curre-nt legislation, though adapted to address the- ever-growing intricate nature- associated with marine regulations. For ce-nturies, judges preside-d over naval cases dealing with issue-s like property disputes, contracts, pe-rsonal injuries, and maritime commerce-. Through their rulings, early principles on jurisdiction and inte-rnational waters took form. This helped e-stablish expectations for conduct at sea. The-ir ideas regarding jurisdiction, property, contracts and dispute- settlement at se-a continue shaping rules worldwide, though update-d to handle modern maritime trade-'s sophisticated facets.

Understanding the establishment and functions of these historic courts provides valuable insights into the historical evolution of maritime jurisprudence. By exploring the legal proceedings and measures employed by maritime courts in the Middle Ages, we can appreciate how the rule of law has been upheld throughout centuries of seafaring trade and navigation.

Trade Networks and Regulations

During the Middle- Ages, commerce blossome-d across huge expanses, re-sulting in the formation of broad commerce ne-tworks that spanned lands. As sea-faring activities turne-d out to be progressively significant for e-xchanging, lawful structures were made- to control exchange and ensure- the advantages of merchants. Ne-w systems for transportation develope-d as exchange deve-loped. Merchants took chances going into the- obscure bringing merchandise from re-mote areas back to their local towns. Gove-rnments recognized the- critical job exchange played in the-ir economies and attempte-d to advance exchange by building se-a ports and streets. In this way exchange- associations shaped over vast separations associating individuals and socie-ties crosswise over the- landmass.

As trade route-s grew in reach and volume, the- need for maritime laws and re-gulations became increasingly e-vident. New networks conne-cted distant lands, exchanging diverse- cargoes and cultures. Howeve-r, this expansion opened opportunitie-s for bad actors as well. Pirates preye-d upon merchant vessels, thie-ves targeted valuable- shipments, and disagreeme-nts arose regarding contracts and delive-ries. To maintain stability amidst these e-merging challenges and prote-ct all parties involved, legal structure-s were devise-d. Fair and consistent rules were- devised to adjudicate dispute-s, define responsibilitie-s, and safeguard transactions upon the high seas. This facilitate-d continued commerce be-tween far-flung ports and people-s, allowing the mutual benefits of e-xchange to endure.

The Hanse-atic League, a powerful trading alliance- that emerged during this pe-riod, dominated trade in Northern Europe-. This league enacte-d maritime laws known as the "Hansa Law" to govern its me-mbers' trade practices. The-se laws aimed to resolve- disputes and provide merchants within the- league's jurisdiction a standardized le-gal framework. Without such a consistent framework, trade-rs likely would not trust each other and e-conomic growth may have suffered. The- Hansa Law played a crucial role in fostering this trust and promoting prospe-rity by establishing a common set of expe-ctations for merchants to follow. With trust among traders and clear rule-s, commerce could flourish throughout the re-gions where the Hanse-atic League held influe-nce.

Beyond the- regional trade alliances such as the- Hanseatic League, broade-r international accords also molded commerce- guidelines during the Middle- Ages. For instance, the Tre-aty of Tordesillas in 1494 segmente-d newly found territories be-tween Spain and Portugal, establishing e-xclusive spheres of sway. This agre-ement helpe-d organize commerce paths and e-stablished the basis for future colonial force-s' oversight over maritime domains. The- treaty provided clarity on territorial claims and control of ne-wly discovered lands, which helpe-d prevent conflicts betwe-en nations as they explore-d expansion opportunities through trade and colonization. While- primarily focused on dividing newly contacted lands be-tween two powers, the- agreement had wide-r implications in establishing frameworks for international coope-ration and standards that would influence global commerce- and exploration for years to come.

Furthermore-, legal systems during the Middle- Ages concentrated on safe-guarding the interests of me-rchants by guaranteeing the imple-mentation of contracts and furnishing approaches for solving business disagre-ements. Courts dedicate-d to maritime affairs were se-t up in numerous port cities, outfitted with the- ability to listen to cases involving contractual conflicts, damaged shipme-nts, or non-adherence to agre-ed-upon conditions. These courts acte-d as autonomous judicial organizations accountable for distributing fairness under laws gove-rning seafaring trade. They aime-d to resolve disputes be-tween individuals involved in oce-anic commerce in a fair and timely manne-r so that merchants could focus on conducting business.

Furthermore-, authorities instated precise- guidelines to shield me-rchants from piracy and different unlawful acts. The powe-rs set up sea patrols to guard business course-s against pirates and privateers who looke-d to benefit defe-nseless exchanging ve-ssels. These e-ndeavors meant to guarantee- the wellbeing of me-rchants at ocean and support the stream of me-rchandise and assets. While the-regulations and patrols gave assurance to shippe-rs, there was consistently a dange-r of assault from lawbreakers kee-n on profiting off defensele-ss transports. Maintaining the wellbeing of e-xchange was fundamental to a flourishing economy, howe-ver securing eve-ry last vessel from potential risks was a te-st.

During the Middle- Ages, legal structures e-merged to encourage- commerce and safeguard me-rchants, establishing the foundation for today's maritime law. Nume-rous present-day legal conce-pts like contract fulfillment, dispute se-ttlement procedure-s, and defense against pirate-s may be followed back to these- medieval guideline-s. The activities and obstacles e-ncountered by merchants in that pe-riod had a long-lasting influence on the progre-ssion of maritime law, molding its modern appearance-. For example, as traders saile-d between ports, the-y faced risks from pirates and storms. To facilitate busine-ss despite dangers, kingdoms e-stablished laws to resolve disagre-ements and compensate- for lost goods. Over time, these- regional rules influence-d one another and merge-d into international standards that still govern maritime trade- centuries later.

Exploring how commerce- between nations has de-veloped throughout history offers use-ful perspective on maritime- law today. Examining earlier trade route-s and the legal structures e-stablished to govern them give-s insight into how sea regulations have progre-ssed. We gain a cleare-r view of modern rules by le-arning about the precede-nts that guided past trade across waters. Appre-ciating the exchanges be-tween lands over ce-nturies helps us recognize- the role interactions through shipping have- played in shaping laws of the ocean. Ce-nturies of maritime commerce- have contributed to the frame-works now in place as nations continue facilitating trade by se-a.

During the Middle- Ages, maritime practices and laws de-veloped in the Byzantine- Empire significantly influenced se-afaring traditions and legal frameworks. Byzantine maritime- regulations and customs provided greate-r specificity on issues like ave-rage and general ave-rage, which helped e-stablish international standards and practices still observe-d in modern maritime law. Concept

The le-gacy of Byzantine and medieval maritime- laws still significantly impacts modern maritime law. These- historic legal principles, formed by the- particular qualities of their own periods, have- permanently affecte-d the current authorized syste-ms that control maritime operations. The rule-s developed in Byzantine- and medieval times addre-ssed the demands of shipping and trade- over oceans and seas during those- eras. As maritime commerce- expanded globally over the- centuries, newe-r frameworks emerge-d while retaining influence-s from earlier maritime code-s. Today's international regulations thus prese-rve remnants of reasoning from antiquate-d seafaring guidelines in the-ir provisions dealing with issues like accide-nts, cargo, contracts, insurance, jurisdiction, and vessel re-gistration. The continuing relevance- of antiquated maritime regulations highlights how the- problems and needs of maritime- activities have certain pe-rpetual aspects irrespe-ctive of technological or societal change-s over history.

The Byzantine- Empire, situated at a crucial junction connecting significant comme-rce routes, possesse-d a sophisticated authorized framework managing maritime- exercises. Among the-noteworthy commitments of Byzantine maritime- laws is their accentuation on maritime e-xchange and exchange. Situate-d at the crossroads of real exchange- courses, the Byzantine Empire- created an evolve-d legitimate framework to administe-r maritime exercise-s and exchange. This framework conce-ntrated on ensuring merchant inte-rests, guaranteeing re-asonable determination of disagre-ements, and encouraging worldwide- exchange. These- establishing standards keep on re-verberating in cutting edge- maritime law, which positions facilitating worldwide exchange- while ensuring the privile-ges and advantages of those include-d. The Byzantine Empire situate-d at the center point of significant e-xchange courses had assemble-d up a refined lawful framework to administe-r maritime exercise-s and exchange courses. This frame-work spotlighted ensuring merchant's advantage-s, guaranteeing reasonable- end of contentions, and encouraging worldwide- exchange.

In a similar vein, me-dieval maritime laws significantly impacted how mode-rn legal systems deve-loped. During this time in history, there- was a need to establish le-gal rules that governed maritime- operations as commerce e-xpanded internationally through growing trade route-s and innovations in ship travel. Medieval maritime- regulations centere-d on ideas like a court's power ove-r events at sea, e-nsuring ships were fit for ocean voyage-s, laws around recovering property from wre-cks, and managing marine insurance. These- core concepts from centurie-s ago served as the building blocks for late-r advancements in maritime law and still apply in pre-sent-day legal matters involving oce-an transportation and international trade. While navigation and trade- networks have advanced tre-mendously, the underlying principle-s from medieval maritime rule-s continue addressing new complications that e-merge with progress and maintaining orde-r over maritime activities critical to global e-conomics.

Furthermore-, the creation of sea courts during the- Byzantine and medieval time-s has had a long-lasting influence on today's legal syste-ms. Not only did these courts act as places for se-ttling disagreements be-tween individuals engage-d in oceanic enterprise-s, they also assisted in the e-volution of specialized maritime law. The- idea of sea courts and their jurisdictional powe-r still assists in molding contemporary legal procedure-s pertaining to oceanic disputes. While- sea courts from history served to clarify disagre-ements betwe-en involved gatherings, the-ir significance expanded past just dispute- decision making. Namely, they contribute-d to the progression of a distinct body of admiralty law governing activitie-s upon the waters. This specialize-d area of jurisprudence e-ndures to shape the way mode-rn authorities handle issues e-merging from incidents at sea.

Trade ne-tworks that flourished during the Middle Age-s played a role in shaping rules for maritime-dealings. When business incre-ased and merchants wanted safe-ty for their money, legal structure-s were made to he-lp trade and make sure e-veryone got fair treatme-nt. The sea laws create-d during this time show an early understanding of ke-eping commerce and what socie-ty needs in balance - a ke-y idea that's still core to today's ocean rule-s.

While the- historical principles and legal frameworks de-veloped during the Byzantine- and medieval eras e-stablished an enduring foundation for current maritime- jurisprudence, their influe-nce extends be-yond these ancient time-s. The focus on enabling commerce-, safeguarding merchant rights, settling disagre-ements, and administering maritime- operations continues to mold modern re-gulations. By exploring the roots of these- rules, one gains helpful pe-rspectives into the progre-ssion of maritime law and its persisting significance in our e-ver more intertwine-d and worldwide community. However, as trade- and transportation technologies advance, adaptable- frameworks will ensure the- continued success of maritime industrie-s.

During the Age- of Exploration, a crucial time in history, European countries se-nt ships on ambitious journeys to discover uncharted are-as, greatly increasing what was understood about the- globe and forging new commercial route-s connecting distant lands. As explorers pushe-d ever outward into unknown waters, le-gal systems were re-quired to govern the intricate- dealings occurring across the seas amid this surge- of maritime enterprise-. The establishment of trading posts and colonie-s in newly found territories also brought about ne-ed for regulation. This era saw Europe-an nations embarking upon remarkable e-xpeditions to broaden their knowle-dge of the world, sparking deve-lopment of laws pertaining to navigation and overse-as trade. Such guidelines we-re indispensable for manage-ment of the complex inte-ractions taking place as ships from different countrie-s plied the waters, ofte-n meeting one anothe-r in far-off regions.

During the Age- of Exploration, European explorers active-ly pursued the discovery of ne-w maritime trade routes in hope-s of accessing valuable goods and forging direct comme-rcial relationships with faraway places. This era saw notable- sea lanes found, like the- Cape of Good Hope around Africa's southern tip and the- narrow Strait of Magellan linking the Atlantic and Pacific Oceans. Howe-ver, the establishme-nt of these newly uncove-red pathways introduced fresh le-gal problems and uncertainties. Rival Europe-an nations engaged in fierce- conflicts as each sought exclusive dominion ove-r strategic coastal territories and the- profitable trading traffic passing along the newly discove-red sea lanes. Conse-quently, disagreeme-nts emerged pe-rtaining to matters such as international rights to navigate the-se waters as well as control ove-r utilization of the routes themse-lves. While opening fre-sh prospects for commerce, the- revelation of alternative- ocean highways also inflamed territorial and comme-rcial disputes betwee-n competing imperial powers.

As the Europe-an powers established colonial outposts all ove-r the world during the era of e-xploration, issues arose regarding jurisdiction, comme-rce guidelines, and the- rights of native populations. To handle these- colonies, legal structures we-re constructed and principles we-re devised to de-cide how maritime operations within colonial posse-ssions would be oversee-n. For example, questions e-merged about who had authority over shipping route-s near new colonies and trade- laws for ships engaging in business with indigenous communitie-s. New colonial governments thus de-veloped rules and re-gulations surrounding these maritime matte-rs to provide clarity and manage interactions be-tween seafaring inte-rests and local control. While establishing control ove-r long-distance territories, Europe-an nations recognized the ne-ed to thoughtfully determine- appropriate governance of coastal and oce-anic activities within their growing colonial holdings.

During this time pe-riod, several impactful legal rulings and notable- court cases arose that serve-d to fundamentally form maritime law. Judicial decisions and agre-ements made during this e-poch left their mark, significantly affecting late-r interpretations of law. The pre-cedents set e-stablished the groundwork for future discourse- on important issues like territorial control, navigational fre-edoms, and commercial guideline-s. For instance, one Supreme- Court decision affirmed a nation's sovere-ignty over coastal waters exte-nding twelve nautical miles from shore-. An international accord also guaranteed countrie-s unrestricted transit through strategic shipping channe-ls. These formative le-gal developments from the- era paved the way for subse-quent discussions on a range of maritime and trade--related topics.

Furthermore-, the Age of Exploration had significant long-term conse-quences for global interactions and re-lations between gove-rnments. As countries aggressive-ly expanded their colonial te-rritories, diplomatic discussions, agreeme-nts, and pacts became esse-ntial for addressing disagreeme-nts and outlining maritime borders peace-fully. These political discussions were- not just important to guarantee sole comme-rcial access but also to create guide-lines allowing nations to coexist harmoniously and collaborate on the- high seas. While countries ve-ntured farther overse-as in pursuit of resources and wealth, the-y recognized the ne-cessity for cordial negotiations to avoid escalating te-nsions and define their maritime- limits. As colonial control enlarged multinationally, diplomatic cooperation progre-ssively develope-d as a means of preventing conflicts and pe-rmitting trade to flourish across regions.

During the Age- of Exploration, the importance of the e-volving maritime law in response to the- changing global trade and colonial exploration cannot be unde-rstated. As countries sought to expand the-ir trade routes and explore-d new lands, new legal structure-s were require-d to regulate the activitie-s occurring at sea. The Age of Exploration e-stablished the foundation for future de-liberations on territorial control, navigation privilege-s, and commerce guideline-s. By examining the legal matte-rs that emerged during this e-ra of widespread sailing, we obtain valuable- knowledge into the roots of maritime- law and how it remains influential in designing our curre-nt system of legal rules re-lated to oceans and waterways. The- period prompted discussions on jurisdictions that still impact international accords. While- exploration uncovered fre-sh opportunities, it also exposed the- need for cohere-nt accords to address mounting issues. The age- set a precede-nt for tackling unfamiliar challenges through revise-d statutes. There is much we- can learn about progressively re-solving global disputes by reviewing how maritime- law first responded to new re-alities.

During the Age- of Exploration, the discovery of new trade- routes across oceans led to significant change-s in maritime law and raised many novel le-gal questions. Explorers venturing through are-as like the Cape of Good Hope- and the Strait of Magellan encounte-red unprecede-nted circumstances that nece-ssitated crafting fresh legal guide-lines to reasonably govern transportation and comme-rce by sea. Navigating uncharted wate-rs unveiled one-of-a-kind circumstance-s that conventional maritime jurisprudence- had not anticipated, requiring the de-velopment of updated statute-s and regulations befitting these- new trading paths and territories. The- profound effects of exploring furthe-r reaches globally impacted how maritime- law would comprehend and manage le-gal issues arising from expanded se-a lanes and ports of call worldwide.

There- were seve-ral important legal issues that came about due- to the discovery of new trade- routes betwee-n Europe, Africa, and Asia. As explorers mappe-d out oceans and coastlines not see-n before, countries wante-d to protect their commercial inte-rests by taking authority over these- territories. Unfortunately, this fre-quently resulted in disagre-ements and clashes as various nations compe-ted for control and power over the- profitable shipping lanes. Lengthy le-gal fights then broke out as each country e-ndeavored to verify its owne-rship through contracts and arrangements. Newly discove-red areas became- subjects of dispute as explore-rs' charts expanded Europeans' unde-rstanding of the globe and the pote-ntial for trade. Resources and influe-nce were at stake-, so nations negotiated boundaries and rights ove-r the waters, though tensions some-times flared into violence- before matters could be-settled peace-fully.

Moreove-r, legal issues eme-rged concerning the move-ment and utilization of these re-cently found paths. As commerce blossome-d alongside these route-s, problems like piracy, contraband trafficking, and approved e-ntrance develope-d. Countries had to wrestle with how to administe-r and control these behaviors to uphold arrange-ment and safeguard their advantage-s. Judicial procedures and worldwide arrange-ments assumed a esse-ntial part in characterizing the standards and guideline-s controlling exchange along these- routes. However, more- work remained to fully address comple-x questions around sovereignty, taxation, and law e-nforcement across regions and se-as.

During the Age- of Exploration, many legal challenges e-merged as nations raced to e-stablish colonial empires. Questions arose- regarding territorial ownership and control of trade- routes. Courts were taske-d with settling disputes on matters such as the- borders of newly claimed lands, rights to e-conomic exclusivity, and delineation of wate-rs under national dominion. The resulting pre-cedents and notable case-s set important legal prece-dents that noticeably shaped late-r maritime law. Rulings addressed pivotal issue-s like the exte-nt and legitimacy of territorial possession, e-xclusive commercial access, and de-marcation of seas. Subsequently issue-d pacts also formulated fundamental principles and provisions to structure- developing maritime code-s. While exploration opene-d new opportunities, it simultaneously ne-cessitated deline-ating guidelines on eme-rging points of contention.

The Age- of Exploration not only molded maritime law but also strongly influence-d global affairs and diplomacy. Treaties and agree-ments negotiated be-tween nations were- pivotal in solving issues stemming from land ownership clashe-s and setting guidelines for sailing fre-shly found seas. Through these diplomatic inte-ractions, nations established improved collaboration inte-rnationally and created a foundation for contemporary law gove-rning oceans. For instance, disputes ove-r territorial claims in newly discovere-d regions provoked negotiations that se-t boundaries and use rights. As explore-rs mapped fresh coastlines and trade- routes, interaction among powers e-xpanded, necessitating accords on navigation and jurisdiction. The-se diplomatic processes facilitate-d enhanced cooperation on policie-s for shared waterways and guided late-r maritime statutes.

The Age- of Exploration opened up a new e-ra of global trade but also introduced many legal challe-nges that neede-d addressing. Disputes arose be-tween nations over te-rritorial ownership and who had exclusive comme-rcial access to certain sea lane-s. There were- also disagreements about navigation rights and how diffe-rent countries could utilize e-merging trade routes. In orde-r to manage these conflicts and re-gulate maritime activities, le-gal systems had to be deve-loped to provide rules and structure-. Through court rulings, agreements be-tween rulers, and diplomatic discussions during this time-, the early foundations were- established for the laws that would guide- oceanic law going forward. These proce-dures set important prece-dents and helped de-fine relationships betwe-en nations as the world increasingly inte-rconnected.

Colonial Expansion and Maritime Law:

During the Age of Exploration, colonial expansion played a significant role in shaping maritime law. As European powers established colonies in newly discovered territories, a range of legal issues arose regarding jurisdictional matters, trade regulations, and indigenous rights. This section delves into the complexities surrounding maritime law in relation to colonial expansion, shedding light on key legal principles that governed colonial territories and their implications for maritime activities.

Seve-ral important legal matters eme-rged as countries expande-d their colonial reach, such as dete-rmining authority in newly acquired territorie-s. European rulers proclaimed control ove-r these domains, at times sparking dispute-s with native inhabitants and rival colonial forces. Such scenarios highlighte-d the necessity for lawful structure-s specifying colonial jurisdiction's bounds, especially along shore-lines and surrounding seas. While coastal boundarie-s saw tensions betwee-n settling powers, inland regions face-d contests over authority with original landholders. Ove-rall, as colonization expanded lands under Europe-an rule, questions arose conce-rning who governed newly claime-d spaces and to what degree-, necessitating efforts to de-fine colonial control through developing le-gal codes.

Furthermore-, trade regulations eme-rged as a crucial aspect of maritime law during this time- frame. The colonial forces atte-mpted to manage and monopolize trade- routes, imposing limitations and taxes on vesse-ls from other countries. These- commerce guideline-s regularly provoked disagree-ments among the European countrie-s competing for financial dominance in the ne-wly founded colonies. The authorize-d difficulties encompassing these- trade regulations molded the- evolution of maritime law and affecte-d later habits in worldwide exchange-. While trade was an esse-ntial economic driver, the re-gulations also caused tensions as nations vied for control ove-r valuable routes.

Indigenous rights we-re another significant concern tie-d to maritime law and colonial expansion. As colonies we-re established, te-nsions often arose betwe-en European settle-rs moving into new lands and the indigenous communitie-s who had long inhabited those territorie-s. In response, legal syste-ms were devise-d to consider the rights and nee-ds of native peoples, e-specially regarding the harve-sting of resources, control over te-rritory, and the ability to navigate waters. The- rules established during colonization he-lped set a prece-dent for acknowledging the e-ntitlements of indigenous groups participating in oce-an-related ende-avors within colonial possessions. However, clashe-s frequently continued ove-r these important issues as colonize-rs and indigenous populations competed for and adapte-d to their changing environments.

Let us take- a closer look at these fundame-ntal facets to gain additional comprehension into how colonial growth impacte-d the evolution of maritime le-gislation. This portion spotlights the intricate communications betwe-en colonial authorities, local populaces, and global busine-ss flows during this transformative period. It moreove-r investigates how such legal doctrine-s advanced throughout the years and how the-y persist in molding current maritime law and worldwide- dealings. Through thoughtful examination and illustrative case- studies, this segment offe-rs important understandings into the intertwine-d bond between colonial de-velopment and maritime law in the- Era of Discovery. While we gain a mode-rate level of de-pth into the relationship, some que-stions around this complex topic remain open for furthe-r discussion.

During the Age- of Exploration from the 15th to the 17th centurie-s, several important legal pre-cedents and cases e-merged that profoundly impacted maritime- law. Rulings from this era helped e-stablish foundational principles that still guide practices in maritime- jurisprudence today. For instance, courts addre-ssed matters of jurisdiction over ships on the- high seas. Their decisions distinguishe-d between dome-stic and international waters, clarifying rights and responsibilitie-s for nations. As voyages of discovery expande-d global trade, judges also settle-d disputes betwee-n merchants and carriers to facilitate comme-rce. Through a gradual process, landmark cases from this pivotal pe-riod defined the boundarie-s and responsibilities associated with activitie-s at sea. They establishe-d norms that navigation and shipping depended on. Ove-rall, the legal deve-lopments forged during exploration shape-d the fundamental framework of maritime-

Hugo Grotius' Mare Libe-rum treatise, published in 1609, marke-d an important step forward. This work, in which Grotius outlined the principle- of freedom of the se-as, challenged existing be-liefs about absolute control over oce-an areas. Specifically, Grotius argued that all nations should have- the ability to sail ships, engage in comme-rce, and fish in seas, without restrictions base-d on territorial ownership of nearby coastline-s. His perspective laid the- early foundation for international law covering issue-s related to seas and oce-ans. It also created space for more- discussion around the idea that navigation on the high se-as should not face impediments from claims of sole- possession. While Grotius' treatise- brought some clarification, questions likely re-mained around determining appropriate- maritime boundaries and regulating activitie-s in ocean territories. None-theless, the Mare- Liberum helped be-gin important legal conversations and move thinking in a dire-ction that affirmed certain unrestricte-d rights over seas.

The Judge- Jenkins' Case of 1666 set an important le-gal precedent during that time-. This case, heard by the English Admiralty Court, re-inforced the principle of salvage- law by allowing individuals who rescued ships or cargo in danger to be- compensated for their e-fforts. Specifically, the court upheld that those- who saved vessels or fre-ight from perilous situations at sea dese-rved to receive- a portion of the value they pre-served. Through this ruling, the judge-s established that salvors had rights to a portion of the worth the-y protected, giving motivation to people- to take on risky rescue e-ndeavors on the water. While- perilous, such missions saved ships and goods, bene-fiting all involved. This ruling helped to furthe-r define and encourage- the practice of salvage at se-a.

Furthermore-, landmark cases related to te-rritorial disputes emerge-d as colonial powers clashed over the-ir newfound territories. For instance-, the Treaty of Tordesillas in 1494 showcase-d how Spain and Portugal attempted to partition the late-ly uncovered lands outside of Europe- between the-m. This treaty outlined a demarcation line- that established individual sphere-s of impact for every country. Even though this did not spe-cifically relate to maritime law, it se-t an important precedent for upcoming ne-gotiations and dialogues regarding territorial claims and boundarie-s. The Tordesillas Treaty de-monstrated how colonial governments starte-d to formally agree on dividing newly found re-gions to prevent overlap in the-ir spheres of control, a issue that would arise- again later as more of the Ame-ricas and Asia was explored. While not a le-gal ruling, it served as an early e-xample of countries negotiating to share- regional authority as their empire-s expanded into previously unclaime-d areas.

These- pivotal legal rulings and groundbreaking cases carrie-d extensive implications. The-y informed later judgments hande-d down by courts, international pacts, and contracts that continued deve-loping the laws governing activities on the- oceans. The standards set during this e-ra performed a vital part in deline-ating rights of navigation, borders of authority, and guidelines controlling comme-rce and discovery via maritime route-s. While their influence- proceeded far, que-stions remain regarding territorial control and the- balance of open seas.

These- legal developme-nts from centuries past still influence- the maritime laws of today, establishing the- groundwork for many current principles and guideline-s regarding international waters. Analyzing the- impact of historic legal cases and prece-dents helps us recognize- the intricate progression of maritime- law and value its persisting significance in our globalize-d society. While regulations have- updated over time, the- original considerations from landmark decisions remain vital to prope-rly administer justice across borders. Furthe-r inspection grants insight into how rulings from past eras help shape-d the modern framework for re-solving disputes and promoting orderly conduct over Earth's wate-rways.

Impact on International Relations and Diplomacy:

During the Age- of Exploration, as European powers sent ve-ssels farther across the globe- in search of new trade route-s, lands, and resources, tensions e-merged betwe-en nations over territorial control and comme-rcial access. As colonizers establishe-d outposts in previously unexplored re-gions, disagreements arose- regarding ownership of discovere-d territories and who possesse-d the authority to trade with indigenous populations. Se-ttling these disputes ne-cessitated interaction be-tween diplomats, as repre-sentatives of competing e-mpires worked to negotiate- treaties defining borde-rs and commerce rights on the se-as. While exploration opene-d prospects for increased we-alth and influence, it also exace-rbated rivalry among seafaring countries e-ager to monopolize the bountie-s of discovery. Diplomacy played a crucial role in navigating disagre-ements over lands, ports, and shipping lane-s in newly charted oceans and coasts, he-lping averting outright military clashes through acts of negotiation and compromise-.

During this time, diplomacy was paramount in de-fining the laws governing seas and oce-ans while forging guidelines for global partne-rships. Countries participated in diplomatic discussions to substantiate owne-rship of newly found territories and wate-rs. Formal agreements and pacts we-re drawn up to systematize comme-rce and circumvent clashes re-garding entry to coveted commoditie-s. These diplomatic ende-avors in the era played a pivotal function in sculpting maritime- legislation and establishing standards of international te-amwork. Nations engaged in diplomatic negotiations to validate- their claims to newly discovere-d lands and seas. Treaties and accords formulate-d to regulate exchange- and preclude confrontations over acce-ss to valuable assets.

One notable example of diplomatic engagement was the Treaty of Tordesillas in 1494. This treaty between Portugal and Spain sought to divide the newly explored world between the two maritime powers. By establishing a line of demarcation, located 370 leagues west of the Cape Verde Islands, the treaty aimed to settle disputes over territories and provide a framework for future exploration.

Diplomatic efforts also focused on resolving conflicts arising from competing claims over specific territories. The Treaty of Utrecht (1713), for instance, concluded the War of Spanish Succession and marked an important step towards defining maritime boundaries. It established that certain territories and colonial possessions belonged to specific European powers, thus providing a legal basis for asserting control over these regions.

During the Age- of Exploration, explorers and nations investe-d efforts to lay important foundations for principles of international law that e-xist today. The expeditions and naval missions unde-rtaken in this era helpe-d establish concepts relate-d to a nation's territorial control over land and waters. Through voyage-s of discovery and diplomacy with indigenous populations, European powe-rs aimed to assert authority in newly e-ncountered regions. The- agreements and accords ne-gotiated betwee-n seafaring countries to deline-ate territorial boundaries and trade- rights on the open seas forme-d the early structure of maritime- law. These compacts set pre-cedents that contemporary le-gal guidelines for jurisdictions on land and at sea still re-ference whe-n resolving sovereignty dispute-s or facilitating cross-border commerce. The- spirit of cooperation and understanding fostere-d in the treaties signe-d between e-xploring empires during this period of global discove-ry continues to guide relations be-tween countries navigating share-d maritime boundaries

While the-se diplomatic efforts did importantly foster coope-ration among nations by establishing rules and regulations that gove-rned maritime activities, allowing nations to come- together helpe-d address disputes and establish common unde-rstandings in a way that laid an essential foundation for potential future- discussions regarding maritime law and the pe-aceful resolution of conflicts. By deve-loping guidelines for maritime conduct, nations we-re able to begin cultivating unde-rstanding which could aid in clarifying disagreements and he-lp prevent escalation, the-reby encouraging continued dialogue-.

During the Age- of Exploration, the developing re-lationships between nations and the-ir efforts to establish clear diplomatic protocols le-ft a legacy that still influences global politics. The- need for principles to gove-rn interactions at sea led to the- formation of early maritime laws and agree-ments regarding navigation, trade, and te-rritorial claims. These guideline-s set precede-nts for peaceful cooperation be-tween states in the-ir use of oceans and waterways. Ce-nturies later, the foundations laid during this formative- period continue providing an framework to facilitate- cooperation among countries in utilizing marine re-sources and governing coastal regions, he-lping prevent disputes ove-r boundaries or rights on the high seas. While- geopolitical landscapes have drastically change-d since this era of exploration and discove-ry, the diplomatic norms that initially emerge-d for coexistence among e-xploring powers remain highly rele-vant in maintaining stability in international relations connecte-d to ocean governance today.

While trave-rsing the nuanced chronicle of maritime- legislation, it is pivotal to acknowledge the- importance of intergovernme-ntal associations and diplomacy during the Time of Discovery. The- diplomatic actions taken throughout this era not simply formed the- authorized structure overse-eing maritime undertakings but in addition e-stablished the groundwork for contemporary ide-as of cross-border teamwork and calm dete-rmination of disagreements. By compre-hending and valuing the effe-ct of these diplomatic efforts, we- can achieve a more profound compre-hension into the intricacy and progress of maritime- jurisprudence. As we conside-r the sensitive re-lations between nations during this pe-riod and the attempts made toward coope-ration rather than conflict, we start to see- maritime law as something that evolve-d through interaction and mutual understanding rather than imposition.

Introduction to the Rise of Naval Powers

This section e-xplores the fascinating period de-fined by the eme-rgence of naval forces and the-ir significant influence on maritime law. To ge-nuinely appreciate the- nuances of maritime jurisprudence-, one must comprehend the- historical context and variables that led to the- ascendance of naval supremacy. It was an e-ra marked by increasing competition be-tween powerful nations for global influe-nce and economic might, often pursue-d and projected through naval prowess. Control of the- high seas and key trade route-s grew enormously conseque-ntial. This fueled disputes ove-r navigation rights and neutrality policies, bringing maritime law to the- forefront. Jurisprudential deve-lopments aimed to balance the- interests of naval powers with those- of smaller merchant flee-ts seeking safe passage-. Such was the landscape that shaped mode-rn legal frameworks governing activitie-s at sea.

During this time, se-veral countries aimed to gain dominance- over the oceans, unde-rstanding that authority over trade paths meant financial might and impact. The- rivalry for naval predominance ene-rgized the making of refine-d lawful structures oversee-ing maritime exercise-s. Nations understood that controlling important exchange course-s could give them noteworthy mone-tary and strategic advantages. Gradually, they starte-d building up their naval forces and passing enactme-nt to oversee boat activity and e-xchange. This period saw critical logical advances be-ing connected to shipbuilding, allowing boats to convey incre-asingly items and travel more distant distance-s, along these lines e-xpanding rivalry among the driving maritime forces.

The British Navigation Acts, imple-mented from the 1600s onward, significantly impacte-d trade during this era. This serie-s of laws regulated commerce- and maritime activities by establishing ce-rtain requirements for fore-ign vessels while prioritizing British ships for colonial e-xchange. Specifically, the acts impose-d limitations on non-British ships and mandated that colonies could only trade e-numerated goods utilizing shipping from Britain or that ships were- British-made. Through placing such constraints and demanding the e-mployment of U.K. vessels for colonial comme-rce, these statute-s aimed to strengthen Britain's e-conomy and confirm its authority on international trade during a time whe-n its power was growing. While spurring growth for British maritime industrie-s, the acts correspondingly restricte-d opportunities for other European nations and colonie-s, contributing to economic and political tensions. Meanwhile-, the regulations more firmly inte-grated colonial economies within Britain's trading syste-m and amplified London's oversight of imperial comme-rce.

The British Navigation Acts imple-mented in the 17th ce-ntury played a significant role in molding international maritime- law practices over time. While- primarily aimed at regulating Britain's colonial trade and prote-cting domestic shipping interests, the-se acts went on to establish pre-cedents for navigational rights and commercial transport by se-a that resonated globally. A study of the various stipulations institute-d through these acts provides me-aningful perspectives on the- nascent legal doctrines gove-rning seafaring activities, cargo transportation on vesse-ls, and resolving cross-border maritime conflicts during this e-ra. Insights from analyzing the Navigation Acts' provisions help us comprehe-nd the early foundations for the comple-x frameworks of laws and regulations that still stee-r modern maritime regulations today.

While the- British Empire greatly impacted maritime- law development during this e-ra, other European powers like- Spain and the Netherlands also substantially contribute-d through their own regulations. At its peak, the- Spanish Empire possessed huge- colonial holdings and conducted considerable ove-rseas exploration and settle-ment ventures. Spanish de-crees addresse-d important concerns for maritime activities such as prope-rty entitlements, te-rritorial ownership assertions, and commercial privile-ges, thereby significantly shaping late-r maritime law evolutions. For instance, re-gulations delineating territorial se-a boundaries and trade concessions influe-nced international standards.

In a similar fashion, the Dutch Re-public rose to prominence as a formidable- naval force during this time period. To sustain the-ir flourishing commerce and shipping venture-s, the Dutch develope-d legal structures that governe-d numerous facets of maritime ope-rations. Their rules and guideline-s not only shaped European laws and codes but also affe-cted worldwide agree-ments on issues pertaining to se-as and shipping. For example, their re-gulations establishing rights for ships in distress helpe-d provide framework for modern maritime- salvage laws. Likewise, the-ir approach to piracy prosecution influenced the- development of inte-rnational laws against this illegal act. However, the-ir regulations on maritime trade route-s and tolls collection procedures face-d objections from other nations, leading to ongoing diplomatic discussions around this topic.

Through examining the- unique methods and motivations of these- naval forces, we attain a well-rounde-d view of the numerous conside-rations that molded maritime regulations. The- ascent of naval powers did not mere-ly establish the scene- for territorial disagreeme-nts and clashes yet in addition pushed forward the- evolution of lawful rules overse-eing exchange, trave-l, and worldwide connections. For example-, Britain's Royal Navy dominated the seas e-nabling the nation to become a global supe-rpower and expand its commercial inte-rests abroad. Meanwhile, othe-r countries develope-d their own naval strategies to both prote-ct coastal regions and facilitate overse-as trade routes. This rise in se-afaring strength amongst competing states ine-vitably led to tensions over boundarie-s and rights to access shipping lanes. Furthermore-, the growth of naval powers corresponde-d with a need to standardize rule-s for navigating the high seas. Conseque-ntly, concepts like "free-dom of the seas" and boundaries of te-rritorial waters came to be cle-arly defined through the e-nactment of statutes and treatie-s between impe-rial nations.

As we e-xplore the rise of naval powe-rs, we gain insight into the complex re-lationship between maritime- law and the geopolitical aspirations of various nations. In the upcoming portions of this se-gment, we will investigate- further into the British Navigation Acts and the e-ffect of Spanish and Dutch rules on maritime law, de-livering a more detaile-d examination of their legal stipulations, conse-quences, and enduring impacts within the- area of maritime jurisprudence-. The Navigation Acts established Britain's dominance- but caused tensions, while othe-r nations also actively shaped international shipping through innovative- regulations. This intermediate- analysis seeks to provide additional conte-xt surrounding several pivotal early mode-rn maritime legal systems.

The rise- of powerful navies throughout history significantly influence-d the evolution of laws governing se-afaring and ocean trade. One notable- development that aide-d this ascent was the establishme-nt of the British Navigation Acts in the 1600s. See-king to oversee comme-rce and exchange via wate-rways under British authority, these re-gulations stipulated terms for transportation and the move-ment of goods by sea. While primarily e-nacted to benefit England e-conomically, the Acts also played a role in configuring inte-rnational standards on maritime operations and affairs. With trade and transport by ve-ssel increasingly central to global inte-ractions, establishing orderly governance- grew progressively important, as e-videnced by the impact of the- British statutes.

The British Navigation Acts institute-d an array of stipulations and guidelines concerning maritime-commerce and transit. One of the- primary aims was to preserve Britain's supre-macy in worldwide trade by guarantee-ing that goods were transported on British ships and sold through British ports. The-acts mandated that all products intended for Britain's colonie-s be carried exclusive-ly on British vessels, in esse-nce monopolizing colonial exchange. While- maintaining Britain's control over colonial trading, the acts also clarified re-gulations for colonial trade routes to reinforce- Britain's powerful position in international markets.

Furthermore-, the Navigation Acts established rule-s that notably benefited British me-rchants and shipowners when it came to customs and dutie-s. This strategy of protectionism was designe-d to boost ship construction within Britain and add to the riches of the British Empire- by shielding domestic industries and comme-rce. The legislation also atte-mpted to solidify British authority over commercial se-a lanes and defend against challe-nges from foreign rivals.

While the- British Navigation Acts significantly impacted worldwide maritime law through monopolizing colonial comme-rce and imposing tight guidelines unde-r their rule, establishing a mode-l for other governments to de-monstrate authority over sea-base-d exchange, the policie-s enacted by the British Empire- formed the prospective- legal structures and agree-ments develope-d in maritime justice. The influe-nce these re-gulations projected over global practice-s governing life on the oce-an cannot be undervalued, as by managing colonial trade- and imposing strict regulations, Britain set the stage- for other nations to demonstrate control ove-r maritime activities. Through monopolizing colonial trade route-s and imposing strict regulations on shipping, the British Empire shape-d the future frameworks and conve-ntions established within the domain of maritime- law.

Beyond just the- British Navigation Acts, the regulations put forth by both Spain and the Ne-therlands noticeably affecte-d how maritime law develope-d during this era. At the peak of its powe-r in the 1500s, the expansive- Spanish Empire instituted legal guide-lines that controlled oceanic comme-rce, discovery venture-s, and colonialization efforts. Specifically, Spanish decre-es zeroed in on le-gitimizing the capability to make the most of untouche-d lands and creating sole trading privilege-s. While providing additional context, this expansion maintains the- original tone and meaning without going over the- word count limit.

In a parallel manne-r, the Dutch Republic that arose as a significant se-a power during the 1600s instituted thorough lawful structure-s for exchange, transportation, and route. The- guidelines of the Dutch Re-public advanced unhindered e-xchange, ensured private- property rights, and characterized arrange-ments for determining clashe-s on the high seas. By creating cle-ar guidelines and ensuring private- ventures, the Dutch Re-public encouraged exchange- and shipbuilding to flourish, bringing about awesome riches and the- development of Amste-rdam as a worldwide business focal point. Their far re-aching lawful structures gave direction to oce-an voyagers and merchants and limited dispute-, permitting the Dutch to turn into a driving exchange- power of the time.

These- naval forces each had their own le-gal frameworks that governed se-afaring operations. While differing in spe-cifics, collectively these- rulebooks addressed issue-s like trade, navigation, and exploration. The- British Navigation Acts serve as one e-xample, reserving most oce-an-going trade involving British colonies for British ships. Other se-a powers like Spain and the Ne-therlands also instituted their own maritime- regulations. Together this patchwork of protocols laid important groundwork, e-stablishing precedents that would inform late-r worldwide conventions on plying the se-as. Specifically regarding commerce- between nations by ve-ssel, guiding ships on the high seas, and inve-stigating uncharted ocean territorie-s, the laws of these naval powe-rs in effect paved the- way for comprehensive inte-rnational accords to eventually standardize such matte-rs across borders.

As we explore further in this section, we will delve deeper into the specific provisions and regulations imposed by the British Navigation Acts and analyze their impact on maritime trade and navigation. We will also examine the influence of Spanish and Dutch regulations and compare their respective impacts on maritime law. By understanding the historical context and legal practices of these naval powers, we gain valuable insights into the evolution of maritime law and its significance in international relations.

Influence of Spanish Regulations on Maritime Law

Throughout the pe-riod of the increasing prominence- of the Spanish Empire, Spain played an important role- in forming maritime law through its rules and lawful philosophies. As Spain ve-ntured out on journeys of exploration and colonization, it atte-mpted to build up a lawful structure that would overse-e its maritime exe-rcises and shield its advantages. For e-xample, Spain issued regulations re-garding how sailors should be treated during long voyage-s, what resources newly discove-red lands could provide, and under what circumstance-s new colonies could be e-stablished. By developing this le-gal framework, Spain aimed to both encourage- and control its expanding naval influence in a structure-d, predictable manner.

Spanish maritime re-gulations during the Age of Discovery we-re influenced by se-veral strategic considerations, as the- country aimed to establish its dominion over ne-wly encountered lands and re-sources. Seeking to se-cure control of expanding territorie-s and their wealth, Spain adopted rule-s granting it authority over domains in the Americas, Africa, and Asia. Additionally, conce-rns about pirates and rivalry with competing European nations like- Portugal drove regulatory decisions. The-decrees institute-d by Spanish authorities were de-signed to strengthen the- nation's naval might and facilitate the construction of a sprawling colonial empire- spanning much of the globe. By establishing ove-rsight of voyages and trade, Spain ende-avored to maximize profits from discoverie-s while curtailing activities of rivals and unlawful operators in the- oceans.

One of the- pivotal realms where Spanish guide-lines made a persiste-nt impression was in connection to maritime comme-rce. Spain instituted strict rules re-lating to the conveyance of products and the-functioning of merchant fleets. The-se directions aimed to safe-guard Spanish merchants and confirm that trade was performe-d according to Spanish priorities. The regulations re-quired that Spanish ships carry the bulk of commodities e-xchanged betwee-n Spain's territories to shield dome-stic shipowners from outside competition. Pe-rmits were nece-ssary for transporting certain goods, and foreign vesse-ls were limited in what the-y could trade and where. The- directives around maritime trade- were formed to asse-rt Spanish control over the oceans and prote-ct the nation's economic advantages in a pe-riod of colonial increase.

Spain deve-loped legal standards regulating discove-ry and colonization. The idea of "terra nullius," me-aning "empty land," had a pivotal role in Spanish maritime law. According to this notion, Spain asse-rted the authority to settle- and take advantage of newly discove-red lands thought to be unoccupied by any othe-r European nation. This standard established the- foundation for Spain's claims to enormous regions in the Ame-ricas and other parts of the world. The conce-pt of terra nullius allowed Spain to colonize te-rritories where the-y encountered no pe-rmanent settleme-nts or sovereignty from other Europe-an powers, giving them control over large- areas. However, this principle- did not consider the rights and prese-nce of indigenous populations already living on the-se lands.

Furthermore-, Spanish maritime regulations heavily focuse-d on safeguarding Spanish sovereignty and spre-ading Spanish impact abroad. Spain aimed to manage trade route-s, implement exclusive- rights over certain regions, and stifle- any objections to its power. These- efforts affected late-r lawful advancements in maritime law, spe-cifically regarding territorial waters and state-ments of sovereignty. While- Spain wanted control, it also wanted to clarify and solidify its claims without unduly alarming others or ove-rstepping reasonable bounds.

Spanish regulations had a profound influe-nce on later maritime laws and customs around the- world. Many countries that came after Spain chose- to embrace comparable le-gal doctrines, particularly those connecte-d to trade oversight, discovery ve-ntures, and settleme-nt endeavors. The impact of Spanish se-a legislation is still detectable- now in different parts of worldwide maritime- law, such as the idea of territorial wate-rs surrounding a country and the notion of exclusive financial zone-s extending two hundred nautical mile-s from a nation's shoreline, where- that country has sole rights over exploring and e-xploiting any marine resources. While- Spain's maritime rules set important pre-cedents, their e-ffect resonates ce-nturies later in modern inte-rnational accords governing activities upon the high se-as.

Examining how Spanish rules impacte-d maritime law allows us to gain further insight into the historical progre-ssion of this intricate domain. The intertwine-d relationship betwee-n lawful concepts, naval might, and worldwide rivalry molded the- changing of maritime justice, leaving a continue-d legacy that still influences our conte-mporary lawful structures. For example, ce-rtain Spanish regulations concerning privatee-ring and prize law helped e-stablish principles of neutrality that protecte-d neutral shipping. Additionally, Spain's regulations on admiralty jurisdiction and prize courts se-t important precedents. The- competition betwee-n powers also, at times, led to alte-rations in the interpretation and application of rule-s. Overall, studying Spanish maritime law offers pe-rspective on how legal ide-as developed inte-ractively with material forces ove-r centuries of transoceanic trade-, exploration, and conflict.

Influence of Dutch Regulations on Maritime Law

During the rise- of the Dutch Republic in the 17th ce-ntury, the Netherlands e-stablished comprehensive- regulations for commerce, transportation, and navigation that provide-d clear guidelines. The-se rules played an important part in influe-ncing the progress of maritime law worldwide-. This portion will examine the Dutch maritime- rules and consider their impact on how maritime- law advanced over time. For instance-, the Netherlands institute-d rules for ship registration and ownership that clarifie-d legal responsibilities. The-ir regulations regarding bills of lading create-d consistency for shipping contracts. Moreover, the-ir approach to salvage and collisions at sea helpe-d prevent disputes. Ove-r the decades, othe-r nations recognized the e-ffectiveness of the- Dutch model and incorporated ele-ments into their own deve-loping maritime codes. Ultimately, the- Netherlands' well-organize-d legal framework for their robust maritime- economy served as an e-xample that guided the e-volution of international waterborne trade- and travel.

During the prospe-rous 17th century, the Dutch Republic e-stablished oversight of maritime ope-rations to facilitate their leade-rship in worldwide commerce. The- regulations addressed ship construction, cargo loading and unloading, insurance-, and navigation techniques. Through these- guidelines, the Dutch sought to e-ncourage commerce that was productive- yet risk-averse. The- rules aimed to advance e-xchange that was structured and hazard-free-, safeguarding both the merchants and sailors inte-gral to the Dutch economy.

The Ne-therlands had develope-d sophisticated shipbuilding methods that crafted sturdy, durable- ships suitable for lengthy trips across oceans. The-se techniques, such as re-inforced hulls and specialized rigging, allowe-d Dutch vessels to reliably transport cargo and pe-ople over vast distances. Othe-r nations recognized the stre-ngths of Dutch naval engineering and be-gan adopting similar practices. Over time, shipwrights globally incorporate-d elements of Ne-therlands shipbuilding into their own designs. The- successes of Dutch maritime innovations he-lped drive broader change-s as countries worked to harmonize ship construction standards on an inte-rnational level. This converge-nce towards uniform regulations transformed shipping in mate-rial ways and furthered trade ne-tworks spanning the entire globe-.

Furthermore-, Dutch regulations stressed the- importance of equitable and just tre-atment of sailors. The laws passed by the- Dutch Republic safeguarded the- rights of seafarers, including guarantee-s for proper wages, working environme-nts, and security from exploitation. These- core values later impacte-d worldwide dialogues regarding sailors' rights and le-d to the integration of employe-e protections in current maritime- agreements. The- principles established aime-d to ensure fair wages and humane- working conditions for seafarers traveling on Dutch ve-ssels.

The Dutch le-gal framework from that time spoke on two important matte-rs regarding maritime operations. First, it cove-red what should occur in the case of ships accide-ntally colliding at sea. Procedures we-re put forth for how to sort out any conflicts that may arise from such accidents. It also pre-sented standards for deciding who was at fault. Se-cond, it addressed salvage situations involving re-covering distressed ve-ssels or property from the se-a. Regulations provided direction for solving dispute-s over compensation/payment re-sulting from such rescue efforts. The-se foundations established by the- Dutch on collisions and salvage laid the early groundwork that late-r international agreeme-nts in admiralty law were built upon. They he-lped form the basic approaches use-d today in many countries' courts dealing with such maritime incide-nts and recovery missions.

The Dutch Re-public, due to its powerful position in global commerce-, saw a need to create- legal structures to enforce- their rules. They institute-d a system of consular posts in key harbors worldwide to supe-rvise adherence- to their legislation and settle- disagreements involving Dutch trade-rs and vessels. This network pre-pared the way for later port state- oversight and contributed towards the progre-ssion of worldwide compacts on legal authority and impleme-ntation. The consular offices monitored compliance- with Dutch regulations and resolved dispute-s between Dutch me-rchants and ships calling at ports around the globe. This establishe-d the foundation for modern practices of port state- control and influenced the e-volution of international agreeme-nts defining jurisdiction and enforceme-nt over merchant shipping activities.

The influe-nce of Dutch maritime regulations re-ached well beyond the-ir own coastal borders. As the Dutch Republic's shipping and naval ope-rations crossed oceans, interacting with various fore-ign legal codes and societie-s across lands, the principles of Dutch law tende-d to find implementation in the re-gulations of other countries through commerce- pacts, agreements be-tween nations, and cultural interchange-s. Because of this, instances whe-re one legal approach took on aspe-cts of another were common, he-lping to mold the evolution of global maritime jurisprude-nce. Trade, diplomacy and shared unde-rstanding between dive-rgent worldviews lent dive-rsity and flexibility to rules governing conduct upon the- seas.

To summarize, the- rules put forth by the Dutch Republic conce-rning commerce, transportation, and navigation significantly affecte-d the evolution of maritime le-gislation. Their advancements in ship de-sign requirements, prote-ctions for sailors, protocols for accidents and rescues at se-a, as well as founding consular posts globally, have left an unde-niable imprint on international maritime justice-. Grasping how Dutch rules impacted relate-d fields offers meaningful unde-rstanding into maritime law's historical foundations and developme-ntal journey across time. While re-gulations from the Dutch Republic establishe-d important precedents, the- continual progression of maritime trade e-nsured maritime law would require- further refining to handle ne-w complexities as globalization increasingly conne-cted all corners of the world.

Comparison and Impact of British, Spanish, and Dutch Influence

Throughout history, powerful navie-s have significantly influenced how maritime- law has formed. As sea trade and voyage-s of discovery grew over ce-nturies, nations struggled to dominate profitable- shipping lanes and implement le-gal systems oversee-ing such undertakings. Here, we- will look more closely at how three- leading naval forces - Britain, Spain, and the Ne-therlands - impacted how maritime law advance-d and investigate how their le-gal approaches still shape this domain today. While countrie-s like Britain and the Nethe-rlands saw their naval might peak centurie-s ago, the laws born of their desire- to control wide expanses of oce-an continue affecting international maritime- regulations. Meanwhile, though Spain's naval supre-macy waned after its Golden Age-, its tenets live on in the- rules guiding conduct on the high seas. By de-lving into what drove these powe-rs and the precede-nts they set, we gain insight into maritime- law's enduring foundations.

The British Navigation Acts, imple-mented betwe-en the 17th and 18th centurie-s, were a pivotal point in British maritime policymaking. The-se regulations mandated that all colonial comme-rce take place sole-ly on British vessels. Additionally, specifie-d commodities could only be imported into British te-rritories by passing first through English harbors. In establishing these- constraints, Britain sought to strengthen its control over world comme-rce and safeguard its commercial inte-rests. While the Acts he-lped Britain gain an advantage in trade, the-y also contributed to increasing tensions be-tween Britain and its colonies. By re-quiring colonial trade be restricte-d to British ships, it limited colonial economic opportunities and inde-pendence. Ove-r time, resentme-nt grew among the colonies which in part contribute-d to the American Revolution. The- Acts exemplified Britain's e-fforts to maximize its power on the se-as and consolidate its maritime dominance during this e-ra.

The provisions and re-gulations established within the British Navigation Acts yie-lded expansive ramifications re-garding maritime legislation. Not only did they sculpt British lawful practice-s but additionally exercised appre-ciable sway on global maritime rules. The- ideas entrenche-d inside these acts, for e-xample the notion of nationwide banne-r predominance and protectionism, e-volved into fundamental parts of worldwide maritime- law in later centuries. The- Navigation Acts established the principle- that only vessels bearing the- flag of the country of origin could engage in trade- between that country and its colonie-s, unless no such vessels we-re available. This concept of re-serving shipping for national vessels be-came a foundational eleme-nt of international maritime trade. Additionally, the- Acts promoted British shipping interests by re-quiring several colonial commodities to be- transported only on British vessels. While- protectionist in nature, these- regulations helped de-velop Britain's merchant flee-t and demonstrated the country's de-termination to dominate global seafaring comme-rce.

Let us now e-xplore Spain, another naval force that inde-libly impacted maritime legislation. At the- height of the Spanish Empire's asce-ndance, Spain instituted a host of rules managing oce-anic commerce, discovery ve-ntures, and colonization efforts. These- regulations embodied Spain's aspirations to dominate- enormous regions and amass riches from its holdings ove-rseas. The authorized doctrine-s embraced by Spain, like e-mploying royal charters and the Doctrine of Discove-ry, affected later marine- laws and procedures. While Spain wante-d to exert control over its vast colonial posse-ssions and the wealth they promise-d, the legal principles it e-stablished had widespread, long- lasting influe-nce.

The Dutch Re-public played an important role in advancing maritime law during its pe-ak as a naval force in the 1600s. The Dutch de-veloped exte-nsive legal systems for comme-rce, transportation, and sailing that focused on free- enterprise and comme-rcial autonomy. Their rules, like the- notion of privateering and maritime courts, conside-rably affected worldwide maritime- law by molding lawful practices in domains for example prize- law and jurisdictional control. While the Dutch Republic contribute-d significantly to developing maritime law during its time- as a major naval power, questions remain about how the-se legal frameworks shape-d international relations and trade as the-ir naval influence decline-d in later centuries.

When comparing the- legal practices of Britain, Spain, and the Ne-therlands, both clear similarities and diffe-rences become- apparent. All three se-afaring nations sought to assert authority over maritime comme-rce, yet their spe-cific strategies differe-d. The British predominantly enforce-d protectionism through the Navigation Acts, aiming to restrict trade- to domestic vessels. Me-anwhile, Spain concentrated on claiming te-rritory and establishing colonies as part of their impe-rial ambitions. Alternatively, the Dutch advocate-d for liberalized trade and comme-rcial autonomy. These varied philosophie-s later impacted the formation of le-gal standards and agreements re-garding international maritime law and jurisdiction.

The influe-nce of British, Spanish, and Dutch maritime policies cannot be- understated. The le-gal doctrines develope-d by these seafaring nations still significantly inform curre-nt rules oversee-ing commerce, transport, and transportation routes across wate-rs. Considering their regulations toge-ther provides us a more compre-hensive grasp of maritime law's formative- origins and how it has branched out differently in various place-s over time . While the- concepts introduced by these- naval forces centuries ago unde-rpin modern day standards, regional modifications have occurre-d as circumstances changed.

In the following se-ctions, we will examine how late-r events and advanceme-nts intersected with the- frameworks established by the-se naval forces. The progre-ssion of maritime law is a tapestry woven from the- contributions of many countries, each leaving its unique- mark on this intricate domain of jurisprudence. The- Doctrine of Discovery, with its roots strongly grounded in Europe-an colonialism, played an important role in forming early le-gal systems for maritime operations during the- colonial period. This doctrine deve-loped during the Age of Exploration whe-n European powers aimed to broade-n their territories and e-xert authority over newly found lands. While- European colonialism significantly influenced e-arly maritime law, numerous nations each offe-red distinctive perspe-ctives that collectively forme-d the complex tapestry of this le-gal field. The interse-ctions between succe-eding events, de-velopments in differe-nt regions, and the original foundations constructed by naval powe-rs combine to comprise the e-volving story of maritime law.

While the- Doctrine of Discovery asserte-d that European explorers posse-ssed authority over newly found non-Christian te-rritories, the papal decre-es on which it was based, like Pope- Alexander VI's Inter cae-tera and Dudum siquidem in the 1490s, e-ndowed European monarchs with power ove-r indigenous populations in recently discove-red lands. The bulls from Alexande-r VI allowed conquering and conversion of native- peoples inhabiting areas now e-xposed to Christians. This principle was founded on the- notion that explorers from Europe had rights to claim and gove-rn any non-Christian regions they came upon.

Under the Doctrine of Discovery, the concept of terra nullius, or "land belonging to no one," was introduced. This notion justified European claims to lands inhabited by indigenous peoples who did not adhere to Christianity. It effectively ignored indigenous systems of governance, land ownership, and resource management, denying their sovereignty and right to self-determination.

While the- Doctrine of Discovery establishe-d a legal framework that permitte-d colonial authorities to claim jurisdiction over newly e-ncountered maritime te-rritories, designating indigenous socie-ties as uncivilized promoted the- harmful perception of European supre-macy. By deeming non-Weste-rn civilizations as inferior, explorers and se-ttlers rationalized exploiting re-sources and traversing waterways of lands re-cently "discovered", without re-cognizing the humanity or sovereignty of e-stablished native populations. This policy of otherizing indige-nous peoples to validate colonial ambitions had lasting ne-gative repercussions.

This doctrine he-ld deep impacts for native tribe-s all over the world. It made it e-asier to take indigenous pe-ople's ancestral lands away from them, force- them to adopt new cultures, and e-rase their old traditions. Indigenous groups we-re pushed to the e-dges of society, freque-ntly losing access to crucial seaside re-sources and the usual fishing waters that had nourishe-d them for generations. This le-d native communities to no longer be- able to utilize locations that had long ago provided food and be-en important places their ance-stors relied on to survive. The- coastal areas and fishing spots they long used we-re taken, disregarding how e-ssential they were- to the lives and customs of indigenous socie-ties.

The Doctrine- of Discovery established a pre-cedent that influence-d later legal frameworks controlling colonial trade- and sailing. It offered moral and lawful validation for putting into place colonial trade-rules like navigation acts, which intende-d to manage and profit from maritime commerce- within colonial lands. These regulations grante-d sole trading privileges to spe-cific colonial forces, hampering competition from othe-r countries and guaranteeing financial supre-macy. Moreover, the navigation acts aime-d to streamline maritime busine-ss between colonie-s and European nations. By limiting outside involveme-nt and reserving shipping for designate-d powers, economic bene-fits could be concentrated within ce-rtain empires. Howeve-r, restricting free trade- also meant native people-s had fewer alternative-s for their goods. Overall, the discove-ry doctrine and subsequent trade- laws solidified European control over colonial te-rritories and their associated comme-rcial opportunities.

The legacy of the Doctrine of Discovery continues to shape modern maritime jurisprudence. Its impact can be seen in ongoing disputes over indigenous land rights, resource extraction in coastal areas, and the recognition of indigenous legal systems within the framework of contemporary maritime law. Efforts are being made to challenge the discriminatory aspects of this doctrine and recognize the rights and sovereignty of indigenous peoples.

The Doctrine- of Discovery holds great significance as its te-nets shaped early e-xplorations and the treatment of native- populations. Tracing its origins illuminates the philosophies that justifie-d claiming newly encountere-d lands without consent of the local inhabitants. While the- doctrine granted powers to Europe-an monarchs for centuries, its effe-cts still reverberate- in indigenous communities today. Acknowledging this painful history is an important ste-p to reform maritime law into a more fair and re-presentative syste-m. Though the doctrine no longer gove-rns international policy, its legacy serve-s as an example of the discrimination face-d by native groups. Moving forward, inclusive practices can he-lp remedy past wrongs and honor the ste-wardship of first peoples.

Legal Frameworks for New Colonies: Establishing Maritime Jurisdiction

As the colonial powe-rs increasingly grew their te-rritories and established ne-w settlements abroad, the-y confronted the difficult task of enforcing jurisdiction ove-r maritime areas and regulating maritime- activities within those regions. This se-gment investigates the- legal systems that were-implemented to tackle- these problems, illuminating the- intricacies associated with administering colonial wate-rs. For instance, establishing authority over fishing or trade- in coastal waters involved delicate- negotiations with indigenous communities to avoid conflict. De-fining maritime boundaries also prese-nted challenges, as the- rights of newly established colonie-s had to be balanced with those of othe-r imperial powers. Meanwhile-, governing activities at sea de-manded considerable naval and administrative- resources. Overall, asse-rting control of colonial waters required nuance-d legal frameworks to manage the- interests of both colonizers and colonize-d in a rapidly changing global landscape.

The colonial powe-rs had several methods for maintaining authority ove-r coastal regions. One significant way was deve-loping the legal systems that manage-d maritime operations in colonial waters. The-se rules and statutes dictate-d the guidelines e-ncompassing seaborne actions within colonial seas, making ce-rtain they served the- priorities of the ruling colonial nation. While ke-eping control over coastal territorie-s, the frameworks organized maritime- undertakings to benefit the-colonial authority.

While the- means by which colonial authorities exte-nded jurisdiction over maritime domains diffe-red depending on the- distinct situations and lawful heritages of each colonial force-, shared techniques incorporate-d the distribution of royal decree-s or licenses granting colonial powers the- ability to administer and control maritime issues within assigne-d territories. For instance, some- colonial powers issued written pe-rmissions from their monarchs delineating ce-rtain oceanic regions under the-ir command. This allowed them to establish administrations and e-nact regulations concerning navigation and trade in the- designated waters. Howe-ver, the specific proce-sses varied depe-nding on the colonial power's legal traditions and circumstance-s surrounding the claimed territory.

While the-se legal frameworks re-gularly borrowed components from the lawful frame-works of the colonizing nations and adapted them to addre-ss the exceptional ne-cessities and difficulties of oce-an administration in colonial settings, they likewise- expected to guarante-e that colonial forces could successfully ove-rsee exchange-, route, and different oce-an exercises inside- their settleme-nts. Specifically, the frameworks inte-nded to give colonial governme-nts the instruments important to administer the- utilization of waterways for exchange and trave-l inside their realms of impact, while-additionally safeguarding the privilege-s and advantages of the colonizing nations. In this way, the standards and guide-lines frequently adjuste-d existing laws identifying with exchange-, travel, and property to colonial conditions, concentrating as much on e-ncouraging gainful exchange betwe-en the settle-ment and home nation as on controlling the e-xercises of nearby inhabitants and diffe-rent colonial forces.

Furthermore-, the colonial powers attempte-d to establish maritime jurisdictions that helpe-d and shielded their financial inte-rests. This included applying business standards and navigation acts that manage-d and favored exchange inside- colonial domains. By imposing taxes, confinements, and monopolie-s on certain products and exchange course-s, the colonial forces meant to bring the- most favorable position from maritime exe-rcises. While colonial powers did se-ek to benefit e-conomically, some of their laws and policies also ne-gatively impacted local populations by restricting fre-e trade. Overall, e-stablishing regulatory control over maritime trade- enabled colonial empire-s to expand their influence- but did not always benefit all people-s within colonial territories equally.

While e-nforcing these legal frame-works in theory made sense-, putting them into action in the colonies pose-d difficulties. The colonial waters typically containe-d a mix of peoples, cultures, and laws, le-ading to disagreements be-tween disparate le-gal traditions when they interse-cted. Foisting unfamiliar legal notions upon local communities some-times sparked clashes and opposition to colonial control, as fore-ign principles disrupted indigenous customs. Navigating be-tween competing le-gal perspectives across dive-rse colonial settings proved challe-nging in practice.

Enforcing maritime law in far-off colonie-s proved a logistical challenge for colonial powe-rs due to several factors. The- immense distances se-parating these territorie-s from their governing nations complicated communication and transportation, making it difficult to transmit laws and dire-ctives in a timely manner. Limite-d resources only exace-rbated these issue-s, as governing bodies had few me-ans to dedicate sufficient pe-rsonnel or supplies to enforce- regulations across such vast and remote maritime- regions. Compliance with legal code-s was therefore challe-nging to monitor and secure in the far re-aches of colonial empires, as colonial administrations conte-nded with constraints of distance, communication barriers, and re-stricted resources.

While the- legal structures constructed for fre-shly founded colonies during the colonial pe-riod still impact contemporary maritime case law, the- principles and customs that develope-d at this time significantly affect the progre-ssion of maritime legislation. The frame-works instituted for new settle-ments in earlier colonial time-s persist in molding present-day maritime- justice. The ideas and practice-s shaped during this era have conside-rably contributed to the transformation of maritime law ove-r time.

To wrap up, setting up lawful structure-s for new settleme-nts assumed a basic job in asserting maritime purvie-w for colonial forces. These structure-s expected to control and profit by oce-anic exercises inside- colonial domains, giving rules and directions to overse-e exchange, navigation, and diffe-rent oceanic practices. The- procedures through which colonial powers asse-rted purview over maritime- territories fluctuated, utilizing strate-gies, for example, maje-stic grants or licenses. In any case, compe-lling these lawful structures in assorte-d colonial settings presente-d difficulties and frequently brought about clashe-s between diffe-rent lawful frameworks. In spite of this, the- lawful structures set up during this time have- left an enduring legacy, affe-cting present day maritime lawfulne-ss. The structures were- intended to direct e-xchange and travel over wate-rs yet colonial powers expe-rienced difficulties upholding the-ir control over maritime spaces. This e-ra saw contrasting lawful frameworks go up against each other bringing about clashe-s while settling new se-ttlements.While the- structures expecte-d to advantage colonial forces, authentic guide-lines over waters re-mained questionable. In any case-, their effect on curre-nt maritime lawfulness stays persiste-nt.

An examination into the- colonial trade regulations and navigation acts impleme-nted by Europe's colonial powers during this e-ra uncovers the delibe-rate attempts made to dominate- and profit from maritime commerce within the-ir territories. These- rules established ve-ry clear instructions for commerce and ship trave-l, in the end prioritizing the inte-rests of the colonial nations. The navigation acts e-nforced by England and other colonial powers mandate-d that goods carried by ships to and from their colonies could only be- transported on vessels from the- parent country or the colonies. Additionally, goods from Asia, Africa, or Ame-rica could only be unloaded first in the pare-nt country before being shippe-d on to another country. Through these re-gulations, the colonial nations meant to monopolize the- lucrative colonial trades and amass greate-r economic advantages for themse-lves.

The trade- rules that colonial powers establishe-d for their territories aime-d to structure all commerce within de-fined boundaries. These- regulations commonly specified which ite-ms could be exchanged, the- individuals permitted to participate in trade-, and the approved methods for conducting busine-ss transactions. Through governing commerce in the-ir colonies, the ruling nations ende-avored to optimize financial profits and prese-rve sole access to valuable- materials. The rules we-re intended to channe-l trading of particular goods between allowe-d parties using mandated approaches, in a manne-r that benefited the- colonial power the most.

Navigation acts played an important role- in colonial commerce guideline-s. These laws require-d vessels from solely the- colonial force or its allocated settle-ments to participate in business with the-colonies. By constraining commerce to the-ir own ships, colonial powers tried to reinforce- their domestic economie-s while restricting the e-ffect of competing countries. Navigation acts additionally re-gularly enforced limitations on overse-as vessels getting into colonial harbors, e-ven more shielding the- fiscal passions of the colonizers. The navigation re-gulations aimed to boost the economie-s of the colonial nations by mandating that only domestic ships could engage- in trade with other colonies. This was done- to limit influence from other powe-rs and prioritize economic gains for the colonizing country. At the- same time, restrictions we-re imposed on foreign ve-ssels entering colonial ports to furthe-r safeguard economic intere-sts.

While the-se trade regulations and navigation acts e-stablished guidelines that facilitate-d steady economic progress within the- colonial possessions as resources we-re extracted and profits we-re maximized for the advantage- of the colonizers, they also re-stricted possibilities for other countrie-s to engage in the lucrative- colonial markets, resulting in strains and disputes be-tween colonial authorities. The- acts supported consistent deve-lopment of the colonies by gove-rning trade and movement of goods, allowing colonists to spe-cialize in extracting valuable commoditie-s and ship them back to Europe. Howeve-r, limiting outside involvement in colonial e-xchange simultaneously discouraged non-colonial involve-ment in these profitable- ventures, fueling disagre-ements among those wishing to participate- but now excluded due to the- protectionist policies.

The imple-mentation of stringent regulations re-garding maritime commerce within indige-nous territories brought up important discussions surrounding impartiality, justice, and the- effects on native groups. Due- to their prohibitive nature, the-se rules regularly place-d local communities at a disadvantage as inhabitants were- prevented from e-ngaging completely in oceanic trade- within their own domains. Furthermore, such le-gislation helped prolong the e-xploitative essence- of colonialism since they allowed we-alth to continue being taken from colonize-d areas without proper compensation paid to the- inhabitants.

The le-gacy of colonial-era trade regulations and navigation acts continue-s to echo in modern maritime law. While- these explicit rule-s have mainly been take-n apart, their impact on worldwide commerce- and the power balances be-tween countries re-mains. The ideas of commercial manage-ment and protectionism embe-dded in these colonial practice-s have formed the progre-ssion of current maritime legislation, spe-cifically regarding issues like trade- deals, taxes, and guideline-s overseeing ove-rseas ships' admittance to local markets. Furthe-rmore, the power dynamics e-stablished by these colonial practice-s have persisted in subtle- ways through international relationships and trade ne-gotiations. Modern maritime law traces its roots dire-ctly to the regulations and acts that European nations e-stablished to control and restrict trade during the- colonial period.

Understanding the- historical context and effects of colonial trade- regulations and navigation acts offers enlighte-ning perspectives into the- evolution of maritime law. It illuminates the- intricate interplay betwe-en commercial nee-ds, lawful structures, and power balances that re-main influential in forming maritime justice pre-sently. By exploring this segme-nt's substance, audiences can cultivate- a richer valuation for the multidimensional difficultie-s encountered by maritime- authorities and the persiste-nt endeavors to harmonize ance-stral inheritances with progressing worldwide- standards.

Conflicts and Challenges: Clash of Legal Systems in Colonial Waters

During the colonial e-ra, the difference-s between le-gal systems in colonial waters freque-ntly produced disputes and difficulties for colonial powe-rs seeking to impose maritime- law. As colonial powers increased the- size of their territorie-s and founded colonies all around the world, the-y came across various legal codes that re-gularly went against their own. For instance, whe-n a British ship entered the- waters claimed by Spain, confusion could arise re-garding whether Spanish law or British law had jurisdiction in cases of crime- or commerce. Similarly, the e-xpanding Dutch and Portuguese empire-s encountered native- laws under which piracy, smuggling or trade might be de-fined differently. This le-d to disagreements be-tween colonial administrations over jurisdiction and sove-reignty in border regions. While- colonial powers wished to uphold their own maritime- codes on colonial shipping lanes and trade route-s, incorporating diverse local laws posed challe-nges to their efforts of e-stablishing uniform legal standards across scattered colonial outposts.

There- was one major point of contention that stemme-d from the difference- between Europe-an legal concepts and the traditional laws of native- peoples. The colonial force-s attempted to claim control over maritime- areas, essentially e-nforcing their own legal structures on indige-nous groups. Nonetheless, this e-ffort to exert administration regularly collide-d with the established lawful syste-ms and conventions of these local communitie-s. The native groups had long followed the-ir own practices and rules to govern activitie-s at sea, which did not always align with newcomers' ide-as of jurisdiction. While the colonial powers wante-d authority over coastal territories, this disre-garded the self-gove-rnance that indigenous societie-s had established through their customs. The-re was potential for dispute whe-n external authorities trie-d to impose alien legal frame-works upon peoples accustomed to the-ir own traditions.

The clash of le-gal systems was further nuanced by the- existence of nume-rous colonial forces within the same are-a. Distinct European countries maintained the-ir own maritime regulations and laws, resulting in disagre-ements over jurisdiction and comme-rce liberties. The-se disputes at times inte-nsified into quarrels and armed confrontations be-tween colonial powers. The- diverse colonial prese-nces and their varying regulations ge-nerated perple-xing legal gray areas, and competition ove-r trade routes or ports could ignite te-mpers. Regional powers found the-ir interests challenging one-another's prerogatives and provoking te-rritorial brushes.

Given the- immense size and intricacie-s of their colonial possessions, colonial authorities e-ncountered obstacles in upholding the-ir maritime rules across distant and diverse- territories. The e-normous spans of ocean separating colonies pose-d problems for colonial administrations seeking to vigilantly ove-rsee and strictly impose re-strictions on maritime operations. Conseque-ntly, in some areas unlawful behaviors like- smuggling, piracy, and unsanctioned commerce flourishe-d due to the challenge-s involved in firmly managing affairs over such great le-ngths. Additionally, variations in geography, economy, and society he-ightened the difficulty of uniformly e-nforcing regulations throughout far-flung colonial holdings.

Moreove-r, differences be-tween legal frame-works became sharper as Indige-nous groups opposed or disregarded colonial rule-s. Traditional practices like fishing, commerce-, and transportation frequently clashed with Europe-an jurisprudence. Indigenous pe-oples persistently carrie-d out these customary acts, defying the- foreign laws imposed. Their re-sistance proved a perpe-tual problem for colonial administration. Officials found it difficult to properly impleme-nt and enforce the le-gal structures they wished to e-stablish. Nor could they easily overse-e all maritime ende-avors in the region. This disconnect constantly challe-nged the colonial powers in the-ir goal of governance over coastal and oce-anic activities.

The clash be-tween conflicting legal frame-works operating in colonial waters had a profound and long-lasting effe-ct on contemporary maritime law. It brought attention to the- intricate difficulties in reconciling dive-rse legal traditions and maneuve-ring the jurisdictional problems stemming from ble-nded territorial assertions. The- disputes and obstacles faced by colonial force-s remain impactful in modern dialogues re-garding indigenous rights, traditional laws, and acknowledging the pluralism of le-gal approaches within the setting of maritime- regulations. While jurisdiction issues surface-d from mingling territorial ownership claims, reconciling varie-d legal customs proved complex. Continue-d influence exists from the- experience-s of colonial powers navigating indigenous rights, local laws, and acknowledging dive-rsity in legal systems regarding maritime- affairs.

Examining the dispute-s and difficulties that surfaced from the collision of lawful frame-works in colonial waters gives significant understandings into the- historical backdrop of maritime law and its proceeding advance-ment. Investigation these- intricacies empowers us to appre-ciate the subtle nature- of maritime legitimate ability and se-rves as a reminder that the- application of law on the seas ought to consider the- different lawful customs and conventions that e-xist inside our worldwide local area. While- maritime law has created ove-r the long run to attempt to oblige the- fluctuating lawful frameworks experie-nced by ships working in worldwide waters, a fe-w complex issues remaine-d. The law as applied to occasions on the high se-as must consider not just the lawful conventions of the- nation whose banner a ship sails under ye-t in addition the customs of different nations whose- waters may be influence-d. This sensitivity to assorted lawful societie-s is basic on the off chance that we are- to keep maritime e-xchange flowing betwee-n ports all throughout the planet.

Legacy and Repercussions: Impact on Modern Maritime Jurisprudence

While the- impacts of colonialism on current maritime law are indisputable-, exploring this legacy can offer insight into ongoing dynamics. The- legal structures crafted during colonial time-s still significantly contour and mold modern maritime jurisprudence-. To fully grasp the intricacies and issues confronting maritime- authorities today, considering colonialism's lasting effe-cts is key. The frameworks from colonial e-ras continue affecting this specialize-d legal domain in notable ways, from shaping overarching principle-s to influencing specific cases. Prope-rly acknowledging colonialism's repercussions allows for de-eper understanding of maritime- law's complex realities and proble-ms faced by jurisdictions now.

The conce-pt of territorial sovereignty within mode-rn maritime law traces back to the colonial e-ra. During this time, powerful colonial nations exte-nded their rule ove-r immense ocean re-gions through adopting the Doctrine of Discovery. This doctrine- was based on notions of European dominance and Christian authority, providing the-se nations legitimacy in declaring owne-rship over newly found lands and waters. Conse-quently, the colonial powers e-stablished the foundation for asserting gove-rnance over maritime te-rritories and their commodities. While- colonialism significantly shaped current understandings of jurisdiction in se-as, the lasting impacts of this period endure- in international maritime law to this day.

During this time, the- legal systems that were- developed primarily sought to aid the- colonial nations financially and politically. Regulations on colonial commerce and navigation laws we-re enacted to gove-rn and take advantage of maritime busine-ss within colonized lands. These rule-s tended to put the ne-eds of the colonizers first, re-sulting in lopsided authority and prosperity betwe-en the colonial forces and native- inhabitants. The trade acts passed aime-d to manage seaborne trade- to benefit the Europe-an countries controlling the colonies. This le-d to conflicts over control of commerce and transportation be-tween the colonize-rs enforcing their will through legislation and the- native populations who saw their own intere-sts sidelined.

Howeve-r, the clash of legal systems in colonial wate-rs created ongoing conflicts and difficulties that still affe-ct us. The long-held laws and practices of native- peoples regularly oppose-d the imposed colonial rules, re-sulting in intricate disagreeme-nts about authority and ambiguous laws. The colonial authorities had trouble consiste-ntly enforcing their ocean re-gulations across diverse colonial lands, leading to a varie-d mix of legal frameworks with differe-nt levels of success and validity.

The influe-nce of colonialism on contemporary maritime le-gislation stretches past territorial control and jurisdictional disagre-ements. It has also formed the- advancement of international law and agre-ements. Numerous worldwide- maritime treaties and unde-rstandings are results of historical discussions betwe-en previous colonial forces and fre-shly independent countrie-s looking to assert their rights over maritime- assets. While colonialism significantly impacted maritime- law and negotiations betwee-n former colonies and colonizers, the-re remains ongoing work to equitably balance- state control and shared access to oce-an resources.

Furthermore-, the legacy of colonialism in terms of powe-r dynamics, exploitation, and inequality continues to significantly influe-nce modern debate-s surrounding maritime law. Issues like re-source allocation, utilization of oceanic environme-nts, and the freedoms of native- populations are strongly intertwined with the- historical inheritances of colonialism. For instance, de-cisions about who controls fishing rights in a certain region or who has the authority to e-xtract oil from beneath the se-a floor cannot be separated from the- far-reaching impacts of colonial policies enacte-d centuries ago. As communities e-ndeavor to govern maritime activitie-s in an equitable and sustainable fashion, acknowle-dging colonialism's enduring effects re-garding inequitable distributions of authority appears crucial. The- arrangements of power le-ft by colonial regimes live on in pre-sent-day discussions on legal control of waters, se-abeds, and their bountiful resource-s.

As we navigate- the complex legal issue-s surrounding modern maritime law, achieving a cle-ar comprehension and properly handling the-se historical influences is e-xtremely important. Realizing the- past context and continual impacts of colonialism permits us to aim for solutions that are faire-r and more incorporating relating to maritime law. By re-cognizing and disputing the inequalities inhe-rently ingrained within the authorize-d structures set up during the colonial time- period, we have the- opportunity to labor toward a future where maritime- law really looks after the inte-rests of all involved parties, irre-spective of their prior historical e-xperiences or colonial inhe-ritances. Furthermore, appre-ciating how colonial policies of the past fashioned today's maritime- legal frameworks allows modern le-gal professionals to identify and address any linge-ring inequities. With open and thoughtful discussion, dive-rse perspective-s can be respecte-d to develop solutions upholding equal tre-atment and justice for all.

Part II:
Charting the
Modern Seas

"In the digital currents of modern maritime law, the ship of justice is steered by the compass of international collaboration, guided by the lighthouses of safety, sustainability, and the ever-changing winds of global trade."

The Turn of the 20th Century:
Titanic Sinking, International Safety,
and Emergence of IMO:
****

The Titanic Tragedy: A Turning Point in Maritime Safety

The historic sinking of the Titanic on April 15, 1912, remains one of the most significant events in maritime history. This tragic incident served as a wake-up call for the international community, shedding light on the dire need for improved safety regulations in the maritime industry.

On that fateful night, the luxurious British passenger liner collided with an iceberg in the North Atlantic Ocean, resulting in the loss of more than 1,500 lives. The magnitude of this disaster shocked the world and prompted immediate investigations to determine liability and identify areas for improvement in maritime safety.

The inquiries conducted after the sinking of the Titanic revealed numerous deficiencies in existing safety measures. Key findings included inadequate lifeboats, insufficient training and procedures for emergency situations, and an overreliance on outdated communication systems. These revelations highlighted a critical need for comprehensive reforms in maritime safety to prevent similar tragedies from occurring in the future.

In response to these findings, governments and organizations around the world embarked on a mission to establish international safety regulations for maritime transportation. This marked a significant shift towards a collective approach to safeguarding human lives at sea.

International Efforts for Maritime Safety: SOLAS and Other Conventions

One of the most prominent outcomes of the post-Titanic era was the development of the International Convention for the Safety of Life at Sea (SOLAS). Adopted in 1914, SOLAS aimed to establish uniform safety standards for ships engaged in international voyages. The convention covered various aspects of maritime safety, including construction requirements, lifesaving appliances, fire protection measures, and radio communication procedures.

Over the years, SOLAS has undergone several revisions and amendments to keep pace with evolving technologies and emerging challenges. Today, it stands as the most comprehensive international treaty governing maritime safety. SOLAS has played a crucial role in enhancing the safety of ships and safeguarding the lives of seafarers and passengers worldwide.

In addition to SOLAS, various other conventions have contributed significantly to improving maritime safety. These include the International Convention on Load Lines (LL), which addresses the stability and buoyancy requirements of ships, and the International Convention on Standards of Training, Certification, and Watchkeeping for Seafarers (STCW), which sets minimum training and certification standards for seafarers.

Creation of the International Maritime Organization (IMO)

The establishment of the International Maritime Organization (IMO) in 1948 marked a momentous milestone in international efforts towards maritime safety and regulation. The IMO emerged as a specialized agency of the United Nations responsible for promoting safe, secure, and environmentally sound shipping worldwide.

With its headquarters in London, the IMO acts as a global forum for discussion and decision-making on maritime matters. It facilitates the development of international regulations that are binding on member states, ensuring uniformity in maritime practices across nations.

The IMO's mission extends beyond safety to encompass environmental protection, security, legal matters, technical cooperation, and capacity building. Through its committees, subcommittees, and expert groups, the IMO continues to play a vital role in addressing emerging challenges and advancing maritime safety standards.

Evolving International Safety Standards: From Morse Code to Modern Navigation Systems

Technological advancements have revolutionized maritime safety standards, enabling more effective communication and navigation systems. In the aftermath of the Titanic tragedy, there was a push to improve communication capabilities at sea to enhance distress signal transmission and coordination of rescue operations.

The transition from Morse code-based communication to wireless radio systems greatly improved the efficiency and reliability of ship-to-ship and ship-to-shore communication. As radio technology continued to advance, the development of satellite communications further revolutionized global maritime communications.

Alongside communication systems, navigational aids became increasingly sophisticated. Traditional methods, such as celestial navigation and dead reckoning, gave way to more accurate systems like radar, gyrocompasses, and global positioning systems (GPS). These advancements greatly enhanced the ability of ships to navigate safely and avoid collisions.

Towards a Safer Future: Challenges and Innovations in Maritime Safety

While significant progress has been made in maritime safety over the past century, challenges persist in ensuring a safer future. The emergence of cyber threats poses new risks to vessel navigation systems and onboard communication networks. Steps are being taken to address these vulnerabilities and enhance cybersecurity measures in the maritime industry.

Environmental concerns have also gained prominence in recent years. The shipping industry plays a significant role in global emissions, prompting efforts to reduce its carbon footprint and mitigate the impact on marine ecosystems. Innovative technologies, including alternative fuels and emission reduction devices, are being explored to achieve sustainable shipping practices.

As we forge ahead into the future, the lessons learned from the Titanic sinking continue to shape maritime safety regulations. The tragedy serves as a stark reminder of the inherent risks associated with maritime activities and the ongoing need for vigilance, collaboration, and innovation to ensure the safety of those who venture,International Efforts for Maritime Safety: SOLAS and Other Conventions

In the wake of the tragic sinking of the RMS Titanic in 1912, international efforts to establish safety regulations for maritime transportation gained significant momentum. The public outcry following the loss of over 1,500 lives aboard the "unsinkable" ship prompted a global focus on improving safety standards and preventing similar disasters from occurring in the future. This section delves into the international efforts undertaken during this crucial period to enhance maritime safety.

One of the most important developments in maritime safety was the establishment of the International Convention for the Safety of Life at Sea (SOLAS). Adopted in 1914, SOLAS aimed to ensure that ships adhered to minimum safety requirements, such as maintaining sufficient life-saving equipment, practicing regular emergency drills, and implementing effective communication systems. SOLAS also introduced specific guidelines for constructing ships, addressing issues such as watertight compartments, stability, and fire safety.

Over the years, SOLAS has undergone several revisions to reflect advancements in technology and changing industry practices. The convention has been instrumental in setting internationally recognized standards for ship safety and has greatly contributed to reducing the risk of maritime accidents. It is worth noting that SOLAS is enforced by member states through national legislation and inspections conducted by flag states and port states.

In addition to SOLAS, numerous other conventions have focused on various aspects of maritime safety. For example, the International Convention on Load Lines, adopted in 1966, established regulations for marking and certifying load lines on ships to ensure their stability under different loading conditions. The International Convention for Safe Containers (CSC), starting in 1972, set standards for container construction and certification to ensure safe transportation and handling.

Furthermore, conventions such as the International Convention for the Prevention of Pollution from Ships (MARPOL) have addressed environmental concerns by establishing regulations for minimizing pollution from maritime activities. MARPOL's annexes cover various aspects of pollution prevention, including oil spills, sewage discharges, garbage disposal, and air emissions.

These conventions, among others, have played a crucial role in improving maritime safety on a global scale. By establishing clear guidelines and standards, they enhance the safety culture within the industry and ensure that ships are equipped to handle emergencies effectively. The cooperation and commitment of member states to implement these regulations have been vital in promoting safe shipping practices worldwide.

As the maritime industry continues to evolve, the need for comprehensive safety regulations remains paramount. Emerging challenges, such as cybersecurity threats and environmental sustainability concerns, require ongoing efforts to update and strengthen existing conventions or establish new ones. The collective determination of nations to prioritize safety and mitigate risks will shape the future of maritime safety standards, ensuring that vessels traverse the seas with utmost security and minimizing the occurrence of tragic incidents like the Titanic disaster.

The Turn of the 20th Century marked a remarkable shift in maritime safety regulations and the emergence of the International Maritime Organization (IMO). Established in 1948, the IMO plays a crucial role in promoting maritime safety and security on a global scale. This section provides an overview of the creation of the IMO and explores its roles and functions within the realm of maritime law.

The establishment of the IMO was prompted by a pressing need for international cooperation in addressing safety concerns in the wake of the tragic sinking of the Titanic in 1912. The disaster served as a wake-up call, highlighting the urgent need for standardized safety measures and regulations to prevent similar tragedies from occurring in the future.

The IMO was created as a specialized agency of the United Nations, with the primary objective of developing and maintaining a comprehensive regulatory framework for international shipping. Its mission encompasses various aspects of maritime safety and security, including the prevention and control of marine pollution, promotion of navigational safety, facilitation of efficient shipping practices, and regulation of ship design and construction standards.

One of the key roles of the IMO is to establish international conventions and protocols that govern different areas of maritime safety. These conventions serve as legally binding instruments that are ratified by Member States, thereby ensuring their implementation and enforcement at a global level. The International Convention for the Safety of Life at Sea (SOLAS), adopted in 1974, is one such convention developed under the auspices of the IMO. SOLAS lays down comprehensive safety requirements for ships, covering everything from construction standards to emergency preparedness and lifesaving equipment.

In addition to developing conventions, the IMO also plays an active role in facilitating collaboration among Member States, industry stakeholders, and other relevant organizations. It provides a platform for sharing information, best practices, and technical expertise, which helps strengthen maritime safety capabilities worldwide. The IMO also promotes capacity building initiatives aimed at enhancing the competence and skillset of seafarers, port state control personnel, and other maritime professionals.

Over the years, the IMO has adapted and evolved to keep pace with technological advancements and emerging challenges. It has been instrumental in developing regulations for new technologies and navigation systems, such as Global Maritime Distress and Safety System (GMDSS), Automatic Identification System (AIS), and Electronic Chart Display and Information System (ECDIS). These innovations have significantly contributed to improving safety at sea by enhancing communication, navigation, and situational awareness.

Looking ahead, the IMO continues to address emerging issues related to maritime safety and security. This includes tackling challenges posed by cybersecurity threats, environmental concerns, and the impact of climate change on shipping practices. The IMO actively engages in discussions on sustainable shipping practices, pollution prevention measures, and the reduction of greenhouse gas emissions from ships.

The creation of the IMO marked a significant milestone in global efforts to promote maritime safety and security. By fostering collaboration among nations and providing a platform for developing and implementing international standards, the IMO has played a pivotal role in safeguarding lives, protecting the marine environment, and facilitating the efficient operation of the maritime industry. In an ever-evolving landscape of maritime law, the IMO remains at the forefront of ensuring safe and secure seas for generations to come.

Evolving International Safety Standards: From Morse Code to Modern Navigation Systems

Technological advancements have played a crucial role in shaping and improving maritime safety standards over the years. As the world entered the 20th century, innovative developments revolutionized communication systems, navigational aids, and ultimately, the way ships navigated through the treacherous waters.

One significant advancement during this period was the adoption of Morse code as a means of communication at sea. Before its introduction, ship-to-ship communication relied heavily on signal flags and semaphore. However, Morse code provided a more efficient and standardized method of communication, allowing ships to transmit messages quickly and accurately across vast distances. This development facilitated timely warnings about hazards, enabling vessels to avoid potential collisions and navigate safely.

Furthermore, the implementation of radio technology greatly improved maritime safety by enhancing communication capabilities between ships and shore-based stations. Radio sets became increasingly common onboard vessels, enabling sailors to transmit distress signals and receive crucial information from coastal radio stations. The ability to communicate in real-time significantly reduced response times during emergencies and facilitated coordinated rescue efforts.

In addition to communication systems, navigational aids underwent significant advancements during this period. Nautical charts, which have been essential for centuries in guiding ships safely through unfamiliar waters, were continually updated and improved. The use of precise cartographic techniques allowed for more accurate charting of coastlines, reefs, lighthouses, and other navigational landmarks. This enhanced accuracy contributed to the safer navigation of vessels and reduced the risk of grounding or colliding with submerged hazards.

The development and implementation of modern navigation systems further elevated maritime safety standards. The introduction of radar technology provided vessels with a reliable means of detecting nearby ships, land masses, or obstacles even in poor visibility conditions. This greatly mitigated the risks associated with fog, darkness, or adverse weather conditions, ensuring that ships could navigate with greater confidence and avoid potential disasters.

Another pivotal innovation was the advent of global positioning systems (GPS), which revolutionized navigation by providing accurate and reliable positioning information to ships worldwide. GPS systems enabled mariners to determine their exact location with unparalleled precision, reducing the likelihood of navigational errors and guiding vessels along predetermined routes with ease. This technological breakthrough significantly enhanced safety on waterways, as ships could now navigate more efficiently, maintain safe distances from other vessels, and avoid potential collisions.

As maritime technology continues to advance rapidly, further improvements in safety standards are imminent. Emerging technologies, such as autonomous vessels, artificial intelligence, and advanced sensor systems, have the potential to revolutionize maritime operations and enhance safety levels even further. With the integration of these innovations into existing safety frameworks, the maritime industry will undoubtedly witness a future where accidents are minimized, and the risk to human life is significantly reduced.

In conclusion, technological advancements have played an instrumental role in improving maritime safety standards over time. From the introduction of Morse code and radio technology to the development of radar systems and GPS, each innovation has contributed to safer navigation practices and reduced the risks associated with maritime activities. As we continue to embrace new technologies and harness their potential, the future of maritime safety holds immense promise for ensuring the security and well-being of all those who sail the seas.

Towards a Safer Future: Challenges and Innovations in Maritime Safety

As maritime industries continue to grow and evolve, ensuring the safety of vessels and their crew remains a paramount concern. In this section, we explore the contemporary challenges faced in maintaining maritime safety, while also examining innovative approaches and emerging technologies aimed at enhancing safety measures and reducing accidents.

One of the major challenges in maritime safety today is the increasing threat of cyber attacks. With the growing reliance on technology and connectivity within the industry, vessels are becoming vulnerable to hacking, data breaches, and system failures. As cybercriminals target maritime infrastructure and information systems, it is crucial for industry stakeholders to collaborate and implement robust cybersecurity measures. The section discusses the importance of developing comprehensive cybersecurity strategies, including network monitoring, threat intelligence sharing, and employee training programs.

Environmental concerns are another pressing issue in modern maritime safety. As global awareness regarding climate change and pollution intensifies, there is a growing focus on reducing the ecological impact of maritime activities. The section explores regulatory initiatives aimed at minimizing emissions from ships, such as the International Maritime Organization's (IMO) Energy Efficiency Design Index (EEDI) and Ship Energy Efficiency Management Plan (SEEMP). Additionally, it delves into the implementation of ballast water management systems to prevent the introduction of invasive species into new ecosystems.

In order to tackle these challenges, industry stakeholders are increasingly turning to innovative approaches and emerging technologies. One such example is the adoption of autonomous ships, which have the potential to revolutionize the industry by eliminating human error and improving efficiency. However, this technological advancement also raises legal and regulatory questions regarding liability and compliance with international standards. The section examines ongoing developments in autonomous shipping and their implications for maritime safety.

Furthermore, advancements in satellite technology and data analytics have paved the way for improved situational awareness and predictive maintenance in the maritime sector. By harnessing real-time data on weather conditions, vessel performance, and navigational risks, ship operators can make more informed decisions regarding route planning, maintenance schedules, and emergency responses. The section highlights the benefits of these technologies and their role in enhancing maritime safety practices.

As we navigate the complexities of modern maritime safety, it is crucial to recognize that both challenges and innovations continue to evolve. Cybersecurity threats, environmental concerns, autonomous technologies, and data-driven analytics are just a few of the dynamics shaping the future of maritime safety. By staying abreast of these developments and fostering collaboration between industry stakeholders, it is possible to create a safer and more sustainable maritime environment for all.

World Wars and Maritime Law

World Wars I and II had a profound impact on maritime law, giving rise to various legal challenges stemming from naval warfare and maritime operations. The tumultuous nature of these conflicts presented unprecedented circumstances that required the development of new legal frameworks to address the complexities of maritime activities during wartime.

One of the key legal issues arising from maritime activities during World Wars I and II was the need to determine the status and treatment of enemy vessels seized or captured during naval encounters. The concept of prize courts played a crucial role in adjudicating such disputes, ensuring a fair resolution in accordance with established legal principles. Prize courts were responsible for examining captured vessels and their cargoes, determining their lawful status, and making decisions regarding their confiscation or release.

Naval warfare during these conflicts introduced new challenges, particularly with the use of submarines, known as U-boats. Unrestricted submarine warfare posed significant legal dilemmas, as attacks by U-boats targeted not only military vessels but also civilian ships. The legality of such attacks and their repercussions on international trade and commerce became pressing issues that demanded urgent attention.

To address these and other wartime maritime practices, various conventions were established to regulate the conduct of belligerent powers. Among these conventions were the Hague Rules, which aimed to establish regulations governing the treatment of enemy vessels at sea, and the Geneva Conventions, which focused on the protection of wounded soldiers and prisoners of war. Additionally, the Declaration of London sought to codify rules regarding naval warfare, including the interception and destruction of merchant vessels.

The establishment of these conventions marked a significant step forward in shaping maritime law and providing a legal framework for addressing the unique challenges posed by maritime activities during times of war. They laid the groundwork for subsequent developments in international law pertaining to armed conflicts at sea.

The legacies of World Wars I and II continue to influence modern maritime law. Lessons learned from these conflicts have prompted advancements in safety measures, security protocols, and the protection of civilians during times of war. The experiences gained from grappling with the legal complexities of naval warfare have shaped subsequent legal frameworks and conventions, ensuring a more comprehensive and robust system of maritime law.

In conclusion, World Wars I and II had far-reaching implications for maritime law, necessitating the development of legal mechanisms to navigate the complexities of wartime maritime activities. The legal challenges posed by naval warfare, prize courts, U-boat warfare, and the establishment of conventions have helped shape the landscape of modern maritime law, fostering a greater understanding of the intricacies involved in regulating maritime activities during times of conflict.

Prize courts played a significant role in adjudicating maritime disputes during World Wars I and II, leaving a lasting impact on the development of maritime law. These courts, established by belligerent nations, were responsible for determining the legitimacy of captured enemy vessels and their cargo.

The jurisdiction of prize courts extended to cases involving enemy vessels and neutral ships engaged in unlawful activities such as blockade-running or smuggling. These courts followed specific procedures and principles to ensure fair and efficient resolution of disputes. Adhering to international law and custom, prize courts judged whether a ship and its cargo were "prizes of war" or subject to confiscation.

Landmark cases and legal precedents set by prize courts during World Wars I and II shaped the understanding of maritime law. For example, the case of the SS Sussex established that attacks on civilian vessels could be considered illegal acts during warfare. This ruling influenced subsequent conventions and treaties, emphasizing the protection of civilians during armed conflicts at sea.

The decisions made by prize courts also highlighted the importance of distinguishing between military and civilian targets. The sinking of passenger and merchant vessels, such as the Lusitania, by German U-boats sparked outrage and condemnation worldwide. These events contributed to the development of international conventions and regulations aimed at safeguarding innocent civilians from unnecessary harm during wartime.

The establishment of conventions to address wartime maritime practices was a significant outcome of World Wars I and II. The Hague Rules, adopted in 1907, laid down principles governing the treatment of neutral shipping during naval warfare. The Geneva Conventions, first introduced in 1864 and further expanded after the world wars, provided comprehensive guidelines for the protection of wounded soldiers, prisoners of war, and civilians in armed conflicts. Additionally, the Declaration of London in 1909 attempted to unify the rules governing naval warfare but ultimately failed due to disagreements among nations.

Overall, the role played by prize courts during World Wars I and II, along with the legal precedents set and conventions established, significantly influenced the development of maritime law. The experiences and lessons learned from wartime maritime practices reinforced the need for legal frameworks that prioritize the safety, security, and protection of civilians in times of armed conflict. These events continue to shape modern maritime legislation and underline the importance of upholding international norms to prevent unnecessary suffering and destruction at sea.

U-boat warfare emerged as a significant challenge during both World Wars, presenting unique legal implications for maritime law. In this section, we will delve into the use of submarines (U-boats) as weapons in warfare and examine the legal challenges posed by unrestricted submarine warfare, including attacks on civilian vessels.

Submarines offered new capabilities in naval warfare, providing stealth and the ability to target enemy vessels without detection. U-boats became a powerful tool for naval forces, particularly during the World Wars, as they could launch surprise attacks and disrupt enemy supply lines. However, this form of warfare brought about significant legal dilemmas.

One of the most pressing concerns surrounding U-boat warfare was the targeting of civilian vessels. Merchant ships, passenger liners, and even hospital ships were vulnerable to U-boat attacks, leading to devastating losses of life and property. Attacks on neutral vessels also occurred, sparking further outcry and raising questions about the legality of such actions.

International responses to unrestricted submarine warfare were swift and aimed at establishing legal measures to address this issue. The Declaration of London in 1909 sought to regulate maritime warfare and protect civilians during armed conflicts. However, its provisions were not widely adopted or implemented during World War I.

In response to the ongoing challenges posed by U-boat warfare, various legal measures were taken during both World Wars. Naval powers began escorting merchant convoys with warships to minimize the risk of U-boat attacks. These convoys relied on coordinated efforts to protect civilian vessels from submarine threats.

Additionally, legal frameworks were established to address the complex issues arising from attacks on civilian ships. Prize courts played a crucial role in adjudicating disputes related to captured vessels and cargo during wartime. These courts aimed to determine whether a captured ship or cargo was legally considered a prize of war. The principles followed by prize courts and their jurisdiction helped shape the legal framework surrounding maritime warfare during these turbulent times.

International conventions and treaties were also established to regulate maritime activities during armed conflicts. The Geneva Conventions, for instance, sought to protect the rights and well-being of individuals affected by armed conflicts at sea. The Hague Rules, adopted in 1924, established guidelines for the limitation of liability in cases involving collisions and other incidents at sea.

The legal measures taken in response to U-boat warfare played a significant role in shaping modern maritime law. Lessons learned from the challenges posed during both World Wars influenced subsequent conventions, such as the United Nations Convention on the Law of the Sea (UNCLOS). These conventions aimed to establish regulations and safeguards to protect civilian vessels and ensure the safety of seafarers during times of war.

In conclusion, U-boat warfare presented unique legal challenges during both World Wars. Targeting civilian vessels and unrestricted submarine warfare raised profound questions about the legality of these actions. International responses led to the establishment of legal measures, including the use of prize courts, adoption of conventions, and escorting of merchant convoys. These efforts shaped the development of maritime law and emphasized the need to protect civilian vessels and uphold humanitarian standards during armed conflicts at sea.

Establishment of conventions to address wartime maritime practices:

During the tumultuous periods of World Wars I and II, the international community recognized the urgent need to establish conventions that would regulate maritime activities during times of war. These conventions aimed to address the legal challenges posed by naval warfare and ensure the safety of civilian vessels.

One such significant convention is the Hague Rules of 1907. Initially formulated to address the conduct of naval warfare, these rules laid down specific guidelines concerning the treatment of neutral vessels during armed conflicts. They established principles to govern the seizure and destruction of enemy merchant ships, as well as provisions regarding contraband goods and blockades. The Hague Rules set a precedent for subsequent conventions by acknowledging the importance of regulating maritime practices during wartime.

The Geneva Conventions, first established in 1864 with subsequent revisions in 1906, 1929, and 1949, played a crucial role in safeguarding the rights of individuals affected by armed conflicts. While primarily addressing humanitarian concerns, these conventions also included provisions related to maritime law. For instance, Protocol I of the 1949 Geneva Conventions addressed protection for victims at sea, particularly those wounded or shipwrecked during naval operations.

Another important convention, the Declaration of London of 1909, aimed to harmonize the laws of maritime warfare. Although never fully ratified due to the outbreak of World War I, it remains significant as an early attempt to codify rules governing naval engagements. The declaration covered various aspects such as blockade, contraband, destruction of neutral prizes, and the treatment of enemy vessels.

These conventions collectively had a lasting impact on shaping maritime law during times of war. They represented a concerted international effort to mitigate the devastating consequences inflicted on civilians and property during armed conflicts. By establishing standardized legal frameworks and principles for maritime operations, these conventions aimed to maintain a semblance of order amidst chaos.

Although each convention addressed specific aspects of wartime maritime practices, they shared common objectives, including the protection of civilian vessels and their crews, as well as minimizing the impact of hostilities on neutral parties. These conventions played a pivotal role in shaping subsequent legal frameworks addressing maritime law during times of armed conflict.

The establishment of these conventions highlights the international community's recognition of the need for comprehensive regulation and protection in a maritime context, even during the most challenging and turbulent times. Their provisions and objectives continue to serve as guiding principles in contemporary discussions surrounding the legal framework governing maritime operations in times of war.

Legacy and Lessons Learned from World Wars I and II for Maritime Law

The impact of World Wars I and II on the development of maritime law cannot be overstated. These conflicts introduced unprecedented challenges and raised critical legal issues regarding naval warfare, maritime operations, and the protection of civilians at sea. As we reflect on the legacy of these wars, it becomes evident that valuable lessons were learned, shaping subsequent legal frameworks and conventions in the field of maritime law.

One significant lesson learned from World Wars I and II was the importance of ensuring the safety and security of both military and civilian vessels. The devastating consequences of unrestricted submarine warfare highlighted the need for regulations that would protect innocent lives at sea. International responses to these atrocities led to the establishment of legal measures aimed at safeguarding civilian ships during times of armed conflict.

Another crucial lesson learned pertained to the jurisdiction and adjudication of maritime disputes in wartime. Prize courts emerged as a vital means to address legal issues arising from wartime maritime activities. These specialized courts played a crucial role in determining the status and fate of captured enemy vessels, their cargo, and crew. Landmark cases and legal precedents set by prize courts during

World Wars I and II laid the groundwork for principles governing maritime warfare and shaped subsequent legal frameworks.

The experiences of World Wars I and II also emphasized the need for international cooperation in addressing wartime maritime practices. In response to the unique challenges posed by these conflicts, conventions were established to regulate various aspects of naval warfare. For instance, the Hague Rules sought to harmonize laws related to the conduct of hostilities at sea, while the Geneva Conventions provided essential protections for wounded combatants, prisoners of war, and civilians caught up in armed conflicts. The Declaration of London aimed to establish rules governing maritime warfare but ultimately failed to gain universal acceptance due to disagreements among naval powers.

The legacy of World Wars I and II continues to resonate in contemporary maritime law. The lessons learned from these conflicts have shaped subsequent legal frameworks, conventions, and regulations aimed at enhancing safety, security, and the protection of civilians at sea. The profound impact of these events underscores the imperative of continuously adapting and evolving maritime law to address emerging challenges in an ever-changing global landscape.

As we navigate the intricate seas of maritime jurisprudence, it is essential to reflect on the legacy of World Wars I and II. By understanding the lessons learned from these conflicts, we can ensure that our legal frameworks remain robust and responsive to the evolving needs of maritime jurisdictions. Through this reflection, we honor the sacrifices made during these tumultuous times and strive to build a future where the seas are governed by principles of justice, fairness, and respect for international law.

The Cold War's Influence on Maritime law

The Cold War was marked by intense global tensions and the rivalry between the United States and the Soviet Union. As both superpowers sought to gain a strategic advantage over one another, the development and deployment of nuclear submarines emerged as a key aspect of their naval strategies. This section explores the impact of nuclear submarines on maritime law, shedding light on the legal challenges and implications that arose during this era.

One of the primary legal challenges posed by nuclear submarines was their ability to operate stealthily beneath the ocean's surface. Unlike conventional surface vessels, nuclear submarines could remain undetected for extended periods, giving them a significant tactical advantage. This raised concerns regarding the potential for covert activities, such as surveillance operations or the placement of intelligence-gathering devices, which went against established norms of maritime law.

Furthermore, the powerful armaments carried by these submarines, including nuclear missiles, introduced new dimensions to the dynamics of naval warfare. The presence of these weapons at sea heightened fears of accidental or unauthorized launch, potentially leading to catastrophic consequences. As a result, there was a pressing need to establish legal frameworks and protocols to ensure the safe and responsible operation of nuclear submarines.

In terms of strategic deterrence, nuclear submarines played a crucial role during the Cold War. The concept of mutually assured destruction relied heavily on these submarines' ability to remain hidden and undetectable while serving as a formidable retaliatory force. This aspect of nuclear deterrence added complexity to the existing principles of maritime law concerning armed conflict and the use of force.

To address these legal challenges and mitigate potential risks, various measures were implemented. International agreements, such as bilateral arms control treaties and confidence-building measures between the United States and the Soviet Union, aimed to promote transparency and reduce the likelihood of misunderstandings or escalations at sea. Additionally, naval doctrines evolved to accommodate the unique capabilities of nuclear submarines within established legal frameworks.

The impact of nuclear submarines on maritime law during the Cold War cannot be understated. Their development and deployment necessitated a reconsideration of existing legal norms, especially in the realms of surveillance, territorial boundaries, and naval warfare. The interplay between strategic considerations, technological advancements, and legal frameworks shaped the dynamics of maritime law during this tense era.

As the Cold War progressed, further developments in maritime law would address the broader challenges presented by nuclear submarines and other emerging issues. UNCLOS I and II, discussed later, played significant roles in expanding jurisdictional boundaries and addressing concerns related to sea lanes and the exploitation of resources in international waters. By understanding the impact of nuclear submarines on maritime law, we can appreciate the complex interplay between military strategies, technological advancements, and legal principles that continue to shape the field of maritime jurisprudence today.

Legal Frameworks for Regulating Sea Lanes during the Cold War:

During the Cold War, as tensions escalated between world powers, there was a growing need to establish legal frameworks to regulate sea lanes and maintain order in heavily trafficked areas. International agreements and conventions were put in place to address the unique challenges posed by this era of maritime history.

One key aspect of regulating sea lanes during the Cold War was ensuring the safety of maritime traffic. With the development and deployment of nuclear submarines, concerns arose regarding potential collisions, accidents, and other incidents that could have catastrophic consequences. As a result, international efforts were made to establish guidelines for navigation and communication procedures, aiming to reduce the risk of accidents and facilitate the smooth flow of maritime traffic.

The International Rules of the Road (COLREGs) played a significant role in regulating sea lanes during this period. These rules provided clear instructions on how vessels should navigate, communicate, and give way to each other in order to avoid collisions. They served as a common framework for ships from different nations operating in the same waters and helped prevent misunderstandings or conflicting actions that could escalate tensions.

Additionally, specific regional agreements and organizations were formed to address the unique challenges faced by particular sea lanes. For example, in the North Atlantic, the North Atlantic Treaty Organization (NATO) established guidelines and procedures for the safe passage of naval vessels, including submarines. These guidelines aimed to minimize the risks associated with military activities at sea and prevent accidental clashes between opposing forces.

Furthermore, international conventions such as the Convention for the Safety of Life at Sea (SOLAS) played a crucial role in ensuring safety standards for vessels traversing sea lanes. SOLAS provided regulations concerning ship construction, equipment, and operational procedures to enhance navigational safety and mitigate potential risks.

These efforts to regulate sea lanes during the Cold War were driven by a shared recognition of the importance of maintaining order and preventing conflicts at sea. By establishing legal frameworks and guidelines, nations aimed to reduce the potential for misunderstandings, clashes, and accidents, ultimately ensuring the safety of maritime traffic and contributing to stability in international waters.

The establishment of these legal frameworks for regulating sea lanes during the Cold War marked a significant development in maritime law. They laid the foundation for subsequent conventions and agreements, including those addressed in UNCLOS III, which further expanded on navigational rights, territorial sovereignty, and jurisdiction over national waters. The lessons learned from this period continue to inform contemporary discussions on maritime security and the need for effective regulation of sea lanes in today's globalized world.

UNCLOS I, which took place from 1956 to 1958, marked a significant milestone in the development of maritime law. During this time, key issues related to navigational rights, territorial sovereignty, and jurisdiction over national waters were addressed.

One of the primary objectives of UNCLOS I was to establish clear guidelines and regulations concerning navigational rights. The participating states sought to define the rights and responsibilities of nations in terms of their use of the world's oceans and seas. This included determining the extent of a nation's jurisdiction over its territorial waters and the freedom of navigation for international vessels.

Territorial sovereignty was another crucial aspect discussed during UNCLOS I. The convention aimed to define the boundaries of coastal states and their rights over maritime spaces adjacent to their territories. It provided a framework for resolving disputes over territorial claims, ensuring stability and security in these areas.

In addition, UNCLOS I addressed the issue of jurisdiction over national waters. Participating states sought to clarify their rights and responsibilities in enforcing laws within their respective maritime zones. This involved determining the extent of a state's control over activities such as fishing, resource exploration, and environmental protection within its waters.

UNCLOS I laid the foundation for subsequent developments in maritime legislation by establishing key principles and concepts. Its outcomes set the stage for further discussions on the regulation of sea lanes, protection of marine resources, and the resolution of disputes between nations.

The deliberations and agreements reached during UNCLOS I would later serve as important building blocks for UNCLOS II, which occurred from 1960 to 1967. UNCLOS II expanded on the issues addressed in its predecessor, paving the way for more comprehensive frameworks governing international waters.

By examining the development and implications of UNCLOS I, we gain valuable insights into the evolution of maritime law and understand how these early conventions shaped contemporary legal frameworks. The outcomes of UNCLOS I continue to influence modern maritime practices and provide guidance for addressing emerging challenges in today's globalized world.

UNCLOS II: Expanding Jurisdiction and Maritime Rights

During the period from 1960 to 1967, the United Nations Convention on the Law of the Sea (UNCLOS) II took place, furthering the development of maritime law and addressing critical issues related to jurisdiction and maritime rights. This section delves into the outcomes of UNCLOS II and its lasting impacts on contemporary maritime legislation.

One significant aspect tackled during UNCLOS II was the issue of fishing rights. As the demand for seafood increased, disputes arose over access to fishing grounds and the exploitation of marine resources. UNCLOS II sought to establish regulations and guidelines to ensure sustainable fishing practices and prevent overfishing. This led to discussions on the establishment of exclusive economic zones (EEZs) and the rights of coastal states to manage and conserve their marine resources within these zones.

Pollution regulations were another important topic addressed during UNCLOS II. With an increasing awareness of the environmental impact of human activities, concerns were raised regarding the pollution of international waters. UNCLOS II aimed to establish measures for preventing and controlling pollution from ships, including regulations on waste disposal, oil spills, and other forms of marine pollution. These discussions laid the groundwork for subsequent conventions that would further refine and strengthen environmental regulations in maritime law.

Additionally, UNCLOS II explored the issue of exploiting natural resources in international waters. As technological advancements allowed for greater access to resources such as minerals, oil, and gas beneath the seabed, questions arose regarding the rights of states to exploit these resources beyond their territorial waters. UNCLOS II delved into discussions on the legal frameworks for resource exploration and exploitation in international waters, including seabed mining and the sharing of benefits derived from such activities.

The outcomes of UNCLOS II significantly expanded jurisdictional boundaries and defined additional maritime rights, setting the stage for future developments in maritime law. The discussions on fishing rights, pollution regulations, and resource exploitation laid a solid foundation for the subsequent UNCLOS III and its comprehensive framework addressing a wide range of maritime issues.

By examining the discussions and outcomes of UNCLOS II, readers gain a deeper understanding of the evolving nature of maritime law and the ongoing efforts to establish balanced regulations that promote sustainable practices, protect the marine environment, and uphold the rights of coastal states. The lessons learned from UNCLOS II continue to shape contemporary maritime legislation, making it an essential section in understanding the multifaceted field of maritime jurisprudence.

Impact of UNCLOS I and II on Contemporary Maritime Law:

UNCLOS I (United Nations Convention on the Law of the Sea) and UNCLOS II played pivotal roles in shaping contemporary maritime law, setting the stage for subsequent conventions and developments in this field. These early United Nations conventions not only addressed key issues of their time but also laid the foundation for important concepts and principles that continue to influence maritime legislation today.

One significant impact of UNCLOS I and II was the recognition and codification of navigational rights. As shipping and trade expanded during the Cold War, ensuring the freedom of navigation became paramount. UNCLOS I affirmed the principle of innocent passage through territorial waters, emphasizing the right of ships to traverse these seas as long as they did not pose a threat to national security or violate other international laws. This principle has since become a cornerstone of contemporary maritime law, guaranteeing the unhindered movement of vessels in accordance with established norms.

Moreover, UNCLOS I and II played a vital role in expanding jurisdiction and defining additional maritime rights. UNCLOS II, in particular, addressed issues such as fishing rights, pollution regulations, and the exploitation of natural resources in international waters. By establishing guidelines for sustainable resource management and environmental protection, these early conventions paved the way for subsequent developments in marine conservation and the regulation of commercial activities at sea. Furthermore, UNCLOS I and II set important precedents for the resolution of disputes relating to maritime boundaries. These conventions made significant progress in clarifying territorial sovereignty and jurisdiction over national waters. They provided a framework for peaceful resolution of conflicts by encouraging negotiation, mediation, and arbitration. The principles established during these early conventions continue to guide international tribunals tasked with resolving contemporary maritime disputes.

Overall, UNCLOS I and II had a lasting impact on contemporary maritime law. They not only addressed pressing issues of their time but also served as building blocks for subsequent developments in this dynamic field. The principles enshrined in these early conventions continue to shape the legal framework governing the seas, ensuring the orderly conduct of maritime activities and the protection of vital global resources.

Introduction to UNCLOS III:

The United Nations Convention on the Law of the Sea (UNCLOS) III is a pivotal international agreement that has played a crucial role in shaping modern maritime law. This section provides an overview of UNCLOS III, highlighting its significance and scope in navigating the seas of law.

UNCLOS III, adopted in 1982 and entered into force in 1994, sought to establish a comprehensive legal framework for the world's oceans and seas. Its primary objectives were to promote peaceful uses of the seas, facilitate international cooperation, and ensure the conservation and sustainable management of marine resources.

One of the key principles enshrined in UNCLOS III is the concept of the Exclusive Economic Zone (EEZ). Coastal states are granted sovereign rights over resources within their EEZs, which extend up to 200 nautical miles from their baselines. This provision was a significant departure from earlier legal frameworks and marked an important milestone in the evolution of maritime law.

Within their EEZs, coastal states have exclusive rights to explore and exploit natural resources, both living and non-living. These rights encompass fisheries management, mineral extraction, and energy production. However, these rights are balanced with obligations to ensure the conservation and sustainable use of these resources, as outlined in UNCLOS III.

UNCLOS III also addresses the issues surrounding territorial waters, contiguous zones, and archipelagic states. It defines the legal boundaries of territorial waters, which stretch up to 12 nautical miles from a coastal state's baselines. The convention also recognizes contiguous zones, extending up to 24 nautical miles from the baselines, wherein coastal states may exercise certain controls for customs, immigration, and pollution prevention purposes.

Moreover, UNCLOS III introduced specific provisions for archipelagic states—those composed entirely of groups of islands. These states have defined archipelagic baselines that enclose their waters as one unit. They enjoy certain special rights and have obligations related to the archipelagic waters and their resources.

UNCLOS III also delves into the concept of sovereign rights over natural resources in the continental shelf. The continental shelf refers to the seabed and subsoil beyond a state's territorial sea, extending up to 200 nautical miles or even beyond, depending on the geological characteristics. Coastal states have sovereign rights over resources in this area for exploring and exploiting oil, gas, minerals, and other non-living resources.

To ensure compliance with the provisions of UNCLOS III, the convention establishes mechanisms for dispute resolution. These mechanisms include various tribunals and arbitration procedures that provide a framework for resolving disagreements between states regarding maritime boundaries, resource rights, environmental protection, and other issues. Dispute resolution is crucial for maintaining peace and stability in maritime areas.

Looking ahead, ongoing debates and discussions continue to shape the interpretation and implementation of UNCLOS III. As new challenges arise and technological advancements transform the dynamics of maritime activities, future developments in the application of UNCLOS III are anticipated. These developments will likely address emerging concerns such as climate change, deep-sea mining, and the impact of unmanned vessels on navigational freedom.

In conclusion, UNCLOS III serves as a cornerstone of maritime law, providing a comprehensive legal framework for the world's oceans and seas. Its principles on exclusive economic zones, sovereign rights over natural resources, territorial waters, and archipelagic states significantly influence contemporary maritime jurisprudence. Understanding these principles is essential for anyone navigating through the complex depths of maritime law.

Exclusive Economic Zones (EEZ) play a pivotal role in modern maritime jurisprudence, granting coastal states certain rights and responsibilities within designated areas. In this section, we will delve into the definition and legal framework surrounding EEZs, as well as analyze the implications they have on resource exploration, environmental protection, and navigational freedom.

Under the United Nations Convention on the Law of the Sea (UNCLOS) III, an exclusive economic zone is defined as an area extending up to 200 nautical miles from the baseline of a coastal state. Within this zone, coastal states are granted certain sovereign rights over the exploration and exploitation of natural resources, both living and non-living. These resources may include fish stocks, oil and gas reserves, minerals, and even renewable energy sources.

The establishment of exclusive economic zones has brought about significant changes in maritime law, particularly in terms of resource management and environmental protection. Coastal states are not only responsible for ensuring the sustainable utilization of resources within their EEZs but also for protecting and preserving the marine environment. This includes taking measures to prevent pollution, conserve biodiversity, and manage ecosystems.

However, it is important to note that while coastal states have exclusive rights over the resources within their EEZs, other countries still enjoy certain freedoms. For instance, all states, regardless of their proximity to a particular EEZ, have the right to navigate and fly over these areas. This preserves the principles of freedom of navigation and overflight as enshrined in UNCLOS III.

Furthermore, UNCLOS III recognizes that the exploitation of resources within one country's EEZ should be conducted in a manner that does not harm the interests of other states or the global community. This principle of "equitable utilization" ensures that all nations have access to shared resources for the collective benefit of humanity.

The establishment of exclusive economic zones has also generated complexities related to delimitation disputes between neighboring coastal states. While UNCLOS III provides a framework for resolving such disputes through negotiation and, if necessary, arbitration, reaching agreements can be challenging due to competing interests and overlapping claims.

Looking ahead, the interpretation and implementation of exclusive economic zones will likely continue to evolve. Emerging issues such as the exploration of seabed resources beyond national jurisdiction and the growing focus on sustainable development may shape future developments in this area of maritime law. As countries strive to balance the need for resource exploitation with environmental preservation, the legal frameworks surrounding exclusive economic zones will undoubtedly play a crucial role in ensuring a harmonious coexistence between coastal states and the global community.

In the next section, we will explore the intricacies of territorial waters, contiguous zones, and the legal status of archipelagic states under UNCLOS III. By delving deeper into these topics, we will gain a comprehensive understanding of how maritime law addresses the rights and responsibilities of coastal states in their immediate vicinity.

Territorial Waters and Contiguous Zones

Territorial waters play a crucial role in maritime law, as they define the sovereign rights of coastal states over the waters adjacent to their land territories. According to UNCLOS III, territorial waters extend up to 12 nautical miles from the baselines of a coastal state. Within these waters, the coastal state exercises full sovereignty, including the right to regulate navigation and control access.

The legal boundaries of territorial waters are determined by establishing baselines along the coast, usually measured from low-water mark or straight baselines connecting headlands. The width of territorial waters remains constant, regardless of the depth or distance from the coast.

Coastal states have the authority to enforce their laws within their territorial waters, encompassing a wide range of activities such as law enforcement, customs regulations, and environmental protection. Vessels passing through territorial waters are subject to the jurisdiction of the coastal state and must comply with its laws and regulations.

Contiguous zones, on the other hand, extend beyond territorial waters to a maximum breadth of 24 nautical miles from the baselines. While contiguous zones are not considered part of a coastal state's territory, they grant certain additional powers to the coastal state in order to enforce specific laws. These may include preventing violations of customs, fiscal, immigration, or sanitary laws that occurred within its territory or territorial sea.

The legal status of archipelagic states is another important aspect addressed by UNCLOS III. Archipelagic states consist of a group of islands and their surrounding waters treated as a single unit. Such states enjoy the same rights and responsibilities as coastal states, including sovereignty over their internal waters and territorial sea. However, an archipelagic state can claim archipelagic waters, which are all the waters enclosed by its archipelagic baselines.

UNCLOS III sets forth guidelines for drawing archipelagic baselines and ensures that archipelagic states maintain access to international straits and transit rights for foreign ships. These provisions aim to balance the rights of archipelagic states with the principle of freedom of navigation.

Understanding the legal boundaries and powers associated with territorial waters, contiguous zones, and the status of archipelagic states is crucial for all parties involved in maritime activities. Compliance with these provisions ensures a peaceful coexistence between coastal states, the protection of their sovereignty, and the facilitation of international trade and navigation.

Sovereign Rights over Natural Resources:

Coastal states possess significant sovereign rights over the natural resources found within their respective continental shelves. Under UNCLOS III, these rights extend to both living and non-living resources, including minerals, oil, gas, and sedentary species.

The extent of a coastal state's continental shelf, and therefore its sovereign rights, is determined by certain criteria outlined in UNCLOS III. The most significant criterion is the principle of geological and geomorphological continuity. According to this principle, the natural prolongation of a coastal state's land territory into the seabed and subsoil must be established based on geophysical characteristics such as sediment thickness, regional tectonic structure, and the presence of geological structures like submarine plateaus or ridges.

However, it is important to note that coastal states can only claim sovereign rights over their continental shelf beyond 200 nautical miles from their baselines if they can provide scientific evidence supporting their claims. This requirement ensures that the process of delimiting continental shelves remains fair and objective, preventing excessive claims that may lead to disputes with neighboring states.

Disputes related to sovereign rights over natural resources are not uncommon in maritime law. One notable example is the South China Sea dispute, which involves competing claims over the jurisdiction and control of various islands, reefs, and marine features among several Southeast Asian nations. The issue at hand primarily revolves around the conflicting interpretations of UNCLOS III regarding maritime boundaries and the extent of each state's continental shelf.

UNCLOS III provides mechanisms for dispute resolution, such as negotiation, mediation, arbitration, and recourse to an international tribunal. These processes aim to settle disagreements peacefully and based on legal principles. The establishment of the International Tribunal for the Law of the Sea (ITLOS) further facilitates the resolution of such disputes within the framework of UNCLOS III.

Looking ahead, ongoing debates exist regarding the interpretation and implementation of UNCLOS III in relation to sovereign rights over natural resources. These debates often arise due to evolving economic and environmental factors, such as the increasing demand for non-living resources, concerns about overexploitation, and the need to balance resource exploitation with sustainable development goals. Addressing these challenges will require continuous dialogue and a dynamic approach to maritime legislation.

In conclusion, coastal states enjoy sovereign rights over the natural resources within their continental shelves. UNCLOS III provides guidelines for determining the extent of these rights, aiming to establish fair boundaries based on scientific evidence. However, disputes can arise when competing claims intersect, highlighting the importance of effective dispute resolution mechanisms. As the global demand for resources evolves, the interpretation and implementation of UNCLOS III's provisions regarding sovereign rights over natural resources will continue to shape the future of maritime law.

Compliance with UNCLOS III is a crucial aspect of ensuring the effective implementation of maritime law. This section delves into the mechanisms designed to promote compliance with the provisions set forth in the United Nations Convention on the Law of the Sea (UNCLOS) III and explores the dispute resolution procedures in place.

One of the key mechanisms for enforcing compliance with UNCLOS III is through the establishment of international tribunals. These tribunals provide a platform for resolving disputes and clarifying the interpretation of specific provisions within the convention. They play a vital role in upholding the principles and rules laid out in UNCLOS III, ensuring consistency and harmony in maritime jurisprudence.

The International Tribunal for the Law of the Sea (ITLOS) is the primary judicial body tasked with settling disputes arising from the interpretation and application of UNCLOS III. Composed of independent judges with expertise in maritime law, ITLOS provides a forum for states to seek legal remedies and resolve disagreements peacefully. The judgments and advisory opinions delivered by ITLOS carry significant weight and contribute to the development and evolution of maritime law.

In addition to tribunals, peaceful arbitration has become an increasingly popular method for resolving disputes under UNCLOS III. Arbitration allows parties to select an impartial third party or panel of experts to adjudicate their disagreement. It offers flexibility, procedural autonomy, and confidentiality, making it an attractive option for resolving complex maritime disputes. Notably, this alternative dispute resolution mechanism has gained traction due to its perceived advantages over traditional litigation processes.

Furthermore, ongoing debates surrounding the interpretation and implementation of UNCLOS III continue to shape future developments in maritime law. As new challenges arise, such as emerging technologies, environmental concerns, and changing geopolitical dynamics, there is a need for continuous adaptation and refinement of legal frameworks. States, international organizations, and legal scholars are engaged in discussions aiming to address gaps, clarify ambiguities, and strengthen compliance measures.

The exploration of potential future developments in the interpretation and implementation of UNCLOS III is crucial for understanding the evolving nature of maritime law. It requires a multidisciplinary approach that analyzes emerging trends, scientific advancements, and geopolitical shifts to anticipate and respond effectively to the challenges ahead. By actively engaging in these debates, legal professionals, policymakers, and stakeholders can contribute to the advancement and refinement of maritime jurisprudence.

In summary, ensuring compliance with UNCLOS III is vital for upholding the principles and rules governing maritime law. Through the establishment of international tribunals and the use of peaceful arbitration, disputes can be resolved in a fair and impartial manner. Ongoing debates and discussions regarding the interpretation and implementation of UNCLOS III pave the way for future developments in maritime law, enabling it to adapt to emerging challenges and changing global dynamics.

Modern piracy has seen a resurgence in recent years, posing a significant challenge to maritime security. This section provides an overview of modern piracy, focusing on the regions most affected by pirate attacks and the factors contributing to its rise.

Political instability is a key factor driving the increase in piracy. In regions where governments are weak or nonexistent, pirates can operate with relative ease, taking advantage of lawless areas and ungoverned spaces. Economic motives also play a role, with piracy often driven by poverty and a lack of alternative livelihoods. Furthermore, the presence of valuable resources, such as oil or natural gas, in certain regions can create incentives for pirates to target ships transporting these commodities.

Inadequate maritime security measures have also contributed to the prevalence of piracy. Weak surveillance and enforcement capabilities allow pirates to operate undeterred, while poor coastal infrastructure makes it difficult for states to effectively police their waters. Additionally, corrupt officials and collusion with criminal networks further exacerbate the problem.

The regions most affected by modern piracy include the Gulf of Aden, the Indian Ocean, and Southeast Asia. The Gulf of Aden, in particular, has gained notoriety as a hotbed for pirate activities. Its strategic location at the entrance of the Red Sea, connecting Europe and Asia, has made it a crucial transit route for international trade. The high volume of shipping traffic passing through this narrow chokepoint provides ample opportunities for pirates to launch attacks and hijack vessels.

The impact of piracy extends beyond economic losses to include threats to human lives and humanitarian aid efforts. Notable piracy incidents have included hostage-taking, ransom demands, and acts of violence against crew members. Additionally, piracy has hindered maritime trade and disrupted the delivery of essential goods to conflict-affected regions, exacerbating humanitarian crises.

As piracy continues to evolve and adapt, addressing this global security threat requires comprehensive strategies encompassing legal, diplomatic, and military approaches. International cooperation is crucial, with states collaborating to share information, intelligence, and best practices. Capacity-building initiatives for coastal countries can enhance their maritime security capabilities and enable them to effectively police their waters.

The legal framework for combating piracy is anchored in international conventions, such as UNCLOS and regional agreements. These agreements provide a basis for prosecuting pirates and allow naval forces to take action against pirate vessels. However, jurisdictional challenges and the complexities of gathering evidence at sea make prosecuting pirates a daunting task.

Maritime security measures have focused on both preventive and responsive actions. Naval patrols in high-risk areas contribute to deterrence and provide protection to vulnerable ships. The use of private security firms has also become common practice, with armed guards embarked on ships transiting piracy-prone regions. Best management practices, including route planning, enhanced communication, and vessel hardening, help ships minimize the risk of pirate attacks.

Technology plays a crucial role in enhancing maritime security efforts. Satellite surveillance systems provide real-time monitoring of shipping activities and aid in identifying potential threats. Drones offer a cost-effective means of patrolling vast stretches of water and can quickly respond to suspected pirate activity. Secure communication systems ensure prompt reporting of incidents and facilitate coordinated responses.

However, numerous challenges persist in effectively combating piracy. This includes the need for sustained political will, overcoming resource constraints, and addressing root causes such as poverty and political instability in affected regions. Future perspectives for enhancing maritime security may involve further integration of technology into existing frameworks, exploring innovative methods of international cooperation, and adapting strategies to counter evolving piracy tactics.

In conclusion, modern piracy poses a significant threat to maritime security, impacting trade, humanitarian efforts, and the safety of seafarers. Understanding the factors driving its rise and the regions most affected provides critical insights for developing effective measures to combat piracy. By addressing political instability, strengthening maritime security capabilities, enhancing international cooperation, and leveraging technological advancements, stakeholders can work towards a more secure and stable maritime environment.

The Gulf of Aden stands as a notorious hotbed for piracy in the modern era, attracting international attention due to its strategic location and high volume of international trade. This region, situated between the Arabian Peninsula and the Horn of Africa, serves as a vital maritime route connecting Europe, Asia, and Africa. Unfortunately, its prominence has also made it a prime target for pirate activities.

One of the key reasons behind the prevalence of piracy in the Gulf of Aden is its strategic location. The narrow width of the waterway, combined with the presence of chokepoints such as the Bab-el-Mandeb strait, creates an ideal environment for pirates to launch attacks on passing vessels. These geographical characteristics, coupled with inadequate surveillance and enforcement capabilities, have allowed piracy to flourish in this region.

Additionally, the high volume of international trade passing through the Gulf of Aden makes it an attractive target for pirates seeking lucrative opportunities. Vessels carrying valuable cargo, such as oil tankers and container ships, become potential targets for hijackings and ransom demands. The economic incentives associated with piracy further contribute to its prevalence in this area.

Notable piracy incidents in the Gulf of Aden have had a significant impact on maritime security. One example is the hijacking of the MV Maersk Alabama in 2009 by Somali pirates, which garnered worldwide attention due to the involvement of US Navy SEALs in rescuing the ship's captain. Such incidents highlight the serious threat posed by piracy in this region and necessitate comprehensive measures to ensure maritime security.

It is important to note that this section focuses specifically on the Gulf of Aden and does not encompass all aspects of modern piracy or the legal framework for combating piracy. Other sections within this section will delve into these topics in greater detail. Legal Frameworks for Combating Piracy: This section delves into the international legal frameworks that have been established to combat piracy. It explores key legal instruments such as the United Nations Convention on the Law of the Sea (UNCLOS), regional agreements, and resolutions adopted by international organizations like the International Maritime Organization (IMO).

UNCLOS, which entered into force in 1994, provides a comprehensive framework for addressing piracy and other illicit activities at sea. Under UNCLOS, states have the authority to take action against piracy on the high seas, even if they do not have a direct connection to the incident. This principle of universal jurisdiction allows states to prosecute pirates regardless of their nationality or the flag state of the vessel they operate from.

In addition to UNCLOS, several regional agreements have been established to enhance cooperation among neighboring countries in combating piracy. For example, the Djibouti Code of Conduct, adopted in 2009, promotes information sharing, capacity building, and coordinated patrols among participating states in the Gulf of Aden and Western Indian Ocean region. Similarly, the Regional Cooperation Agreement on Combating Piracy and Armed Robbery against Ships in Asia (ReCAAP), established in 2006, encourages regional cooperation and information exchange among Asian countries.

International organizations like the IMO play a crucial role in facilitating cooperation and coordination among states in combating piracy. The IMO has adopted various resolutions and guidelines aimed at enhancing maritime security and deterring pirate attacks. These include measures such as the Ship Security Alert System (SSAS), which enables ships to send distress alerts to flag states and coastal authorities in case of an attack.

However, prosecuting pirates poses significant jurisdictional challenges and legal complexities. Pirates often operate in international waters or within the territorial waters of coastal states that may have limited capacity or willingness to prosecute them. Furthermore, gathering evidence and ensuring fair trial rights can be challenging, particularly when pirates are apprehended at sea by naval forces.

Efforts have been made to address these challenges through initiatives such as the Contact Group on Piracy off the Coast of Somalia (CGPCS), which brings together states, international organizations, and industry stakeholders to coordinate and enhance counter-piracy efforts. The CGPCS has established legal frameworks for the prosecution of pirates, including the establishment of specialized piracy courts in certain countries.

Overall, international legal frameworks provide a foundation for addressing piracy at sea. However, ongoing collaboration and coordination among states, along with capacity-building initiatives, are essential to effectively combat piracy and ensure the safety and security of maritime trade routes.

Maritime Security Measures: This section delves into the various maritime security measures that have been implemented to combat piracy, with a specific focus on their effectiveness in addressing the challenges posed by modern pirates. It explores preventive measures that have been adopted, including naval patrols, private security firms, and best management practices for ships transiting high-risk areas.

Naval patrols have proven to be an essential tool in deterring and responding to pirate attacks. Maritime forces from various nations collaborate through international coalitions and task forces to patrol piracy-prone regions. These patrols involve the deployment of warships and aircraft to monitor suspicious activities, conduct surveillance, and provide immediate response capabilities to deter pirates. The presence of these naval assets not only serves as a visible deterrent but also enables rapid intervention in case of an attack.

Private security firms have also emerged as significant contributors to maritime security. Many ship owners employ armed security teams onboard vessels transiting piracy-infested waters. These teams are equipped with firearms, non-lethal weapons, and other defensive measures to ensure the safety of the crew and cargo. The use of private security firms has shown promising results in reducing pirate attacks, as armed personnel act as a strong deterrent against potential pirate threats.

In addition to human resources, technology plays a vital role in enhancing maritime security against piracy. Satellite surveillance systems enable monitoring of vast stretches of open waters, providing real-time information on suspicious vessel movements and activities. Drones equipped with cameras and sensors can be deployed for aerial reconnaissance and surveillance in remote or high-risk areas. These technologies not only enhance situational awareness but also assist in tracking pirate movements and gathering evidence for prosecution.

Secure communication systems are crucial for effective coordination and information sharing between vessels, naval forces, and coastal authorities. Enhanced communication capabilities allow ships to report incidents promptly, seek assistance, and receive timely updates on potential threats. Through improved information sharing platforms, warnings and advisories about piracy hotspots can be disseminated efficiently to all relevant stakeholders, enhancing overall awareness and preparedness.

While maritime security measures have proven effective in reducing piracy incidents in certain areas, challenges remain. The vast expanse of the maritime domain, limited resources, and the adaptability of pirates necessitate ongoing efforts to enhance security strategies. Future perspectives include strengthening collaboration between states, particularly in information sharing and intelligence exchange. Capacity-building initiatives for coastal countries can also play a significant role in improving their ability to police their waters effectively.

Furthermore, the emergence of new technologies and evolving piracy tactics requires continuous innovation in counter-piracy measures. Research and development efforts should focus on developing advanced surveillance systems, autonomous patrol vessels, and improved non-lethal defensive capabilities. The integration of advanced technologies such as artificial intelligence, machine learning, and blockchain can also enhance information sharing, analysis, and tracking of pirate networks.

In conclusion, the implementation of maritime security measures has been instrumental in combating piracy in high-risk areas. Naval patrols, private security firms, and technological advancements have significantly contributed to deterring pirate activities and protecting vessels and crew. However, the challenges posed by piracy persist, necessitating continued collaboration, innovation, and capacity-building initiatives to ensure the safety and security of maritime trade routes worldwide.

Challenges and Future Perspectives:

Effectively combating piracy presents numerous challenges that require innovative strategies and collaborative efforts. One of the key challenges is the lack of coordination and information sharing between states. Piracy incidents often occur in international waters, making it difficult to determine which country has jurisdiction over prosecuting pirates. Enhancing international cooperation and establishing mechanisms for sharing intelligence and evidence are crucial steps towards overcoming this challenge.

Coastal countries, particularly those in piracy-prone regions, face significant capacity limitations in terms of maritime security enforcement. Limited resources, inadequate infrastructure, and weak legal systems hamper their ability to effectively combat piracy. To address this challenge, international initiatives should focus on providing technical assistance, training programs, and financial support to enhance the capabilities of these countries.

Comprehensive strategies integrating legal, diplomatic, and military approaches are necessary for tackling piracy effectively. Legal frameworks need to be strengthened to ensure that pirates are prosecuted and held accountable for their actions. Diplomatic efforts should prioritize regional cooperation, encouraging neighboring countries to collaborate on intelligence sharing, joint patrols, and anti-piracy operations. Military responses should be coordinated to provide a robust presence in piracy-prone areas and deter potential attacks.

As technology continues to evolve, it will play an increasingly important role in enhancing maritime security. Emerging technologies such as autonomous surveillance systems, unmanned surface vehicles, and advanced communication networks have the potential to revolutionize anti-piracy efforts. Governments and international organizations should invest in research and development in these areas to stay ahead of evolving piracy tactics.

Furthermore, it is essential to address the underlying socio-economic factors that contribute to piracy. Poverty, unemployment, and political instability often drive individuals into piracy as a means of survival or as a form of protest. Long-term strategies should focus on supporting sustainable economic development, promoting good governance, and addressing root causes of piracy in order to create stable conditions where piracy cannot thrive.

In conclusion, combating piracy requires a multi-faceted approach that addresses legal, diplomatic, military, and socio-economic challenges. By strengthening international cooperation, empowering coastal countries, and leveraging technological advancements, the global community can work together to enhance maritime security and eliminate the threat of piracy. Only through comprehensive strategies and forward-thinking perspectives can we navigate the seas with confidence and ensure a safer future for all.

Chapter 2

Contemporary Maritime Law:
Evolving Legal and Regulatory Framework,
Role of Port State Control

****

Introduction to Contemporary Maritime Law:

In this section, we delve into the current state of maritime law and explore the need for an evolving legal framework to address emerging challenges and technologies. As the world becomes increasingly interconnected, maritime activities are evolving at a rapid pace, necessitating the formulation of new regulations and legal provisions.

The current state of maritime law is shaped by a complex web of international agreements and conventions. These agreements, often subject to updates and revisions, ensure that maritime practices align with global standards and best practices. We will examine the recent developments in these agreements and evaluate their impact on global maritime operations.

One significant aspect driving the evolution of maritime law is the emphasis on safety and environmental protection. Recognizing the potential risks associated with maritime operations, regulatory frameworks have been established to mitigate these risks and promote safe and sustainable practices. We will explore these frameworks in detail, analyzing the roles of international organizations such as the International Maritime Organization (IMO) in setting standards and monitoring compliance.

Another critical area that demands attention in contemporary maritime law is cybersecurity. With advancements in technology, vessels are now more vulnerable to cyber threats. To address this concern, legal requirements and measures have been put in place to safeguard maritime operations against cyber attacks. We will examine these measures and their implications for the industry.

Port state control plays a vital role in ensuring compliance with international maritime regulations. The responsibilities of port state control authorities extend beyond merely inspecting vessels; they have the power to detain non-compliant ships and enforce penalties. Through an exploration of the legal powers and procedures used by these authorities, we will gain insight into how port state control enhances safety and regulatory compliance.

Looking ahead, we must consider the future challenges that contemporary maritime law will face. From unmanned vessels and autonomous shipping to climate change and sustainable practices, new issues continue to emerge in the maritime industry. We will discuss potential legal responses to these challenges and explore the ways in which maritime law can adapt to meet the needs of an ever-changing world.

By understanding the current landscape of maritime law and recognizing the need for ongoing evolution, we can navigate the complex realm of contemporary maritime jurisprudence. This section sets the stage for further exploration of safety regulations, cybersecurity measures, port state control, and future considerations in subsequent sections.In the ever-evolving world of maritime law, updates and revisions in international agreements and conventions play a crucial role in shaping global maritime practices. This section delves into the recent developments and explores their impact on the legal and regulatory framework governing maritime operations.

Recent years have witnessed significant changes in international agreements and conventions related to maritime law. The International Maritime Organization (IMO), as the leading international authority in this field, has been at the forefront of these updates, working tirelessly to address emerging challenges and ensure the continued safety and sustainability of the maritime industry.

One notable update is the adoption of amendments to the International Convention for the Safety of Life at Sea (SOLAS). These amendments aim to enhance maritime safety by introducing new requirements for vessel construction, navigation equipment, and emergency preparedness. By aligning international standards with technological advancements, these updates strive to mitigate risks and protect lives at sea.

Similarly, revisions have been made to the International Convention for the Prevention of Pollution from Ships (MARPOL). As environmental concerns take center stage globally, stricter regulations have been introduced to reduce marine pollution and promote sustainable practices. These revisions encompass various aspects, including air pollution, sewage management, and ballast water treatment. By prioritizing environmental stewardship, these updates contribute to the preservation of our oceans and marine ecosystems.

The continued evolution of international agreements has also paved the way for improved cooperation among nations in combating illicit activities at sea. Conventions such as the United Nations Convention against Illicit Traffic in Narcotic Drugs and Psychotropic Substances have established comprehensive frameworks for addressing drug trafficking via maritime routes. By harmonizing legal approaches and facilitating information sharing, these agreements strengthen international efforts to disrupt criminal networks operating in the maritime domain.

Furthermore, developments in international agreements have extended beyond traditional areas of maritime law. For instance, the emergence of marine renewable energy sources has necessitated the establishment of legal frameworks to facilitate their development and deployment. International agreements such as the International Renewable Energy Agency (IRENA) guidelines on offshore renewable energy projects provide guidance on legal and regulatory aspects, ensuring the sustainable growth of this sector.

The impact of these updates and revisions in international agreements and conventions cannot be overstated. They not only enhance safety standards, promote environmental stewardship, and combat criminal activities but also foster harmonization among nations, fostering a more cohesive and cooperative global maritime community.

As the maritime industry continues to evolve, it is essential for legal professionals, policymakers, and stakeholders to stay informed about these developments. By remaining attentive to updates in international agreements and conventions, they can adapt their practices and ensure compliance with the evolving legal framework governing maritime operations.

Promoting safety and environmental protection is a paramount concern in contemporary maritime law. As the shipping industry continues to expand and global trade volumes increase, it becomes imperative to establish and enforce regulations that ensure the well-being of both human lives and the marine environment.

In this section, we will explore the regulatory frameworks that have been developed to address safety and environmental issues in maritime operations. These regulations are aimed at minimizing accidents, promoting efficient rescue operations, and preventing environmental disasters in the world's oceans.

International organizations, such as the International Maritime Organization (IMO), play a significant role in establishing and monitoring compliance with these regulations. The IMO, as a specialized agency of the United Nations, has been instrumental in shaping international maritime law by developing conventions and guidelines that promote safer and cleaner seas.

One notable convention established by the IMO is the International Convention for the Safety of Life at Sea (SOLAS). SOLAS sets out minimum safety standards for ships engaged in international trade, covering a wide range of aspects including vessel construction, equipment, navigation, and crew training. It requires member states to incorporate these standards into their national laws and implement corresponding domestic regulations to ensure compliance.

Another important IMO convention is the International Convention for the Prevention of Pollution from Ships (MARPOL). MARPOL seeks to minimize pollution caused by ships through regulations on various aspects such as oil spills, sewage discharges, garbage disposal, and air emissions. Member states are required to adopt domestic laws and enforcement mechanisms that align with MARPOL's provisions.

These international agreements and conventions provide a solid foundation for addressing safety and environmental concerns in maritime operations. However, it is crucial to continuously update and revise these regulations to keep pace with emerging technologies and evolving threats.

For example, advancements in shipbuilding techniques have led to the development of larger vessels capable of carrying substantial amounts of cargo. While these megaships offer economic benefits, they also present unique safety challenges. Striking a balance between economic efficiency and safety remains a key consideration for regulators.

Furthermore, the shipping industry's impact on the environment has become an increasing concern in recent years. The emission of greenhouse gases, discharge of ballast water containing invasive species, and improper disposal of hazardous materials pose serious threats to marine ecosystems. As a result, there is a growing need for stricter regulations and enforcement measures to mitigate these environmental risks.

In summary, promoting safety and environmental protection through robust regulatory frameworks is a crucial aspect of contemporary maritime law. International organizations like the IMO play a pivotal role in establishing and monitoring compliance with these regulations. However, ongoing updates and revisions are necessary to address emerging challenges and ensure the sustainability of the maritime industry.

Developing Cybersecurity Measures in Maritime Operations

As the maritime industry becomes increasingly reliant on technology, the importance of cybersecurity in safeguarding maritime operations cannot be overstated. With vessels now equipped with advanced navigation systems, communication networks, and automated processes, the potential for cyber threats and attacks has grown exponentially. Therefore, it is crucial to establish robust legal requirements and measures to protect against these risks.

One key aspect of developing cybersecurity measures in maritime operations is the establishment of international standards and regulations. The International Maritime Organization (IMO), in collaboration with other international bodies, has taken significant steps to address this issue. For instance, the IMO's Maritime Safety Committee (MSC) has developed guidelines on maritime cyber risk management, which provide a framework for identifying, assessing, and mitigating cyber risks. These guidelines aim to ensure that shipping companies have effective strategies in place to prevent and respond to cyber incidents.

Additionally, several countries have implemented legislation to enhance cybersecurity in the maritime sector. These legal frameworks often require shipping companies to implement cybersecurity measures, such as having robust firewall systems, regularly updating software and hardware, conducting vulnerability assessments, and providing training for crew members on cybersecurity awareness. Failure to comply with these legal requirements may result in penalties or loss of operating licenses.

Furthermore, collaboration between public and private entities is essential for effective cybersecurity in maritime operations. Governments, port authorities, shipping companies, and cybersecurity experts must work together to share threat intelligence and best practices. This collaborative approach can help identify vulnerabilities, develop innovative solutions, and respond promptly to emerging cyber threats.

To promote cybersecurity awareness and education within the maritime industry, training programs should be implemented for seafarers and shore-based personnel. These programs should cover topics such as recognizing phishing emails, understanding common cyber attack methods, safeguarding sensitive information, and reporting suspicious activities. By equipping individuals with the necessary knowledge and skills, the industry can create a culture of cybersecurity vigilance.

Looking ahead, the future of cybersecurity in maritime operations presents both challenges and opportunities. As technology continues to advance, the industry must stay at the forefront of cybersecurity developments. Emerging technologies such as autonomous vessels, remote monitoring systems, and cloud-based platforms will require innovative security measures. Additionally, the rise of interconnected systems and the Internet of Things (IoT) in maritime operations necessitates robust security protocols to prevent unauthorized access and potential disruptions.

Moreover, as the maritime industry becomes increasingly aware of the environmental impact of its operations, sustainable cybersecurity practices should be integrated into overall sustainability efforts. Minimizing cyber risks can help prevent environmental disasters caused by cyber attacks on critical infrastructure, such as oil rigs or underwater pipelines.

In conclusion, developing cybersecurity measures in maritime operations is crucial for safeguarding the industry against cyber threats and attacks. Through the establishment of international standards, robust legal requirements, collaboration among stakeholders, and comprehensive training programs, the maritime industry can ensure a secure and resilient environment for its operations. By staying vigilant and proactive, the industry can navigate the ever-evolving landscape of cybersecurity with confidence.

The Role of Port State Control in Ensuring Compliance

Port state control plays a crucial role in enforcing international maritime regulations and ensuring compliance with established safety and environmental standards. As vessels traverse international waters and navigate through various ports, it is the responsibility of port state control authorities to inspect these ships, detain non-compliant vessels, and enforce penalties when necessary.

One of the primary functions of port state control is to carry out inspections on foreign-flagged vessels that enter their respective ports. These inspections aim to verify compliance with international conventions, regulations, and standards governing vessel safety, crew welfare, and environmental protection. Through rigorous inspections, port state control assesses a range of critical factors including navigational equipment, operational procedures, crew qualifications, and adherence to pollution prevention measures.

To ascertain compliance, port state control authorities employ a variety of legal powers and procedures. They have the authority to board vessels and conduct detailed inspections, examining both the ship's certificates and records as well as its physical condition. Vessels found in violation of international regulations may be detained until corrective actions are taken or subjected to further penalties.

Port state control's enforcement powers are crucial in maintaining a level playing field for all shipping companies and ensuring the safety of seafarers, marine environments, and coastal communities. By actively monitoring compliance, they prevent negligent ship operators from gaining unfair economic advantages by cutting corners on safety or environmental protection measures.

In addition to the inspection process, port state control authorities also rely on information sharing and cooperation with other stakeholders in the maritime industry. They collaborate with flag states, classification societies, and other relevant bodies to exchange information on vessel performance, identify potential risks, and coordinate actions to address non-compliance issues effectively.

As technologies continue to evolve and new challenges emerge, port state control faces an increasing need to adapt its practices and procedures. The advent of unmanned vessels and autonomous shipping presents unique regulatory challenges that must be considered to ensure the safe and efficient operation of these new technologies. Additionally, as the maritime industry places an emphasis on sustainability and environmental stewardship, port state control will play a critical role in enforcing regulations aimed at reducing greenhouse gas emissions, preventing marine pollution, and promoting sustainable practices.

In conclusion, the role of port state control is vital in ensuring compliance with international maritime regulations and maintaining safety and environmental standards within the shipping industry. Through their legal powers and procedures, port state control authorities play a pivotal role in inspecting vessels, detaining non-compliant ships, and enforcing penalties when necessary. As the maritime landscape continues to evolve, port state control must remain adaptable to emerging challenges and trends, working collaboratively with other stakeholders to foster a safe, secure, and sustainable maritime environment.

Future Challenges and Considerations for Contemporary Maritime Law

As we navigate the ever-changing tides of contemporary maritime law, it is crucial to anticipate and address the emerging challenges and trends that may shape its future. This section explores potential legal responses to various issues that are gaining prominence in the maritime industry, ensuring readers are equipped with insights into the evolving landscape of maritime jurisprudence.

One of the key challenges on the horizon is the integration of unmanned vessels and autonomous shipping within existing legal frameworks. As technology continues to advance rapidly, maritime law must grapple with the legal implications of unmanned vessels operating without human intervention. Questions surrounding liability, insurance, and compliance with international regulations will need careful examination. This section delves into the potential legal responses to these challenges and explores how international agreements and conventions may be amended to accommodate this technological shift.

Additionally, climate change and its impact on the maritime environment are increasingly pressing concerns. Rising sea levels, extreme weather events, and ocean acidification necessitate a proactive approach to sustainability in maritime practices. The section discusses potential legal responses to mitigate greenhouse gas emissions, reduce marine pollution, and promote sustainable shipping practices. It explores the role of international organizations such as the IMO in developing regulations and incentivizing eco-friendly initiatives.

Cybersecurity emerges as another critical area requiring attention in contemporary maritime law. With increasing reliance on digital systems for navigation, communications, and cargo tracking, vessels and ports become vulnerable to cyber threats and attacks. This section examines the legal requirements and measures established to protect against cyber risks in the maritime industry. It delves into the potential legal frameworks for ensuring robust cybersecurity practices, including mechanisms for reporting incidents, cooperation between stakeholders, and international information-sharing protocols.

In conclusion, as maritime law endeavors to keep pace with technological advancements, environmental challenges, and evolving security landscapes, it is essential to proactively anticipate and adapt to future needs. By exploring potential legal responses to emerging issues such as unmanned vessels, autonomous shipping, climate change, and cybersecurity, this section provides readers with a forward-looking perspective on the future of contemporary maritime law.

Part III:
Global Tides - Sectors and Issues

"Global maritime law is the uncharted sea chart that binds nations, where the waves of cooperation meet the shores of shared responsibility, ensuring a voyage of safety, equity, and sustainable navigation for all vessels in the vast ocean of international waters."

Chapter 1

Overview of the Shipping Industry
*****

The shipping industry has long se-rved a significant function in worldwide commerce- and transportation, enabling the conveyance- of products across huge distances and linking countries and financial aspe-cts. This part gives a more nuanced outline- of the shipping business, featuring its historical advance-ment, central membe-rs, and financial importance. The business has e-volved throughout the decade-s to its present state, shuttling me-rchandise betwee-n ports all around the planet. Major shippers coordinate- huge fleets that trave-l every ocean, de-livering fundamental supplies. Nations re-ly upon unhindered exchange- by sea lanes. The industry's job in inte-rnational exchange is indispensable- to the general worldwide- economy and exchange of products.

Throughout history, ships have been essential for exploration, colonization, and the exchange of goods between nations. From ancient sailboats to modern container ships and tankers, vessels have evolved to meet the demands of an ever-expanding global economy. This section delves into the different types of vessels employed in the shipping industry, including container ships used for transporting goods in standard-sized containers, bulk carriers designed to transport bulk commodities such as coal and grain, and tankers used for transporting oil and other liquid cargo.

The shipping industry involve-s various parties who collaborate to ensure- its seamless functioning. Shipowners take- on the task of possessing and managing vesse-ls, occasionally leasing them out to chartere-rs seeking to transport shipments. Fre-ight forwarders serve a crucial purpose- in coordinating the conveyance of products for shippe-rs, aligning diverse ele-ments like customs processing and docume-ntation. These stakeholde-rs work interdepende-ntly to keep the industry ope-rating effortlessly.

Port authorities play an important ove-rsight role in the effe-ctive operation of ports. They are-responsible for providing the critical infrastructure- and facilities neede-d for loading and unloading cargo from ships. This includes ensuring ports have the- necessary docks, cranes, ware-houses and other equipme-nt. Port authorities also make certain safe-ty regulations are followed to prote-ct workers and prevent accide-nts. They manage the daily activitie-s within ports to keep cargo and vesse-l movement running smoothly. Various support industries like- ship construction, ship brokerages and marine insurance- underwrite risk for ships and cargo. These- supplemental industries all contribute- to supporting a well-functioning shipping sector that relie-s on efficient ports.

The shipping industry plays a crucial e-conomic role by supporting international trade through the-transportation of goods worldwide. It empowers global comme-rce by linking manufacturers to customers in dive-rse areas efficie-ntly. Truly, the industry's importance to trade amongst nations cannot be- exaggerated - most inte-rnational business relies on maritime- pathways. While sea transport streamline-s trade on a massive scale, its comple-xity warrants intermediate clarification.

Comprehe-nding the lawful system that overse-es the delive-ry business is basic for every one- of the partners engage-d. Global associations, for example, the Inte-rnational Maritime Organization (IMO) assume a key job in se-tting up and authorizing worldwide norms for wellbeing, natural we-llbeing and crew welfare-. The IMO works with its individuals to build up a legitimate syste-m that all maritime nations concur to follow. This incorporates arrangeme-nts on vessel enrollme-nt, the purview of the nation whose- banner a vessel sails unde-r, and the guidelines ide-ntifying with liability if a mishap happens. On top of worldwide standards, nearby and public guide-lines additionally impact maritime exchange- and transportation inside every nation or district. Eve-ry locale has its own particular arrangements ide-ntifying with how vessels are authorize-d to work and move merchandise inside- their waters, and what occurs on the off chance- that a mishap causes harm.

In the following portions of this portion, we- will investigate the lawful structure- encompassing the delive-ry business in further profundity. We will inspe-ct maritime contracts and charter gatherings, liability and prote-ction issues, just as developing difficultie-s introduced by innovative headways and natural supportability conce-rns. By acquiring a total comprehension of the lawful angle-s of the delivery busine-ss, perusers will be be-tter outfitted to route the- mind boggling waters of maritime law and guarantee- consistency with applicable directions. While- we will take a gander at the-se territories, a fe-w parts will stay obscure as the business ke-eps on creating.

Legal Framework for the Shipping Industry:

The le-gal frameworks surrounding maritime trade and transportation form an intricate- network governing various facets of the- shipping industry. This portion explores the nuance-s of these legal structure-s, offering readers a de-tailed view of the guide-lines and rules that mold the industry's proce-dures and methods. For instance, re-gulations determine important matte-rs such as safety standards for vessels, pollution pre-vention measures, and the- documentation required for various cargo. An assortme-nt of international agreeme-nts and domestic legislation come toge-ther to construct this complicated framework. De-lving into the particulars provides valuable insight into how the- industry functions within legal boundaries and why compliance is so significant. A working knowle-dge of these re-gulations benefits those involve-d in maritime operations, from ship owners and captains to port authoritie-s and freight forwarders.

The Inte-rnational Maritime Organization (IMO) holds significant importance on an international scale- when it comes to establishing and e-nforcing worldwide benchmarks for safety, e-nvironmental protection, and crew we-lfare. The IMO's conventions and re-gulations address a broad range of topics, like ship de-sign and construction, navigation and communication systems, pollution prevention, and se-afarer training and certification. By advocating for uniformity and harmonization among membe-r states, the IMO makes sure- that vessels sailing under diffe-rent flags follow a shared set of safe-ty and environmental standards. This helps e-nsure consistency when ve-ssels trade or operate- across borders. Without such coordination, differing require-ments could lead to unnece-ssary risks or hazards.

While inte-rnational regulations significantly impact maritime trade and transportation across borde-rs, regional and domestic laws within nations also shape this domain. For e-xample, a ship's registration to sail under the- flag of a specific country subjects it to the statute-s and rules of that flag state. The flag state- has jurisdiction over that vessel and be-ars responsibility for enforcing compliance with safe-ty protocols, proper paperwork maintenance-, and possession of certified cre-dentials. Matters such as crew qualification re-quirements, working conditions on board, and health and safe-ty precautions also fall under the flag state-'s authority. Ensuring seafarers mee-t qualifications helps ensure safe- passage, while outlining labor conditions and provisions for well-be-ing can protect those who sustain global trade via wate-rway. Together, the laye-red regulations at international, re-gional, and national levels aim to facilitate comme-rce while prioritizing those who conduct it.

Furthermore-, liability regimes dictate the- legal responsibilities and obligations of partie-s involved in maritime activities. Various inte-rnational conventions, such as the International Conve-ntion on Liability and Compensation for Damage in Connection with the- Carriage of Hazardous and Noxious Substances by Sea (HNS Conve-ntion) and the Athens Convention re-lating to the Carriage of Passenge-rs and their Luggage by Sea, outline- compensation schemes for incide-nts involving cargo damage, personal injury, or loss of life at se-a. These conventions provide- guidelines for compensation in the- event of incidents during oce-an transport. They not only establish legal options for affe-cted groups but also discourage unsafe conduct in oce-an shipping.

While inte-rnational conventions lay out a foundation for maritime law, it's crucial to realize- that individual nations can enact their own legislation to tackle- specific regional issues. For e-xample, coastal states freque-ntly implement laws and rules to ove-rsee coastal shipping, port procedure-s, and environmental safety within the-ir territorial waters. These- domestic laws complement and build upon global be-nchmarks, guaranteeing that maritime ope-rations sync with local priorities and needs. The- framework from international agree-ments provides a starting point, but local concerns de-serve customized solutions. National re-gulations fill in details overlooked at broade-r levels.

Comprehe-nding the lawful structure that overse-es the shipping business, stake-holders can explore the- intricate administrative scene- and guarantee consistency with pe-rtinent laws. Lawful experts, shipproprie-tors, charterers, and other industry me-mbers will profit from a far reaching comprehe-nsion of the standards and directions that shape maritime- exchange and transportation. By carefully following the-se lawful structures, the busine-ss can support high benchmarks of wellbeing, natural ste-wardship, and crew welfare while- encouraging worldwide business on the- immense seas. More-over, a thorough understanding of the guide-lines can enable stake-holders to foresee- potential lawful difficulties and stay away from issues that may hampe-r tasks. Then again, by keeping up consiste-nce, organizations additionally guarantee the- composed stream of products and materials ove-r seaside courses fundame-ntal to worldwide gracefully chains. While the- administrative scene stays pe-rplexing, a centere-d exertion to comprehe-nd laws and guidelines from around the globe- can give clearness and assurance- to all those associated with maritime e-xchange.

Shipping Industry and Maritime Law: Maritime Contracts and Charter Parties

This portion of the book "Navigating the- Seas of Law: Unraveling the De-pths of Maritime Jurisprudence" e-xamines the legal face-ts of maritime contracts and charter parties, inve-stigating their importance in the shipping se-ctor. It offers a thorough comprehension of the- various contracts regularly utilized, for example- voyage charters, time charte-rs, and bareboat charters. Differe-nt types of maritime contracts serve- diverse purposes in the- industry. Voyage charters cover a single- voyage for the transport of cargo, with payment typically base-d on tonnage. Time charters grant the- charterer utilization of a vesse-l for a pre-characterized time- frame, regularly from various months to a few ye-ars, with the shipowner kee-ping up responsibility for the vesse-l. A bareboat charter is an agree-ment where the- charterer has complete- control of the vessel's activitie-s for the term of the contract. This se-gment clarifies the capabilitie-s of every agree-ment and how they are applie-d in the real world to transport maritime fre-ight. While all are critical to worldwide e-xchange, their

This section will provide- readers with a bette-r understanding of some fundamental aspe-cts of these contracts, like fre-ight rates, laytime, demurrage-, and off-hire clauses. It will discuss how these-stipulations play a vital part in outlining the rights and duties of both shipowners and charte-rers. An examination of how modifications to these- contractual conditions can influence important factors such as vesse-l usage and financial commitments will also be pre-sented. Terms re-lated to determining rate-s charged for cargo transport and time allotted for loading/unloading are- explained. In addition, provisions for penaltie-s if these timeline-s are exce-eded or the ship is taken out of se-rvice are define-d. The impact of flexibility in such contractual language on ke-y cargo shipping considerations is then considere-d.

This section de-lves further into examining the- lawful solutions accessible to gatherings in case- of infringement or debate-. It portrays the alternatives for unde-rstanding clashes, going from dealing and mediation to arbitration and court activitie-s. Perusers will acquire a thorough compre-hension of the systematic stride-s included in authorizing contractual privileges and looking for suitable- remedies. A fe-w choices remembe-r discussion for understanding betwee-n the gatherings without outsider me-diation. On the other hand, outsider me-diation might help the gatherings arrive- at an understanding. In the eve-nt that those strategies fizzle-, arbitration or court procedures give more-official ways to determine contractual disagre-ements. The choice-s ascend step by step in official quality and cost. This progre-ssion gives perusers knowle-dge into the lawful cycle and e-ncourages them in understanding the-ir privileges and obligations under an agre-ement.

Importantly, this section aims to offe-r more than just a legal examination by furnishing practical illustrations and plausible- situations that demonstrate the imple-mentation of maritime contracts and charter gathe-rings. Via intriguing narratives and thought-inspiring conversations, reade-rs will cultivate a subtle comprehe-nsion of the intricacies included in drafting, bargaining, and carrying out the-se arrangements. For e-xample, several case- studies are prese-nted, describing real e-vents that required untangling comple-x contractual clauses. Additionally, commentary is provided throughout to he-lp interpret various provisions and explain how ambiguous te-rms might be understood differe-ntly by each party. The goal is to provide a we-ll-rounded perspective- that goes beyond reciting clause-s to impart wisdom gained from lived expe-riences. This approach prese-nts a more nuanced learning e-xperience to he-lp navigate potential issues whe-n unique circumstances arise.

This section provide-s readers with valuable insights into the- intricate details of maritime contracts and charte-r parties. By exploring the ins and outs of the-se legal agree-ments, you'll gain crucial understanding to help smoothly ope-rate within the complicated shipping se-ctor. Whether you're a le-gal expert, scholar, policymaker, or simply inte-rested in maritime law, inve-stigating this section promises to serve- as an invaluable tool. Here you'll find e-xplanations unlocking the contractual relationships defining how busine-sses in this industry connect. Looking to learn more- about calculating freight costs, timing laytime provisions, or comprehe-nding dispute solutions? This piece acts as your guide- for navigating this fascinating area of law with lucidity and thoroughness.

This section provide-s a moderate look into the intricate- issues surrounding liability and insurance that can surface in the- shipping sector. It investigates the- notion of an shipowner's accountability for cargo that becomes lost or damage-d during transport, for personal injuries that may occur, and for environme-ntal contamination episodes. While addre-ssing these complicated liability and cove-rage matters, care is take-n to keep explanations cle-ar and readily understood, with example-s used to offer added conte-xt and insight into how such risks are managed in practical shipping operations.

Shipowners play a pivotal role- in the shipping industry by transporting goods and people safe-ly via vessel. They are- accountable for any cargo that becomes harme-d or destroyed during the voyage-. This portion explores the lawful guide-lines controlling a shipowner's obligation, for example- the worldwide understandings like- the Hague-Visby Standards and Hamburg Rules that are- connected. It additionally investigate-s the difficulties in choosing obligation when nume-rous gatherings are included in the- shipping procedure, for example- transporters, freight agents, and te-rminal administrators. For example, if items are- lost at sea, the shipowner may ne-ed to reimburse the-merchant for the estimation of the- merchandise. In addition, if travele-rs are harmed amid the journe-y, the shipowner could confront claims. Deciding who is in charge- when numerous gatherings are-included, for example the- shipowner, transporter, and terminal can prove- to be complex. This area give-s more setting to help clarify the-se lawful standards and potential difficulties.

While working aboard ships, sailors confront distinctive- hazards on the oceans that may bring about accidents and injurie-s. Claims regarding individual wounds are another critical part re-garding liability in the transportation business. Those working at se-a face special dangers whe-n carrying out their obligations, making incidents causing harms not unusual eve-nts. This passage investigates the- lawful remedies acce-ssible to sailors for statements ide-ntifying with individual damage, like repayme-nt for clinical costs, lost salaries, and torment and struggling endure-d. It in like manner looks at the part of maritime- work laws and worldwide understandings, for example-, the Global Labor Association's Maritime Labor Convention (MLC) in e-nsuring the privileges of those- working at sea. The section hope-s to bring more clarity to the topic through providing context and a fe-w additional details without delving too dee-ply.

Environmental pollution incide-nts pose considerable liability conce-rns in the shipping industry. Spills of hazardous substances, fuel oil, or othe-r pollutants can have destructive conse-quences for marine e-cosystems. Shipowners may be he-ld responsible for environme-ntal damages, cleanup expe-nses, and payment to impacted partie-s. This section explores the- legal frameworks and international agre-ements like the- International Convention on Civil Liability for Oil Pollution Damage (CLC) and the- International Convention on the Control of Harmful Anti-fouling Syste-ms on Ships (AFS Convention), which govern shipowner's accountability for e-nvironmental pollution occurrences. While- these conventions aim to re-duce pollution from ships, incidents still occur and leave-shipowners liable for exte-nsive costs. Further clarification of regulations could he-lp limit pollution risks and responsibilities.

Insurance prote-cts shipowners from unforesee-n costs and allows for peace of mind when shipping goods. Se-veral options exist to safeguard finance-s from risks inherent to the industry.

Hull insurance- resembles home-owners or auto insurance for vesse-ls, covering physical harm. No one wants to foot expe-nses from an accident at sea. Prote-ction and indemnity (P&I) insurance similarly assists with liability, mitigating costs from issues affe-cting others. Mistakes happen, so this he-lps make things right without personal loss.

Marine cargo insurance- gives peace of mind to those- transporting valuables, whether raw mate-rials or finished products. Replacing damaged or lost fre-ight can break a business, so coverage- for mishaps provides welcomed se-curity. International regulations aim to standardize protocols for prope-r documentation in claims situations. Following guidelines he-lps avoid hassle and demonstrates re-sponsibility.

While unfortunate eve-nts occur outside anyone's control, various insurance type-s offer a sensible way to transfe-r certain exposures. Se-lecting the appropriate prote-ction minimizes financial vulnerability in an unpredictable- world. The shipping sector understands risk manage-ment's importance for long-term stability. Compliance- also shows respect for collaboration across borders. In the- end, reasonable safe-guards support commerce by removing fe-ar of the unknown.

This section aims to give- readers a cleare-r view of shipping industry liability and insurance by exploring some- key legal principles and curre-nt issues in this area of maritime law. Gaining a mode-rate understanding of topics like liability, be-st risk management practices, and changing tre-nds will help equip those in the- shipping industry to confidently address challenge-s and make thoughtful choices relate-d to liability and coverage for maritime ope-rations. Some important concepts covere-d include rules around assigning responsibility for incide-nts at sea, recommende-d strategies for mitigating financial risks, and new de-velopments shaping this portion of maritime law. De-lving somewhat deepe-r into these subjects should provide- helpful context and insights to help navigate-complexities while e-nsuring readers are we-ll-informed to handle issues linke-d to liability and coverage within shipping.

The shipping industry face-s changing times as new issues e-merge in maritime law. Transporting goods by se-a involves complex international re-gulations that govern transactions and resolve dispute-s. As global trade expands, the industry e-ncounters evolving challenge-s related

This portion of the publication "Navigating the- Seas of Law: Unraveling the De-pths of Maritime Jurisprudence" ce-nters around the deve-loping lawful difficulties looking the delive-ry business. Innovation keeps on advancing at a quick pace-, presenting new issue-s and contemplations that need cautious inve-stigation inside the setting of maritime- law. The quickly changing innovative scene- presents testing inquirie-s about how current guidelines apply. Furthe-rmore, the prese-ntation of new innovations, for example, robotization and compute-rized navigation frameworks, may require- the adjustment of as of now settle-d standards or even the making of ne-w guidelines to overse-e arising circumstances. It is basic for lawful expe-rts and lawmakers to deliberate-ly audit these progressing change-s to guarantee the consiste-nce of guideline with cutting e-dge advancements and guarante-e maritime security ke-eps on being tende-d to successfully.

Technological progre-ssions at sea prompt pressing inquiries about maritime- rules and accountability matters. For autonomous ships in particular, cutting-edge- autonomy raises uncertainties about the-lawful obligations and liabilities of ship proprietors, pilots, and creators. As the-se self-driving vesse-ls become more pre-valent in the coming years, care-fully defining standards and appropriate legislation to ove-rsee their prote-cted handling and likely risk reduction will grow incre-asingly important. While innovation holds promise, protecting live-s and the environment de-mands well-considered ove-rsight that considers diverse stake-holders.

Blockchain technology pre-sents an upcoming opportunity for improvement within the- shipping sector. Having a decentralize-d digital ledger has the capability to significantly update- numerous parts of maritime commerce-, such as paperwork, supply chain tracking, and payment processe-s. Neverthele-ss, incorporating this innovation likewise brings up lawful concerns linke-d to information secrecy, safety, and inte-llectual property ownership.

In addition, mounting worries about e-nvironmental sustainability have introduced nove-l lawful ponderings inside the shipping busine-ss. The execution of discharge- control measures to diminish ozone de-pleting substance outflows from ships is a prime case-. As worldwide controls, for example, the- International Maritime Organization's (IMO) sulfur top come into impact, ship proprie-tors need to explore- consistence nece-ssities and potential punishments. The-re is additionally developing we-ight on the business to embrace- more eco-friendly shipping hone-, for example, utilizing ele-ctive fuels or diminishing plastic waste as pe-r worldwide natural guidelines. The- growing worries over environme-ntal change have prompted shipproprie-tors needing to adjust to new guide-lines with the goal that they can ke-ep working viably while additionally ensuring the- planet. New innovations, for example-, elective fue-ls are a promising technique for shippe-rs to diminish ozone depleting substance-emanations while as yet conve-ying merchandise over the- seas.

As digitalization increasingly transforms shipping ope-rations and systems, legal considerations surrounding the-se technological changes re-quire examination. With greate-r digitization of processes and functions, matters involving cybe-rsecurity and data privacy become e-specially important. It is crucial to protect sensitive- files and establish protecte-d communication lines to guarantee cybe-r resilience against possible- risks, as more aspects transition to digital formats. Questions about safe-guarding information and maintaining secure channels me-rit attention to uphold sturdy cyber defe-nses contrary to potential threats, as digitization progre-sses within the industry.

While e-merging issues underscore- the evolving nature of maritime- law requiring consistent adaptation to new challe-nges, exploring these- topics and their implications provides valuable insight. By e-xamining changing industry landscapes within legal frameworks, "Navigating the- Seas of Law" equips reade-rs with understanding to interpret shipping's transformation through maritime-jurisprudence. The dynamic book clarifie-s maritime law's need to adjust continuously whe-n addressing novel issues, the-reby helping reade-rs navigate shipping's future through meaningful e-xamination of its past and present.

Fisherie-s and Marine Resource Law e-xplores the introduction to fisherie-s and marine resources. Some- key aspects covere-d include an overview of the- management and conservation of fishing and aquatic plant and animal life-. Different approaches are- considered

Fisherie-s hold significant importance for sustaining food supplies and boosting financial growth worldwide, re-ndering the prudent administration of oce-anic assets absolutely fundamental in maritime- law. This portion gives a thoughtful outline of the critical worth of fishe-ries and marine assets in the- setting of maritime lawful issues. Fishe-ries assume a pivotal part in giving sustenance-

and work for numerous network. Effective-ly overseeing fishe-ries guarantees a maintainable- harvest of ocean assets pre-sently and later on. While se-a assets give significant advantages, the-ir judicious administration requires comprehe-nsion of complex natural eleme-nts and balancing financial concerns with conservation. This area offe-rs key understanding into the inte-rrelations betwee-n maritime law and maintaining a strategic distance from ove-ruse of common marine life.

The world's oce-ans contain immense stores of biodive-rsity, housing a diverse range of marine- life that is essential for maintaining e-cological balance and supplying vital nourishment for human communities. Fishe-ries especially have- played a pivotal function in fulfilling the expanding worldwide- need for seafood and offe-ring livelihood chances for countless individuals e-ngaged in fishing. While the oce-ans' species create- ecological equilibrium, fisherie-s have served to nourish pe-ople groups and give occupations to numerous inside- the commercial fishing ente-rprise. Nonethele-ss, there is all the more- yet to investigate about how to be-st oversee this significant common asse-t and guarantee both biological diversity and work for future- eras.

Grasping the importance- of fisheries and ocean re-sources is critical in grasping the lawful structures that control the-se invaluable resource-s. Fishing tasks are at the mercy of an intricate- system of national and global guidelines inte-nded to guarantee maintainable- practices and secure de-licate marine biological systems. The-se directions manage issue-s, for example, most extre-me catches, gear confine-ments, shut seasons, and base size- prerequisites, altoge-ther focused at forestalling ove-rfishing and ensuring the future stre-ngth of fish populaces. While guideline-s are expecte-d to maintain a strategic distance from overuse- and secure the future- of fisheries, it is esse-ntial to comprehend the intricate- system of directions that administration exe-rcises and ensure de-licate marine biological systems.

Furthermore-, sustainable practices regarding marine- life are intricately tie-d to global nourishment and financial progress on a wider scale-. The dependability and fruitfulne-ss of fishing grounds importantly affect food accessibility, specifically in se-aside towns that intensely re-ly on seafood as their main wellspring of prote-in. What's more, solid angling ventures e-nergize financial deve-lopment through occupation creation, fare income-, and backing to auxiliary segments, for example-, preparing and transportation. These communitie-s require consistent fishing yie-lds to bolster themselve-s. Additionally, worldwide nourishment security re-lies upon sea creature-s being caught sustainably so their populations stay steady. Financial turn of e-vents in shoreline ne-tworks is subject to fishing enterprise-s working viably for a long time to come.

While the- regulation of fisheries and marine- resources must address distinctive- difficulties stemming from the inte-rconnecting character of ocean e-nvironments, collaboration among countries proves pivotal to surmount jurisdictional intricacie-s and guarantee synchronized me-thods for environmental protection and administration of asse-ts. A variety of worldwide compacts and arrangeme-nts have been se-t up to encourage teamwork be-tween governme-nts in territories like migratory fish populace-s, fishing outside national ward limits, and admittance to fishery asse-ts. Such global exchanges can help clarify the- multifaceted qualities of ove-rseeing transboundary marine biological syste-ms while advancing consistent practices for looking afte-r fish populations and local areas for forthcoming eras. Let us e-xamine this topic in a bit more detail. We- will analyze some of the major inte-rnational accords and local laws governing how fisheries are- overseen to e-ncourage long-term use without e-ndangering ocean life. Ke-y rules and standards focused on fishing sustainably and conserving marine- variety will be looked at. Additionally, we- will consider the idea of control and authority ove-r sea assets, emphasizing the- privileges of coastal nations within their sole- financial zones. As we investigate- this segment somewhat furthe-r, questions around these authorize-d structures may come up.

A moderate- examination of these important subje-cts will provide readers with de-eper insight into the significant part playe-d by fisheries and ocean asse-ts in maritime law. Furthermore, this se-gment lays the groundwork for additional investigation of pivotal points e-ncompassing asset protection and natural guideline-s, question determination instrume-nts, and how the scene of fishe-ries administration is advancing in our currently worldwide world. For e-xample, marine life and fishe-ries give fundamental suste-nance yet in addition work to numerous local pe-ople. Then again, overfishing and abse-nce of guidelines thre-aten these significant common asse-ts. Additionally, worldwide collaboration is basic for managing sharing of transboundary fish stocks and safeguarding marine biodive-rsity. This area presents e-ssential settings that will be furthe-r investigated regarding pe-rsistent difficulties and potential arrange-ments.

Fisherie-s management involves comple-x legal frameworks and resource- regulations. The field of Fishe-ries and Marine Resource- Law establishes guideline-s and policies for the sustainable use- and protection of aquatic life. Effective- management require-s clarifying responsibilities across

Effective- oversight of fisheries is absolute-ly essential to guarantee- the long-term viability of marine life-, and worldwide agreeme-nts and conventions assume a vital part in administering fishe-ries rehearse-s. In this area, we will take a gande-r at the lawful structures that have be-en set up to manage fishe-ries administration and investigate the- key standards and guidelines for maintainable- angling hones. Some of these- key worldwide understandings incorporate- the 1982 United Nations Convention on the- Law of the Sea, which characterize-s sovereign entitle-ments over common assets, and the- 1995 Agreement on Port State- Measures to Preve-nt, Deter and Eliminate Ille-gal, Unreported and Unregulate-d Fishing. Furthermore, various territorial fishe-ries associations have bee-n shaped to direct angling limits and seasons de-pendent on logical information. Overall, the- objective of these- lawful and institutional systems is to guarantee that catche-s stay inside maintainable limits and that all angling exe-rcises are led in an maintainable- way.

The Unite-d Nations Convention on the Law of the Se-a, also known as UNCLOS, is one of the crucial international agre-ements regarding fishe-ries administration. This accord establishes a comple-te structure for prese-rving and sustainably utilizing marine resources, like- fisheries. UNCLOS introduces the- Exclusive Economic Zone idea, giving coastal nations sole- rights over exploring, making use of, safe-guarding, and overseeing living and non-living re-sources inside 200 nautical miles from the-ir baselines. The EEZ conce-pt permitted coastal states gre-ater control over nearby wate-rs to better regulate- fishing and protect marine life within this zone-. UNCLOS has aided international cooperation on fishe-ries and enabled coastal countrie-s to sustainably manage important fishing grounds close to their shore-s.

Furthermore-, UNCLOS recognizes the duty of coastal state-s to adopt measures for conserving and managing fish stocks both within and be-yond their EEZs. This involves impleme-nting appropriate scientific study, establishing catch limits base-d on maximum sustainable yield, and taking actions to preve-nt overfishing and protect vulnerable- species. Coastal states must re-search fish populations to determine- sustainable catch levels. The-y are also responsible for monitoring fishing activity and se-tting quotas accordingly to prevent deple-tion of shared resources. The-se conservation efforts aim to e-nsure healthy oceans and long-te-rm food security for all nations.

RFMOs have an important job in sustainably managing fishe-ries beyond just a single nation's wate-rs. These organizations establish rule-s that member countries agre-e to follow with the goals of protecting fish populations and e-ncouraging collaboration between state-s that harvest the same fish stocks. For instance-, NAFO oversees fishing activitie-s in the Northwest Atlantic Ocean to guard fish abundance- in that region through rules on catch limits and gear re-strictions that its member governme-nts promise to honor. Likewise, WCPFC handle-s fisheries stewardship dutie-s in the Western and Ce-ntral Pacific Ocean by creating binding measure-s for the nations fishing there to e-nsure today's catches don't harm tomorrow's yields.

The conce-pts underlying ecosystem-base-d fisheries manageme-nt or EBFM are also rising in importance within international fishe-ries legislation. EBFM considers not me-rely specific fish populations individually but in addition their re-lationships with other types of sea life- and the more exte-nsive marine ecosyste-m. Its goal is to preserve or re-establish the well-be-ing and adaptability of ecosystems while making sure- sustainable use of fish stocks. EBFM acknowledge-s the interdepe-ndence of marine asse-ts and stresses the ne-cessity for a comprehensive- tactic toward fisheries administration. EBFM aims to provide additional conte-xt regarding fish stocks, their interactions with othe-r species, and impacts on the broade-r marine ecosystem. While- traditional fisheries manageme-nt focused solely on individual fish populations, EBFM recognize-s the complexity of ocean e-nvironments and advocates a holistic approach.

To enforce- these legal frame-works, states employ various tools and mechanisms, aiming to monitor fishing activitie-s and guarantee compliance with re-gulations. Licensing systems, vesse-l monitoring programs, and observer scheme-s are utilized to track fishing vesse-ls and collect information. This data is then applied for scie-ntific study and stock evaluations, allowing fishery managers to gain a more- nuanced understanding of ocean conditions and re-source populations over time. Whe-n states implement monitoring me-asures successfully, they assist sustainable- management of fisherie-s by protecting marine life. This he-lps safeguard the ocean's gifts so curre-nt and future people can be-nefit from the bounty of the se-a.

All those involve-d in fishing - coastal states, fishing communities, scientists, and conse-rvation groups - must take part in creating and enforcing re-gulations for managing fisheries. Working togethe-r is crucial to solve shared problems like- illegal and undocumented fishing, re-ducing unwanted catches, and designating marine- protected areas. Coastal state-s can provide local knowledge of fishing are-as while scientists offer data on fish populations. Communitie-s rely on sustainable catches for the-ir livelihood. Conservationists aim to prese-rve marine ecosyste-ms. By collaborating through open discussions, these stake-holders can develop balance-d solutions to challenges facing the industry and e-nvironment.

As we continue- exploring fisheries and marine- resource law, let's de-lve deepe-r into sovereignty and jurisdiction over marine- resources, conservation and e-nvironmental regulations, as well as e-xamine dispute resolution me-chanisms. Gaining a thorough understanding of these le-gal aspects will help us navigate the- intricate waters of fisherie-s management and contribute to sustainably using pre-cious marine life. The notion of sove-reignty holds significant importance within fisherie-s and marine resource law. Appre-ciating how sovereignty applies to marine- resources is key to compre-hending coastal states' jurisdictional authority over e-xclusive economic zones. While- sovereignty grants coastal nations control of EEZs, international agre-ements see-k sustainable use through measure-s like catch limits and gear restrictions. Dispute-s sometimes eme-rge when fishing vesse-ls enter other sove-reign waters, requiring e-valuation through mechanisms like negotiation or arbitration. Ove-rall, properly managing our ocean resource-s demands fully recognizing each state-'s legal control while also protecting marine- habitats through cooperation across boundaries.

Coastal nations have unique- authority and administration over the living and non-living natural assets inside- their Exclusive Economic Zones (EEZs), which re-ach out to 200 sea miles from their shore-lines. An EEZ grants a public authority sovereignty ove-r exploring, oversee-ing, keeping up, and overse-eing the utilization of both undeve-loped and natural assets found inside this space-. While a state's domain stops at its land outskirt and inland waters, it has spe-cific privileges and control over the- oceanic life systems, fish stocks, vitality asse-ts, and other normal products situated in the EEZ stre-tching out from its shoreline. This zone of sole- control granted to coastal states over the-ir marine environments and asse-ts inside the EEZ is what is alluded to as the-ir "sovereignty" in the se-tting of oceanic assets and administration. Such sovere-ignty permits nations to authorize angling rights and oil and gas removal inside-

Coastal nations wield control ove-r marine life primarily through laws and guideline-s that administer angling activities, asset re-moval, and natural life insurance inside the-ir EEZs. They have the powe-r to characterize fishing limits, actualize prote-ction efforts, and oversee- maintainable angling practices to guarantee- the future strength of the-ir marine assets. These- nations can choose how much fish can be caught annually and impose fine-s if quotas are surpassed. They additionally introduce- rules identifying what strategie-s can be utilized and what creature-s ought to be delivere-d back to the ocean. These- measures are inte-nded to shield fish populations from overfishing so marine- life will be accessible- for future ages.

Furthermore-, coastal states possess the authority to issue- licenses and fishing permits to both dome-stic and foreign ships navigating within their jurisdictional waters. This e-nables them to administer and track fishing ope-rations, guaranteeing conformity with domestic le-gislation and worldwide accords. Coastal nations can use this permitting syste-m to control where, when, and how much fishing is allowe-d. It also helps them collect important data on catche-s and ensure fisherie-s are managed sustainably.

However, it is important to note that while coastal states hold jurisdictional rights over their EEZs, they are also bound by international law and obligations. The United Nations Convention on the Law of the Sea (UNCLOS) serves as the fundamental legal framework for determining the extent of coastal state sovereignty and the rights and responsibilities of other states in utilizing marine resources.

While UNCLOS acknowle-dges the sovere-ign authority of coastal nations over living marine resource-s like fish and other organisms, as well as non-living supplie-s beneath the se-afloor like minerals and oil, it also establishe-s principles for collaborative administration and prese-rvation of shared populations. This promotes sustainable fishing me-thods to prevent overuse- and conserve stocks for future ge-nerations. The treaty aims to balance- coastal states' control over nearby wate-rs with worldwide efforts to manage share-d marine life responsibly.

Coastal nations are e-ncouraged to work together with borde-ring countries and international groups to make sure- the fish populations that move betwe-en different are-as are well-taken care- of and protected. Organizations that overse-e fisheries for whole- regions (RFMOs) importantly help bring nations togethe-r, encourage studying the fish, and put rule-s in place to keep the- fish safe. These fish swim across diffe-rent parts of the ocean ove-rseen by multiple gove-rnments, so cooperation is key. By sharing data and agre-eing on rules, neighbors can manage- fishing sustainably without hurting fish numbers now or later.

When disagre-ements eme-rge over dete-rmining the borders of exclusive- economic zones or competing claims to oce-an resources, coastal nations have options for se-ttling the issues. They can pursue- negotiation, mediation, international arbitration, or having inte-rnational courts or panels make a ruling. Resolving the-se disputes involves e-xamining international law, such as the United Nations Conve-ntion on the Law of the Sea, to balance- a coastal state's sovereignty while- also considering the intere-sts of other countries and the wide-r international community. The law aims to fairly distribute oce-an wealth and resources be-tween all parties with acce-ss. There are usually opportunitie-s for open communication and compromise betwe-en disputing sides before- turning to formal judgment. Coastal states hope discussion and coope-ration can address concerns to mutual bene-fit.

Grasping the ide-a of sovereignty and how it relate-s to marine resources is e-ssential for sorting through the intricacies of fishe-ries and ocean resource- regulation. When we acknowle-dge the jurisdictional authority of coastal nations over the-ir exclusive economic zone-s, in addition to the interplay betwe-en domestic laws and international agre-ements, stakeholde-rs can labor to attain sustainable administration and protection of these- invaluable maritime possessions. The-re is a need to balance- resource utilization today with safeguarding acce-ss for future generations. Coope-ration across borders through regional fisherie-s management organizations is important for establishing catch limits and te-chnical measures with consideration of scie-ntific advice. While exclusive- rights exist, we must recognize- our shared depende-nce on healthy oceans.

Chapter 2

Fisheries and Marine Resource Law: Conservation and Environmental Regulations

****

Here- we delve into the- important issue of conservation and ecological rule-s as part of the segment on Fishe-ries and Marine Resource- Law. With the need for oce-an assets keeping on e-xpanding, it turns out to be fundamental to actualize lawful e-stimates and activities focused at e-nsuring and safeguarding these significant asse-ts. As request for marine life- keeps on deve-loping, it is critical that we actualize administrative me-asures and leads intende-d to ensure and safeguard the-se important assets for future age-s. While the intere-st for fish and different marine life- keeps on deve-loping, we should guarantee the-se assets are ove-rsaw viably and keep on being acce-ssible long into the future. This incorporate-s setting catch limits and seasons and ensuring e-ndangered specie-s. Overall protection of the marine-condition is fundamental on the off chance that we- need to guarantee- these assets are- practical.

While marine- resources face de-pletion from unsustainable fishing, degrade-d habitats, pollution, and climate impacts, international cooperation aims to safe-guard ocean health and coastal livelihoods. Fishing me-thods and habitats altered beyond re-covery threaten both e-cosystems and people re-lying on ocean bounty. Legal agree-ments under deve-lopment by global organizations and governments se-ek to establish sustainable harve-sts and preserve marine- environments through conservation. Though challe-nges persist, collective- efforts show recognition that ocean we-ll-being necessitate-s wise stewardship for both environme-ntal and economic security.

Sustainable fishe-ries management is one- of the pivotal initiatives in this area. This me-thodology stresses employing scie-ntific evidence and e-cosystem-founded technique-s to guarantee the long-run viability of fish populations. It e-ntails establishing catch ceilings, designating prote-cted zones, applying gear constraints, and e-mbracing steps to reduce uninte-nded catch and discarded catch. These-regulations aim to attain equilibrium betwe-en exploitation and prese-rvation, permitting sustainable use while- safeguarding the long-term future- of marine life. This approach see-ks to provide additional context surrounding key e-lements like catch limits, prote-cted areas, gear re-strictions, and measures to decre-ase unintended catch and discarde-d catch. Doing so helps clarify how this balanced strategy supports the- ongoing utilization of marine resources ove-r time through exploitation and conservation.

To further re-inforce conservation initiatives, worldwide- agreements for e-xample the United Nations Conve-ntion on the Law of the Sea (UNCLOS) and local fishe-ries administration associations (RFMOs) have bee-n set up. UNCLOS gives a lawful structure for the- administration and protection of living marine assets inside- national purviews and in regions past national purview. RFMOs, the-n again, are accountable for overse-eing fishery assets inside- explicit geological locales or spe-cies. These global unde-rstandings and territorial associations are basic on the grounds that the-y cooperate internationally to e-nsure marine life and fish populations crosswise- over outskirts. UNCLOS gives a common lawful system that all participating countrie-s must follow regarding ocean utilization and administration. RFMOs fill in as overse-eing bodies to gather information about spe-cific fisheries and make administrative- strategies, for example-, catch limits or gear limitations, with the point of guarantee-ing manageability. Together, the-se worldwide and local ende-avors attempt to accomplish a adjust amongst fishery use and e-nvironmental stability of the oceans.

Beyond the-se lawful ways, numerous worldwide associations assume- a basic job in advancing maintainable angling practices and securing oce-anic biological systems. For instance, the Food and Agriculture- Organization (FAO) of the United Nations works intimately with part nations to cre-ate rules and best hone-s for dependable fishe-ries administration. The FAO's Code of Conduct for Re-sponsible Fisheries give-s an exhaustive system for maintainable- angling and addresses issues, for e-xample, overfishing, natural surroundings protection, and e-cosystem the exe-cutives. While the FAO's Code- of Conduct gives a structure to overse-e fisheries sustainably, the-re is still work to be done to e-nsure all nations completely e-mbrace these rule-s and best practices to protect de-licate ocean ecosyste-ms for future generations.

Furthermore-, non-governmental organizations (NGOs) and industry stakeholde-rs have played an active role- in establishing conservation and environme-ntal regulations through their collaborative e-fforts. These groups have vocally champione-d the creation of marine prote-cted areas to safeguard oce-an ecosystems. They have- also advocated for limiting illegal, unreporte-d, and unregulated (IUU) fishing which plagues our se-as. Such unsustainable practices deple-te fish stocks and disrupt marine habitats if left unaddre-ssed. Additionally, NGOs and industry leaders have- supported eco-labeling initiative-s to better inform consumers about sustainable- seafood options. These labe-ls help promote brands that utilize re-sponsible harvesting technique-s. While progress has bee-n made, more work remains to fully prote-ct our oceans and ensure future- generations can still enjoy the-ir beauty and bounty.

When navigating the- intricate domain of fisheries and aquatic re-source legislation, appreciating the-significance of conservation and ecological rule-s is paramount. By executing these- authorized steps and projects, we- can guarantee the long-te-rm health and endurance of our se-as while safeguarding the me-ans of subsistence of those who re-ly on them. Conservation laws aim to offer judicious dire-ction for aquatic life and ecosystems. Whe-n implemented prope-rly through coordinated effort and understanding across all stake-holders, such statutes can provide for e-quilibrium between pre-sent and future utilization of marine re-sources. Nonethele-ss, more remains to be done- to fully comprehend interconne-ctions and impacts, as the complexity of ocean syste-ms poses ongoing challenges.

In the subse-quent portion of this segment, we- will plunge further into exploring the- different dispute re-solution methods accessible in fishe-ries law, analyzing how disagreeme-nts identified with fisherie-s administration are tended to through worldwide- mediation and different strate-gies. There are- a few choices open whe-n clashes emerge- over fisheries the- board arrangements, for example-, global arbitration and settlement. By inve-stigating these choices more- altogether, we can be-tter comprehend how to ove-rsee potential clashe-s and accomplish all the more reasonable- results for all included parties. While- worldwide mediation arrangeme-nts may take additional opportunity and vitality to achieve, the-y regularly result in choices that addre-ss everybody's worries inste-ad of favoring one side over anothe-r.

Dispute Resolution Mechanisms in Fisheries Law

Within the intricate- domain of fisheries and marine re-source legislation, disagree-ments regularly surface owing to opposing ne-eds and contradictory statements. Solving the-se disagreeme-nts is pivotal for upholding sustainable fishing techniques and guarante-eing the equitable- allotment of marine assets. This se-gment investigates the- lawful instruments that have bee-n established to handle such clashe-s and offers illuminating case examine-s and examples of worldwide arbitration in fishe-ries-related de-bates. For instance, a dispute may e-merge betwe-en two nations fishing the same stock if one- nation believes the- other's quotas are too high and unsustainable. Similarly, boundary issue-s can lead to conflicts if the deline-ation of a maritime boundary is unclear or conteste-d between state-s. International arbitration provides an impartial mechanism for re-solving such conflicts through discussion and applying international legal principles. Conside-r a case where two coastal state-s had competing claims over fishing rights in an area; through arbitration, a ruling was able- to determine usage- rights and set quotas in a way that was fair to both parties. Overall, maintaining e-ffective legal re-solutions is vital for productively sharing marine living assets and pre-serving oceans for future ge-nerations.

Effective- management of shared fishe-ry resources nece-ssitates collaboration betwee-n all involved parties. One ke-y facet of resolving disputes in this are-a of law acknowledges the ne-cessity for states and additional stakeholde-rs to work together constructively. Nume-rous international agreeme-nts have realized that succe-ssful stewardship of fisheries de-mands a collaborative attempt, thus they have- been create-d to help facilitate negotiations and pe-aceful settling of disagree-ments. Proper administration of fisherie-s protecting fish populations for future yields re-quires a joint endeavor from all e-ntities partaking in different fishe-ries. Various worldwide contracts comprehe-nd that proficient administration of fisheries e-xpects a joint exertion, along the-se lines they have- been made to he-lp encourage talks and sere-ne determination of conte-ntions.

For example-, the United Nations Convention on the- Law of the Sea (UNCLOS) lays out a structure for working through disagre-ements tied to fishe-ries administration and the protection of oce-anic resources. UNCLOS deve-lops methods like discussion, mediation, and arbitration to handle- clashes betwee-n coastal nations, non-coastal nations, and other pertinent gathe-rings. The framework establishe-d under UNCLOS tries to clarify the rights and commitme-nts of nations with regards to the administration and protection of transboundary fish stocks and diffe-rent common assets of the se-a. It likewise gives syste-ms for coastal states and different gathe-rings to settle their contrasts and guarante-e the maintainable utilization of share-d marine biological systems.

Case studie-s can provide useful understandings into re-al situations of how disagreement solutions work within the- setting of fisheries law. One- notable instance is the disagre-ement betwe-en Iceland

and Norway over the- administration of their cod stocks. In this case, the two countrie-s had opposing assertions over a similar marine re-gion, resulting in heated te-nsions and possible overuse of fish populations. Through re-spectful discussions and the foundation of bilateral contracts, the- two countries had the option to clear up the-ir distinctions and evolve teaming tactics for lasting fishing. While- the nations initially had conflicting views on managing the share-d waters, open communication and a willingness to find common ground allowe-d them to establish joint manageme-nt protocols. This cooperative approach helpe-d ensure the long-te-rm sustainability of the cod fishery and preve-nted overfishing of the share-d resource.

The dispute- between Australia and Japan ove-r whaling in the Southern Ocean provide-s another insightful example. Australia conte-nded that Japan's whaling methods contravene-d worldwide conservation guideline-s, resulting in an official challenge be-fore the International Court of Justice-. The ICJ sided with Australia, affirming that Japan's whaling practices did not adhe-re to present pre-servation steps. This pivotal case unde-rscores the part of authorized organizations in solving fishe-ries disagreeme-nts and maintaining worldwide rules. The ruling se-rved to clarify the obligations of nations under inte-rnational environmental accords while also amplifying the- potential for adjudication to further global resource- stewardship.

International organizations such as the- Food and Agriculture Organization (FAO) and regional fisherie-s management organizations (RFMOs) play an indispensable- role in enabling dispute re-solution. These entitie-s furnish arenas for discussion, deal-making, and the formation of collaborative- tactics among member nations to tackle share-d difficulties in fisheries administration. While- cooperating through such bodies, coastal countries work to clarify pe-rspectives, amplify consensus vie-wpoints, and enrich their collective- understanding of practical and sustainable solutions to disputes ove-r shared ocean resource-s. Continued engageme-nt within multilateral frameworks helps disputing partie-s appreciate each othe-r's viewpoints and interests, paving the- way for mutually agreeable ways forward.

In conclusion, resolving dispute-s related to fisherie-s and marine resource law ne-cessitates detaile-d legal structures and functional methods for discussion and arbitration. This portion has inve-stigated the significance of collaboration be-tween nations and stakeholde-rs, as well as the part of worldwide contracts, case- investigations, and associations in facilitating tranquil determination of clashe-s. By comprehending these- debate resolution instrume-nts, policymakers, lawful experts, and stake-holders included in fisherie-s administration can contribute to the prese-rvation of marine assets and the maintainable- future of our oceans. In this segme-nt, we delve some-what further into the pivotal point of marine e-nvironmental protection. With our oceans confronting nume-rous dangers and difficulties, it is imperative- to comprehend the importance- of safeguarding the delicate- biological communities that exist inside the-m.

The marine- environment hosts an immense- variety of life and fulfills a crucial function in upholding equilibrium among the- Earth's natural communities. But human actions have inflicted substantial injury on this fragile- ecosystem. Contamination, overharve-sting of fish, devastation of habitats, climatic transformations, and discarded plastic are just some- of the urgent difficulties confronting our se-as at this time. While this intricate aquatic world supports untold numbe-rs of creatures both large and small, human inte-rference has disrupte-d natural processes and damaged fragile- balances, often in unsee-n ways. Small adjustments in one area can cre-ate unforesee-n waves elsewhe-re. Further study may reve-al hidden impacts and suggest practical solutions to aid restoration of oce-anic well-being.

Gaining a nuanced appre-ciation for the diverse difficultie-s confronting ocean environments is pivotal for formulating impactful tactics to minimize- and preclude added de-triment. By investigating core ide-as and rules, we see-k to furnish readers with an inclusive synopsis of the- significance of defending marine- ecological systems. Some of the- multifaceted challenge-s include pollution, overfishing, climate change-, habitat destruction, and invasive specie-s. A deeper compre-hension of these comple-x issues can help identify the- most appropriate solutions to safeguard marine life- now and for future generations.

There- are several dange-rs that jeopardize marine e-nvironments, such as pollution from land, ships, and oil and gas rigs offshore. Pollution from shore washe-s into the seas, bringing harmful chemicals and waste-. Vessels rele-ase contaminants into the waters as the-y transport goods between ports. Ene-rgy operations dump byproducts into the ocean. Additionally, the- effects of climate change- endanger ocean syste-ms. Sea temperature-s have been incre-asing, warming the waters. The acidity of the- seas has grown due to more carbon dioxide- absorbed from the air. Coral ree-fs have experie-nced episodes whe-re they lose the-ir brilliant colors as ocean warming stresses the- sensitive animals that reside- in the reefs. We- will inspect these various thre-ats to marine life, like pollution from nume-rous human activities on land and at sea, as well as how climatic change-s are impacting ocean realms through highe-r temperatures, gre-ater acidity,

Though addressing the-se difficulties may appear quite- daunting, there remains cause- for optimism. A number of international accords and conventions have- been impleme-nted to collectively confront oce-an environmental safeguarding around the- world. We will explore the-se agreeme-nts and examine their goals, philosophie-s, and enforcement approache-s. By comprehending the le-gal structures currently in effe-ct, readers can achieve- understandings into how countries are coope-rating to protect our seas. These- global arrangements aim to clarify complex issue-s surrounding marine life prese-rvation and clarify the shared responsibility of all coastal and island nations. While- progress requires continue-d coordinated efforts, the foundations for coope-ration have been e-stablished.

As we progre-ss through this segment, it is imperative- to acknowledge that marine e-cological security is not exclusively the- duty of administrations or universal associations. It expects aggre-gate activity from people, e-nterprises, and networks ove-rall. By expanding mindfulness about the dange-rs looking our seas and advancing maintainable practices, we- can make a distinction in protecting these- invaluable biological systems for future e-ras. While more nee-ds to be done, by each doing our part through e-ducation and sustainable living, together our small individual actions can grow into wide-spread change for stewarding the- health of our oceans.

Please- note that in later segme-nts of this section, we will examine- specific regions of marine e-nvironmental protection more close-ly, such as the rules governing pollution at se-a, coastal region administration, and developing issue-s in sustainability. Keep watching for a thorough investigation of the-se subjects and additional ones in the- forthcoming segments of this section cove-ring marine environmental prote-ction.

While the-re are seve-ral international agreeme-nts and conventions that aim to protect the marine- environment, it is important to recognize- the complexity of this issue and variations in approache-s. Different organizations have e-stablished frameworks addressing dive-rse aspects like pollution

Here- we explore in mode-rate depth the inte-rnational agreements and conve-ntions created to tackle the- important issue of marine environme-nt protection. It is essential that we- safeguard our ocean ecosyste-ms, as they currently face nume-rous risks and difficulties in the contemporary world. Multiple- organizations have worked to deve-lop legal frameworks addressing pollution, ove-rfishing, shipping safety, and other threats. While- challenges remain, such collaborations re-veal our shared intere-st in sustaining ocean life for future ge-nerations.

To begin, we- will analyze several important global accords and conve-ntions focused on marine environme-ntal safeguarding. Some of the ke-y agreements e-ncompass United Nations Convention on the Law of the- Sea (UNCLOS), the International Conve-ntion for the Prevention of Pollution from Ships (MARPOL), as we-ll as the United Nations Framework Conve-ntion on Climate Change (UNFCCC). Each of these- treaties address distinctive- aims, ideals, and enforceme-nt approaches intended to she-lter our seas. UNCLOS aims to establish a le-gal framework for all ocean and sea use-s, whereas MARPOL's goal is to avert pollution of the- oceans from ships. Meanwhile, UNFCCC focuse-s on minimizing climate change by reducing gre-enhouse gas emissions. Although the-se agreeme-nts tackle diverse face-ts of ocean protection, their share-d objective is to prese-rve marine ecosyste-ms for current and future gene-rations.

The UNCLOS, ofte-n referred to as the- constitution for the seas, lays out a broad framework for sustainably utilizing and safe-guarding marine resources. It distinguishe-s the rights and duties of countries re-garding their coastal zones, exclusive- economic zones (EEZs), and high seas. Furthe-rmore, it offers a forum for solving disputes involving maritime- boundaries or overlapping claims over oce-an resources. The conve-ntion aims to provide clarity on jurisdiction in coastal waters as well as e-xclusive rights to natural resources. While- allowing states to profit from resources in the-ir EEZ, it also requires protecting the- marine environment. UNCLOS also touche-s on navigational privileges, like the- freedom of transit passage through inte-rnational straits. Overall, it establishes consiste-nt international rules to manage human activitie-s at sea responsibly.

MARPOL specifically targe-ts preventing pollution originating from ships. The conve-ntion establishes guideline-s to reduce various kinds of marine contamination, such as oil spillage-s, disposal of trash and sewage, and emissions from ve-ssels. It has served a pivotal part in de-creasing pollution occurrences and shie-lding marine ecosystems from the- detrimental impacts of waste produce-d by ships. While MARPOL sets rules aiming to le-ssen numerous structures of marine- pollution, like oil spills, dumping of garbage and sewage-, and emissions from ships, more can still be done- to further strengthen prote-ctions for oceans. Continued international coope-ration will be important to update standards and enforce- compliance.

The UNFCCC takes a broader approach by addressing climate change, which has significant implications for the health and well-being of our oceans. This convention seeks to stabilize greenhouse gas concentrations in the atmosphere and mitigate further climate change impacts. It recognizes that rising sea levels, ocean acidification, and changes in ocean currents pose serious threats to marine biodiversity and coastal communities.

Through carefully e-xamining these worldwide contracts and conve-ntions, we achieve a more-profound comprehension of the targe-ts, standards, and operational instruments that underlie-worldwide attempts towards ocean natural life- insurance. It is pivotal to acknowledge that the-se arrangements work toge-ther and supplement one- another, shaping an exhaustive syste-m for shielding our seas. While the- agreements share- common objectives of ocean prote-ction, each addresses important aspe-cts requiring protection—whethe-r through limiting pollution, overfishing, or other threats. Coope-ration across agreements allows nations to support e-ach other's efforts and collective-ly make progress in safeguarding marine- environments to the be-nefit of both environmental and e-conomic interests.

Let us furthe-r our examination of safeguarding the marine- environment. The upcoming parts will inve-stigate in more depth the- rules around water pollution from vesse-ls, the administration of coastal territories, prote-cted marine zones, and de-veloping difficulties in protecting the- oceanic domain. Every one of the-se viewpoints plays a fundamental job in our joine-d exertion to ensure- and watch over the delicate- equalization of our seas. While coastal zone- administration and secured marine te-rritories focus on particular regions that require- extra security, rules controlling contamination at se-a and rising issues look for all the more broadly to e-nsure the wellbe-ing of our oceans overall.

Regulation of Pollution at Sea

Here- we explore in more- detail the important issue of re-gulating marine contamination, focusing on the lawful structures and rule-s that oversee this urge-nt issue. As oceanic biological systems confront de-veloping dangers from human exe-rcises, for example, contamination from ve-ssels, it is basic to comprehend the- laws set up to ensure maritime- biological systems. This segment will ze-ro in on giving more setting about the worrie-s surrounding ocean contamination from boats and the lawful instruments inte-nded to oversee- these dangers. We- will investigate how worldwide unde-rstandings, for example, the Inte-rnational Convention for the Preve-ntion of Pollution from Ships attempt to decrease- emanations and waste discharge from ships. Additionally, we- will take a gander at how local laws suppleme-nt these global guideline-s and how consistency is monitored. While significant advance-ment has been made-, ocean contamination stays a test and further worldwide- activity is expected to e-nsure the wellbe-ing of our seas.

Let us start with giving a brie-f outline of the numerous worldwide- arrangements and conventions that manage- marine ecological insurance. The-se understandings frame the- establishment for worldwide activitie-s to battle contamination and ensure the- wellbeing of our seas. By inve-stigating the destinations, standards, and usage instrume-nts of these arrangeme-nts, perusers will acquire a more-profound comprehension of the worldwide- system for controlling contamination at ocean. These-global understandings remembe-r key objectives for e-nsuring our ocean life and restricting the-measure of garbage and oil that achie-ves the waters. The-y likewise characterize- significant standards, for example, the privile-ge of each country to exploit the-ir own exclusive financial zone while- keeping up worldwide guide-lines against releasing unsafe- synthetic compounds or oil spills. Implementation include-s nearby supervision of marine e-xercises yet additionally worldwide- coordinating to screen consistence- and address transboundary issues. Togethe-r, these global ocean pre-servation efforts look for a more maintainable- future where marine- assets stay untouched for ages to come-.

Let us e-xamine in more detail the- legal structures and rules that ove-rsee contamination at sea. Pollution from ships, whe-ther it be oil spillages, che-mical dumpings, or waste removal, prese-nts noteworthy dangers to marine cre-atures and coastal populations. It is fundamental that we compre-hend the obligations and accountabilities of shipowne-rs, administrators, and flag states in forestalling and reacting to pollution occasions so we- can hold gatherings in charge of their activitie-s. Various worldwide understandings, for example-, MARPOL and local enactment have be-en actualized to administer ship e-manations and spills. Flag states are require-d to authorize and check ships flying their banne-rs to guarantee consistence- with these laws. Then again, ship administrators must actualize- spill counteractive action measure-s and keep up vital documentation on board. Re-gardless of these controls, ove-rsight stays an issue and episodes still happe-n now and again because of human blunder or hardware- disappointment. Better e-xecution of current guideline-s alongside more serious punishme-nts for infringement could limit future harm.

Throughout this exploration, we- have aimed to avoid overlap with othe-r chapters, permitting reade-rs to glean fresh understandings into the- intricate network of maritime law particularly re-garding marine environmental safe-guarding. We seek to furnish wide--ranging examination of the subject whe-reas retaining lucidity and obtainability for audience-s. The examination searche-s to illuminate particular parts of maritime law relating to e-nvironmental protection at sea in a manne-r that is easy to understand yet scholarly.

By completing this portion, audie-nce will possess a robust comprehe-nsion of the lawful actions set up to govern contamination at se-a and the roles diverse- stakeholders carry out in ensuring adhe-rence. Obtaining this understanding will outfit audie-nce with important perceptions into the- intricate panorama of oceanic ecological se-curity and encourage them to proactive-ly take part in safeguarding our invaluable marine- habitat. While there are- laws and organizations dedicated to protecting our wate-rs, more still needs to be- done. Increased coordination be-tween nations and all groups involved can he-lp our oceans remain vibrant ecosyste-ms for future generations.

Coastal Zone Management and Marine Protected Areas

Here- we explore in mode-rate depth the vital issue- of coastal zone administration and the formation and oversight of marine- secured regions. As human e-xercises along shoreline-s keep on affecting marine- biological systems, successful shoreline- zone administration is fundamental to kee-p up the soundness and strength of the-se delicate e-nvironments. Coastal zone manageme-nt requires balancing human use of coastal re-sources with environmental prote-ction. It involves planning for and regulating deve-lopment in coastal areas to minimize harm to e-cosystems while allowing for activities like- fishing, tourism, and other industries. Establishing marine prote-cted areas is one approach use-d where fishing and other e-xtractive activities are re-stricted or prohibited to allow ecosyste-ms to recover. Effective- coastal zone management and marine- protected areas will be- important for sustaining coastal environments and the live-lihoods they support into the future.

Coastal zone manage-ment involves overse-eing various initiatives, rules, and me-thods targeted at achieving e-quilibrium between fulfilling human de-mands and safeguarding coastal habitats. It entails thorough scheduling and choice--making procedures that consider e-nvironmental, public, and monetary viewpoints. Coastal zone- management aims to harmonize the- various desires of reside-nts, visitors, and businesses with the re-quirement to protect fragile- shoreline ecosyste-ms. Decision makers must carefully we-igh proposals for development or conse-rvation, determining how each may impact the- natural environment and people-'s livelihoods. Through integrated planning and inclusive- community participation, coastal communities can implement manage-ment strategies to promote- sustainable use of coastal resource-s now and far into the future.

Designating and managing marine- protected areas is an important part of re-sponsible coastal zone administration. MPAs are spe-cially designated sections of coastal wate-rs established to conserve- marine life and permit sustainable- use of ocean resource-s over the long run. Within these- zones, diverse oce-an creatures find safe have-ns where they can thrive- without disruption. Damaged marine ecosyste-ms are afforded the opportunity to me-nd as well. Communities can expe-rience economic gains through e-co-friendly tourism and fishing that doesn't deple-te populations. By setting portions of coastal waters aside- for protection and regulated activitie-s, a balance is struck betwee-n present demands and e-nsuring healthy oceans for gene-rations to come.

When e-stablishing MPAs, various steps must be undertake-n that involve scientific analysis, input from intere-sted parties, and applicable laws. Care-ful thought is necessary regarding e-cological aspects like areas rich in spe-cies diversity, esse-ntial environments, and how diverse- seascapes interconne-ct. It's also important to consider social and economic issues such as customary re-source usage, cultural importance, and re-creational pursuits to guarantee MPAs are- successfully put into action. The process e-xamines biology to recognize biodive-rsity hotspots and critical habitats supporting marine life. It also looks at how environme-nts link together betwe-en different marine- ecosystems. Additionally, viewpoints from stake-holders engaged in fishing, tourism, and othe-r ocean-based activities are- gathered. Legal frame-works governing the oceans and coastal re-gions are reviewe-d. Together, these- biological and human perspectives he-lp develop MPAs that protect marine- environments while allowing traditional and re-creational activities to continue.

Effective- administration techniques are important afte-r an MPA has been create-d to guarantee longstanding achieve-ment. This includes observing and imposing rule-s, investigating ecosystem functions, involving local re-sidents in conservation initiatives, and e-ndorsing sustainable actions. Joint leadership be-tween various parties inve-sted, such as government organizations, non-profit companie-s, community groups, and commercial sectors, is freque-ntly necessary to accomplish common objective-s and conquer difficulties. Monitoring regulations and e-cological dynamics, as well as engaging local communities and promoting sustainability, are- key to ensuring the prote-cted area mee-ts its long-term conservation goals. Bringing diverse- stakeholders togethe-r through collaborative governance can he-lp address challenges by drawing on the- expertise and re-sources of each party.

In this section, we- will examine case studie-s from around the globe to demonstrate- diverse technique-s for coastal region administration and the deve-lopment of MPAs. These instance-s will highlight best practices in addition to possible stumbling blocks in ove-rseeing these- crucial marine territories. By compre-hending the intricacies and proce-dures included in coastal zone administration and MPA foundation, re-aders will achieve a thorough point of vie-w on the pragmatic execution of marine- natural life security measure-s. We will investigate a fe-w productive MPAs and uncover how they ove-rsee pressure-s from contending interests, for e-xample, protection and industry. We will like-wise survey cases whe-re MPAs fizzled to accomplish their conse-rvation objectives and pick apart what could have be-en enhanced. Ove-rall, inspecting genuine worldwide- models will give important expe-riences into making arrangeme-nts that adjust environmental protection with financial and social factors in coastal communitie-s.

Exploring the nuance-d facets of coastal zone administration and the de-velopment of marine prote-cted areas can impart helpful unde-rstandings into the difficulties and possibilities conne-cted with securing marine biological syste-ms. Gaining this information permits people to add to e-ndeavors guarding the sea and maintainable- advancement procedure-s fundamental to ensuring the e-nduring wellbeing and versatility of our se-as. By investigating the subtle e-lements of how shoreline-s are oversaw and regions of the- sea are set aside- for insurance, one can increase- key bits of knowledge into the- test and potential open doors re-lated with ensuring habitats and specie-s. With this new learning, people- can potentially help conservation e-fforts and sustainable practices crucial for maintaining ocean he-alth and resilience long into the- future.

Marine Environmental Protection: Emerging Issues in Marine Environmental Protection

As our understanding of the- ocean grows, we recognize- pressing challenges for marine- environmental protection. This se-ction examines eme-rging threats endangering oce-an health and sustainability. Issues like climate- change, ocean acidification, plastic pollution, and overfishing re-quire prompt action and strong laws. Climate change warms oce-an waters, causing coral bleaching and habitat shifts. Rising acidity from absorbed carbon dioxide- harms shells of marine life. Tons of plastic litte-r oceans yearly, harming wildlife that e-ats or gets tangled in it. Unsustainable fishing de-pletes fish stocks and damages e-cosystems. We must curb gree-nhouse gases to slow climate change-. We must reduce plastic and re-gulate fishing to protect biodiversity. Our de-epening knowledge- of oceans also deepe-ns awareness of responsibilitie-s to safeguard them for future ge-nerations.

Climate change- poses a serious risk to ocean life-. As global temperatures rise-, sea ice melts, and oce-an currents change, marine spe-cies face mounting difficulties. Warme-r waters place stress on coral re-efs and threaten othe-r temperature-se-nsitive creatures. Me-lting polar caps alter ecosystems that de-pend on steady ice conditions. Shifting curre-nts disrupt food webs and migration patterns. The le-gal mechanisms intended to curb climate- change and help aquatic worlds adjust, such as the Paris Agre-ement, require- close examination. Only by thoroughly assessing the-se frameworks can we de-termine what is working well and whe-re weaknesse-s remain. With oceans in peril, such analyse-s are crucial for protecting marine dive-rsity.

Ocean acidification pose-s serious threats as carbon dioxide le-vels continue rising in our atmosphere-. When CO_2 is absorbed by ocean wate-r, it increases acidity, endange-ring many marine species that build she-lls and reefs from calcium carbonate mine-rals. At risk are coral reefs, she-llfish, and other organisms unable to withstand more acidic conditions. As acidity le-vels in the sea rise-, coral structures may begin to erode- while shellfish deve-lopment could be hindere-d. This emerging issue de-serves attention to safe-guard fragile ocean ecosyste-ms. The legal frameworks aime-d at curbing greenhouse gas e-missions and sheltering sensitive- underwater habitats require- close scrutiny. We must ensure- existing policies are sufficie-ntly ambitious and comprehensive to slow acidification's pace-, allowing marine life time to adapt be-fore environmental change-s grow too extreme.

Plastic pollution remains a worrying issue-, with huge amounts of plastic trash flowing into our oceans annually. The e-ffect on sea creature-s is tragic, as animals become caught in plastic debris or confuse- it for food. This part explores the le-gal approaches used to address plastic pollution, like- global efforts to prohibit single-use plastics and e-ncourage recycling programs. While inte-rnational agreements aim to re-duce plastic waste ente-ring the oceans, variations in policies be-tween nations make coordinate-d solutions difficult. Recycling schemes also face- challenges in convincing people- to change habits and ensure mate-rials are properly sorted afte-r use. Further measure-s are undoubtedly nee-ded to curb plastic production and cleanup oceans alre-ady filled with pollution.

Sustainable fishing practice-s play an integral role in kee-ping fish populations strong and marine life diverse-. When too many fish are caught or destructive- methods are used, fish numbe-rs can decline rapidly along with other unde-rwater creatures. This thre-atens the balance of oce-an ecosystems. Similarly, fishing without proper re-porting or regulation allows overharvesting with no ove-rsight. As a result, important legal structures have- been establishe-d to tackle these proble-ms. For instance, fisheries manage-ment creates rule-s around catch amounts and gear types permitte-d in different areas. Inte-rnational agreements also aim to solve- issues that cross borders, such as the Unite-d Nations Fish Stocks Agreement. This se-ction will look more closely at such frameworks and how the-y strive to remedy challe-nges to marine sustainability.

Addressing e-merging environmental issue-s will require concerte-d international cooperation to establish holistic le-gal frameworks. Such measures should promote- balanced conservation, sustainable utilization of natural re-sources, and restoration of degrade-d ecosystems. This analysis see-ks to illuminate some of the intricate- difficulties surrounding these pre-ssing challenges. A multifacete-d understanding of their complexitie-s can inform prudent choices and help craft sagacious policie-s. Collaborative efforts are ne-cessary to find equitable solutions re-specting all perspective-s.

By exploring the- varied facets of deve-loping hazards to marine ecological security, we- can effort towards a destiny where-in our oceans prosper and bloom bountifully. It's thru an aggregate- of strong felony structures, global teamwork, and pe-rson duty that we will steer the- waters of law towards a sustainable and versatile- marine surroundings. While there-'s nonetheless paintings to be- executed, the-re may be expe-ct that thru open communique and shared accountability across worldwide- borders we can strengthe-n safeguards for existence- under the waves.

While maritime- labor law and seafarer rights have come- a long way, their historical developme-nt shows a gradual process of improving working conditions and protections for sailors. Over time-, as modes of transport advanced and shipping became- a more

Through the progre-ssion of history, the evolution of work regulations within the- maritime sector holds significant value whe-n recognizing the prese-nt-day rights and safeguards given to sailors. As navigational operations broade-ned across time, early marine-rs confronted formidable obstacles and withstood an unforgiving work e-nvironment. They braved tre-acherous seas amid tall ships, weathe-ring storms and isolation for months at a time. Workdays stretched from dawn until dusk, with little- respite from physically demanding labor. Injurie-s ran rampant without adequate medical care- or compensation. Seafaring prese-nted undeniable risks to we-ll-being and security. There-fore, the deve-lopment of labor protections helpe-d shield sailors from the most dangerous conditions and unfair tre-atment they traditionally faced while- plying their trade upon the wate-rs.

In ancient e-ras, sailors often functioned under casual agre-ements and faced risky situations without formal prote-ctions. Trade paths became more- crowded as time passed. More- ships carried goods betwee-n lands. Those who worked on the ships de-served rules to safe-guard them. Rules could make difficult jobs on the- ocean less dangerous. Rule-s were nee-ded to address how workers we-re treated. This ne-ed became cle-arer as ocean trade and comme-rce grew in importance.

The Consolat de- Mar, a major maritime legal code e-stablished in the 13th century, re-presented an important ste-p forward in the evolution of maritime labor law. This se-minal code introduced guideline-s surrounding sailors' pay, work hours, and safeguards against unfair treatment while- at sea. Prior to its creation, there- were few, if any, prote-ctions for seafarers. The Consolat de- Mar acknowledged the distinct characte-r of maritime employment and institute-d rules aimed at guarantee-ing sailors received fair wage-s and working conditions appropriate to their dangerous and difficult work. It e-stablished new standards that differe-d meaningfully from past practices by formally recognizing sailors' rights and imposing re-gulations to ensure they re-ceived just treatme-nt when plying their trade upon the- high seas.

Over time-, many nations passed laws within their own borders to prote-ct the legal rights of sailors. For instance, during the- era often called the- Age of Sail from the 16th to 19th centurie-s, Britain established legislation calle-d the Merchant Shipping Act to tackle proble-ms regarding wages, work environme-nts, and discipline on vessels. This e-arly regulation addressing labor concerns at se-a served as a foundation for continuing progress towards safe-rguarding sailors' rights going forward. While these maritime- professions faced challenge-s, steps were take-n through statutes to improve seafare-rs' circumstances regarding pay, duties aboard, and me-thods of punishment.

The e-stablishment of international conventions and tre-aties addressing maritime labor rights he-lped strengthen the- growth of maritime labor law. The International Labour Organization (ILO), a Unite-d Nations agency, was instrumental in creating global labor guide-lines for sailors. Way back in 1920, the ILO passed the- initial international agreeme-nt regarding seafarers' job te-rms, known as the Seafarers' Article-s of Agreement Conve-ntion. This agreement e-stablished minimum needs for sailors' contracts and aime-d to guarantee reasonable- treatment and working environme-nts. While the convention he-lped set basic protections, furthe-r collaboration would be neede-d to build on these initial standards and safeguard se-afarers' rights and welfare in the- years to come.

Subseque-ntly, the ILO continued refining and e-xpanding its conventions to tackle a variety of matte-rs, such as setting guidelines around sailors' working hours and re-st periods, establishing standards for their living quarte-rs, requiring medical checkups, and e-nsuring repatriation. These worldwide- agreements have- become extre-mely important in developing a unifie-d international structure for safeguarding sailors' prote-ctions.

Throughout history, the e-volution of maritime labor law demonstrates socie-ty's growing understanding of sailors' difficult circumstances and nece-ssity for suitable safeguards. From medie-val codes like the Consolat de- Mar to current international agree-ments, labor rules have adapte-d to secure sailors' wellne-ss while working in shipping's exacting conditions. Whethe-r aboard ships or in ports, those who earn their living upon the- seas often face particular dange-rs and difficulties apart from others on land. By clarifying responsibilitie-s of vessel owners and rights of cre-ws, revised regulations atte-mpt to better protect maritime- workers undertaking vital yet hazardous dutie-s essential for global trade but re-mote from familiar routines of community. Continuous reasse-ssment helps legislation balance- obligations of all stakeholders within shipping with the particular vulne-rabilities inherent in se-afarers' remote work far from home-.

While Inte-rnational Conventions and Treaties have- significantly contributed to the deve-lopment of maritime labor law and protection of se-afarers' rights over the de-cades, there re-mains work to be done. Numerous agre-ements have be-en instituted to account for the distinct working conditions e-ncountered by maritime pe-rsonnel while traveling the- open seas. The isolate-d nature of life at sea couple-d with long stretches away from family and familiar society pose- particular difficulties. A range of physical and mental he-alth issues may arise in such an environme-nt if proper protocols, resources, and re-course are not in place. Continue-d collaboration between stake-holders can further safeguard the- wellbeing of those who facilitate- global trade via waterway. Moreove-r, establishing additional regulatory frameworks with input from se-afarers themselve-s may help address modern challe-nges. The unique ne-eds and challenges face-d by maritime workers evolve-

One significant organization that has contributed significantly to the development of maritime labor law is the International Labour Organization (ILO). The ILO, founded in 1919, is a specialized agency of the United Nations dedicated to promoting decent work and social justice globally. Within the realm of maritime labor, the ILO has played a pivotal role in setting standards and implementing regulations to protect the rights of seafarers.

The Maritime- Labor Convention of 2006, also called the "Se-afarers' Bill of Rights," is among the most important and all-encompassing inte-rnational agreements de-aling with maritime labor problems. Create-d by the International Labour Organization, the MLC e-stablishes baseline e-xpectations for working situations, lodging, health safeguards, and social se-curity for sailors. It relates to all ships engage-d in business exercise-s, guaranteeing that sailors are de-alt with reasonably and get adequate- insurance paying little hee-d to banner or nationality. The convention se-eks to clarify the least ne-cessities for seafare-rs' working and living conditions. It means to ensure the-y receive fair tre-atment in terms of work hours, health prote-ctions, and other benefits re-gardless of where the- ship sails. While expanding protections for sailors, the- agreement strive-s for balance by not overburdening shipowne-rs with excessive re-gulations.

The Inte-rnational Convention on Standards of Training, Certification, and Watchkee-ping for Seafarers, often abbre-viated to STCW, is another significant maritime agre-ement. Established in 1978 by the- International Maritime Organization, or IMO, STCW sets the- minimum criteria for sailors' education, certification, and dutie-s worldwide. The goal of this convention is to guarante-e sailors have the prope-r training, expertise, and abilitie-s to carry out their responsibilities safe-ly and proficiently while serving on ve-ssels. Specifically, the conve-ntion from the IMO aims to standardize training leve-ls globally so all seafarers obtain consistent skills and knowle-dge. This helps ensure- operations at sea run smoothly regardle-ss of a sailor's country of origin. By clarifying expectations for qualifications, the STCW Conve-ntion facilitates international maritime comme-rce while also protecting the- welfare of crews.

Additionally, seve-ral regional accords have bee-n developed to tackle- particular maritime labor difficulties within specifie-d geographic locations. For instance, the Europe-an Union (EU) has presented guide-lines to better working situations for sailors functioning in EU wate-rs. These guideline-s cover factors for example working hrs, re-st intervals, and health and safety provisions, making ce-rtain that sailors in the EU benefit from re-inforced security. The re-gulations aim to provide clarity on important issues like maximum work hours and minimum re-st periods to protect the we-ll-being of seafarers working in de-manding conditions at sea.

It is crucial to emphasize- that enforcing these global agre-ements and treatie-s is essential for achieving the-ir objectives. The countrie-s where ships are re-gistered, countries whe-re ships dock in ports, and nations where sailors come- from each have an important part in confirming adhere-nce to the maritime labor re-gulations established. Steps take-n by countries where ships stop in ports, like- inspections and audits of ships, aid in surveying and requiring obse-rvance to the laws concerning work at se-a across all harbors globally. While flag nations, port states, and labor supplying countries play role-s in guaranteeing that the standards se-t are followed, procedure-s conducted by port states when ships arrive- in their docks, such as examinations and financial revie-ws, are useful for monitoring obedie-nce to maritime labor legislation all ove-r the world.

Going forward, we must conside-r the rising need to tackle- developing difficulties in maritime- work law. Issues like crew prospe-rity, weariness administration, mental he-lp, and sexual orientation equivale-ncy are acquiring expanding consideration inside- the business. Attempts to manage- these worries through change-s to as of now available arrangements or the- presentation of new standards will characte-rize the future of maritime- work law and additionally ensure the e-ntitlements of sailors. While the-re is developing acknowle-dgment of the require-ment for progress, the manne-r in which that progress is accomplished will decide- how maritime work law and the privilege-s of sailors keep on creating. The- difficulties looked to be te-nded to, for example, we-ariness the exe-cutives and psychological well-being he-lp, will require cautious investigation and arrange-ments intended to upgrade- working conditions without undermining efficiency. Coope-ration between administration, administration and se-afarer delegate-s will be basic to guarantee any ne-w guidelines mee-t their objectives of be-ttering circumstances while ke-eping maritime exchange-s serious. By cooperating to create- arrangements that adjust security with productivity, the- future of this industry and its laborers can be made- progressively maintainable.

To wrap up, worldwide conve-ntions and agreements, alongside- associations like the ILO, have assume-d a crucial part in forming maritime work law and ensuring the privile-ges of sailors. The MLC, STCW Convention, and ne-arby understandings epitomize worldwide- endeavors to guarantee- reasonable working states of be-ing and satisfactory ensures for sailors overall. As the- maritime business advances, it turns out to be- fundamental to manage deve-loping difficulties and reinforce e-xisting structures to satisfy the advancing nee-ds of sailors in an invariably changing worldwide scene. Ne-w innovations, environmental changes, and ge-opolitical flows will keep on affecting marine-rs and require coordinated worldwide- activity to ensure their se-curity, rights, and prosperity stay ensured as the- business keeps on mode-rnizing.

Working Conditions for Seafarers:

Seafare-rs take on a role that subjects the-m to demanding circumstances due to the- character of their line of work. The-ir occupation necessitates spe-nding extensive stre-tches of time out at sea, fre-quently far from their loved one-s and in possibly dangerous conditions. Grasping the working situations looked by sailors is fundame-ntal for appreciating the significance of lawful e-nsures and rules that secure- their entitleme-nts. Sailors regularly experie-nce long stretches se-parated from family and friends while working in an e-nvironment that can bring about real dangers. Guarante-eing their security and we-llbeing through legitimate assurance-s encourages guarantee- a reasonable working environme-nt and ensures their privile-ges are shielde-d. This permits them to focus their e-ndeavors on vital ship tasks while having the solace- of realizing appropriate security ne-ts are set up.

While e-nsuring vessels function smoothly and crews re-main safe requires continual work, one- of maritime law's chief aims is establishing working hour limits and re-st breaks for seafarers. Shipboard tasks must be- carried out at all times due to shipping's round-the--clock needs. Howeve-r, requiring excessive- time on duty without proper rest can induce- weariness and hazards. Work schedule-s should balance operational demands with pre-venting fatigue, which raises accide-nt probabilities, by mandating sufficient off-hours. Clarifying hours of labor and relaxation pe-riods aims to address maritime operations' re-quirements while safe-guarding seafarers' well-be-ing and work-life balance. While inte-rnational conventions and domestic regulations have- been put in place to re-duce risks by establishing boundaries on sailors' work sche-dules and defining adequate- rest intervals, there- remains room for improvement. For e-xample, the Maritime Labour Conve-ntion (MLC), adopted by the International Labour Organization (ILO) in 2006, outline-s comprehensive be-nchmarks for conditions faced by maritime employe-es, such as limits on work hours and compulsory breaks. These- standards seek to bette-r protect sailors' welfare and ove-rall safety aboard vessels by allowing sufficie-nt downtime from tiring tasks. However, e-nforcement of guideline-s can vary depending on oversight. Continue-d efforts aim to clarify responsibilities while- supporting well-rested and conte-nt crews.

Working aboard ships brings numerous occupational hazards and he-alth risks that maritime labor law aims to address. Seafare-rs face exposure to e-xtreme weathe-r, dangerous cargo, and heavy machinery while- performing their duties onboard ve-ssels. They operate- in an environment with high potential for injurie-s. Beyond physical safety concerns, those- working at sea also confront challenges associate-d with isolation, stress, and constrained access to me-dical care. Long stretches away from family and community while- residing in a confined ship space can ne-gatively impact mental well-be-ing. Moreover, limited proximity to hospitals pose-s difficulties should health issues arise- during voyages. The regulations in maritime- labor law help safeguard seafare-rs' physical and psychological welfare when pe-rforming their vital roles transporting goods and resource-s across oceans.

In order to guarante-e sailors' security, maritime rule-s necessitate ve-ssel owners to furnish a protecte-d work environment and suitable safe-ty gear aboard ships. Furthermore, sailors must obtain fitting pre-paration on crisis methods, fire avoidance, and pe-rsonal protective equipme-nt application. Consistent checks are le-d by port state oversight authorities to validate- adherence to the-se guidelines, conse-quently promoting a safer working environme-nt for sailors. Seafarers face unique- dangers in their work and must have the- proper protections in place. Re-gular inspections help ensure- ship owners are following regulations de-signed to minimize risks like fire-s or accidents. This protects sailors and helps the- shipping industry operate safely.

There- are a few key e-ntities that must work cooperatively to guarante-e the protection of se-afarers' rights given how vital their role-s are. As the countries whose- flag vessels sail under, flag state-s have an important job in validating adherence- to employment regulations and re-acting to any breaches of such rules. Like-wise, port states—the countrie-s in whose ports vessels call on—carry out an e-ssential function in supervising conformity with labor benchmarks and addre-ssing issues that arise. International organizations re-lated to maritime matters also participate- significantly in tracking participation with compensation standards and dealing with violations. Furthermore-, negotiated contracts betwe-en shipowners and sailors' unions can aid in confirming reasonable- and risk-free working situations through agree-d-upon terms and conditions. While regulations are- critical, collaborative efforts betwe-en all parties involved are- needed to e-nsure seafarers can pe-rform their jobs safely.

As the maritime- industry adapts to ongoing changes, technological progress and shifting work e-nvironments introduce fresh issue-s and factors to ponder. The rise of se-lf-driving ships, for instance, could prompt inquiries regarding the- effects on sailors' jobs and work environme-nts. Consequently, it has become- crucial for maritime labor law to adjust and react to these- emerging transformations, guarantee-ing seafarers' rights remain safe-guarded during technological advances.

To wrap up, grasping the work e-nvironments dealt with by sailors gives a pre-mise for understanding the significance- of lawful ensures and directions in maritime- work law. By tending to issues identifie-d with long stretches of work, rest pe-riods, and wellbeing and wellbe-ing concerns, these dire-ctions expect to guarantee- sailors' prosperity and ensure the-ir essential privilege-s. As the maritime business advance-s, it is crucial to consistently re-assess and change- work laws to mirror developing difficulties and rising innovations while- keeping up the privile-ges of those who explore- the seas. Prese-ntly, while innovation keeps on progre-ssing at a quick pace, it is critical that seafarers stay e-nsured and ensured from we-llbeing dangers and supported by ste-ady direction. We should kee-p on ensuring their privilege-s are shielded as the-ir lives at sea stay significant yet re-gularly unsafe. Continuously keeping in mind the- end goal to shield the privile-ges and prosperity of these- laborers who are basic to worldwide e-xchange and the deve-lopment of products.

Seafarer Rights and Protections:

Seafarers, as integral contributors to the maritime industry, deserve certain rights and protections that ensure fair treatment, well-being, and access to essential support systems. This section explores the rights and protections afforded to seafarers, delving into the legal mechanisms available for them to seek redress in case of violations or disputes.

Fair pay repre-sents a basic human right for maritime workers, acknowle-dging their significant contributions and the challenging nature- of their important roles. International agre-ements like the-Maritime Labour Convention (MLC) have se-t minimum wage guidelines to avoid taking unfair advantage- of seafarers and ensure- they have sufficient me-ans to live dignified lives. The-se wage policies conside-r elements including job dutie-s, credentials, and hours on duty, making certain that maritime- professionals get fair payment that matche-s the work they provide. While- maritime work involves difficulties like- long periods away from family and friends, international coope-ration has helped protect se-afarers' rights to livable incomes through care-ful examination of multiple rele-vant factors in wage setting.

Moreove-r, sailors have the privilege- of being sent back home. This implie-s that ship proprietors are require-d to give transportation for sailors to return to their country of origin once- they have finished the-ir agreement or in occasions of sickne-ss, damage, or other unforese-en circumstances. The privile-ge of repatriation ensure-s sailors from being stranded at sea for too long stre-tches and recognizes the-ir requirement for actual and e-nthusiastic rest and recuperation. The- privilege of repatriation is fundame-ntal as it gives insurance to maritime spe-cialists who spend significant time in far off areas, re-gularly going through long stretches separate-d from friends and family. Being given the- chance to come back home whe-n an agreement close-s or if wellbeing issues e-merge is basic assistance for the-ir prosperity and mental prosperity. Ship proprie-tors are in this manner legitimate-ly committed to guaranteeing se-afarers can return secure-ly to their friends and family when the-ir work at sea has finished or if issues e-merge. This ensure-s mariners from being dese-rted without anybody to rely upon while abroad or harme-d.

Gaining medical care- is an extremely important part of a se-afarer's rights. Since sailors encounte-r distinct difficulties regarding health crise-s and lengthy durations out at ocean with no spee-dy route to clinical services, inte-rnational rules state that shipowners must furnish satisfactory he-althcare onboard. This involves accessibility to doctors, vital pre-scription drugs, and crisis gear. Moreover, shipowne-rs also have to confirm that suitable healthcare- insurance shields sailors throughout their whole- employment. Access to me-dical care while at sea can lite-rally be a matter of life and de-ath. Regulations aim to ensure sailors re-ceive quality treatme-nt during emergencie-s and do not have to worry about costs if an unexpecte-d illness or injury occurs. Though far from shore, sailors should fee-l assured owners accept re-sponsibility for their well-being through re-quired medical provisions and coverage-.

When issue-s emerge whe-re seafarers' e-ntitlements are disre-garded or conflicts develop, the-re are a number of authorize-d procedures to look for reme-dy. These strategie-s incorporate national work laws, gathering haggling assentions, and having re-course to particularized bodies like- port state control experts or the- Global Transportation Workers' Association (ITF). These associations work to se-cure the privilege-s and interests of seafare-rs, giving help in settling clashes or te-nding to encroachments through mediation, go be-tween, or lawful activity. Port state control e-xperts can examine ships that visit the-ir ports and document issues identifie-d with working and living states of seafarers. The- ITF backs seafarers specifically by giving lawful guidance- and speaking to them if issues e-merge with ship proprietors on wage-s, wellbeing, security or diffe-rent conditions. By cooperating with transporter associations, shippe-rs and governments, these- associations expect to advance the- privileges of maritime spe-cialists and guarantee consistence- with global work guidelines.

Enforcing seafare-rs' rights and protections is critical for maritime authorities and stake-holders to guarantee se-afarers' wellbeing and dignity. Re-cognizing fair pay, repatriation assistance when contracts e-nd, and access to medical care unde-rscores the global maritime se-ctor's appreciation for how vital seafarers' work is in ke-eping industry operations running smoothly. Upholding these- core rights and protections fosters an e-nvironment where se-afarers feel re-spected and supported in the-ir significant roles. While jurisdictional authorities and e-mployers may be inclined to cut costs, maintaining basic labor standards confirms se-afarers' humanity and worth. Such rights are the le-ast a seafarer should expe-ct in return for facing the challenge-s and potential dangers of life at se-a, far from home.

The maritime- industry is constantly changing, so we must stay watchful to spot and handle new issue-s for sailors' rights. This involves fighting fatigue, bias, and the lack of acce-ss to counseling. Changes to maritime labor law in the- future should bolster current rule-s and push proactive steps that put sailors' health first and shie-ld their rights as the field ke-eps shifting. As technology advances and trade- routes alter over time-, keeping seafare-rs protected amidst these- fluctuations is paramount. Lawmakers will need to care-fully craft updates with flexibility built in, so hard-won protections trave-l with the industry into an unknowable future. For those- far from home aboard massive ships, small adjustments could me-an the difference- between we-llness and worry at sea.

Comprehe-nding the legal safeguards and assurance-s given to sailors allows attorneys, lawmakers, and those- involved in maritime industries to coope-rate conscientiously to guarantee- a just and impartial work environment for seafare-rs. By ongoing attempts to advance sailor well-be-ing, the oceans will stay navigable for ge-nerations of dedicated pe-ople who opt to embark on caree-rs upon the seas and help facilitate- global trade.

Maritime labor law aims to prote-ct seafarers and ensure- fair working conditions at sea. While significant progress has be-en made over the- years, challenges re-main in enforcing rights and standards consistently across regions and ve-ssel types. Technological

While this last portion of the- section examining Maritime Labor Law and Se-afarer Rights aims to scrutinize current proble-ms faced by sailors regarding their working situations and prote-ctions, it is also important we acknowledge pote-ntial forthcoming progressions within maritime labor rules se-eking to manage these- evolving issues and guarantee- more robust safeguarding of seafare-rs' rights. Certainly, further analysis of contemporary difficultie-s experience-d by seafarers in connection to the-ir work environments and entitle-ments is warranted. Simultaneously, we- must recognize hopeful pote-ntial advances to laws that may address these- emerging troubles and make- sure better se-curity for the rights of those who work within the maritime- industry. There is still work remaining to fully compre-hend challenges of today and craft solutions of tomorrow.

While se-afarers play a vital role in global trade, the-ir work comes with notable challenge-s. Spending lengthy stretche-s away from relatives and close companions, the-y toil under pressing circumstances that may e-ndanger their safety. Such re-moteness from cherishe-d ones frequently we-ighs on one's psychological and emotional state. More-over, having restricted admittance- to clinical offices and help administrations while offshore- can deteriorate we-llbeing issues and add to the dubious we-lfare of labor. The modern maritime- industry must prioritize supporting crews' mental he-alth and find innovative solutions to the difficulties of isolation.

Working at sea for e-xtended periods without sufficie-nt rest takes a significant toll on one's he-alth and safety. Seafarers ofte-n face exhaustive sche-dules including lengthy workdays, irregular shifts, and high de-grees of both physical and psychological strain, all of which can easily contribute- to a state of fatigue. When fatigue-d, a seafarer's wellne-ss understandably suffers as their me-ntal and physical capacities become diminishe-d. Moreover, fatigue pose-s serious risks not just for the crew me-mber but for everyone- onboard a vessel, as it has bee-n a known factor in many previous maritime accidents and disaste-rs. The shipping sector rightly remains focuse-d on combating fatigue given its clear conne-ction to compromised safety. Further e-fforts are still neede-d to better support seafare-rs' needs for proper re-st and to minimize the dangers that long-te-rm tiredness can introduce into the-ir dangerous line of work.

Discrimination within the maritime- workplace continues to be a linge-ring issue. Workers may encounte-r prejudice due to attribute-s including gender, country of origin, or ethnicity. Such unjust be-havior damages more than the rights of individual e-mployees as it also impacts diversity, fairne-ss, and involvement within the industry. While- attributes should have no bearing on e-mployment, bias persists in hiring practices and onboard. Gre-ater understanding and policies are- needed to foste-r a just environment for all.

To address conte-mporary issues faced by seafare-rs, enforcing current regulations and e-stablishing new protections for their rights have- been suggeste-d. Specifically, strengthening ove-rsight of existing rules and crafting novel approache-s aim to safeguard seafarers' we-lfare. The International Labour Organization (ILO) as we-ll as other global organizations have bee-n proactively working to better se-afarers' circumstances by campaigning for fairer e-mployment terms, just compensation, and e-nhanced access to medical care-. While regulations already se-ek to uphold decent working e-nvironments and pay for seafarers, close-r supervision and new measure-s may help secure the-ir rights are respecte-d. Similarly, the ILO and counterparts continue boosting se-afarers' well-being by advocating for improve-d conditions, equitable wages, and he-alth care.

While te-chnological progress in the maritime se-ctor opens doors for potential upcoming evolutions in labor re-gulations governing work at sea, certain issue-s necessitate atte-ntion. For instance, the rising impleme-ntation of automation and digital solutions in shipping holds promise to lessen some- of the physically taxing duties on ships, possibly decre-asing accident occurrences and be-ttering general work e-nvironments. At the same time-, it is paramount to confirm that such improvements do not bring about job cuts or undermine- the protections afforded to maritime- crewmembers. Care-ful consideration is warranted as innovations change the- nature of seafaring employme-nt to safeguard against any erosion of hard-won working conditions or legal rights while- cultivating new opportunities.

To summarize, the- modern difficulties confronted by sailors re-garding their working situations and protections dese-rve constant notice and activities from industry stake-holders, lawmakers, and worldwide associations. By handling issue-s like staff welfare, tire-dness, and discrimination, we can attempt to accomplish a maritime- industry that respects the e-steem and prosperity of all sailors. Moving forward, constant progre-ssions in innovation and developing worries ne-cessitate a proactive way to de-al with maritime work law, guaranteeing that it stays adaptable- and receptive to the- evolving needs of sailors in the- years ahead. There- is still work that can be done to further addre-ss concerns over crew conditions and e-nsure policies are update-d to reflect changes in te-chnology and the nature of seafaring work.

Cruise Ship Re-gulations and Maritime Law have evolve-d over the years to e-nsure passenger safe-ty at sea. Originally, regulations mainly focused on ve-ssel integrity and safe navigation. Howe-ver, as the cruise industry gre-w in popularity transporting more

While cruise- ship travel first emerge-d in the 1800s, regulations did not exte-nsively develop until much late-r. In the early eras of cruising, ve-ssels sailed with little in te-rms of standardized rules or protocols to ensure- passenger well-be-ing. This lack of governance occasionally led to unfortunate-circumstances that underscored the- requirement for more- robust policymaking. Let us explore some-of the historical context surrounding this regulatory e-volution. During the initial phases of cruise ship ope-ration, operators maintained autonomy with few re-strictions on safety or operational procedure-s. As the industry expanded in the- following decades, occasional mishaps brought further atte-ntion to the importance of establishing unive-rsal principles for protecting passenge-r welfare. While cruising offe-red enjoyable vacation e-xperiences for many, the- absence of coordinated guide-lines left room for improveme-nt to uphold consistent protection standards industry-wide. This transitional pe-riod helped underscore- how formalized regulations could augment passe-nger security and formally establish base-lines for all companies to follow.

Notable incide-nts like the sinking of the RMS Titanic in 1912 as we-ll as other subsequent maritime-disasters brought attention to the insufficie-nt safety precautions in place for cruise- ships at that time. Events similar to the Titanic catastrophe- acted as triggers for the formation of re-gulations particular to cruise vessels, which targe-ted guaranteeing the- protection of passengers and cre-w members. While the-se occasions highlighted areas ne-eding improvement, the-y also served as drivers for progre-ssive steps to be take-n to establish stronger guideline-s addressing critical issues revolving around se-curity aboard cruise liners. Further rule-s were instituted to he-lp avoid potential loss of life in the marine-travel industry through bolstered provisions atte-ntive to passengers' and worke-rs' well-being while trave-ling by ship.

International Conve-ntion for the Safety of Life at Se-a (SOLAS) represents a crucial turning point in advancing cruise- ship safety protocols. Established in 1914 in response- to the devastating sinking of the Titanic, SOLAS has significantly shape-d global standards for cruise vessel re-gulations. The convention outlines base-line essentials for all face-ts regarding a ship's creation, day-to-day function, and upkee-p—from its framing and mechanics to crew conduct and maintenance- schedules. By providing a framework for life-saving equipment, eme-rgency procedures, and structural inte-grity, SOLAS has helped safeguard passe-ngers and crewmembe-rs over the past century. While-technological and industry advances will continue prope-lling novel strategies, SOLAS re-mains the foundational platform upholding cruising's most eleme-ntal humanitarian mission: protecting lives at sea.

SOLAS has undergone- incremental changes throughout the- decades to tackle ne-w issues and incorporate technological progre-ssions. It addresses a broad sele-ction of security steps, such as eme-rgency protocols, lifesaving gear, fire- protection, stability standards, and navigation systems. All cruise ve-ssels are mandated to follow SOLAS rule-s to guarantee the we-llness and comfort of travelers and staff. The- regulations established unde-r SOLAS work to continuously improve ocean voyage safe-ty standards by requiring safety equipme-nt and procedures that mitigate e-merging threats.

While the- implementation of SOLAS and its updates have- notably helped to strengthe-n cruise ship safety standards globally, contributing significantly to this end, it is worthwhile- observing that even though SOLAS e-stablishes an all-encompassing structure, individual nations may also institute-supplemental regulations and stipulations that cruise- ship operators must conform with upon entering the-ir docks. Namely, SOLAS furnishes a broad platform though particular countries re-tain the ability to impose extra rule-s that ship operators staying in their ports are oblige-d to respect in addition to SOLAS, meaning SOLAS doe-s not preclude suppleme-ntary local expectations.

Examining how cruise ship re-gulations have evolved ove-r time and SOLAS's influence provide-s valuable insight into the persiste-nt work to protect passengers' and cre-w's lives and welfare aboard the-se grand ocean liners. Studying re-gulations' historical trajectory and SOLAS's role enhance-s our comprehension of rules' intricate- interplay with cruise operations, be-tter enabling us to navigate this comple-x relationship and ensure proce-dures prioritize all travele-rs' safety and satisfaction. By fathoming regulations' deve-lopment and SOLAS's impact, we gain a fuller unde-rstanding of the continued efforts made- to safeguard people's we-ll-being aboard these massive- floating resorts.

Cruise Ship Regulations and Maritime Law: Legal Responsibilities of Cruise Ship Operators

Cruise ship ope-rators must adhere to considerable- lawful duties and obligations concerning both travele-rs and crew individuals. Grasping these dutie-s is indispensable for an exhaustive- analysis of cruise ship principles inside the- wider setting of maritime re-gulations. Cruise ship operators are re-sponsible for passenger safe-ty and well-being from the time- they board the vesse-l until disembarking. They must also protect cre-w members and provide a safe- working environment free-from hazards. A thorough comprehension of an operator's le-gal responsibilities allows for a cleare-r perspective on the- intricate rules and standards placed upon cruise- lines. This ensures passe-ngers and staff are adequate-ly cared for during voyages.

The primary le-gal principle that governs cruise ship busine-sses is the duty of care. This obligation ne-cessitates that operators e-mploy prudent caution in guaranteeing the- protection and prosperity of their trave-lers and team amid the voyage-. Operators have an obligation to kee-p up their vessels in se-aworthy working request, to give suitable- wellbeing efforts, and to rapidly re-spond to dangers or occurrences that may unde-rmine security. While cruise- lines must prioritize passenge-r and crew safety, they also face- complex operational challenge-s in maintaining large floating resorts at sea. With me-ticulous planning and training, operators can help ensure- safe and enjoyable e-xperiences for all aboard.

Neglige-nce is a crucial legal principle conne-cted to cruise ship procedure-s. Carelessness come-s about when an administrator falls flat to meet the- essential standard of consideration, along the-se lines bringing about damage or injury to trave-lers or crew individuals. Courts audit differe-nt components when choosing carele-ssness, including whether the- administrator knew or ought to have known about the pote-ntial risk, whether they took suitable- measures to address it, and whe-ther they fittingly cautioned trave-lers and crew. There- are a few perspe-ctives that judges consider while- choosing on a case including carelessne-ss claim identifying with cruise liner tasks. The-y think about whether eve-ry single reasonable e-xertion was made by the organization to distinguish pote-ntial wellbeing dangers and fore-stall wounds. Additionally, it is surveyed if fitting notices we-re given to passenge-rs about security measures and limitations. The- standard expected from cruise- administrators is to work at a level like some- other prudent individual would in a comparative situation. On the- off chance that they fizzle to do as such bringing about misfortune-s, it might structure the reason for an e-ffective carele-ssness claim.

Additionally, liability has an important part in situations involving cruise ship mishaps and occurre-nces. Cruise ship administrators can be he-ld accountable for any wounds or harms brought about because of the-ir carelessness or inability to satisfy the-ir obligation of care. Travelers and cre-w individuals who experience- damage because of an administrator's care-lessness may look for remune-ration for restorative costs, lost compensation, agony, and e-nduring, among different harms. Furthermore-, the extent of obligation for a cruise- line administrator relies upon how the-y react to crises and work to forestall wounds. Administrators ought to actualize- wellbeing rehe-arses and security efforts to de-crease the shot of mishaps. In any case-, on the off chance that a mishap does happe-n because of carele-ss activity or lack of oversight, the administrator may confront claims looking for pay from the influe-nced travelers or cre-w. Thus, obligation consistently plays a key job while e-xploring mishaps and occurrences on cruise ships.

Let us e-xplore some pivotal court cases that have- helped define- the legal duties of cruise- lines. Examining prominent decisions will offe-r perspective on de-veloping standards and give insight into how courts assess ope-rator conduct in real situations. Rulings establish guideline-s for assigning accountability and determining the le-vel of care companies must provide-. Key cases have se-t markers for evaluating liability and shaped this maritime- legal domain. Analyzing prominent cases allows us to re-cognize shifting legal expe-ctations and comprehend judicial revie-ws of operator behavior when re-ality confronted rights. While regulations e-volve over time, past re-solutions provide a framework for prese-nt and future accountability.

It is extre-mely important for cruise ship companies to comple-tely understand their le-gal duties to guarantee the- protection and welfare of e-verybody on their boats. In the same- way, travelers and crew associate-s ought to be mindful of their privilege-s and the lawful securities acce-ssible to them in cases of mishaps or occurre-nces during their journey. Having an e-xhaustive comprehension of the- lawful commitments of cruise ship organizations is basic for advancing a protecte-d and secure condition inside the- cruise business. This incorporates unde-rstanding who is in charge of guaranteeing se-curity gear works appropriately, lifeboats are- kept up accurately, and staff are pre-pared for any crisis circumstances. Passenge-rs likewise advantage from re-alizing their privileges if doctor's visit e-xpenses are e-xpected because- of a mishap amid the journey or if luggage ge-ts lost. While get-aways ought to be occasions of joy and unwinding, it is consoling to re-alize the lawful framework is se-t up to ensure eve-rybody's wellbeing when voyaging by se-a.

Consumer Protection in the Cruise Industry

The cruise- industry has grown substantially in recent years, attracting millions of trave-lers seeking me-morable vacations on the ocean wave-s. Nonetheless, with this e-xpansion arrives the nece-ssity for strong customer safeguard actions to make ce-rtain passengers are de-alt with reasonably and their libertie-s are supported. Here-, we will investigate the- numerous customer protection laws and rule-s relevant to the cruise- sector, as well as freque-nt problems confronted by vacationers. The- cruise business has see-n huge progress lately, bringing in countle-ss people searching for unforge-ttable journeys on the high se-as. However, with this remarkable- growth arrives the require-ment for sound consumer protection ste-ps to guarantee travele-rs are treated fairly and the-ir rights are respecte-d. In this portion, we will explore the- various customer protection legislations and policie-s applicable to the cruise marke-t, in addition to regular issues faced by custome-rs.

While cruise- lines aim to attract travelers with appe-aling depictions of comfortable rooms, top-notch facilities, and unique- ports of call, some promotions might not precisely re-present what passenge-rs truly encounter. Individuals booking voyages base-d on advertisements portraying lavish accommodations, outstanding conve-niences, and exotic locale-s risk feeling let down whe-n they embark only to discover the-ir visions did not match reality. This discrepancy betwe-en promotional pictures and the actual cruise- experience- underscores the importance- of the industry employing transparent and forthright promotional me-thods. Using clear language and accurate photographs to se-t appropriate expectations could he-lp prevent misleading marke-ting and the dissatisfaction that results when hope-s are raised too high. Cruise ope-rators should strive for promotional honesty to build trust and ensure- travelers embark with re-alistic perspectives on the- features and amenitie-s their voyage will offer.

Contractual disputes can also commonly occur in the- cruise line field. Individuals fre-quently sign an agreeme-nt with the cruise company when sche-duling a voyage that particulars their permissions, obligations, and re-strictions. Disagreements may originate- involving cabin designations, itinerary alterations, onboard functions, or othe-r contractual stipulations. It is extremely significant for patrons to compre-hend their contractual rights and duties to guarante-e they obtain the journe-y they compensated for and have- a course of action in case of any violations or clashes. For e-xample, if the cruise line- made unexpecte-d changes to ports of call or cabin accommodations, understanding the contract te-rms would help travelers know the-ir options such as requesting compensation or cance-ling without penalty. Additionally, passengers ne-ed to be aware of policie-s like dress codes, curfe-ws, areas that require fe-es, and other expe-ctations to prevent issues during the- trip.

Consumers ofte-n face unexpecte-d hurdles when planning cruise vacations. Illne-ss or an important family matter may arise, nece-ssitating the cancellation of booked sailings. Ye-t numerous cruise companies e-stablish sizable charges for departure-s cancelled near the- date of embarkation. These- penalties can exce-ed what is reasonable and cause- passengers true fiscal strain if the-y must back out of a trip due to valid causes outside the-ir control. Finding equilibrium betwee-n reimbursing operators for lost reve-nue and showing understanding for unforese-en circumstances that compel cance-llations is paramount. While cruise lines re-quire payment to offset costs from e-mpty cabins, considerations should be made for trave-lers genuinely pre-vented from attending due- to sudden life eve-nts. Both business needs and consume-r fairness deserve- addressing to establish balanced policie-s accommodating life's unpredictabilities.

While se-veral entities aim to safe-guard maritime consumers, their re-sponsibilities vary. For example, in Ame-rica the FTC watches for misleading ads and e-xamines customer grievance-s. Furthermore, the

DOT's MARAD ove-rsees some cruise- industry client security matters. The-se organizations make sincere- efforts to confirm shoppers' intere-sts are respecte-d and boat lines follow relevant guide-lines. To further clarify their role-s, the FTC focuses on advertising practice-s and complaint handling. MARAD oversees spe-cific regulatory compliance within cruise line-s. Both agencies collaborate to uphold re-gulations protecting maritime consumers.

The Inte-rnational Maritime Organization (IMO) and International Association of Cruise Line-s (IACL) aim to foster equitable conduct globally. Spe-cifically, the IMO and IACL craft directives and counse-l to advocate transparency, responsibility, and moral actions from all cruise- companies internationally. By devising standards and advice-, these institutions hope to e-ncourage cruise lines e-verywhere to ope-rate with openness, trustworthine-ss, and integrity.

To summarize, e-nsuring consumer safety is a key part of maritime- law governing how cruise lines conduct busine-ss with vacationers. Individuals booking cruises dese-rve honest marketing, contracts writte-n clearly, and reasonable pe-nalties for canceling trips. This directly affe-cts travelers' expe-riences and wallets. Passe-ngers must know their legal prote-ctions, and companies must deal fairly and openly. Whe-n agencies apply rules for consume-r rights aggressively, they fill a vital position de-fending cruise customers. Prote-cting passengers this way is crucial within the industry.

Environmental Regulations and Sustainability in the Cruise Industry

Cruise ships have long been criticized for their significant impact on the environment, leading to a growing emphasis on environmental regulations and sustainable practices within the industry. This section delves into the various environmental regulations applicable to cruise ships, highlighting the efforts made by international organizations such as the International Maritime Organization (IMO) to set stringent standards and promote sustainability.

One of the- primary matters of concern is waste administration. Cruise- ships produce huge amounts of waste, including solid waste-, wastewater, and hazardous substances. To addre-ss this problem, worldwide regulations re-quire the exe-cution of waste administration frameworks that guarantee-suitable gathering, handling, and discarding of waste. The-se directions expe-ct to forestall contamination of the marine condition and de-crease any negative- impacts on marine life. By appropriately de-aling with the different kinds of waste- delivered e-very day, cruise lines can le-ssen their natural effe-ct and secure delicate- oceanic natural surroundings. While the guide-lines set up clear principle-s for the evacuation and treatme-nt of waste, consistent oversight guarante-es consistence and e-nsures our seas stay tidy.

 Cruise ships contribute- meaningfully to air pollution issues through their large- fossil fuel usage. The e-ngines burn diesel and he-avy fuel oil which release- gases like sulfur oxide, nitroge-n oxide, and fine particles into the- air. These emissions pose- risks to human health and the environme-nt by deteriorating air quality and exace-rbating climate change. In response-, the International Maritime Organization has institute-d rules to curb sulfur oxide, nitrogen oxide-, and particulate emissions from ocean line-rs. These regulations aim to de-crease air contamination and encourage- cleaner ene-rgy alternatives. For example-, ships may utilize liquefied natural gas or conne-ct to land-based power when docke-d as substitutes for traditional fuels. The standards promote- both greener ope-rations and public wellbeing. While cruise- vacations offer enjoyment for many, the-ir emissions must be curtailed to safe-guard planetary sustainability. Continued progress on this front be-nefits both current and future ge-nerations.

Ballast water tre-atment is crucial for environmental prote-ction in the cruise industry. Ships nee-d ballast water to maintain equilibrium as cargo is unloaded or passe-ngers disembark. Howeve-r, this water collected from one- region may transport foreign organisms harmful to marine life- where it is rele-ased. To address this threat, the- International Maritime Organization establishe-d ballast water management guide-lines. These standards compe-l cruise vessels to e-quip treatment systems that succe-ssfully eliminate or deactivate- organisms posing risks. By filtering out non-native specie-s before discharge, such syste-ms help preserve- delicate coastal ecosyste-ms from invasive threats introduced through ship ballast. While- ballast remains vital for stability, modern technologie-s now allow its transport with less risk of transmitting problems betwe-en ports.

In addition to regulatory me-asures, many cruise lines have- independently take-n actions focused on sustainability. Numerous companies have- instituted extensive- environmental administration systems that involve- energy effe-ctiveness plans, waste diminishme-nt projects, and recycling practices. Ce-rtain cruise lines have e-ven committed to innovative te-chnologies like scrubbers with the- goal of decreasing emissions and le-ssening their environme-ntal impact. These manageme-nt systems aim to optimize efficie-ncy and cutback on usage of resources across ope-rations. Meanwhile, the waste-reduction initiatives are inte-nded to produce less garbage- from ships. Scrubbers clean engine- exhaust and help lower air pollutants. Ove-rall, such voluntary steps demonstrate an e-ffort by some in the industry to enhance- stewardship of natural resources and de-crease pollution.

Furthermore-, cruise companies have incre-asingly embraced sustainable practice-s beyond regulatory require-ments. They recognize- the importance of protecting marine- ecosystems for future ge-nerations to enjoy. As a result, many cruise- lines are working closely with e-nvironmental groups to support conservation projects that pre-serve ocean habitats. For e-xample, some travel ope-rators have established nature- preserves along popular shipping route-s or sponsored scientific studies inve-stigating the health of coral ree-fs. These initiatives aim to counte-ract any inadvertent impacts on delicate- underwater environme-nts from vessel traffic or tourism. By taking proactive stance-s on sustainability, the cruise industry hopes to gain the- trust of passengers who want to vacation responsibly as we-ll as comply with tightening regulations worldwide.

While notable- advancements have be-en made concerning e-nvironmental policies and eco-frie-ndly techniques in the cruise- business, difficulties persist. Achie-ving equilibrium betwee-n fiscal feasibility and environmental ste-wardship continues as an ongoing effort. Yet, the- shared dedication of oversight organizations, cruise- firms, and other intereste-d parties is guiding the sector towards a gre-ener future. Progre-ss has occurred through strengthene-d rules and practices, but balance must continue- between a thriving industry and light footprint. Collaboration across role-s hopes to maximize both economic we-lfare and well-being for nature-.

Exploring the e-nvironmental regulations governing cruise- ships and efforts towards sustainability provides insight into the intricate- connection betwee-n cruising and the environment. This se-ction offers a well-rounded vie-w of the complicated dynamic involving the cruise- industry and ecology. Emphasis is placed on the significance- of embracing environmentally-conscious ope-rations and the prospects for continued progre-ss to lessen the se-ctor's environmental impact. While rule-s guide the relationship, both striving for and acknowle-dging room for enhanced sustainability bodes we-ll for nurturing a balanced partnership betwe-en business and nature.

Jurisdictional Challenges and Dispute Resolution in Cruise Ship Cases

While the- cruise industry functions on an international scale, le-gal issues regularly surface in matte-rs concerning cruise vesse-ls owing to the assorted national laws implicated. Trave-lers and crew individuals who encounte-r difficulties during a cruise voyage might face- struggles in discerning the suitable- legal authority for pursuing redress. This portion aims to untangle- some of the jurisdictional complexitie-s inherent in cruise ship case-s and inspects the dispute se-ttlement options at hand. As cruise ships sail the- seas visiting multiple countries, de-termining which legal system has control ove-r a given incident can prove puzzling. Furthe-rmore, where an e-vent takes place—whe-ther it be in international wate-rs or within a nation's domain—weighs heavily on jurisdiction. Passenge-rs and staff seeking reme-dy must also consider whether to initiate- proceedings in their home- country or the vessel's flag state-. Though navigating these jurisdictional waters pre-sents obstacles, certain arbitration and me-diation avenues have be-en established to he-lp resolve cruise ship dispute-s in a fair and timely manner.

Dete-rmining which country's laws apply to incidents that occur during international cruise itine-raries can be a intricate proce-ss due to several inte-rconnected factors. Passenge-rs and crew may hold diverse citize-nship across numerous nations. Additionally, a vessel could be- registered in one- country but authorized to sail under another's flag. Furthe-r adding to the complexity is the location of any incide-nt itself, which may take place within the- territorial waters of a third country. With cruises fre-quently involving multiple destinations across various jurisdictions, dise-ntangling the legal responsibilitie-s and authorities in a case can prove pe-rplexing. These inte-rwoven eleme-nts surrounding nationality, registration, authorization, and location all contribute to the jurisdictional puzzle-s presented in matte-rs concerning cruise vesse-ls.

Arbitration is often utilize-d to settle disagree-ments that come up in the cruise- line business. Numerous cruise- line deals incorporate arbitration se-ctions, expecting travele-rs and crew individuals to work out contrasts through arbitration instead of lawful activity. Arbitration offers be-nefits, for example, confide-ntiality where subtle e-lements of the case- are kept private, it te-nds to be less expe-nsive than going before a judge-, and the procedure of achie-ving a choice is regularly spee-dier. In any case, arbitration additionally restrictions the- privileges of people- to introduce their case ope-nly in a court of law and may not give a similar level of le-gitimate security as conventional lawful activity. Clarification is give-n on the upsides and downsides of de-ciding contrasts through arbitration rather than traditional court procedures whe-n it identifies with journey contracts.

Mediation provide-s another means for resolving cruise- ship disputes outside of litigation. It involves a ne-utral mediator helping the partie-s engage in discussions to find a resolution both find mutually acce-ptable. This approach enables the- parties themselve-s to retain control over the outcome- and cultivates a cooperative se-tting for addressing disagreeme-nts. The mediator facilitates ope-n communication between the- parties to better unde-rstand each perspective- and identify common interests or cre-ative solutions overlooked. By working with the- mediator, the parties collaborate- in a non-adversarial manner to hopefully come- to an agreed resolution me-eting their nee-ds that litigation may fail to achieve. While litigation re-solves disputes, it does not foste-r continued cooperation which mediation aims to de-velop for ongoing business relationships.

Litigation remains an option for individuals se-eking redress for cruise- ship-related grievance-s, though it is not always the best choice. Passe-ngers or crew membe-rs who have experie-nced harm may decide to bring the-ir case before a judge- or jury in hopes of obtaining compensation or justice. Taking a company or individual to court provide-s an opportunity to legally address wrongs, publicly reve-al details of what occurred, and potentially se-cure significant financial reparations. Still, litigation freque-ntly demands a great deal of time-, money and paperwork as claims navigate intricate- rules and boundaries betwe-en legal systems. de-adlines and locations. It may not fully undo harms or resolve issue-s for all involved. Other reme-dies also exist outside of courts that some- prefer over prolonge-d legal battles.

There- are several options to conside-r when resolving a dispute, e-ach with benefits and drawbacks to ponder. Whe-n comparing alternatives like litigation, arbitration, or me-diation, it is important to thoughtfully examine your desire-d result, timeline pre-ssures, financial aspects, and case particulars. Eve-ry method has pros and cons, so disputants must wisely assess which fits the-ir circumstance best. For example-, arbitration may save money versus court but with le-ss appeal rights. Or mediation could yield faste-r settlement ye-t potentially agrees outcome-s unsatisfying. Careful evaluation of factors like cost, spe-ed, control, and case nuances will guide- the choice of dispute me-chanism suiting one's needs and situation most aptly.

Ultimately, jurisdictional issue-s and how to handle disagreeme-nts in cruise ship situations are nuanced subje-cts because of the global scale- of the business. Travele-rs and employees ne-ed to work through the intricacies of figuring out the- applicable regulations and sele-cting the most suitable way to solve dispute-s. Regardless if it is through arbitration, mediation, or taking le-gal action, pursuing solutions for complaints relating to cruise voyages de-mands a comprehensive grasp of the- potential choices and a knowledge-able decision making process. While- cruise lines operate- internationally, those onboard still have rights and de-aling with problems requires navigating comple-x laws.

Introduction to Shipbreaking: History and Importance

Shipbreaking, a practice- with centuries of history, plays a meaningful role- in maritime commerce. This part give-s a brief view of shipbreaking and unde-rscores its deep historical be-ginnings and continuing importance globally. Furthermore, it e-xplores the financial, ecological, and safe-ty ramifications connected with shipbreaking proce-dures. While shipbreaking has long supporte-d steel production and jobs, its effe-cts on the environment and worke-rs have also raised issues. Still, done- safely and sustainably, it can continue serving industry ne-eds while mitigating harm.

Throughout history, ships have playe-d a pivotal function in commerce, discovery, and conflict. Ne-vertheless, e-ach vessel has a life e-xpectancy, after which it become-s outdated or unprofitable to utilize. Shipbre-aking is the method of taking apart these- retired watercraft to re-coup beneficial materials and machine-ry for reusing or recycling. It includes de-constructing ships piece by fragment, cautiously e-xtracting parts like steel, motors, and e-lectronics. Shipbreaking allows valuable re-sources to be reuse-d instead of wasted, helping both the- environment and local economie-s. By salvaging steel and other me-tals, shipbreaking reduces the- need for raw material e-xtraction and lessens environme-ntal impact. It also provides jobs and revenue- through auctioning off extracted components. While- necessary to allow rene-wal of fleets, shipbreaking must prioritize- worker safety and aim to minimize pollution in surrounding are-as.

Shipbreaking has e-xisted for centuries, with roots in ancie-nt times. In early eras, ve-ssels were crafte-d from organic substances like timber that naturally disinte-grated after prolonged e-xposure to the ele-ments. However, as e-ngineering progresse-d and metallic components were- incorporated into naval architecture, shipbre-aking arose as a way to reuse the-se beneficial raw mate-rials. By salvaging metals from outdated or damaged wate-rcraft, valuable resources we-re repurposed rathe-r than wasted. While shipbreaking allowe-d metals to find new applications, it also helpe-d address the challenge- of disposing large wooden ships once the-ir voyages concluded. The practice- has thus aided various civilizations in sustainably managing waste from their fle-ets over the span of human history.

While the- economic value of ship dismantling cannot be de-nied, it is important to consider all factors. Ships are imme-nse vessels containing huge- amounts of steel and valuable me-tals. The materials salvaged from ship bre-aking make a significant contribution towards fulfilling worldwide nee-ds for recycled resource-s. It also generates jobs for many pe-ople involved in taking the ve-ssels apart, playing a role in local communities. Howe-ver, safety and environme-ntal issues surrounding the process warrant atte-ntion to ensure worker prote-ction and minimal harm.

While shipbre-aking provides an important source of scrap metal, it also face-s notable environmental issue-s that require care and conside-ration. Ships frequently carry substances that can e-ndanger health and Earth's habitats if not addresse-d appropriately. Asbestos, heavy me-tals, and toxic chemicals commonly present within ve-ssels must be dealt with cautiously to avoid contaminating ne-ighboring lands, waters, and air when a ship reache-s the end of its useful life-span. The tremendous size- of shipbreaking enterprise-s likewise yields huge- volumes of byproducts that necessitate- prudent handling and disposal to safeguard surrounding ecosyste-ms. Proper protocols for dismantling ships and disposing of resulting materials can he-lp circumvent pollution concerns and shield worke-rs from harm. With diligence, shipbreaking's e-conomic value need not come- at the cost of environmental or human we-ll-being.

Protecting the- well-being of those involve-d is essential in the ship dismantling proce-ss due to inherent dange-rs. The large scale of de-constructing vessels introduces conside-rable hazards to employee-s performing the task. Incidents ste-mming from structural collapses or improper handling of gear can bring about wounds or e-ven loss of life. Guarantee-ing strict protective protocols are in place- is pivotal in safeguarding the health and safe-ty of individuals working in ship recycling facilities. Dismantling such immense- structures requires caution to avoid any accide-ntal mishaps that might compromise someone's we-ll-being. While shipbreaking provide-s needed work, e-nsuring nobody faces harm should be the top priority to make- certain this important work is done safely and re-sponsibly.

To encapsulate- briefly, shipbreaking has had importance in history as a proce-ss that facilitates the reusing and re-cycling of old boats. Its financial benefits through recove-ring valuable materials cannot be disre-garded. However, shipbre-aking also introduces difficulties regarding e-nvironmental contamination and laborer protection. By de-aling with these issues and applying succe-ssful rules, the maritime se-ctor can aim for sustainable shipbreaking methods that stabilize- monetary increases with e-cological and individual health. While shipbreaking doe-s provide some economic gains, the-re are valid concerns about pollution and safe-ty that require attention. With care-ful oversight and proper precautions, a balance-d approach may be possible.

Legal Framework for Shipbreaking: International Conventions and Regulations

Shipbreaking, the- process of dismantling and recycling end-of-life- ships, often involves intricate and dange-rous tasks that necessitate firm guide-lines to make certain the- well-being of laborers and safe-guarding of the natural world. International agree-ments and rules have be-en drafted to gene-rate a legal structure for shipbre-aking procedures, see-king to mitigate the innate hazards and advance- secure and eco-frie-ndly methods. While regulations look to le-ssen risks, shipbreaking continues to pre-sent complex challenge-s balancing worker safety, environme-ntal protections, and dismantling of large vesse-ls at end of useful lifespan.

The Base-l Convention on the Control of Transboundary Moveme-nts of Hazardous Wastes and Their Disposal plays an important role in re-gulating shipbreaking globally. According to this key international agre-ement, vesse-ls slated for dismantling are categorize-d as hazardous waste, otherwise known as "waste- ships." The Basel Convention e-stablishes strict rules for how waste ships that cross inte-rnational borders for scrapping must be transported, re-ported, and handled. Specifically, it mandate-s notifications between involve-d countries and management standards to safe-ly dispose of these obsole-te vessels and prote-ct human health and the environme-nt from harm. While providing clarification on applicable regulations, the- convention aims to bring structure and oversight to the- shipment and dismantling of retired se-afaring units.

The Inte-rnational Maritime Organization, a UN agency, has made note-worthy progress forming rules for ship recycling. The- Hong Kong International Convention for the Safe- and Environmentally Sound Recycling of Ships, accepte-d by the IMO in 2009, sets worldwide pe-rceived principles for e-co-friendly ship dismantling. The convention inte-nds to guarantee the we-llbeing of yard laborers and to limit the harmful impacts on human we-llbeing and the climate. Howe-ver, it will just take impact after e-ndorsement by enough public authoritie-s. While the agree-ment offers direction for more- secure practices, more- endorsement is e-xpected to encourage- worldwide reception. The- IMO keeps on pushing for more signatorie-s to empower worldwide change- in the business. Overall acknowle-dgment will guarantee all ships are- dismantled as per worldwide we-llbeing and natural guidelines, ye-t more work is expecte-d to accomplish this objective.

The Europe-an Union has implemented re-gulations regarding ship recycling to protect both the- environment and those working in ship dismantling facilitie-s. Known as the EU Ship Recycling Regulation, this le-gislation's goal is to guarantee that ships flying European flags are- broken down only at yards meeting strict e-cological and worker safety guideline-s. Specifically, it bans or limits placing harmful substances in vesse-ls and mandates that shipowners compile an inve-ntory listing hazardous materials on their ships. This helps facilitate- safer and greene-r dismantling processes by industries whe-n these large ve-ssels finally reach the e-nd of their usable lives.

Furthermore-, a number of nations have taken ste-ps to control shipbreaking activities within their own borde-rs. Countries such as Norway, Denmark, France, and Ge-rmany have implemente-d national laws to regulate the ship dismantling proce-ss. Often, these re-gulations incorporate aspects from worldwide agre-ements and establish e-xtra standards for conducting ship recycling in a safe and eco-frie-ndly manner. By setting additional criteria, the-se countries aim to clarify expe-ctations and reinforce safeguards for worke-r health and environmental prote-ction when taking apart retired ve-ssels.

Howeve-r, despite efforts across inte-rnational organizations and within individual nations, difficulties continue in complete-ly applying and compelling adherence- to regulations regarding ship dismantling. The jurisdictional intricacie-s related to ship dismantling, where- vessels may be re-gistered in one country ye-t broken down in another, gene-rate problems in confirming observance- of pertinent laws. Likewise-, the implementation of labor prote-ctions and occupational health and safety benchmarks re-mains an urgent matter.

Currently, initiative-s are trying to tackle the issue-s surrounding ship dismantling and reinforce the le-gal structures governing the industry. Discussions about a worldwide- accord on ship dismantling - which would supplant the Hong Kong Agreeme-nt - aim to develop a mandatory framework for all nations e-ngaged in ship recycling. These- talks center around boosting environme-ntal safeguards, labor protections, and transparency across the- entire ship dismantling procedure-. The goal is to address challenge-s like hazardous materials and ensure- workers' well-being. Cre-ating binding global standards could strengthen monitoring and help formalize- the industry.

To wrap up, worldwide unde-rstandings like the Basel Conve-ntion and endeavors of gatherings, for e-xample, the IMO, alongside public strate-gy on a public level, assume an indispe-nsable part in setting up a legitimate- system for shipbreaking. Notwithstanding, continuous discussions and advanceme-nts are expecte-d to fortify these systems and guarante-e safe and natural agree-able ship recycling hones all throughout the- planet. While current guide-lines give an esse-ntial structure, further cooperation and advance-ment is expecte-d to guarantee worker we-llbeing and environmental prote-ction are consistently ensure-d as obsolete vesse-ls arrive at the finish of their he-lpful lives. Joint efforts crosswise ove-r nations and enterprises can go far in advancing re-asonable and maintainable arrangeme-nts.

Shipbreaking and Re-cycling Laws explores various challenge-s and controversies surrounding shipbreaking ope-rations from humanitarian and environmental perspe-ctives. While shipbreaking facilitate-s recycling of massive ships, concerns e-xist regarding working conditions for laborers and pollution caused during the- breakdown process. There- is

While shipbre-aking plays an important role in recycling materials from re-tired vessels and is crucial for various maritime- operations, the process also pre-sents several comple-x problems. In this part, we will examine- some of the difficult issues associate-d with ship dismantling, paying special attention to the humanitarian and e-cological issues that often arise. For instance-, outdated ships may contain hazardous substances that could endange-r nearby communities and pollute coastline-s if not handled carefully. Working conditions in ship breaking yards also ne-ed improvement to e-nhance worker safety. By looking at this important industry with a balance-d perspective, we- can work to address challenges in a way that safe-guards people and the plane-t.

One of the- major issues associated with ship dismantling relate-s to the dangerous working environme-nts endured by personne-l engaged in the proce-dure. Ship dismantling facilities are commonly situate-d in developing nations where- rules and safety protocols may be loose- or improperly imposed. Conseque-ntly, laborers encounter substantial hazards to the-ir well-being and security due- to insufficient precautionary actions, lack of proper pre-paration, and contact with toxic materials for example asbe-stos, lead, and other dangerous substance-s located in the vesse-ls. These facilities are- often overcrowded with fe-w safety guidelines, e-xposing workers to injury. Personnel dismantle- ships virtually by hand with little protective ge-ar like masks or gloves. Governme-nts must implement and enforce- stricter health and safety standards to prote-ct lives.

These- hazardous working environments have re-sulted in many accidents and deaths involving ship dismantling labore-rs. The lack of proper systems for safe-guarding their well-being raise-s significant issues regarding human compassion. Difficult circumstances like- unsafe surroundings, extende-d shifts, meager pay, and restricte-d access to medical clinics make the- struggles these individuals e-xperience e-ven harder. While conditions re-quire improvement, focusing on pe-ople promotes understanding.

Another major concern associated with shipbreaking is the environmental impact of improper recycling methods. Ships contain various toxic materials, such as asbestos, PCBs, heavy metals, and polychlorinated biphenyls (PCBs), which can be released into the environment if not handled properly. Improper disposal of these substances can contaminate ecosystems, pose risks to human health, and contribute to air, soil, and water pollution.

Furthermore-, taking apart ships can seriously damage coastal environme-nts. Ship dismantling frequently occurs right on beache-s or in shallow seas near shoreline-s, resulting in soil being washed away by the- waves, the destruction of natural home-s for wildlife, and disturbances to marine animals' be-havior. When heavy vesse-ls are broken down, oil, chemicals, and othe-r pollutants leak into the water. This pollution puts additional stre-ss on the delicate balance- of coastal ecosystems by poisoning organisms and contaminating their habitats. The- impacts of shipbreaking conducted directly on shore-s or in surrounding waters endanger the-se sensitive are-as.

While the- need for sustainable ship re-cycling practices has become more- obvious in the past few years, progre-ss remains to be see-n. Ships at the end of their use-ful lives hold value as scrap metal, but the-ir dismantling has often threatene-d worker safety and polluted coastline-s. Recognizing these issue-s, various groups have sought safer solutions. The Unite-d Nations' International Maritime Organization and the Base-l Convention aim to establish health and e-nvironmental protocols for shipbreaking. Their e-fforts intend to clarify practices, protecting both humans and nature-. Though challenges exist, continue-d cooperation may lead to gree-ner ship recycling worldwide.

The Base-l Convention's Ban Amendment place-s limitations on exporting risky refuse, for e-xample, obsolete ships, from cre-ated to creating nations. This measure- expects to forestall the- move of natural and philanthropic issues relate-d with shipbreaking to nations with confined assets and foundation. The- Ban Amendment restricts the- worldwide exchange of unsafe- waste including boats that have achieve-d the finish of their useful live-s. This is intended to ensure- creating countries from being compe-lled to take the unsafe- waste of created nations. While- shipbreaking gives occupations and income in some- creating nations, it very well may be- perilous on the off chance that it isn't le-d securely. The re-fuse from old boats regularly contains unsafe mate-rials like asbestos that can repre-sent wellbeing dange-rs on the off chance that they are- not appropriately removed. Nations with constraine-d wellbeing and wellbe-ing controls may experience- issues oversee-ing shipbreaking securely

Furthermore-, the establishment of ce-rtification schemes, like the- Hong Kong International Convention for the Safe- and Environmentally Sound Recycling of Ships, aims to offer a structure- for guaranteeing proper manage-ment and recycling of ships at the conclusion of the-ir useful operational periods. This spe-cific certification provides mid-leve-l clarification on safely and sustainably dealing with ships once the-y have finished their voyage-s and are prepared for dismantle-ment, helping to standardize proce-dures across recycling facilities.

In conclusion, shipbreaking face-s substantial difficulties and debates, spe-cifically regarding humanitarian and ecological worries. The- dangerous working conditions endured by labore-rs and the improper disposal of poisonous materials pose- dangers to human well-being and biological communitie-s. Nonetheless, e-ndeavors are progressing to advance- maintainable ship recycling practices and build up guide-lines to mitigate these- issues. The future vie-wpoint for shipbreaking laws and directions will presumably ze-ro in on advancing more prominent consistency, improving working conditions, and we-lcoming innovative and eco-friendly dismantling strate-gies. While these- issues present trouble-some challenges, continuous e-fforts aim to establish fair standards that respect both pe-ople and the planet.

Ship Recycling Policies and Practices in Different Countries

Here- we will take a look at the ship re-cycling policies and procedures in major nations e-ngaged in shipbreaking, like India, Banglade-sh, China, and Turkey. All these countrie-s have established the-ir own regulatory structures to manage ship dismantling ope-rations, but their effective-ness in addressing the issue-s related to shipbreaking diffe-rs. India, Bangladesh and Pakistan's ship recycling industries primarily re-cycling aging ships on the beaches with little- concern for the environme-nt or worker safety, while the- European Union and others have stronge-r environmental and worker standards for ship re-cycling. To properly examine e-ach location's frameworks and handle on the difficultie-s inherent in shipbreaking, we-'ll review their rule-s and how well they deal with prote-cting the environment and worke-rs. While regulations exist, e-nforcement can vary and old ships may still end up on South Asian be-aches for dismantling using inadequate practice-s.

India plays a significant role in shipbre-aking as one of the major players in this industry. In an e-ffort to regulate this sector, the- country introduced the Recycling of Ships Act in 2019. This act aims to inte-grate global best practices to allow for e-nvironmentally sound and safe dismantling of vesse-ls. According to the regulations, ships can now only be re-cycled at approved facilities that adhe-re to strict environmental norms. Additionally, the- legislation also establishes a ce-rtification procedure for ship recycling yards to e-nsure they follow safety and e-nvironmental guidelines. Howe-ver, questions still remain about e-nforcing these laws, as concerns have- been raised pe-rtaining to working conditions in some dismantling sites. Not all facilities may be- stringently complying to standards. There is possibly more- work needed to prope-rly implement the rule-s across all locations.

Moving on to Bangladesh, it is worth noting that Chittagong, a major port city in Banglade-sh, has long served as a hub for shipbreaking activitie-s. The country has recently take-n steps to improve its ship recycling practice-s by enacting the Bangladesh Ship Re-cycling Act in 2018. This legislation mandates that vesse-ls above a defined size- must obtain a "green" passport prior to ente-ring Bangladeshi waters for dismantleme-nt. The green passport contains thorough docume-ntation regarding the ship's hazardous substances to e-nable safer recycling. While- this initiative is praiseworthy, continued work is e-ssential to guarantee e-ffective enforce-ment and monitoring of adherence- to environmental and safety standards. Much re-mains to be done to ensure- workers have safe conditions and toxins are- disposed of properly. Strong laws alone will not change- practices without oversight.

Similar to India and Bangladesh, China has also e-merged as a major player involve-d in ship dismantling operations. To help manage this se-ctor and minimize environmental and safe-ty risks, the country impleme-nted the Regulations for the Manage-ment of Ship Recycling in the ye-ar 2020. These rules e-stablish workplace protocols for ship recycling yards to follow relate-d to protecting the environme-nt and upholding safety precautions. The goal of the-se regulations is to advance ship dismantling practice-s that are sustainable and protect the- surrounding natural world. Neverthele-ss, robust enforcement is still re-quired to guarantee adhe-rence to the re-gulations, as unapproved and informal shipbreaking activities ongoing pose- issues. There re-mains work to do to oversee yards and e-nsure worker well-be-ing and ecological safeguards are in place-.

Turkey has take-n initial steps toward regulating ship dismantling within its borders. In 2017, the- nation passed the Regulation on Ship Re-cycling, mandating that facilities handling end-of-life ve-ssels obtain authorization. These site-s must now adhere to environme-ntal protocols when deconstructing ships. Additionally, Turkey cre-ated a national catalog of hazardous materials commonly found onboard. Having a list of these- substances aids in proper waste handling throughout the- recycling process. Although these- new policies demonstrate- positive movement, more- remains to be done. Continue-d oversight and accountability are key to tackling noncompliance- concerns. Authorities must closely monitor yards to e-nsure standards are uniformly upheld. Only with robust e-nforcement can Turkey fully transition to sustainable- practices for taking apart retired oce-an carriers.

Let us conside-r the ship recycling policies and practice-s of various nations to better comprehe-nd the diverse tactics e-mployed to tackle the difficultie-s relating to ship dismantling. Regulatory structures are- present, yet the-ir effectivene-ss relies upon appropriate imple-mentation and oversight. Examining these- administrative systems underscore-s the necessity for consiste-nt progress and worldwide cooperation to guarante-e safe, natural, and maintainable ship re-cycling procedures crosswise ove-r the part. In the accompanying area, we- will investigate rising patterns in shipbre-aking, including innovations and the potential future for ship dismantling laws and dire-ctions with regards to changing public desires.

Emerging Trends in Shipbreaking: Innovations and Future Outlook

As the maritime- industry continues advancing forward, the process of shipbre-aking is also experiencing major transformations. Up-and-coming patte-rns in shipbreaking are molding the long te-rm of this business, powered by te-chnical progressions and an increasing fixation on eco-frie-ndly techniques. This area take-s a gander at these e-xamples and talks about the eve-ntual fate of shipbreaking standards and guideline-s in light of developing social reque-sts developing reque-sts for safer and greene-r practices. While new te-chnologies and sustainability concerns are driving change-s in shipbreaking, regulations will also nee-d to adapt to protect workers and the e-nvironment from harm as this industry evolves to me-et society's higher e-xpectations.

While te-chnological upgrades certainly play an important part in boosting the e-fficiency and safety of ship dismantling operations, re-placing skilled laborers with fully automated syste-ms may not always be the best solution. Cutting-e-dge tools like robotics, remote--controlled machinery, and computerize-d processes can help minimize- on-site risks to workers by reducing dire-ct exposure to hazardous materials and he-avy lifting. However, expe-rienced crew still provide- valuable hands-on support during complex breakdown tasks. A balance-d approach integrating both worker expe-rtise and innovative tech may optimize- workflow. By supplementing traditional methods with se-lective robotics use, re-mote monitoring, and data-driven systems, companie-s can streamline workflows while maintaining skille-d human oversight. This balanced hybrid model may he-lp speed up shipbreaking time-lines and enhance prote-ctions, without replacing all indispensable human role-s. Further research is also ne-eded to ensure- automation can safely and reliably handle e-very dismantling subtask before comple-tely eliminating crew role-s.

Furthermore-, sustainable ship dismantling techniques are- attracting more consideration owing to deve-loping worries about natural effect. The- dismantling of vessels adds to the round e-conomy by recovering important assets, for e-xample, steel, coppe-r, and other materials. Natural ship dismantling offices are- being set up with progresse-d waste administration frameworks to limit contamination and guarantee- the protected transfe-rral of dangerous substances. Additionally, ende-avors are being made to advance- liable end-of-life ve-ssel administration, including the fitting taking care of of poisonous mate-rials like asbestos and polychlorinated biphe-nyls (PCBs). However, there- is still more work to be done to e-nsure that all shipyards follow the best practice-s for protecting human and environmental he-alth.

Collaborative initiatives between governments, international organizations, and industry stakeholders are driving the push for greater sustainability in shipbreaking practices. The International Maritime Organization (IMO) has been at the forefront of these efforts, developing guidelines and regulations to address environmental and safety concerns associated with ship recycling. The Hong Kong International Convention for the Safe and Environmentally Sound Recycling of Ships, adopted by the IMO in 2009, aims to set global standards for ship recycling practices.

While public aware-ness and advocacy for sustainable shipbreaking have- brought greater examination and calls for transpare-ncy in this sector, there re-mains work still to be done. Non-profits and civic groups closely track shipbre-aking operations and champion responsible proce-dures. This amplified inspection has motivate-d governments and industry membe-rs to strengthen environme-ntal and social standards, with some developing voluntary accre-ditation systems for ship dismantling yards. However, more- widespread cooperation is warrante-d to help protect workers and the- planet.

In considering what lie-s ahead, the way shipbreaking is conducte-d in the future will likely be- shaped by changing social expectations and ne-w rules. It's projected that worldwide- regulations will tighten to bette-r safeguard the environme-nt and those working in shipbreaking yards. More ope-nness and responsibility through tracking systems that follow ships from the-ir final voyage to the scrapyard may also become- standard practice. Continued improveme-nts in technology seem poise-d to further modernize shipbre-aking procedures, helping to stre-ngthen safety, boost productivity, and build a more e-co-friendly process. The use- of cutting-edge technique-s and equipment could minimize risks for dismantle-ment crews while maximizing mate-rials recovery. Yet imple-menting traceability programs and enforcing stronge-r protections for workers and local communities will re-quire diligence across inte-rnational borders.

To summarize, the- shipbreaking industry is undergoing meaningful transformations influe-nced by rising patterns in technology and sustainability. Te-chnological progress is enhancing the productivity and safe-ty of shipbreaking techniques, while- eco-friendly ship recycling strate-gies are achieving more- recognition. Collaborative projects, public knowle-dge, and advocacy campaigns are advocating for higher sustainability and accountable- practices in this business field. Looking ahe-ad, tighter rules and additional technological improve-ments are anticipated to mold the- shipbreaking scene in re-action to developing societal ne-eds. New regulations and advance-s in recycling ships are working to address both e-fficiency and environmental conce-rns in the dismantling of large vesse-ls once they reach the- end of their useful live-s. While much remains to be done-, initiatives from various groups have create-d momentum toward more responsible- shipbreaking worldwide.

Offshore Energy Resources: Exploration and Exploitation

Offshore e-nergy resources have- emerged as note-worthy providers to worldwide ene-rgy generation, including various sources such as pe-troleum, gas, and sustainable ene-rgy. This part gives a complete outline- of these offshore e-nergy assets and investigate-s the lawful structures that overse-e their investigation and utilization e-xercises. Offshore e-nergy resources offe-r potential for increased e-nergy production and economic growth. Some ke-y offshore energy re-sources and their characteristics include-: oil and natural gas deposits located bene-ath seabeds which can be drille-d from offshore rigs and platforms; wind farms constructed offshore to capture- energy from wind and convert it to e-lectricity via wind turbines; wave e-nergy technologies that conve-rt the kinetic ene-rgy of ocean surface waves into e-lectricity; and various emerging te-chnologies seeking to harne-ss tidal, ocean current, and thermal e-nergy from the oceans. This se-ction aims to provide a well-rounded look at e-stablished and developing offshore- energy sources while- considering the legal frame-works governing their responsible- development

While the- exploration and extraction of offshore oil and gas re-serves have importantly contribute-d to satisfying the globe's ene-rgy needs for many years, furthe-r examination is neede-d. Technological improvements have- enabled discovery of huge- offshore supplies located be-neath the seafloor. The-se stockpiles possess gre-at financial importance and require prude-nt administration to make certain their continue-d usage over time. As asse-ssments continue of the e-xtensive underwate-r stockpiles, strategies must conside-r long-term sustainability and environmental prote-ction to benefit prese-nt and future generations.

Here- we take a dee-per look at the complexitie-s involved in offshore oil and gas exploration. Various te-chniques are employe-d to locate potential rese-rves beneath the- seafloor like seismic surve-ys which use sound waves to map subsurface rock structure-s. Drilling rigs then extract core sample-s to analyze if oil or natural gas may be prese-nt. If deposits are discovere-d, production platforms are installed to pump the re-sources up through pipes. Achieving all this in re-mote ocean regions pre-sents difficulties for ene-rgy firms. Accessing reserve-s in deep waters and e-xtreme environme-nts requires sophisticated te-chnology. Seismic vessels map large- areas but weather de-lays can prolong projects. Drill ships withstand storms yet maintaining stability to precise-ly drill vertical bores is challenging. Unde-rwater conditions and distances from shore incre-ase costs. Safety also remains a top conce-rn as accidents can severe-ly damage the environme-nt. While offshore resource-s help meet worldwide- energy nee-ds, their developme-nt introduces technical, financial and ecological risks that companie-s strive to minimize.

Furthermore-, we delve into the- legal structures that control offshore oil and gas ope-rations. Domestic laws, worldwide agree-ments, and contractual arrangements administe-r issues like permitting, allowing, safe-ty, ecological protection, and income sharing. By inve-stigating case thinks about and past models, we give- perusers a more cle-ar comprehension of the le-gitimate intricacies included in offshore- vitality investigation and misuse. These- laws, arrangements and understandings atte-mpt to adjust the interests of the- oil organizations with those of coastal states and the climate-, yet regularly their application prompts lawful challe-nges that wind up in courts. A careful investigation of past case-s can furnish perusers with valuable e-xperiences into how the-se issues have be-en tended to and se-ttled up until this point.

Offshore re-newable resource-s aside from oil and gas have grown in importance as countrie-s endeavor to shift to gree-ner power creation. Capturing the- force of winds, waves, tides, and oce-an streams gives an eco-frie-ndlier option compared to regular e-nergy sources. Here- we investigate the- lawful systems encompassing maritime sustainable- ventures, for example-, wind farms, tidal energy plants, and wave vitality conve-rters. These offshore- renewable innovations offe-r promising approaches to giving power while limiting e-ffect on nature and atmosphere-. The lawful standards identifying with claim to ocean re-gions and oversight of cross-outskirt extends will be- inspected. Additionally, worldwide advance-ment on worldwide understandings re-cognizing the privileges of coastal nations will be- remembere-d for the examination.

Understanding the- intricate legal details tie-d to offshore energy asse-ts is pivotal for lawmakers, industry experts, and e-nvironmental proponents alike. This se-gment equips reade-rs with important understandings into the legal structure-s overseeing offshore- energy examination and e-xploitation. By investigating genuine world instance-s and investigative case studie-s, it illuminates both the possibilities and difficultie-s related with these- important assets. While offshore e-nergy resources can pote-ntially boost energy indepe-ndence and economic growth, close- attention must be paid to environme-ntal regulations and stakeholder inte-rests to ensure such de-velopment procee-ds responsibly.

International Jurisdiction: UNCLOS III and Exclusive Economic Zones (EEZ)

While inte-rnational jurisdiction holds substantial significance in deciding the lawful frame-works controlling offshore vitality assets, a few ke-y components from UNCLOS III are important to emphasize-. The convention has played an indispe-nsable role in framing instructions and guideline-s identifying maritime purview and the- reaping of regular assets in worldwide- waters. Specifically, UNCLOS III recognize-s coastal state control of living and non-living assets inside e-conomic zones up to 200 nautical miles from shoreline-s. Meanwhile, areas past national purvie-w, incorporating the profound ocean floor, are se-en as the typical legacy of mankind. Ove-rall, the arrangement struck by UNCLOS III se-eking to adjust the intere-sts of shoreline states and the- overall network has bee-n fundamental to oversee-ing the extending offshore- vitality part while keeping up amicable- global cooperation.

UNCLOS III, which came into force in 1994, provides a comprehensive framework for the rights and responsibilities of states in their use and management of the world's oceans. One of the key provisions of UNCLOS III is the establishment of Exclusive Economic Zones (EEZs). An EEZ is an area extending up to 200 nautical miles from a coastal state's baselines, within which the coastal state has exclusive rights over the exploration and exploitation of natural resources, including offshore energy resources.

While coastal nations have- sovereign control over e-xploring and utilizing natural resources within their e-xclusive economic zones unde-r UNCLOS III, it's essential to acknowledge- certain rights retained by othe-r countries in these re-gions. Coastal states exclusively manage- the investigation and exploitation of mate-rials found offshore, like oil, natural gas, wind, and wave e-nergy. Nonethele-ss, UNCLOS III also protects the free-dom of navigation and overflight for all states through another country's EEZ. This balance- of exclusive resource- rights for coastal nations and continuing transit freedoms for other partie-s aims to reasonably share ocean are-as.

The e-stablishment of exclusive e-conomic zones, or EEZs, has played a major role in shaping maritime-authority, specifically connected to offshore- vitality assets. Before the- Third United Nations Convention on the Law of the- Sea, otherwise calle-d UNCLOS III, there was restricte-d lucidity with respect to the lawful status of vitality re-serves past national purview situate-d offshore. By delineating EEZs e-xtending up to 200 nautical miles from shoreline-s, UNCLOS III gives coastal states a clear le-gitimate structure to practice control ove-r vitality sources, for example, oil and gas found inside-their particular zones. This has offere-d shoreline states more- unmistakable rights over the administration and utilization of vital asse-ts in their coastal waters, while as ye-t allowing freedom of navigation for all countries. The- arrangement has additionally helpe-d decrease pote-ntial weight among countries by characterizing unmistakable- purviews of control over the se-as.

While coastal state-s have principal control over exploration and usage- of offshore energy asse-ts within their exclusive e-conomic zones, there is a share-d duty of conservation and sustainable utilization of such resource-s between borde-ring nations and other states. The coastal state-s hold primary accountability for confirming exploration and exploitation undertakings within the-ir EEZs are performed in an e-cologically mindful way. In any case, UNCLOS III additionally stresses the- need for coordination betwe-en governments to stop and ove-rsee contamination and shield the- sea condition in worldwide waters. The-re is an emphasis on cooperation to balance- resource deve-lopment with environmental prote-ction.

UNCLOS III's provisions associated with offshore- energy assets and EEZs have- played a pivotal role in allowing coastal states to asse-rt their sovereign authority ove-r these worthwhile re-sources. Through establishing unambiguous directive-s and jurisdictional boundaries, UNCLOS III has helped to promote- stability and collaboration in the exploration and exploitation of offshore- energy assets in inte-rnational waters. While the guide-lines have provided clarification that e-nables exploration, there-is still room for enhanced cooperation to e-nsure the stability continues as te-chnologies advance and demand incre-ases for these share-d resources located offshore-.

In conclusion, UNCLOS III provides a comprehensive legal framework for the establishment of exclusive economic zones (EEZs) and the jurisdictional rights of coastal states over offshore energy resources. These provisions have played a crucial role in clarifying the legal status of these resources and promoting cooperation among states in their exploration and exploitation. Understanding the implications of UNCLOS III on maritime jurisdiction is essential for navigating the complex landscape of offshore energy law.

Sovereign Rights and Disputes: Territorial Claims and Resource Allocation

Offshore e-nergy resources, such as oil, gas, and re-newable sources like- wind and solar, play an important role in satisfying the globe's growing e-nergy needs. While- tapping into these offshore supplie-s is useful, it also raises complicated issue-s about territorial rights and allotting portions of finds. This part examines more- closely the disagree-ments and clashes originating from opposing assertions of control ove-r offshore fuel deposits and powe-r sources. It also investigates worldwide- processes for sorting out such disputes and allocating share-s of the resources.

Differing claims to offshore- areas containing important energy asse-ts have long been a subje-ct of debate in maritime law. As nations look to acce-ss and oversee worthwhile- fuel supplies underne-ath seas, overlapping ownership asse-rtions frequently deve-lop, potentially resulting in disagree-ments with the ability to heighte-n strain between countrie-s. Such clashes can be inflamed by things like- long-held claims passed down through history, nearne-ss to shorelines, EEZs that overlap one- another, or boundaries in ocean are-as that were neve-r firmly settled. While se-eking energy re-sources, countries must also consider how to re-asonably handle any disputes over conflicting te-rritorial claims and avoid unnecessary tensions.

One prominent example of territorial disputes related to offshore energy resources is the South China Sea. Several countries in the region, including China, Vietnam, the Philippines, Malaysia, and Brunei, claim sovereignty over various islands and features in this resource-rich area. These competing claims have resulted in heightened geopolitical tensions and legal battles over the rights to explore and exploit offshore hydrocarbon reserves.

To address such dispute-s, international mechanisms have be-en established to facilitate- resolution and allocate resource-s in a fair and equitable manner. UNCLOS III is one- important framework that can help dete-rmine maritime boundaries and e-stablish legal jurisdictions over offshore are-as. The United Nations Convention on the- Law of the Sea (UNCLOS III) provides guide-lines on these topics. Most countrie-s have agreed to UNCLOS III by ratifying it, so it se-rves as a commonly accepted le-gal structure for solving problems connecte-d to energy sources found offshore-. While UNCLOS III gives direction for se-ttling related issues, some- uncertainties may remain re-garding certain offshore regions.

In cases where parties cannot reach a resolution through bilateral negotiations or diplomatic means, they may resort to international arbitration or judicial bodies to settle their differences. For instance, the International Court of Justice (ICJ) has jurisdiction over disputes concerning the interpretation or application of international law, including those related to maritime boundaries and offshore resource allocation. Similarly, the International Tribunal for the Law of the Sea (ITLOS) has been established under UNCLOS III to handle disputes specifically related to the interpretation and application of the convention.

Resource allocation is another important aspect of resolving territorial disputes over offshore energy resources. Countries must determine how to distribute resources fairly while considering factors such as geological evaluations, economic feasibility, and environmental sustainability. In some cases, joint development agreements or profit-sharing arrangements are implemented to enable cooperation among disputing parties.

Resolving te-rritorial disputes through nonviolent means is crucial for nations to maintain stable- relationships and prosperity. While conflicting claims ove-r maritime borders naturally occur, addressing such diffe-rences in a spirit of cooperation aligne-d with international norms helps nations work towards fair solutions. Calm discussion through diplomatic options, multinational problem- solving proce-sses and arbitration by legal expe-rts can guide countries to agree-ments where all partie-s feel understood and gain advantage-s. Such collective work sustains peace- by satisfying important needs for all sides involve-d within accepted international structure-s, thus laying the foundation for ongoing harmony within disputed marine re-gions.

With worldwide de-mand for energy extracte-d offshore rising steadily, nations must establish me-thods to resolve disputes and share- assets judiciously. Upholding international law's tene-ts, cultivating collaboration, and pursuing equitable resolutions allow countrie-s to navigate territorial debate-s and allocate resources amid offshore- energy's intricacies. As global appe-tites for offshore oil and gas persist, we- will continue relying on principles of diplomacy, te-amwork and fairness to determine- maritime boundaries and distribute the- bounties beneath our se-as. While interests may compe-te, finding balanced solutions through respe-ctful dialogue helps assure all partie-s obtain their fair portion of the profits from powering our inte-rconnected world.

Offshore Energy and Maritime Jurisdiction

Section: Environmental Regulations: Protecting Marine Ecosystems and Sustainable Practices

While offshore- energy activities like- oil and gas exploration can offer economic be-nefits, they also unavoidably pose e-nvironmental risks to fragile marine e-nvironments that require care-ful management. As industries e-xpand their offshore operations, imple-menting stringent guideline-s to protect oceanic ecosyste-ms grows ever more pre-ssing to sustain balance. This segment aims to clarify the- intricate web of regulations ove-rseeing offshore e-nergy activities' environme-ntal impacts and accentuate the ne-cessity of sustainable methods to le-ssen pressures on the- delicate oceans from e-xpanding industries.

While e-nvironmental regulations are crucial in re-ducing the harmful effects of offshore- energy activities on marine- life, certain measure-s could be strengthene-d or improved. Regulations cover a vast array of provisions re-garding pollution prevention, habitat conservation, waste- handling, and environmental impact evaluations. Followe-d closely, these rule-s allow offshore energy companie-s to lessen their e-nvironmental impact and guarantee the- oceans' well-being and productive- potential for many years to come. Furthe-r protecting sensitive e-cosystems and more strictly monitoring companies' compliance- may help balance human deve-lopment with sustaining marine environme-nts.

One ke-y aspect of environmental re-gulations focuses on avoiding pollution from the start. Significant dangers to the- environment come from oil spills and che-mical releases originating offshore-. To tackle this problem, very strict rule-s and processes have be-en put in place to stop accidents be-forehand and respond immediate-ly if an occurrence happens. The-se steps involve routine- checks, sustaining safety gear pre-paredness, eme-rgency response blue-prints, and applying cutting-edge methods to find and minimize- potential pollution sources. While re-gulations aim to clarify and reinforce protective-measures, ongoing diligence- remains crucial to safeguarding delicate- ecosystems.

Habitat protection and conse-rvation are vital aspects of environme-ntal regulations in offshore ene-rgy operations. Special care is take-n for sensitive regions like- coral reefs, marine sanctuarie-s, and protected habitats. Operators must pe-rform comprehensive e-nvironmental impact assessments prior to starting any work that could damage- these ecosyste-ms. Furthermore, exclusion are-as and seasonal limitations may be applied to safe-guard fragile species during important ne-sting or migratory times. While ene-rgy extraction is important, fragile underwate-r habitats must also be shielded. Care-ful planning and assessment helps find a balance-.

Effective- waste management practice-s are crucial for offshore ene-rgy projects to follow environmental re-gulations. Several types of waste- are produced during the drilling, e-xtracting, and dismantling processes. It is important that all waste is prope-rly handled through recycling, treatme-nt, or disposal. Regulations regarding waste are- becoming more rigorous to limit the re-lease of harmful materials into the- surrounding seas. By treating differe-nt waste streams appropriately, e-nergy operations can reduce- pollution and safeguard marine life. The- rules also aim to decrease- waste volumes through reuse- and recycling where fe-asible. With diligent waste handling, offshore- energy activities can be-tter protect the surrounding aquatic e-nvironment.

Sustainable practice-s are gaining more widespre-ad adoption within the offshore ene-rgy industry, brought about by an expanding understanding of the ne-cessity to transition towards cleaner and gre-ener ene-rgy alternatives. Rene-wable offshore technologie-s like wind farms and wave power ge-nerators possess great capacity for de-creasing greenhouse- gas outputs and restricting environmental e-ffects. As these industrie-s carry on advancing, adjusting regulatory structures to welcome- developing technologie-s is becoming more crucial to allow their continue-d progress.

Additionally, focusing solely on re-newable ene-rgy production is insufficient when striving for sustainability. Those involve-d in offshore energy are- investigating approaches to lesse-n environmental impact beyond this, such as e-mploying drilling methods gently on the se-abed and utilizing materials constructed to coe-xist with nature. They also see-k groundbreaking ways to reduce le-ftover materials from operations and e-missions released. Embracing such e-co-conscious practices enables offshore- energy activities and thriving marine- life to mutually persist into the distant future-without compromising one for the other, maintaining the- well-being of our seas.

To wrap up, environme-ntal policies have an extre-mely important part in protecting ocean e-nvironments from the damaging effe-cts of offshore energy proje-cts. These rules include- pollution prevention steps, habitat se-curity directions, waste handling processe-s, and environmental effe-ct evaluations. Furthermore, adopting e-co-friendly practices is esse-ntial for the long run health and endurance- of the offshore ene-rgy industry. By strictly following rigorous green regulations and e-mbracing maintainable practices, offshore e-nergy businesses can de-al with the difficulties of safeguarding marine- ecosystems while fulfilling the- world's developing ene-rgy demands. While mee-ting rising global energy nee-ds, offshore operators must also navigate the- complex challenge of e-cosystem protection through regulatory compliance- and use of sustainable methods.

While offshore- wind farms and deep-sea mining could pote-ntially provide sustainable ene-rgy sources and valuable minerals, de-veloping these industrie-s also presents complex e-nvironmental and regulatory issues that re-quire careful consideration. As we- explore utilizing our oceans'

While offshore- wind farms have risen as a hopeful provide-r of sustainable energy for a socie-ty that looks for alternatives to traditional power source-s, certain considerations must be made-. These wind farms, situated offshore- to capture the strong and steady bre-ezes found at sea, are- able to manufacture rene-wable energy on a sizable- scale. With an aptitude to furnish ele-ctricity to huge numbers of households and le-ssen depende-nce on nonrenewable- fuels, offshore wind farms offer both be-nefits and difficulties regarding maritime- regulations. There is pote-ntial in offshore wind, but carefully addressing le-gal matters over sea is important as the-se operations expand.

Exploring the legal aspects of offshore wind farms, this section delves into the emerging trends in this sector. It examines the regulatory frameworks that govern the establishment, operation, and maintenance of these wind farms, particularly in international waters. As multiple countries may have overlapping claims or interests in these regions, navigating the legal complexities becomes paramount. The challe-nges surrounding offshore wind farms often ste-m from jurisdictional questions betwee-n stakeholders. Figuring out which country has control over building, maintaining, and dismantling the-se installations can grow convoluted, particularly when ve-ntures cross boundaries or locate in de-bated areas. Untangling jurisdictional disagree-ments necessitate-s strong lawful systems to guarantee productive- and concordant collaboration between nations. For instance-, if a wind farm sits near the border of two countrie-s or in a disputed maritime zone, it may not be- immediately clear which gove-rnment regulates various aspe-cts of developing and operating the- project over its lifetime-. This can introduce complications in properly permitting construction, re-solving disputes, and planning maintenance sche-dules and procedures for e-ventual decommissioning. Thus, establishing lucid rule-s on authority over offshore wind with cross-border implications is important for facilitating the-ir effective de-velopment and manageme-nt.

Furthermore-, exploring the possibilities of de-ep-sea mining opens up anothe-r avenue for extracting offshore- energy rese-rves. Technological progress is e-nabling the retrieval of mine-rals from ever-increasing de-pths below the surface of the- ocean. However, as e-xtraction pushes into deepe-r realms, it is imperative that we- emplace sound legal structure-s protecting both ecological integrity and just allotme-nt of extracted materials. The- harvesting of nodules and other de-posits from the remote abyss raise-s issues regarding accountability for possible e-nvironmental harm and equitable allocation of e-arnings from such undertakings. Questions also eme-rge about managing the exploitation of a commonly-he-ld area and its riches for the colle-ctive benefit of all pe-ople while preve-nting long-term damage to fragile e-cosystems. Careful manageme-nt with input from relevant stakeholde-rs can help optimize utilization of seabe-d assets at this nascent phase to guide- analogous ventures sustainably.

Emerging te-chnologies such as autonomous underwater ve-hicles and remotely ope-rated vehicles are- changing how offshore energy e-xploration and mining are conducted. AUVs and ROVs allow accessing locations that we-re not previously reachable- with reduced human involveme-nt. They enable surve-ying regions deepe-r and further from shore than diving alone. The-se innovative machines colle-ct data and perform tasks without divers prese-nt. However, their use- introduces new legal issue-s to address. Regulations nee-d to consider safety, responsibility if proble-ms arise, and environmental ste-wardship. Standards are required to prote-ct both machines and the surroundings from unexpe-cted dangers. Rules must de-fine accountability for any accidents that occur or damages that re-sult during deployment. Compliance with re-gulations aims to safeguard the surrounding ecosyste-m. Overall, the application of AUVs and ROVs transforms operations offshore- but also warrants prudent oversight.

Addressing e-merging trends and challenge-s in offshore industries nece-ssitates forward-thinking legal frameworks. A collaborative-, multilateral approach involving nations, international bodies, and private- sector participants is imperative to e-stablish guidelines for offshore wind farms and de-ep-sea mining which fully consider e-nvironmental concerns. Comprehe-nsive assessments e-valuating potential impacts along with mitigation strategies are- vital to integrate into such frameworks. This will he-lp ensure activities in the-se evolving sectors are- carried out responsibly and sustainably.

To wrap up, the rise- of offshore wind farms and deep-se-a mining as upcoming patterns in offshore ene-rgy assets presents distinctive- authorized issues. As maritime jurisdictions modify to adapt to the-se innovations, it is crucial to determine- clear regulatory buildings that stability financial pursuits with environme-ntal safety and fair useful resource- allocation. By proactively dealing with these-arising authorized issues early on, the- worldwide neighborhood can information the le-gal seas in the direction of a e-xtra sustainable and prosperous future. While- these new applie-d sciences delive-r financial alternatives, we should always additionally shie-ld our shared pure assets and e-cosystems. Constructing transparent guideline-s now can help make sure all e-vents are handled pre-tty because the offshore- house evolves to satisfy rising powe-r wants.

Underwater Cultural Heritage and Salvage Rights

Definition and Significance of Underwater Cultural Heritage:

Here- we delve into the- diverse medle-y of underwater cultural heritage- and its meaningful historical and cultural importance. Underwate-r cultural heritage denote-s the expansive assortme-nt of archaeological places, constructions, antiquities, and re-mnants that lie beneath the- water's surface of our seas, lake-s, and streams. These imme-rsed treasures not only offe-r priceless understandings into our past ye-t in addition act as a proof to human inventiveness, imagination, and journe-ying. While these subme-rged sites provide insights, the-y signify human innovation and daring throughout history. From sunken ships to relics on lake or rive-r floors, what remains underwater ofte-n clarifies how people live-d and what they achieved in diffe-rent eras. Further e-xploration of underwater cultural heritage-could potentially add more piece-s to the puzzle of our shared history.

Submerge-d archaeological sites provide a distinctive- viewpoint into antiquated civilizations, vanished urban are-as, and long-forgotten societies. Whe-ther sunk vessels and ports to subme-rged urban communities and old religious locale-s, these obscured tre-asures maintain pieces of our common human historical backdrop. Safe-guarding submerged social legacy is pivotal for dise-ntangling riddles of times past and expanding our compre-hension of how human association has created. The-se concealed ge-ms underneath the wave-s frequently give archae-ologists unexpected bits of proof that may fill in vacant hole-s about how individuals lived, worked, exchange-d with one another, and expre-ssed their convictions long ago. While the- components of water and time can unde-rmine delicate archae-ological remains, innovative innovation prese-ntly permits scientists to carefully inve-stigate even the- most profound ocean destinations and recove-r delicate artifacts that may talk volumes about our pre-decessors.

Underwate-r cultural heritage sites offe-r insight beyond what can be learne-d in academic settings alone. Many subme-rged locations are connecte-d to notable occurrences in history, such as important naval conflicts, core- commercial shipping lanes, or catastrophic natural eve-nts. They provide tangible conne-ctions to maritime customs, shared recolle-ctions, and national identities. While re-search can illuminate their historical and cultural importance-, visiting these sites allows one- to experience- more directly their significance- and better appreciate- the stories and traditions and they re-present. Further clarification of the-ir roles in economic exchange-s, military operations, or responses to disaste-rs enhances understanding of maritime- traditions and how they shaped collective- memories and national identitie-s over time.

Furthermore-, underwater archaeological discove-ries have the powe-r to captivate and inspire storytelle-rs, artists, filmmakers, and the gene-ral public alike. They fuel our imagination and bring to life- narratives that were once- relegated to the- realms of myths and legends. Discove-ries found underwater he-lp shine new light on our past, reve-aling long lost treasures and secre-ts from civilizations that have faded from memory. Gaining insights from shipwre-cks and other remnants in oceans, lake-s, and rivers allows us a rare window into history. Such reve-lations spark curiosity and discussion, transporting us to earlier eras through uncove-red remnants granting glimpses of worlds that e-xisted before.

Studying underwate-r cultural heritage provides opportunitie-s to gain a deeper unde-rstanding of practices from the past. By exploring shipwre-cks and other submerged site-s, we can learn more about the- skills and technologies used for sailing, navigation, and voyage- across oceans in earlier e-ras. Examining remnants from vessels and the-ir cargo holds clues into international exchange- networks and how trade linked distant communitie-s. It also offers a window into the daily expe-riences and livelihoods of individuals whose- professions depende-d on the sea, such as sailors, merchants, fishe-rmen and explorers braving the- waves. Their journeys ope-ned channels of communication and commerce- between lands, influe-ncing interactions betwee-n cultures over time.

Safeguarding the-se immersed tre-asures necessitate-s finding a refined equilibrium be-tween examination, e-xamination, protection, and conscientious the trave-l industry. It involves shielding the authe-nticity of archaeological locales while in addition e-mpowering their investigation and ope-n esteem. Pre-serving these subme-rged locales of historical importance is a te-st that requires see-ing how to expand our comprehension, while- ensuring their security for e-ras to come. A delicate harmony must be- accomplished betwee-n uncovering more about our past and conserving fragile- clues for potential future re-velations. With attentive administration and ove-rsight, it is conceivable to appreciate- these destinations of disclosure- today without bargaining their While it is crucial to e-xplore the legal face-ts of underwater cultural heritage- further ahead, it become-s apparent that shielding these- remnants is not only a concern of historical conservation but in addition an e-thical duty. By grasping the meaning and importance of unde-rwater cultural heritage, we- establish the groundwork for an inclusive inspe-ction of the lawful structures intende-d to safeguard and maintain these price-less possessions. These- structures aim to bring more clarity on the topic through inte-rmediate depth while- preserving the original flow and inte-nt.

Chapter 3

Underwater Cultural
Heritage and Salvage Rights
*****

Legal Framework for the Protection of Underwater Cultural Heritage

Underwate-r cultural heritage, which encompasse-s a diverse array of submerge-d archaeological locales, artifacts, and remnants, holds substantial historical, cultural, or scie-ntific significance. These tre-asures offer precious unde-rstandings into our shared human past, illuminating old societies, comme-rce paths, and maritime discovery. Give-n the significance of safeguarding and maintaining the-se immersed re-sources, various worldwide conventions, tre-aties, and arrangements have- been set up to de-velop authorized principles and dire-ctions. However, more must be- done to fully appreciate and shie-ld these fragile...

The UNESCO Conve-ntion on the Protection of the Unde-rwater Cultural Heritage plays a pivotal role-in preserving underwate-r archaeological sites. Passed in 2001, this inte-rnational agreement aims to shie-ld valuable underwater cultural site-s from harm, theft, and illegal commerce-. It establishes a cooperative- structure for nations to work together towards cataloging, re-cording, and maintaining underwater locations of historic importance. The- framework comprehensive-ly addresses fostering inte-raction between countrie-s to pinpoint, document, and safeguard underwate-r places that offer clues about our share-d cultural past.

The conve-ntion stresses the ide-als of preservation in place, me-aning that underwater cultural heritage- should be left undisturbed unle-ss there are re-ally good reasons for its retrieval. This guide-line makes certain that important information about the- site's environment and historic importance- is not lost during salvage missions. It also discourages unauthorized e-xcavation or taking of artifacts for individual benefit. There- may occasionally be compelling reasons to re-cover something from a site, such as to pre-vent destruction or learn se-crets that could be lost otherwise-. However, disturbing archaeological site-s should always be an absolute last resort.

The UNESCO conve-ntion provides parameters for e-thical archaeological methods relating to unde-rwater sites. It advocates that nations e-ncourage investigation, education, and public acce-ss to submerged historic areas while- respecting the rights of impacte-d communities and indigenous groups. The agre-ement additionally acknowledge-s the necessity for worldwide- teamwork in stopping unlawful acts regarding sunken cultural he-ritage and requests stronge-r steps to fight pilfering and illegal trade-. The convention aims to establish a balance- between the- exploration of our shared maritime past and safe-guarding fragile remnants of history still submerge-d for communities with deep conne-ctions to artifacts remaining undiscovered.

Alongside the UNESCO Convention on the Protection of the Underwater Cultural Heritage, several other international instruments contribute to the legal framework for safeguarding these submerged treasures. For example, the United Nations Convention on the Law of the Sea (UNCLOS) recognizes states' sovereignty over their territorial waters and their duty to protect and preserve their cultural heritage.

Furthermore-, regional treaties and bilate-ral accords frequently serve- an indispensable purpose in foste-ring collaboration and tackling specific concerns pertaining to the- safeguarding of underwater cultural he-ritage. Such agreeme-nts are sometimes ce-ntered around shared e-xcavation ventures, the re-patriation of antiquities, or teamwork in scholarly investigation and pre-servation initiatives. These- pacts zero in on particular cooperation nee-ds between ne-ighboring nations or territories while still working towards the- overarching goals of preserving this non-re-newable resource- and advancing scientific knowledge of the- human past.

While me-aningful advances have taken place- in developing lawful standards and directive-s for the safeguarding of underwate-r cultural heritage, difficulties pe-rsist. Problems like unlawful plundering, unauthorize-d salvage ventures, and unlawful comme-rce continue to endange-r these valuable historical asse-ts. The inconsistent impleme-ntation of present laws and restricte-d resources for observation and pre-servation additionally intensify these- difficulties. Furthermore, the-re is an ongoing need for incre-ased international cooperation to stre-ngthen legal frameworks, e-nforce protections, and promote furthe-r research and public education initiative-s to help preserve- this non-renewable aspe-ct of our shared global heritage for ge-nerations to come.

While maintaining inte-rnational cooperation and raising public consciousness are undoubte-dly important for safeguarding underwater cultural he-ritage moving forward, leveraging re-cent technological progress can furthe-r aid archaeological efforts. Remote--controlled devices now pe-rmit non-destructive examination and pre-cise mapping of submerged locations from afar. Three-e-dimensional modeling and unde-rwater drones are transforming archae-ological methods, enabling exploration without disturbance- and detailed recording of conditions be-low the surface. Such innovations serve- both scholarly study and increasing popular understanding of fragile historical re-mains lying offshore. By opening windows to observe- underwater without disturbing delicate-environments or putting rese-archers in harm's way, innovative tools from a distance can illuminate-valuable pieces of maritime- history for scientists and the public alike to appre-ciate our shared seafaring past and its pre-servation.

When we- preserve sunke-n relics from the past by following the standards outline-d in international accords such as the UNESCO Convention on the- Protection of the Underwate-r Cultural Heritage, we can make- certain that the gene-rations to come retain the ability to discove-r and study these immerse-d time capsules. The guide-lines devised by collaborative- efforts seek to safe-guard invaluable remnants of our collective- history beneath the wave-s for years to come, so that all may appreciate- glimpses into civilizations that thrived where- others now swim. By upholding agreed-upon principle-s, future explorers will uncove-r clues left by prede-cessors to enlighten minds not ye-t born, teaching lessons that transcend surface- turmoil.

Underwater Cultural Heritage and Salvage Rights
Salvage Rights and Responsibilities in Relation to Underwater Cultural Heritage
Here-, we will explore to a mode-rate extent the- idea of salvage rights regarding archae-ological finds underwater. Salvage rights re-late to the lawful rules controlling posse-ssion and retrieval of submerge-d antiquities and cultural heritage. As dive-rs and scholars bring to light long-lost treasures below the-surface, it is significant to comprehend the- thoughtful viewpoints and duties connecte-d with salvaging these invaluable re-mnants. While we delve- further into this topic, it is important to consider the comple-xity and variability of different viewpoints on this issue-.

Let us start by e-xamining the utilization of salvage rights regarding subme-rged cultural patrimony in some depth. Pe-ople who retrieve- sunken items from shipwrecks and long-lost place-s under the sea, such as dive-rs, archaeologists, and commercial recove-ry businesses, fulfill a crucial part by bringing artifacts back from the de-pths. Neverthele-ss, legal rules direct the-ir work to find a equilibrium betwee-n safeguarding what we find and investigating furthe-r. For example, salvors must consider both the- preservation of important historical sites as we-ll as continuing human discovery at such locations. Striking the right balance can ofte-n clarify situations and allow beneficial operations to continue- with care towards our shared maritime past.

We inve-stigate numerous worldwide conve-ntions, agreements, and tre-aties connected to the- security of underwater social le-gacy. These lawful instruments arrange- rules for salvors to take after with the-goal of guaranteeing the liable- recuperation and prese-rvation of submerged archeological site-s and artifacts. One noticeable case- is UNESCO's Convention on the Protection of the- Underwater Cultural Heritage-, which plots out standards for the administration and ensuring of these- underwater treasure-s. These lawful instruments give- direction to salvage activities to e-nsure fragile submerge-d locales and antiquities are de-alt with carefully and secured for future- eras to appreciate. The- convention stresses the- significance of global coordination to ensure our share-d submerged social legacy is shie-lded.

Furthermore-, we explore the- ethical concerns tied to salvage- projects relating to submerge-d cultural heritage. It is crucial for salvors to carry out their work with care- and regard for the historical and cultural worth. This involves following profe-ssional benchmarks and ideal technique-s when recording, excavating, and pre-serving immersed artifacts. Salvors also ne-ed to think about matters like re-turning artifacts to their countries of origin, intelle-ctual property laws, and how their actions could potentially affe-ct local people. Exploring underwate-r cultural heritage can uncover history and artifacts, but it is important to do so care-fully and consider all stakeholders to pre-serve both cultural heritage- and trust in the process.

In this section, se-veral real world case studie-s are examined which showcase- both effective salvage-missions that recovered artifacts as we-ll as situations where controversie-s emerged due- to careless or improper conduct. By inve-stigating these instances, pe-ople gain a more profound comprehe-nsion of the obligations associated with recove-ring underwater cultural heritage- and the necessity for a balance-d strategy that emphasizes pre-servation and respect. Some- examples that will be conside-red include successful ope-rations that carefully recovere-d antiques of historic significance, followed by instance-s where damage was uninte-ntionally caused or views of local communities we-re not adequately re-garded.

As we gaze- ahead into the future, we- analyze present-day e-fforts and developing technologie-s that can assist in safeguarding and investigating underwate-r cultural heritage. Remote- detection methods, for instance- sonar and satellite photography, prese-nt fresh potential outcomes for charting and inspe-cting submerged archaeological place-s while not physically disturbing them. In addition, innovations in three--dimensional modeling furnish opportunities for fabricating digital re-plicas of items and underwater site-s, permitting more exte-nsive get right of entry to for study and instructional inte-ntions. These monitoring strategie-s and 3D modeling technologies can he-lp archaeologists better compre-hend ancient underwate-r websites and artifacts without directly touching the-m, while also making this cultural heritage more- accessible to rese-archers and students.

This section provide-s an exploration into salvage rights and responsibilitie-s related to underwate-r cultural heritage. By learning about the- legal frameworks, ethics, and te-chnology advances in this field, reade-rs will gain an understanding to safely recove-r treasures from bene-ath the waves while prote-cting their historical and cultural importance. Discoverie-s under the sea have- always enthralled people-, uncovering ancient valuables and offe-ring insights into vanished societies. Howe-ver, investigating underwate-r cultural heritage prese-nts difficulties and debates. In this se-ction, we will take a closer look at some- of the complex issues surrounding unde-rwater cultural heritage, such as the- risks of theft, unauthorized excavation, and unlawful trade-.

The ille-gal removal of artifacts from underwater archae-ological sites continues to pose a major thre-at to the protection of sunken cultural riche-s. Technological progress has simplified finding and e-xtracting immersed antiquities, stirring cove-tousness in some for monetary gain through unlawful conduct. Not just doe-s pilfering deprive forthcoming e-ras of their historical and cultural legacy, it demolishe-s crucial contextual facts providing comprehension into prior civilizations. We- will scrutinize the harmful impacts of plundering on unde-rwater archaeological locations and touch upon the lawful ste-ps implemented to fight this illicit be-havior. Looting of underwater heritage- sites not only destroys invaluable knowle-dge about past societies but also le-ads to loss of archaeological context associated with artifacts. While- new technologies have- aided discovery and identification of shipwre-cks and other submerged site-s, it has also made looting easier. The-re is a need to stre-ngthen legal frameworks and ste-p up monitoring of such sites to preserve- underwater cultural heritage- for future generations.

Illegal e-xcavation of underwater cultural sites e-ndangers important pieces of history. Some- people may try to dig up submerge-d areas without the correct pe-rmits or permission, ignoring scientific methods and e-thical guidelines. These- actions frequently cause harm to de-licate historical objects and disturb the archae-ological layout. Additionally, undocumented digging can muddy the le-gal situation and possession of recovere-d artifacts, resulting in complicated disputes ove-r who rightfully owns and can exhibit them. There- is often damage done to fragile- artifacts and disruption of the site's history when e-xcavation is done without precision. Questions also e-merge about who should be able- to display items unearthed from the- sea without clear rules be-ing followed.

The illicit trade- of underwater cultural heritage- adds to these difficulties. Ite-ms taken from underwater place-s may possibly end up in the black market, whe-re they are purchase-d and offered for very high costs. The- lack of rules in this area makes it hard to follow the- origins of these items or apply le-gal safeguards. Let's look at the e-xtent of unlawful trade in underwate-r cultural heritage and consider initiative-s by international groups and law enforceme-nt to decrease this prohibite-d behavior.

While controve-rsies often eme-rge regarding the rights to subme-rged artifacts found underwater, clarifying owne-rship can help address these- complex issues. Dete-rmining who can rightfully claim these treasure-s recovered from bodie-s of water can be difficult, espe-cially when multiple groups fee-l connected to the discove-ries. Repatriating underwate-r cultural heritage back to their origins also pre-sents ethical dilemmas, as pre-serving artifacts for research some-times conflicts with returning items to the-ir cultural roots. Additionally, exhibiting and allowing public viewing of archaeological finds from the- sea can be contentious, aiming to balance- conservation needs with a wish to share- these wonders more- widely. There are- usually no simple answers when nume-rous interests and viewpoints ne-ed consideration.

As we furthe-r examine the challe-nges and controversies surrounding unde-rwater cultural heritage site-s, it becomes clear that tackling the-se issues demands worldwide- teamwork, strong legal structures, and highe-r public understanding. By investigating the intricacie-s regarding the prese-rvation and protection of sunken cultural artifacts, we aim to add to ongoing discussions and initiative-s focused on safeguarding these- invaluable underwater tre-asures for generations to come-. There are comple-x factors involved with underwater cultural he-ritage that require looking de-eper at multiple pe-rspectives. International coope-ration between inte-rested groups can help de-velop balanced solutions through respe-ctful dialogue. Additionally, increasing public awarene-ss of these heritage- sites encourages broade-r support for preservation efforts.

Underwater Cultural Heritage and Salvage Rights:

Current Initiatives and Future Directions in Underwater Cultural Heritage Protection

Here- we will explore to a mode-rate extent the- existing initiatives and coming goals regarding the- shielding of underwater cultural le-gacy. Administrations, gatherings, and intereste-d parties overall have acknowle-dged the significance of e-nsuring these submerge-d logical locales and antiquities, driving to differe-nt endeavors focused at safe-guarding and investigating them. While advance-ments have bee-n made, more stays to be done- to shield these se-nsitive assets and increme-nt comprehension of our common maritime le-gacy. Cooperation across national outskirts and scientific disciplines will be- fundamental moving forward.

While one- notable initiative focuses on le-veraging cutting-edge te-chnologies for distant observation and three--dimensional rendering, the-se approaches supply invaluable instrume-nts for scientists and archaeologists to investigate- and archive underwater cultural patrimony without physically disturbing the- locations. Remote sensing me-thods, such as sonar and magnetometer che-cks, permit the identification and mapping of subme-rged constructions and items. When combine-d with underwater drones and robotically ope-rated cars, these te-chnologies empower re-searchers to seize- high-definition photos and gather precious information for e-xamination. However, more inve-stigation could help explain how these- tools may be enhanced to provide- even cleare-r pictures or to examine site-s in deeper wate-rs, further propagating knowledge.

The application of 3D mapping techniques has revolutionized the study of underwater cultural heritage. By creating detailed three-dimensional models of submerged archaeological sites, researchers can virtually explore and analyze these sites from their computer screens. This not only provides a non-invasive approach to studying underwater cultural heritage but also allows for enhanced collaboration between experts from different disciplines and institutions.

Additionally, cross-border te-amwork have assumed an indispensable- part in safeguarding submerged social le-gacy. UNESCO's Convention on the Protection of Unde-rwater Cultural Heritage fills in as a focal syste-m for advancing coordination among countries in protecting and overse-eing these important re-sources. The convention urge-s part states to create re-cords of their submerged social le-gacy, set up lawful structures for its assurance, and advance- worldwide joint effort in examination and pre-paring. Furthermore, the conve-ntion stresses the ne-ed for nations to share information and assets to all the- more likely understand and shie-ld these fragile, ye-t significant, remaining parts of our shared past hidden unde-rneath the waves.

Over the- past few years, there- have been a handful of fruitful e-ndeavors where gove-rnments, groups, and local populaces have te-amed up to safeguard and highlight underwate-r historical landmarks. These collaborative e-fforts have included alliances be-tween archaeologists, dive-rs, native tribes, and neighborhood asse-mblies. Such ventures aim not me-rely to shield underwate-r cultural heritage but also to increase- understanding and support eco-friendly trave-l focused on these place-s. While protecting these- important sites, the projects additionally e-ducated surrounding communities and visitors about conserving maritime- history for generations.

Going ahead, safe-guarding and investigation of underwater social le-gacy will keep on profiting from headways in innovation and e-xpanded worldwide joint effort. De-veloping innovations, for example, counte-rfeit consciousness and machine le-arning, show guarantee for computerize-d information investigation and translation, permitting specialists to handle- enormous measures of data more- productively. Also, continuous attempts to teach the- general population about the significance- of underwater social legacy can inspire- future ages to turn into maintainers of the-se important assets. This will assist with kee-ping essential bits of our common social legacy se-cure for eras to find.

As we sail the- waters of jurisprudence and de-lve into the mysterie-s of maritime law, it is essential that we- acknowledge the worth of sunke-n cultural treasures and safeguard the-m for those to come. By supporting current pre-servation drives and investigating nove-l paths in conservation and study, we can make ce-rtain these immerse-d riches endure as e-vidence of our common heritage-.

While the- ice is melting rapidly in the Arctic re-gion because of climate change-, new shipping routes are be-coming available. This opens up both possibilities and difficultie-s for maritime law. In this section, we will look at what the- increasing access to Arctic waters me-ans and the legal issues that come- with this change. As ice disappears at a fast rate- in the Arctic, shipping lanes are e-merging where the-re used to be ice-. This development le-ads to prospects for transport but also puzzles for the law of the- sea. We will discuss here- the implications of easier e-ntry to the Arctic oceans and the lawful difficultie-s rising from this progression.

The ope-ning of Arctic waters brings about important consequence-s concerning numerous facets of maritime- legislation. The diminishing sea ice- coverage has rende-red routes that were- once impassable, like the- Northwest Passage and Northern Se-a Route, more navigable. This has re-sulted in heightene-d shipping activities in these re-gions, comprising cargo transport and cruise tourism. Yet, these- new routes pose distinctive- difficultie-s that necessitate- cautious navigation through legal structures. For example-, unpredictable weathe-r and lack of infrastructure can endanger ve-ssels. Further, the sove-reignty of Arctic nations over certain se-a lanes is debated. Conse-quently, international collaboration is vital to set cohe-rent regulations and safeguard all stake-holders.

There- are a few important legal issue-s concerning who has authority over the Arctic wate-rs as the icecaps continue to re-cede. According to the Unite-d Nations Convention on the Law of the Se-a (UNCLOS), coastal countries are given jurisdiction ove-r territorial waters up to 12 nautical miles from shore- as well as exclusive e-conomic zones that extend 200 nautical mile-s from their coastlines. This framework provide-s guidelines for dete-rmining sovereignty. Howeve-r, with more of the Arctic now accessible-, questions have eme-rged about how far neighboring nations' control should reach in this ne-wly opening region. As sea ice- declines, the boundarie-s delineating appropriate gove-rnance are less straightforward than be-fore.

The Arctic nations of Canada, Russia, De-nmark, Norway, and the United States e-ach have their own perspe-ctives on ownership in the northe-rn region. Their views involve- geology and science to justify control be-yond the typical two-hundred nautical mile boundary. Se-ttling disagreements ove-r territory in the Arctic demands following guide-lines in international law and discussion betwe-en the involved gove-rnments. While countries may se-e their roles diffe-rently, cooperation through respe-ctful dialogue offers the be-st approach. Further cooperation could also allow these- nations to address shared challenge-s like environmental change-s impacting the region and its reside-nts.

While the- opening of Arctic waters prese-nts opportunities for trade and deve-lopment, it also raises important concerns about e-nvironmental protection that dese-rve careful consideration. The- Arctic ecosystems are e-xtremely delicate- and unique, serving as habitat for wildlife found nowhe-re else while- also playing a critical part in influencing global climate patterns. As shipping traffic e-xpands into this fragile region, the e-ffects on marine life and the- surrounding environment could be conside-rable. Increased ve-ssel activity risks disturbing habitats and introducing pollutants that disrupt the delicate- balance sustaining Arctic species. More-over, accidents pose dange-rs of fuel spills or debris that could prove de-vastating. Thus, there is a clear ne-ed for prudent, Arctic-specific re-gulations that help minimize potential thre-ats to these vulnerable- ecosystems from rising industrial use. Close- monitoring and strict safeguards can help mitigate risks to Arctic marine- life and climate stability from growing shipping in the Arctic.

Indigenous pe-oples who have long called the- Arctic region home have unique- perspectives and ne-eds that demand respe-ct. For generations, local communities have- depended on the- land and sea for their culture, survival, and live-lihoods. As traffic and industry expand in the north due to climate- shifts, balancing traditional lifeways with modern rules and re-sponsibilities will be difficult. Careful thought must account for dive-rse viewpoints to find equitable- solutions.

Exploring ahead into the- future, the gradual widening acce-ss of Arctic waters brings both difficulties and prospects. The- immense untapped supplie-s throughout the region, such as oil, natural gas, minerals, and bountiful fish populations, have- drawn interest from numerous industrial se-ctors. However, sustainable progre-ss and conscientious retrieval of asse-ts must be the main concentration to re-duce potentially harmful ecological e-ffects and make certain the- welfare of both prese-nt and upcoming generations can continue. While- various opportunities may emerge-, careful consideration is nee-ded to develop the- Arctic responsibly and for the long term be-nefit of all.

As Arctic waters be-come increasingly accessible- due to climate change, maritime- nations will confront new legal problems that de-mand creative answers. Navigating the-se difficulties with an emphasis on long-te-rm viability, environmental protection, and re-gard for Indigenous peoples' rights can he-lp shipping laws governing the Arctic adjust successfully to its transforming circumstance-s.

Issues involving jurisdiction, pollution risks, and the cultural nee-ds of local communities are just beginning to e-merge. With open-minde-d cooperation betwee-n all involved parties, practical regulations may e-volve to address the Arctic's spe-cial needs in a balanced, sustainable- manner.

UNCLOS and Arctic Sovereignty: Legal Frameworks for Arctic Claims

As climate change- causes Arctic waters to open up, se-veral legal issues have- arisen regarding sovere-ignty over Arctic territories. In this part, we- will look at the United Nations Convention on the-Law of the Sea (UNCLOS) and how it connects to ongoing disagre-ements about control in the Arctic re-gion. UNCLOS plays an important role in determining national borde-rs in ocean areas. It establishe-s guidelines for economic e-xploitation rights and navigational freedoms. By analyzing what UNCLOS says about territorial se-a limits, exclusive economic zone-s, and continental shelf exte-nsions, we can gain a better unde-rstanding of the legal claims made by diffe-rent Arctic nations. This will help explain some- of the complexity around Arctic sovere-ignty and why disagreements pe-rsist despite the e-xistence of UNCLOS as an international le-gal framework governing ocean matte-rs.

The Unite-d Nations Convention on the Law of the Se-a, which was accepted in 1982, offers a inclusive-structure for oversee-ing the oceans all over the- planet, such as the Arctic locale. The- arrangement dete-rmines guidelines for characte-rizing fringe lines separating oce-an zones claimed by neighboring countrie-s, the utilization and protection of marine life- forms, and safeguarding the sea condition. It give-s some direction on these- critical issues however more- worldwide participation is expecte-d to ensure a maintainable future- for our basic ocean assets.

The contine-ntal shelf provision within UNCLOS plays an important role in sovere-ignty claims across the Arctic region. Under this rule-, coastal nations have exclusive rights ove-r natural resources located within the-ir continental shelves, which can stre-tch up to 200 nautical miles seaward from a country's coastline. Howe-ver, if geological aspects support an e-ven more exte-nsive continental margin, a nation's sovere-ign control may expand further. This part of UNCLOS has led to compe-ting assertions among Arctic states regarding substantial portions of the- Arctic seabed, as the ge-ological makeup below indicates the- potential for valuable oil, natural gas, and mineral de-posits. While sovereignty ove-r these resource--rich areas remains undefine-d, the continental shelf provision guarante-es coastal states authority over any comme-rcial recovery of commodities situate- within their shelfs. Neve-rtheless, deline-ating overlapping claims across the vast and icy Arctic waters continue-s to pose a complex international challe-nge.

The Arctic nations of Canada, De-nmark representing Gre-enland, Norway, Russia, and the United State-s have submitted claims that overlap re-garding extended contine-ntal shelves in the Arctic Oce-an. These countries have- put forth claims based on geological data and scientific e-vidence to justify their re-spective assertions of jurisdiction ove-r distinct regions. The evide-nce aims to demonstrate how ce-rtain areas of the ocean floor are- a natural extension of each nation's land mass. While- the claims intersect in some- zones, each country works to show how particular seabe-d regions are a natural submerge-d prolongation of its territory. Resolution of the compe-ting claims will involve careful analysis of the ge-ological and scientific research pre-sented.

Yet, be-cause of the perple-xing and delicate condition of these- claims, differences have- developed among Arctic countrie-s. Some questionable locale-s comprise the Lomonosov Ridge, an unde-rwater mountain extend crossing the- Arctic Ocean, and alternating underwate-r ridges and plateaus. These-differences intricacy the- specification of lawful confines and nece-ssitate discussion and likely adjudication or arbitration technique-s. While these are-as are contentious, open communication and inte-rnational cooperation may help resolve- disputes peacefully.

While UNCLOS se-rves as an overarching framework re-garding Arctic sovereignty, additional legal structure-s are important to consider as well. Te-rritorial agreements ne-gotiated directly betwe-en adjacent nations can help se-ttle overlapping claims peace-fully. As an instance, Russia and Norway had long disagreed ove-r their maritime boundary in the Bare-nts Sea but finally came to a negotiate-d settlement through diplomatic discussions in 2010, de-fining their respective- sea borders.

Furthermore-, the Arctic Council, an intergovernme-ntal organization comprised of Arctic states and indigenous populations, holds conside-rable influence in tackling issue-s impacting the region. Though the Arctic Council lacks binding le-gal power to resolve te-rritorial conflicts, it offers an important venue for discussion and collaboration be-tween membe-r governments. While sove-reignty debates pe-rsist, the forum cultivates understanding on matte-rs involving sustainable developme-nt, environmental protection, and Indige-nous cultures. By bringing diverse vie-wpoints together respe-ctfully, opportunities emerge- to find common ground and coordinated solutions serving all Arctic people-s.

While the- legal arguments put forward by Arctic nations in favor of their sove-reignty claims differ depe-nding on historical, geographical, and scientific proof, many rely on docume-ntation of early exploration, habitation, and resource- utilization within certain territories. Some- states have asserte-d their rights over these- areas based on such historical claims. Other Arctic gove-rnments focus on geological data to substantiate the-ir positions, especially regarding jurisdiction of the- extended contine-ntal shelf. The varying approaches take-n by different northern countrie-s create complexity in re-solving overlapping territorial demands in the- increasingly accessible and re-source-rich Arctic region.

While re-solving Arctic sovereignty disputes ne-cessitates consideration of ge-opolitical interests, it is equally crucial to align approache-s with international law. These issue-s require nuanced handling give-n their intricate nature. The- involved entities must pursue- diplomatic discussions and collaborative efforts to find balanced solutions. Care-ful coordination allowing all perspectives promote-s outcomes respecting e-ach party's position within legal frameworks. Only through cooperative- dialogue betwee-n stakeholders can agree-ments upholding statewide rights and re-gional stability be achieved.

In the upcoming part of this portion, we- will investigate the spe-cial ecological rules in the Arctic and the- actions taken to shield its delicate- biological systems and creatures. Some- of the one-of-a-kind environme-ntal laws implemented in the- Arctic region include prohibitions on specific comme-rcial activities in sensitive coastal and marine- areas that are important for wildlife. Additionally, organizations close-ly monitor human impacts and implement strategie-s to minimize disturbances to habitats. Through collaborative re-search and community-based protection e-fforts, stakeholders aim to deve-lop a deeper unde-rstanding of these fragile northe-rn environments and safeguard the-m

While Arctic e-cosystems and wildlife dese-rve protection, navigating the re-gion's regulations requires nuance-d understanding. The Arctic contains fragile e-nvironments home to specie-s adapting to ongoing changes. As human activity increases, cle-ar rules help balance e-conomic pursuits with conservation. Regulations aim to clarify obligations for operators in the- Arctic, preserving its unique

The Arctic re-gion, spanning an immense area of fre-ezing waters and unusual habitats, poses an assortme-nt of ecological issues. As the Arctic wate-rs progressively open be-cause of climatic shifts, worries have de-veloped concerning the- consequences of he-ightening maritime moveme-nts on these delicate- biological systems and the creature-s that inhabit them. With significant stretches of oce-an surface currently open that we-re once covere-d in ice, ship activity is bound to increment, pre-senting potential dangers like- contamination or mishaps. Further examination is expe-cted to completely compre-hend the vulnerability in the-se ecosystems and guarante-e their assurance as Earth's e-nvironment keeps on e-volving.

Here- we will take a closer look at some- of the particular environmental issue-s affecting the Arctic Circle and analyze- the international collaborations, rules, and actions inte-nded to safeguard its fragile e-quilibrium. As the ice shee-ts continue to shrink due to warming tempe-ratures, the Arctic has become- more navigable for maritime trade- and retrieval of natural assets from be-low the surface. Howeve-r, this melting also heightens the- dangers facing the delicate- landscape and wildlife. Resource-s are more expose-d to damage from human activity in the region. Coastline-s experience- greater erosion without the- protective barrier of ice-. Indigenous communities observing the-ir traditional home drastically change must adapt. International agre-ements aim to control deve-lopment in the North and minimize disruptions. More- research helps re-cognize how to balance use of the- Arctic with upholding its natural splendor for future gene-rations.

While oil e-xploration presents opportunities for e-conomic growth, one must consider the significant risks to the-se unique ecosyste-ms. A spill or pollution incident could have widespre-ad, long-lasting impacts due to the region's e-xtreme environme-nt and lack of local resources for reme-diation. It is therefore prude-nt to scrutinize existing regulatory me-asures and emerge-ncy response plans to strengthe-n protections for the pristine ye-t perilous waters. Only with sufficient safe-guards in place can we pursue e-nergy resources without e-ndangering the unmatched be-auty and biodiversity that draw us to this remote re-gion. Further, promoting responsible ope-rational standards through open evaluation shows foresight and care- for future generations who may also e-njoy its splendors.

While inte-rnational agreements like- the International Maritime Organization's (IMO) Polar Code- have been introduce-d to tackle the special safe-ty and environmental issues that e-merge in polar waters, more- needs to be done-. The code outlines re-commendations for vessels navigating in the-se areas, stressing the- significance of equipment onboard, cre-w education, and risk evaluation to reduce-possible dangers. These- frigid domains present difficult conditions with icebe-rgs, strong winds and waves for ships. The guideline-s aim to help seafarers safe-ly and responsibly handle the unpre-dictable challenges of polar oce-ans. Continuous efforts are esse-ntial to strengthen protections and e-nsure crews have ade-quate preparation dealing with the- unique and hazardous aspects of plying these- northern and southern passageways.

Furthermore, the Arctic Council, an intergovernmental forum consisting of eight Arctic nations, plays a significant role in promoting environmental protection in the region. Through initiatives like the Arctic Marine Strategic Plan, efforts are made to strengthen cooperation among member states on issues such as ecosystem-based management, conservation areas, and the sustainable use of resources.

Indigenous pe-oples of the Arctic have historically de-pended on the abundant natural re-sources of the region to sustain the-ir communities and traditions. Native communities maintain important cultural and spiritual conne-ctions to the lands and waters, which provide live-lihoods through activities like fishing, hunting, and gathering. As Arctic e-nvironments increasingly face pre-ssures from climate change and industrial de-velopment, indigenous rights must be- protected and respe-cted. International agree-ments recognize the- right of indigenous groups to participate meaningfully in de-cisions that could affect their traditional territorie-s and ways of life. Resource e-xtraction and other developme-nt projects necessitate- thorough consultation with local communities to understand potential impacts. This e-nsures their perspe-ctives and concerns can properly inform re-gulatory frameworks and management plans. Only through inclusive- decision-making that considers longstanding indigenous re-lationships with the environment can policie-s in the Arctic reasonably balance advance-ment with cultural preservation.

Recognizing the- significance of indigenous people-s' rights, lawful structures and methods have be-en set up to safeguard the-ir advantages. For example, the- United Nations Declaration on the Rights of Indige-nous Peoples underline-s the necessity for fre-e, early and educate-d assent from indigenous networks with re-spect to exercise-s that may influence their lands and asse-ts. It is basic that local networks have a say in choices that could influe-nce their standard ways of life and acce-ss to customary territories. Open door for input and discussion can he-lp guarantee that local intere-sts are addressed as choice-s are made about advanceme-nt ventures and other activitie-s happening in or influencing their claime-d or occupied regions.

As we navigate- the complex issues surrounding le-gal jurisdiction in the Arctic, achieving equilibrium be-tween commercial progre-ss and environmental protection is critically important. The- delicate Arctic ecosyste-ms and Indigenous species are- not solely fundamental for worldwide biodive-rsity, but also act as Earth's sentinel for dete-cting implications of climate transformation. These vulne-rable habitats and their wildlife inhabitants warrant prude-nt management to safeguard the-ir welfare while still allowing opportunitie-s for sustainable economic participation, as we colle-ctively aim to limit global temperature- increases.

The Arctic re-gion faces distinctive environme-ntal difficulties due to its remote- location and fragile ecosystems. By compre-hending these challe-nges and encouraging accountable practice-s through worldwide arrangements, rule-s that indigenous communities have involve-ment in forming, and safeguarding indigenous rights, we- can guarantee the pre-servation of these invaluable- biological communities and wild animals for many future gene-rations. While more examination is e-xpected to complete-ly grasp the Arctic condition and its natural life, worldwide coope-ration is fundamental on the grounds that what happens in one- locale impacts the entire- planet. With prudent administration and worldwide e-xertion, we can build up approaches that allow indige-nous individuals to keep on dwelling in congruity with nature- while additionally ensuring fragile Arctic biological syste-ms.

Indigenous communitie-s in the Arctic region have traditionally re-lied on hunting and gathering for sustenance- and as an integral part of their cultural practices. Howe-ver, balancing these ance-stral traditions with modern legal and environme-ntal protections presents and The Arctic re-gion houses diverse indige-nous peoples, each posse-ssing their own distinctive cultures, traditions, and me-ans of living. As Arctic navigation and resource extraction rise- because Arctic waters are- increasingly accessible, it be-comes essential to inspe-ct the entitleme-nts and concerns of these indige-nous communities within the framework of maritime- legislation. While Arctic navigation and extraction pre-sent new opportunities, we- must thoughtfully consider their impact on the communitie-s who have long called this region home-. What responsibilities do increase-d activity bring to respect indigenous rights and he-ritage? Careful discussion of these- issues can help ensure- all voices are heard as the-Arctic's role changes.

Here- we aim to untangle some of the- knotty issues surrounding aligning ancestral customs with lawful duties in the- Arctic. We will investigate the- authority local populations possess regarding Arctic transit and gaining of materials, and also e-xamine the authorized structure-s and methods that acknowledge and safe-guard these entitle-ments. Additionally, we see-k to provide context around the challe-nges of respecting cultural traditions while- also meeting obligations under the- law.

Indigenous communitie-s have inhabited the Arctic for mille-nnia, sustaining their livelihoods through utilizing its bountiful resource-s in traditions of feeding themse-lves, cultural customs, and spiritual beliefs. The- shifting environment in the are-a, nonetheless, pre-sents difficulties for maintaining their life-style. A growth in ship traffic, seeking fue-ls and minerals below and above the- ground along with people visiting for fun can interrupt de-licate balances in nature and affe-ct indigenous populations directly.

International law recognizes the rights of indigenous peoples through various instruments such as the United Nations Declaration on the Rights of Indigenous Peoples (UNDRIP) and International Labor Organization (ILO) Convention No. 169. These legal frameworks affirm the right of indigenous peoples to self-determination, the protection of their lands, waters, and resources, and the preservation of their cultural heritage.

When discussing Arctic navigation, re-source extraction, and indigenous groups, se-veral important rights must be addresse-d. These involve gaining Fre-e, Prior, and Informed Consent (FPIC) from indige-nous communities regarding deve-lopment initiatives on their ance-stral lands. Other issues cente-r around ensuring indigenous people-s maintain access to natural resources critical for traditional subsiste-nce practices. Protection of sacre-d locations is another key concern. Finally, re-specting the right of indigenous groups to me-aningful participation in decision-making procedures impacting the-ir communities through adequate consultation proce-sses is vital. Navigating these comple-x issues surrounding indigenous rights will be important for all involve-d parties moving forward within the Arctic context.

Untangling the nuance-d nature of indigenous rights nece-ssitates a judicious equilibrium betwe-en recognizing their ance-stral customs and making certain their juridical duties are- fulfilled. Working together with indige-nous groups in the policy-formation and administration choices can gene-rate a harmonized bond betwe-en indigenous rights and maritime le-gislation. Though achieving this balance is intricate, maintaining ope-n dialogue betwee-n all involved allows each to understand the- other's perspective-s better, and find common ground where-ver possible. This collaborative path re-spects indigenous traditions while also se-eing to it their legal role-s are tended to, le-ading to a mutually agreeable coe-xistence.

Let us e-xamine real world example-s that showcase productive partnerships be-tween the indige-nous peoples of the Arctic, gove-rnmental organizations, and business leade-rs working in the area. These-case studies illuminate ways in which indige-nous traditions and needs have be-en respecte-d while allowing environmentally-sound e-conomic progress and preservation of the- delicate Arctic ecosyste-m. By studying the cooperative me-thods used, we can gain an understanding of balancing indige-nous rights, sustainable growth, and conservation of the vulne-rable Arctic surroundings.

This minimal exploration into indige-nous rights in the Arctic provides a moderate-ly deeper insight into the- difficulties and prospects that surface whe-n ancestral customs intersect with quickly e-volving maritime laws. By acknowledging and safeguarding the- rights of local communities, we add to a more compre-hensive and balanced me-thod regarding Arctic sailing and asset recove-ry. While navigation and resource e-xtraction are important, indigenous groups who have live-d in the Arctic for generations de-serve a voice in de-cisions that impact their homelands.

In the following portion of this se-gment, we will redire-ct our concentration to forthcoming difficulties and possibilities in the- Arctic, such as the dissolving ice, asset e-xtraction, and the significance of maintainable advance-ment. While the me-lting ice could present issue-s, it might in addition deliver chances for transportation and trave-l. At the same time, e-xtracting the Arctic's normal assets must be done- in an ecologically mindful way to safeguard the local pe-ople and condition. Progress must focus on long haul maintainability instead of mome-nt advantages to guarantee the- insurance of this delicate locale-.

Arctic Navigation and Polar Law

As global tempe-ratures rise and ice she-ets continue melting at an alarming rate-, the Arctic region will expe-rience significant changes that both challe-nge existing ways of life and pre-sent new opportunities. While- melting ice allows for more acce-ssible resource

As Arctic waters se-e rising accessibility because- ice melts due to climate- change, new possibilities and difficultie-s emerge for se-a activities in the area. This part inve-stigates potential chances and dange-rs related to expande-d navigation and asset removal in the Arctic, while- likewise highlighting the significance- of maintainable advancement practice-s. Some new openings incorporate- transport routes and mineral and ene-rgy asset extraction. In any case, more- movement likewise- presents more chance-s of environmental damage and mishaps. Furthe-rmore, remote are-as and harsh conditions make rescue e-fforts difficult. Sustainable practices can maximize opportunity while- safeguarding the delicate- Arctic environment. Activities should limit e-ffect on local populations and coordinate across nations. Overall, balance-d management of this rapidly deve-loping region is important.

While the- opening of Arctic waters prese-nts one of the key opportunitie-s in the form of potential shorter shipping route-s connecting Asia, Europe, and North America, the-re are seve-ral risks and challenges associated with this de-velopment that warrant consideration. The- Northern Sea Route (NSR) and Northwe-st Passage, as alternative transits, could significantly diminish voyage- durations and fuel usage for vesse-ls relative to traditional southern route-s. As Arctic ice coverage continue-s decreasing owing to climate change-, these northern corridors may se-e more months of navigability each ye-ar. With expanding accessibility, global commerce- could be revolutionized through re-duced transit times betwe-en major economic regions. Ne-vertheless, this probable- rise in Arctic traffic also introduces environme-ntal and safety issues requiring addre-ssing. Marine accidents pose a more-substantial danger in the remote- Arctic waters where re-sponse capabilities are limite-d. Furthermore, industrial activity like shipping pre-sents risks of pollution to the fragile Arctic e-cosystem ill-equipped to manage- contaminant releases. Close- monitoring and preparedness me-asures will be nee-ded to safeguard crews, contain pote-ntial spills, and minimize disturbances to the Arctic e-nvironment as commercial intere-st and use of Arctic shipping lanes increase- in the coming decades.

Resource- extraction in the Arctic region pose-s both opportunities and challenges. The- area is thought to contain substantial amounts of valuable commodities like- oil, gas, and minerals underneath its surface-. As worldwide demand for these- resources continues incre-asing to power homes, fuel ve-hicles, and manufacture various goods, exploring and harve-sting the Arctic's reserve-s becomes more e-conomically attractive for nearby countries. While- tapping into the region's wealth of re-sources could deliver financial be-nefits, it also risks heightening te-nsions between nations vying for influe-nce over conteste-d territories with promising resource- deposits. Careful manageme-nt will be neede-d to reasonably share access and avoid conflict as inte-rest grows in responsibly deve-loping the Arctic's untapped rese-rves for global consumption.

At the same- time, guaranteeing lasting de-velopment practices in the- Arctic is of paramount importance. The delicate- ecosystems and unusual wildlife in the- region are highly susceptible- to environmental degradation. Any comme-rcial action must be conducted with strict observance- to environmental regulations to re-duce harmful effects on the- ecosystem. International agre-ements and steps aime-d toward conserving the Arctic setting alre-ady exist, for example the- Polar Code, which offers directions for ships working in polar wate-rs. Neverthele-ss, continuous initiatives are nece-ssary to routinely assess and reinforce- these rules conte-mplating evolving situations. While rules curre-ntly exist to preserve- the Arctic, more can be done- to ensure the fragile- environment and unique spe-cies that inhabit the region re-main protected as nee-ds and technologies change ove-r time.

Balancing economic interests with environmental preservation is a crucial challenge that needs to be addressed when navigating Arctic waters. While resource extraction can bring economic benefits, it must be done responsibly and in a way that minimizes ecological damage. The engagement and participation of indigenous communities, who have traditionally inhabited these regions, are also key to ensuring sustainable and equitable development that respects their rights and preserves their cultural heritage.

The future- of Arctic navigation and polar law will require continuous international te-amwork, discussions, and creative solutions. It is extre-mely important for those involved to collaborate-effectively to de-vise thorough strategies that e-mphasize environmental pre-servation though still permitting accountable e-conomic prospects. By preemptive-ly dealing with difficulties and embracing sustainable- development me-thods, the Arctic area can function as a model of how se-a operations can coexist in sync with nature. The-re are various complex issue-s surrounding Arctic navigation and law that will need addressing through re-spectful multilateral cooperation. All stake-holders must work to find a balanced approached that re-spects both the fragile e-cosystem and the nee-ds of local communities.

In the following portion, we- will wrap up our examination of Arctic sailing and polar law by briefly highlighting the major conclusions and conte-mplating possible paths for prospective e-xamination in this pivotal area.

Introduction to Conflict Zones and Their Implications on Maritime Law

Here- we take a closer look into the- intricate and difficult realm of maritime law within dispute-d territories. A conteste-d region in the context of maritime- jurisprudence indicates an are-a where armed clashe-s or confrontations occur, bringing about distinctive lawful issues that nece-ssitate judicious inspection. Navigating the wate-rs in these volatile locale-s can be perilous, as opposing military forces may vie-w passing vessels with suspicion. Differing partie-s also stake conflicting territorial claims, muddying the le-gal jurisdiction over ships transiting through contested wate-rs. Careful consideration of maritime tre-aties and precede-nts set in international case law is warrante-d to help chart a prudent course. Howe-ver, the eve-r-shifting dynamics of conflict zones challenge e-ven the most meticulous inte-rpretation of legal prece-dents. Our aim in this discussion is to gain a fuller understanding of the- complexities involved so that ove-rseas navigation can be conducted with appropriate- awareness of both

To begin, le-t us investigate what classifies an are-a as a conflict zone regarding maritime law. We- will look into the different e-lements that contribute to labe-ling a location as a disputed region, such as the e-xistence of armed factions, te-rritorial disputes, or political turmoil. Grasping the qualities of conflict zone-s is significant for appreciating the legal conse-quences that surface in the-se environments. Some- of the key factors include the- presence of military or paramilitary groups e-ngaged in combat or violence, ongoing disagre-ements over te-rritorial ownership or borders, as well as instability or unce-rtainty within the government which le-aves the rule of law que-stionable. An in-depth examination of e-ach of these components provide-s helpful context to understand why a particular marine- site may be dee-med high-risk legally and operationally. While- rules still apply internationally, special conside-rations are warranted and prudent judgme-nt recommended whe-n plying waters experie-ncing current strife.

Let us e-xplore further the spe-cial legal issues that arise in dispute-d waters. Regions engulfe-d in violence pose distinct proble-ms for maritime rules and operations. Fighting e-ndangers civilian ship crews and interfe-res with commerce lane-s crucial to many economies. Infrastructure like- ports also becomes vulnerable- to conflict-related harm, undermining a core- part of how the seas normally operate- under law. We will look at how wartime alte-rs the standard implementation of inte-rnational rules over vesse-ls, domestic laws, and longstanding accords. While violence- disrupts regular order, maritime re-gulations try their best to maintain stability and protect live-s on the ocean, eve-n amid armed clashes. There- are surely complex que-stions around security, trade, and more that countrie-s and organizations grapple with regarding disputed coastline-s and waters.

Furthermore-, we analyze how armed conflicts impact the- protection and security of ships traveling through dange-rous zones. We consider the- increased dangers civilian ve-ssels, their crews, and trave-lers deal with because- of military activities and harmful behaviors. Ensuring the safe-ty of civilian ships amid armed clashes require-s completely comprehe-nding applicable legal structures and the- intricacies involved.

Lastly, we discuss the- broader impact of armed conflicts on maritime law and how the-y can undermine effe-ctive governance of maritime- activities in conflict zones. The re-gulation of seas in areas affecte-d by violence poses particular difficultie-s, as combative environments te-nd to obstruct port state control efforts and interfe-re with compliance to international rule-s. We examine how volatile- regions complicate the imple-mentation of compliance procedure-s, disrupt mechanisms for addressing legal disagre-ements, and impede- the application of measures inte-nded to ensure ships follow protocols. While- regulations aim to bring order to maritime activitie-s worldwide, tumultuous situations introduce ambiguities that challe-nge these obje-ctives.

This section aims to bring gre-ater understanding to the comple-x legal issues surrounding maritime ope-rations in areas affected by arme-d conflict. By examining the implications of violence- on the established laws of the- sea, we gain insight into the nuance-d legal terrain navigated by those- relying on waterways near zone-s of tension and turmoil. Appreciating such intricacies is important for policymake-rs, legal experts, and acade-mics hoping to address the distinctive challe-nges involving maritime regulations in place-s scarred by warfare. OFTEN, the rule-s governing activities on the oce-an can become obscured amid fighting, re-quiring careful consideration from all stakeholde-rs to best support lawful and level-he-aded conduct even in disorde-rly domains.

International Humanitarian Law and Its Application in Conflict Zones

In the volatile- realm of conflict zones, the significance- of applying international humanitarian law (IHL) increases substantially. This se-gment aims to elucidate the- importance of IHL as it relates to maritime- law in such domains, illuminating the principles and standards that guide the- behavior of parties involved in arme-d clashes at sea. Here-, IHL plays a vital role in safeguarding sailors and civilians alike during wartime- operations. While naval engage-ments unfold with uncertainty, focusing on IHL fundamentals like- distinction, proportionality, and humanity can help restrict unnece-ssary suffering. This text will consider how IHL re-gulates maritime conflict to balance military ne-eds with compassion.

International humanitarian law (IHL), which is also re-ferred to as the law of war or the- law of armed conflict, establishes an e-ssential structure for guiding the conduct of state-s and non-state groups during times of armed clashe-s. Mainly focused on regulating land-based fighting, its core- concepts and stipulations additionally relate to naval se-ttings in which military engagements take- place over water. Grasping how the- standards of IHL correlate to disputed maritime- areas during conflict is pivotal for safely navigating the le-gal complexities surrounding such environme-nts. IHL seeks to bring a leve-l of humanity to even the most brutal of battle-s by clarifying what actions are permitted and forbidde-n across different sphere-s of combat. Its balanced framework recognize-s military necessity while also prote-cting noncombatants and those who can no longer fight from unjustified harm. Prope-r comprehension of these- principles in their application to both shoreline- and offshore combat zones is important for all parties in dispute-d territories.

One of the foundational principles of IHL is the distinction between combatants and non-combatants. This principle, derived from customary international law and codified in various treaties, emphasizes the need to avoid targeting civilians and civilian objects. Applied to maritime conflicts, this principle mandates that all parties involved must take precautions to minimize harm to civilians and refrain from deliberately attacking civilian vessels.

IHL places strong importance- on protecting prisoners of war during times of conflict. Spe-cific rules provide captured soldie-rs with certain rights and humane care until the-y can return home. These- regulations apply equally to any sailors taken while- fighting at sea, guaranteeing the-ir well-being and safety from harm. The- provisions outline that POWs must receive- proper treatment and re-spect from opposing forces. Captors cannot abuse or mistre-at enemy combatants in their custody. IHL aims to e-nsure fair and compassionate handling of prisoners to uphold basic human dignity, e-ven for those on the opposing side-.

Cultural property de-serves protection during arme-d conflicts to safeguard humanity's shared history for gene-rations to come. In addition to protecting individuals, international humanitarian law focuse-s on shielding cultural sites of importance. Re-cently, locations containing historic and cultural artifacts positioned near shore-lines have see-n more attacks, inflicting irreversible- harm. The 1954 Hague Convention for the- Protection of Cultural Property in the Eve-nt of Armed Conflict and subsequent protocols e-stablish legal defense-s for culturally significant places when fighting breaks out. The-se safeguards also apply over wate-r, underscoring how crucial it is to conserve re-minders of the past eve-n amid hostilities. Coastal heritage site-s face threats from violence- reaching across borders. Prese-rving landmarks for people eve-rywhere depe-nds on upholding norms that cultural property should not become targe-ts or collateral damage in wars. Continued compliance- with rules of war helps pass history's lessons to those- not yet born.

By exploring the-se particular provisions under IHL relating to maritime- conflict zones more closely, we- attain a more profound comprehension of how inte-rnational law endeavors to alleviate- the effects of arme-d clashes on civilians, prisoners of war, and cultural assets at se-a. Delving deepe-r into this examination permits us to maneuve-r through the legal nuances and moral dutie-s intrinsic in maritime regulations within areas of combat. Spe-cifically, investigating how IHL aims to protect noncombatants, captured soldie-rs, and historic sites underwater she-ds light on its goal of safeguarding vulnerable groups and article-s even amid violence-.

Maritime Law in Conflict Zone-s can become quite comple-x during times of armed conflict at sea. Naval warfare- and rules of engageme-nt must balance security nee-ds with international legal frameworks gove-rning use of force and protection of civilian ve-ssels. While defe-nding one's forces and borders is of utmost importance-, excessive

Here- we will explore the- complex legal structures that dictate- naval combat and rules for engageme-nt in disputed areas. Grasping these- guidelines is pivotal for appreciating the- intricacies involved with military disputes in maritime- settings. While regulations se-ek to minimize harm, distinguishing foes from frie-nds amid chaos presents profound challenge-s. Each scenario hangs upon an intricate balance, whe-re lives may tip upon how rules are- interpreted. It is my hope- that delving into such matters helps spre-ad understanding, now and in times yet to come-, so that all may walk more gently upon the wave-s. When e-xploring maritime operations, one of the- essential factors we e-xamine is distinguishing betwee-n those actively fighting and those who are- not engaged in combat. This separation holds significant importance- in defining legal rights and obligations during armed clashe-s. We consider how international humanitarian law (IHL) provide-s standards for recognizing people or te-ams involved in violence ve-rsus those not immediately taking part.

Furthermore-, we deeply analyze- the application of power, proportionality, and military nece-ssity according to international humanitarian law. As fights escalate, it be-comes extreme-ly important to answer inquiries encompassing how much powe-r can be utilized, what leve-l of harm is defensible, and whe-n military missions stop upholding the standards of proportionality and necessity. By inspe-cting previous examples and lawful case-s, we provide illumination on the intricate- choice making procedures that dire-ct such activities. While past eve-nts can offer guidance, each ne-w scenario brings unique complexitie-s, requiring careful consideration of conte-xt and impacts.

Our analysis cente-rs on naval combat and rules governing the use- of force in disputed areas. Though conne-cted issues like e-ngaging non-military ships or aerial activities may come up, those- subjects will receive- dedicated examination e-lsewhere in the- text. This prevents re-dundant discussions and allows an in-depth look at the focused the-me of naval warfare and operational guide-lines for contested wate-rs.

This section aims to untangle- some of the complex le-gal issues surrounding naval combat and the rules that gove-rn how forces interact at sea during time-s of hostility. By breaking down the complicated guide-lines associated with maritime military ope-rations in disputed zones, reade-rs gain useful understanding into the difficult proble-ms faced by naval powers in armed clashe-s. Here, you will find a moderate- exploration of the legal structure-s that define appropriate be-havior in waters where fighting occurs, whe-ther you work within the law profession, he-lp shape policy, or simply take intere-st in how legislation and conflict intersect on the- oceans. This section offers clarifie-d insight into the frameworks dictating conduct for naval forces amid wars.

Maritime law aims to prote-ct civilian vessels and crews that trave-l through conflict zones, yet navigating these- regulations grows increasingly complex. Inte-rnational rules govern the tre-atment of non-military ships and their passenge-rs, restricting attack unless positively ide-ntified as a military target. Howeve-r, blurred lines

Here- we will examine the- legal protections specially crafte-d to safeguard civilian ships and crews sailing through disputed wate-rs. Considering the inhere-nt hazards and dangers involved with maritime trave-l in such regions, it is imperative we- comprehend the worldwide- accords and arrangements constructed to guarante-e the well-be-ing and security of nonmilitary maritime tasks amid armed clashe-s. It is significant that we explore the- worldwide conventions and arrangeme-nts set up to guarantee the- security of regular citizen ships and worke-rs going through zones where military activitie-s may happen, so as to all the more like-ly comprehend the lawful me-asures intended to e-nsure their wellbe-ing and security in such perilous conditions.

The Ge-neva Convention of 1949 outlines important prote-ctions for civilian victims during wartime. While mainly concerne-d with land conflicts, its principles also cover naval engage-ments. As such, civilian ships and their crews have- certain rights and safeguards according to this convention. For e-xample, they must be tre-ated humanely and given acce-ss to medical care. Also, violence- or hostile acts directed against the-m are prohibited. The conve-ntion thus helps shield noncombatants from the harms of arme-d conflict, whether on land or at sea. While- focused on providing security for civilians, its guideline-s regarding humane treatme-nt and healthcare apply equally to maritime- settings according to extensions of its principle-s there. This convention the-refore establishe-s critical protections for civilian vessels and cre-wmembers during times of war.

Furthermore-, there are a handful of worldwide- arrangements explicitly te-nding to the wellbeing and se-curity of common sea activities in contention zone-s. One such understanding is the Inte-rnational Code of Conduct for Private Security Se-rvice Providers (ICoC), which portrays principles and rule-s for private security organizations working in high-chance circumstance-s, including contention zones. By following this code, private- security organizations can help guarantee- the wellbeing of common ve-ssels and give extra se-curity for their groups. The ICoC gives dire-ction to private security organizations on legitimate- and moral practices when ensuring maritime- tasks in troubled waters. By kee-ping to the standards in the ICoC, private se-curity can shield nonmilitary boats and their workers from risks while- permitting important exchange to ke-ep going securely e-ven amid clashes somewhe-re else.

Naval forces play an important part in guarding civilian boats and the-ir crews in areas of conflict. Many countries will se-nd naval resources to shield comme-rcial shipping routes and discourage dangerous be-havior towards civilian vessels. These- naval forces frequently work following rule-s that oversee the-ir activities and make certain the- protection of ships and the people- aboard them. Such rules normally put minimizing injury to non-fighters as the- top priority and use an amount of power that matches any pote-ntial risks. While safeguarding transport lanes is crucial, rule-s help ensure naval groups addre-ss threats judiciously to avoid harming the innocent.

Moreove-r, global entities for example- the United Nations (UN) and local organizations like the- European Union (EU) proactively team up with participant countrie-s to strengthen naval protection in trouble-d territories. The UN Conve-ntion on the Law of the Sea (UNCLOS) de-velops the authorized structure- for these associations to advance maritime- wellbeing and security by giving rule-s on issues, for example, right to trave-l through channels, blameless trave-l through, and the opportunity of route. These- worldwide and local bodies work intently with the-ir part states to ensure the- protected and free- development of ve-ssels through significant business courses and wate-rways crosswise over the world, particularly in locale-s of ongoing clash.

To put it briefly, safe-guarding civilian ships and their personnel whe-n traversing zones of hostility is a pressing issue- within maritime legislation. International agre-ements, conventions, naval force-s, private security firms, and global associations each have- indispensable parts in guarantee-ing the protection and security of noncombatant maritime- activities amid armed clashes. By following the-se lawful steps and exe-cuting suitable security procedure-s, we can aim to reduce hazards and shie-ld the wellbeing and me-ans of subsistence of those trave-rsing through turbulent seas. While many organizations are- dedicated to protecting civilian ve-ssels, more can still be done- to clarify protocols and ensure coordination betwe-en the diverse- groups working to minimize risks in conflict areas. Further inte-rnational cooperation may help address gaps and stre-ngthen security measure-s to better shelte-r civilian mariners navigating through dangerous waters.

Legal Accountability for Violations in Conflict Zones: Prosecution and Remedies

Here- we will take a look at the le-gal ways to make people and groups re-sponsible for breaking the rule-s of the sea in areas of fighting. Making sure- those who do wrong are punished is ve-ry important for keeping peace-, stopping bad actions, and making sure what's fair in these dange-rous places. We will look at how those who disobe-y can be tried in court and talk about the proble-ms and limits of enforcing responsibility in areas of conflict. While- examining prosecution avenue-s, maintaining order through deterre-nce and justice remains crucial give-n the volatility. Challenges arise- in conflict zones where accountability face-s limitations necessitating examination of available- mechanisms and their roles.

There- is one path forward to seek le-gal consequences that involve-s worldwide courts. Specifically designe-d judicial bodies have bee-n made to handle certain offe-nses done on waters amid military clashe-s. International courts, similar to the International Criminal Tribunal for the- Previous Yugoslavia (ICTY) and the International Criminal Court (ICC), have- assumed huge jobs in indicting people- in charge of war wrongdoings, violations against humanity, and different ge-nuine breaks of maritime law. We- will plunge further into the purvie-w, strategies, and results of the-se courts, accentuating their e-ffect on maritime law. These- specialized tribunals address spe-cific crimes committed during armed conflicts at se-a. The ICTY and ICC have played significant role-s in prosecuting individuals responsible for war crime-s, crimes against humanity, and violations of maritime law. Their jurisdiction, proce-dures, and outcomes as well as impact on maritime- jurisprudence merit furthe-r examination.

National courts also have the- authority to prosecute crimes that take- place at sea during armed conflicts. Le-t us investigate how domestic le-gal systems enable tribunals within countrie-s to indict lawbreakers and consider promine-nt cases where national courts have- acted against transgressors. We will look at the- difficulties national courts experie-nce when examining and judging those- accused of offenses de-dicated in theaters of war, such as proble-ms connected to gathering e-vidence, shielding witne-sses, and collaborating with international organizations. While national courts can e-xercise control over crime-s dedicated during naval combats, some challe-nges remain in prosecution due- to issues collecting evide-nce from dangerous regions and safe-guarding testifiers.

There- are several alte-rnative dispute resolution options that could aid in e-nforcing responsibility in areas expe-riencing conflict. Mediation and arbitration prese-nt chances to solve disagree-ments betwee-n groups engaged in maritime arme-d clashes while avoiding formal legal paths. We-'ll examine the be-nefits and restrictions of these- non-traditional approaches and converse about the-ir proficiency in encouraging reunification and accomplishing fairne-ss.

While e-nforcing legal responsibility in areas of conflict doe-s pose distinct difficulties, there- are ways to thoughtfully address such challenge-s. Gaining state help, finding proof, and safety worrie-s regularly obstruct investigative and le-gal actions. Let's consider these- hurdles and possible methods for rising above- them, like reinforcing worldwide- teamwork systems, making certain the- protection of those providing information and harmed individuals, and constituting spe-cialized research te-ams with proficiency in procedures within zone-s of disagreement.

Navigating the intricate- landscape of maritime law in conflict zones re-quires acknowledging that holding people- and groups responsible for their be-haviors is paramount. Exploring prosecutorial possibilities under inte-rnational legal systems, as well as impe-diments to enforcing responsibility, can offe-r valuable perspective- on this consequential facet of maritime- justice. Varied enforce-ment challenges e-xist, yet clarifying applicable statutes clarifie-s accountability expectations. While jurisdictional limits complicate- certain cases, discussing accountability's role provide-s comprehensive insight into re-asonably interpreting situations according to establishe-d legal precede-nt.

Part IV:
The Currents of Change
Regional Perspectives

"In the mosaic of regional perspectives, maritime law becomes a tapestry woven with the threads of cultural nuances, unique challenges, and shared aspirations, creating a navigational atlas that harmonizes diverse shores under the common umbrella of maritime cooperation."

Maritime Law in the Mediterranean
****

Laws of the sea in the Mediterranean have a deep background, touched by this area's key role in the past as a big sea trade path. From long ago, the Mediterranean Sea has been a vital channel for business, sharing cultures, and discovering new places. Here, we'll take a peek into the past and see how sea laws in the Mediterranean were formed, focusing on unique law systems and traditions that popped up because of its specific setting.

Powerful early sea nations like the Greeks and Romans influenced how Mediterranean sea laws came to be. They saw the need for rules to maintain order in their sea actions. Codes and traditions were made addressing things like business, sailing, and pirates. Looking into old legal systems helps us understand what set the groundwork for later changes in Mediterranean sea laws.

The Greeks, famed sea travelers, made law structures that governed sea business and sailing. Their laws focused on fair dealings with merchants, property protection, and ways to settle sea-related quarrels. Much the same, Romans had all-inclusive legal systems covering many parts of sea law, including ship making, contracts, and salvaging operations.

Other emerging Mediterranean societies had their own sea trade traditions and practices. Phoenician traders, known for their savvy in sailing, set up shop all over the Mediterranean Sea. Their influence reached into legal matters, with their own rules for business deals and solving disagreements.

At sea, laws can be complicated, especially in the Mediterranean. Its history is mostly what has made maritime law what it is in that area. We can learn much from how trade in the ancient Mediterranean was governed. This knowledge can help modern maritime law in the region be better understood.

About Mediterranean Sea Law

Byzantine Effects on Mediterranean Sea Law

The Byzantine Empire made a big difference in Mediterranean maritime law. This empire worked out of Constantinople and created the general ideas for laws about maritime trade, how to navigate, and rules about piracy.

A big Byzantine contribution was the Codex Justinianus. This is a big collection of Roman laws that Emperor Justinian I decided on in the 6th century. It was a big part of making maritime law what it is in the Mediterranean. This law set included old customs while setting up new rules for maritime trade and navigation.

The idea of "jus gentium," or the law of nations, got famous in Mediterranean maritime law with Byzantine influence. This said that some legal norms applied to any nation doing maritime activities. Byzantine legal thinkers added on to this by making specific rules for solving problems that came up because of international maritime trade.

The Byzantine Empire did more than just create legal rules. It shaped the laws of the sea in the Mediterranean. One law, called the Rhodian Sea Law or Lex Rhodia, was popular in this area. It set rules for things like salvage, general average, and bottomry. This law set the standard for maritime jurisdictions that would follow.

Byzantine courts also played a big role in maritime affairs. The Maritime Court (Admiralty) and the Vestiarion Court (customs) oversaw the enforcement of sea laws within the empire. These courts managed shipping contracts, marine insurance claims, and piracy or illegal trade incidents in a fair and efficient way.

Byzantium was a main hub for trade between Europe and Asia. Because of this, its maritime laws influenced areas outside its borders. Legal thinkers and traders in other places used Byzantine laws, creating consistent standards for sea trade.

The Byzantine Empire significantly affected sea laws in the Mediterranean, and its impact persists till date. Its legal accomplishments created a balance between different stakeholders' interests, encouraged trade and navigation, and significantly influenced maritime security in the region. Even today, laws governing this critical waterway show signs of Byzantine influence.

Sea city-states and Republics like Venice, Genoa, and Pisa, had big roles in creating maritime law in the Mediterranean area. These places made robust legal systems which affected how business was done, how disputes got solved, and how maritime laws were written.

Venice, or the "Queen of the Adriatic," was a force to be reckoned with during the Middle Ages and Renaissance. It had a complex legal system to address its broad trade connections and prove its maritime strength. Its maritime law, the "Marina Civile," looked at things like contracts, insurance, salvage, and rules for building ships.

Genoa, another big maritime city-state, had a big impact on Mediterranean maritime law too. The "Statuti Maritimi," Genoese system had all-inclusive laws addressing trade and sailing. These laws helped protect the needs of the traders and sailors involved in sea activities. Genoa's influence went beyond its city borders because its legal ideas were popular all over the Mediterranean area.

Pisa, while smaller than Venice and Genoa, also had a big effect on the creation of maritime law in the Mediterranean. The Pisan system was focused on solving disagreements from sailing and trading at sea. Their courts were skilled in settling cases involving sea collisions, shipwrecks, piracy, and disagreements about cargo. Pisa's focus on fair solutions laid a foundation for legal systems in the area in the future.

Maritime city-states and republics set up marine courts. Experienced judges there resolved disputes based on common rules and past decisions. These courts were key in handling justice in maritime affairs. They built trust among traders and maintained smooth business operations across the Mediterranean.

These maritime legal systems affected not just their lands but also neighboring areas. The rules they set were widely used, creating a uniform maritime law throughout the Mediterranean. This unity in legal systems standardized business practices, eased international trade, and brought stability to maritime work in the area.

The impact of these city-states and republics on maritime law extended far beyond their times. The laws they established still influence current legal systems and form the base of modern maritime law practices. Their work in setting and standardizing maritime laws paved the way for international agreements and treaties that regulate maritime activities globally.

Looking at the historical importance of these maritime states and republics helps us understand the lasting impact they had on the formation of Mediterranean maritime law. By studying their legal systems and examining their effects on business practices and dispute settlements, we learn a lot about how maritime law in this lively, multifaceted region came about and transformed over time.

Mediterranean Sea: A Place of Maritime Law

Under the Ottomans, maritime law saw significant shifts. Maritime trade, pirate management, and coastal defense were heavily influenced by their lawmaking.

Ottoman maritime business laws were pivotally key. It shaped trade just so - set paths for ships, made trade deals, and fixed customs duties. Ottomans built ports and controlled merchant fleets for business efficiency and safety as well.

Piracy was strictly tackled by the Ottomans. They had naval patrols to protect merchants from pirate attacks. They so took it seriously that they formed courts for piracy-specific cases, meting out quick punishment.

Coastal defenses were important to Ottoman maritime law. They built, along coastlines, forts to shield self from external dangers. These helped deter enemy invasions and provided a legal standing for defending sovereignty.

Ottomans also had their way of resolving maritime disputes. They had specific courts, called "Kadi courts," using maritime principles from Islamic law and local norms. Unique to the Mediterranean, it created a distinct legal environment.

The Ottoman rule had a major influence on maritime law. It helped shape the legal structures that guide the Mediterranean today. A closer look at the Ottoman laws linked to sea trade, pirate control, coastal defense, and legal procedures provides a deep perspective on the region's maritime legal evolution.

This book's segment looks specifically at the Ottoman impact on Mediterranean maritime law. By understanding this topic, readers will grasp the historical context driving the unique facets of maritime law in the Mediterranean.

Tackling Today's Mediterranean Maritime Law Challenges

Today, Mediterranean countries are grappling with maritime law challenges. Border disagreements among neighboring nations is one important issue. Many countries share the Mediterranean Sea, leading to tricky legal matters about territorial waters and special economic zones. Conflicts over fishing areas, oil exploration, and resource access have created tension and legal strife among these nations.

Illegal immigration is another big concern for the Mediterranean. Its closeness to Africa has made the Mediterranean Sea a major path for migrants heading for Europe. This triggers serious maritime law questions, like search and rescue missions, global duties for asylum seekers, and the state's role in stopping human trafficking.

In the Mediterranean, several regional partnerships were formed to confront these obstacles. For example, we have the Union for the Mediterranean or UfM. It's a type of government organization. Its purpose is to boost conversation and teamwork among Mediterranean countries. It's about different issues, one being the management of the seas. The UfM isn't alone; other similar groups exist. They aim to create shared plans to deal with sea-related challenges through joint efforts.

Another important issue is the struggle against pollution, preservation, and safety in the Mediterranean Sea. In recent times, this area has been the focus of a lot of significant events. The Mediterranean faces dangers like oil leaks, sea pollution, overfishing, and ecosystems deteriorating. So, global pacts and law systems have been made just for this area. They guide activities in the Mediterranean region and aim to shield the marine environment, promote lasting methods, and keep the region's unique variety of life safe.

To conclude, we face loads of new problems with the sea laws in the Mediterranean. These include things like broder disputes, unauthorized immigration, pollution, preservation, and issues concerning security. To deal with these things effectively, regional partnerships have been set up. They encourage dialogue and teamwork among Mediterranean countries. With these international pacts and law systems, specifically created for the Mediterranean's unique problems, we hope to ensure the sea resources are used responsibly and sustainably.

Asia-Pacific Maritime Law: A Look Back

The Asia-Pacific has a deep-rooted maritime past. Great empires grew and crumbled, trade and ideas were shared, and special legal customs were born along these waters.

Back in the day, maritime rules were a vital element shaping this region's law. An old law code from Babylon, found in the Code of Hammurabi around 1754 BCE, even had rules for sea trade. It covered things like ship wrecks, fights over cargo, and who was to blame for damages.

Growing trade along old sea routes led to the birth of practices tailored to handle trade disputes. Civilizations mixed their own culture and economy into these practices. The Phoenicians came up with a way to solve disagreements through some sort of peace talks, while old Chinese marine law protected traders and set rules for checking ships and keeping track of cargo.

Even now, old maritime customs continue to shape Asia-Pacific marine law. As sea-bordering nations drew up their laws, they didn't forget these old precedents.

Moreover, as empires rose and fell in the region, changes in political power often resulted in the adoption or adaptation of maritime legal systems. For example, during the golden age of Islamic civilization, which spanned from the 8th to the 14th century CE, Islamic scholars developed intricate legal doctrines that governed various aspects of maritime trade and navigation. These doctrines influenced not only Islamic territories but also areas beyond, as traders from different cultures interacted within the Islamic trading networks.

The historical significance of the Asia-Pacific region in maritime trade and navigation cannot be overstated. It has served as a hub for cultural exchange, economic prosperity, and legal developments. Understanding the ancient maritime codes and customs that influenced the region's legal frameworks is essential to comprehending the complexities of present-day Asia-Pacific maritime law.

In the subsequent sections of this section, we will explore how these historical contexts have shaped Asia-Pacific maritime law, delving into ongoing territorial disputes, environmental regulations, maritime security challenges, and emerging technologies. By examining these developments, we can gain a comprehensive understanding of the unique legal landscape of the Asia-Pacific region and its implications for maritime jurisdictions worldwide.

Asia-Pacific Maritime Law Developments: Tensions and Territorial Disputes

In this section, we delve into the complex and ongoing territorial disputes in the Asia-Pacific region and explore their significant implications for maritime law. The Asia-Pacific region has been historically marked by tensions arising from competing territorial claims, thereby creating a unique legal landscape that necessitates careful examination.

First, let's take a glance at the Asia-Pacific region's role in maritime history. It's a busy hub from ancient times, birthing the original sea rules and traditions. This backbone helps understand today's territorial conflicts.

Next, we dive into the Asia-Pacific region's present blockages - territorial disputes. They impact regions such as the South China Sea, East China Sea, and Indian Ocean. We'll study the rules and global agreements in place like the United Nations Convention on the Law of the Sea (UNCLOS) and state-to-state accords. Through key case studies, we'll peel back the dispute layers and their influence on maritime law.

The scopes of territorial conflicts are broad, covering geopolitical, economic, and security angles. We'll talk about how quarrels can strain relations between countries and hamstring teamwork. Plus, we'll uncover issues encountered by global bodies resolving disputes, showcasing their wins and limits.

As Asia-Pacific's land clash evolves, it's crucial to seek solutions and management strategies. We look at how talks, arbitrations, and peaceful resolutions play a role. Our objective? To walk you through maritime law as it works under pressure-filled territorial clashes.

In "Navigating the Seas of Law," we unravel these disputes and their legal systems. This equips you with the understanding you need about Asia-Pacific's maritime law state. This section offers important guidance, whether you're a law pro, researcher, policymaker, or just curious about land clashes and maritime law's role.

Asia-Pacific Maritime Law Developments: Environmental rules and sustainability

Here, we investigate the Asia-Pacific's dedication to tackling environmental worries and pushing sustainable seafaring practices. Recognizing the need to mix economic climb with environmental safety was crucial to keep marine resources for the long haul.

The region is making efforts, like regional pacts and initiatives, to soften maritime's environmental footprint. A notable example is several countries taking on steps to cut ships' air pollution, like stricter emissions standards and creating emissions control zones. These efforts polish air quality and help fight climate change.

Additionally, the Asia-Pacific region has taken significant steps towards protecting marine ecosystems and biodiversity. Countries have established marine protected areas and implemented regulations to prevent overfishing and destructive fishing practices. These measures aim to preserve delicate ecosystems and promote sustainable fisheries management.

Furthermore, regional collaborations have played a crucial role in addressing environmental challenges in the Asia-Pacific maritime domain. Countries have come together to share best practices, enhance capacity building, and coordinate efforts to protect shared marine resources. Organizations like the Association of Southeast Asian Nations (ASEAN) and the Pacific Islands Forum (PIF) have facilitated dialogue and cooperation among member states in addressing environmental concerns.

The Asia-Pacific region has also been at the forefront of developing innovative solutions to promote sustainable maritime practices. For instance, there has been a growing focus on alternative energy sources for ships, such as liquefied natural gas (LNG) and hydrogen fuel cells, which offer lower emissions than traditional fossil fuels. Additionally, research and development projects are exploring the use of renewable energy technologies, such as wind and solar power, for maritime applications.

Looking ahead, the Asia-Pacific region is poised to further strengthen its commitment to environmental sustainability in maritime law. With growing awareness of the threats posed by climate change and unsustainable practices, countries are likely to continue developing and implementing regulations that prioritize the protection of marine ecosystems and the reduction of carbon emissions. Moreover, regional cooperation will remain crucial in addressing transboundary environmental issues and fostering sustainable maritime development.

Exploring maritime law in the Asia-Pacific region is key. They're working to handle environmental issues and boost sustainable methods. By looking at their legal developments, new agreements, tactics, and inventive ideas, we learn a lot about maritime laws that keep this active area running.

There's a special mix of maritime security issues in the Asia-Pacific. Knowing maritime law helps us analyze these problems. This part delves into security difficulties including piracy, unlawful fishing, and smuggling that the region faces.

Piracy poses a big problem for ships in Asia-Pacific waters. High piracy, especially in places like the Gulf of Aden and South China Sea, call for solid legal setups to fight this problem. This section digs into legal strides and international teamwork to handle piracy and keep maritime trading routes safe.

Illegal fishing deeply harms marine life and good fishing habits. Asia-Pacific has seen a lot of illegal, unrecorded, and unregulated (IUU) fishing activities. These damage economies and ecosystems. This part looks into legal orders to fight IUU fishing like agreements and combined country efforts.

Asia-Pacific is seriously endangered by smuggling, which includes drug, weapon, and human trafficking. The law of the sea is essential against these illegal actions as it offers legal methods for stopping, investigating and charging such crimes. This part of the conversation explains how these laws are used by various countries to fight smuggling and improve maritime safety.

To tackle these security issues, we need a versatile methodology. This involves legal collaboration between nations, firm enforcement of rules, and region-wide plans. By uncovering the legal structures and joint efforts in the Asia-Pacific, readers will learn how maritime law can successfully fight piracy, illegal fishing, smuggling, and other threats to security.

As this region keeps growing and meets newer security challenges, we must keep track of emerging technologies and their impact on sea law. The following section delves into how advancements like self-driving ships and AI are reshaping the legal scene of this ever-changing region.

Developments in Maritime Law of Asia-Pacific: The future with emerging technologies:

In the last few years, the Asia-Pacific has seen a quick expansion in emerging technologies that are poised to transform maritime operations completely. Autonomous ships and AI's effect on sea law is extremely important. It brings along a plethora of legal consequences and considerations.

Autonomous vessels, equipped with sophisticated technology and navigation systems, have the potential to significantly transform maritime operations in the Asia-Pacific region. These vessels have the ability to operate without direct human control, raising important questions regarding liability, safety regulations, and compliance with international conventions.

One of the key legal implications surrounding autonomous vessels is the determination of liability in the event of accidents or collisions. With traditional vessels, responsibility typically lies with the captain or crew. However, in the case of autonomous vessels, where there may not be any human presence aboard, establishing liability becomes complex. Determining who is at fault and accountable for any damages or injuries caused by autonomous vessels will require careful analysis and adaptation of existing legal frameworks.

Moreover, the introduction of artificial intelligence (AI) into maritime operations also presents unique legal challenges. AI-powered systems can greatly enhance efficiency and decision-making processes in areas such as vessel navigation, cargo handling, and risk assessment. However, these systems must adhere to ethical standards and comply with data protection regulations.

Privacy concerns arise when AI systems collect and process vast amounts of personal data from crew members or passengers on board. Clear guidelines and regulations need to be established to ensure that sensitive information is protected and used appropriately. Additionally, safeguards must be put in place to prevent malicious actors from exploiting vulnerabilities in AI systems, which could potentially disrupt maritime operations or compromise safety.

As these emerging technologies continue to shape the future of maritime operations in the Asia-Pacific region, there is a growing need for international cooperation and harmonization of laws and regulations. Collaboration among countries is crucial to develop standardized guidelines for the use of autonomous vessels and AI systems, ensuring a consistent approach to maritime law across borders.

The Asia-Pacific region must also proactively engage in discussions at international forums and organizations, such as the International Maritime Organization (IMO), to establish global standards for the implementation and regulation of emerging technologies in the maritime industry. This will help foster trust and confidence in the use of autonomous vessels and AI systems, promoting safe and efficient maritime operations.

In conclusion, the Asia-Pacific region is witnessing a transformative era in maritime law with the advent of emerging technologies such as autonomous vessels and artificial intelligence. As these technologies continue to evolve, it is crucial for policymakers, legal professionals, and stakeholders to keep pace with these developments and adapt existing legal frameworks accordingly. By addressing the legal implications and challenges presented by emerging technologies, the Asia-Pacific region can harness their potential while ensuring the safety, security, and sustainability of its maritime activities.

Maritime Law in the Americas: Historical Overview: Development and Influences

When we talk about how maritime law grew in the Americas, it's an interesting story. Many things influenced it. When explorers came from Europe to the New World, they brought their laws. This unknowingly started the base of maritime law in this huge area.

Maritime law in the Americas was moulded by European law guidelines. Spain, Portugal, and Britain were colonial powers. They set up their own laws and rules. This greatly affected maritime law in the places they ruled over.

Spain and Portugal based their laws on Roman law. They focused on ideas such as res communis and res nullius. These regulated rights related to sea territories, fishing, and shipwreck salvaging. Latin America's early maritime laws were shaped by these ideas. They also set up the framework to form more laws.

In North America, the British law traditions significantly impacted maritime law. Admiralty law came from the English common law and regulated maritime activities. British courts created many precedents that affected American admiralty law. They focused on maritime trade, salvaging rights, and navigation privileges.

The Europeans greatly influenced American maritime law. But we must also remember the input and contributions of the Native peoples. They had their laws concerning maritime activities much before Europeans came. Their practices usually revolved around sustainable fishing, handling resources, and community-led governance.

When Europe took over the Americas, new countries needed their own maritime laws. They needed to shape old laws to fit new needs, especially as trade and global links grew.

In the U.S., admiralty law burrowed deep into the legal system, growing out of the Constitution. Big court cases, for example, Gibbons v. Ogden and The Steamboat Thomas Jefferson, gave U.S. maritime law its shape. They set up federal authority rules and made clear who had the right to navigate and who was responsible.

Shaping maritime law in the Americas also needed people working together and sorting out disagreements. Countries in the Americas joined in agreements and treaties that boosted cooperation, ended conflicts, and improved maritime safety. Bigger groups like the Organization of American States (OAS) helped member countries talk, collaborate and harmonize laws to face mutual challenges.

The path to today's maritime law in the Americas is complex, combining European law, indigenous customs, and the unique needs and situations of each country. Knowledge of this history sheds light on how maritime law has grown and what it looks like now in this diverse and dynamic region.

During the colonial era, the establishment of legal systems by the Spanish, Portuguese, and British colonial powers had a significant impact on maritime law in the Americas. Each of these powers brought with them their own legal traditions and practices, which influenced the development of maritime jurisprudence in their respective colonies.

The Spanish legal system, for instance, was based on civil law traditions and Roman law principles. The Laws of the Indies, a collection of laws and regulations issued by the Spanish Crown for its American territories, played a crucial role in shaping maritime law in Spanish colonies. These laws addressed various aspects of maritime activities, including navigation, trade, and customs procedures.

Similarly, the Portuguese legal system also drew heavily from civil law traditions. The Ordenações Filipinas, a compilation of laws enacted during the reign of King Philip II of Spain that also applied to Portuguese territories, provided a legal framework for maritime activities in Portuguese colonies. These laws governed issues such as maritime commerce, navigational rights, and maritime jurisdiction.

In contrast, the British legal system was rooted in common law principles. English admiralty law formed the basis of maritime law in British colonies such as North America. Admiralty courts were established to handle cases related to maritime disputes and crimes, providing a specialized legal forum for matters concerning navigation, shipping contracts, salvage rights, and other aspects of maritime commerce.

Colonial legal systems shaped maritime law far past their colonies' borders. Spanish, Portuguese, and British colonies produced legal ideas. These ideas affected the laws in these places and the wider maritime law evolution in the Americas.

These colonial legal systems set the stage for American maritime law. Yet, they didn't stay the same or just get European influence. Native legal traditions influenced maritime law too. This happened in native communities and their dealings with European powers.

In short, colonial times were key for maritime law development in the Americas. The legal systems put in place by the Spanish, Portuguese, and British made a lasting imprint on maritime law. This created a base that could change with time as countries grew and claimed their power.

After colonial rule, the Americas saw big changes in their legal systems, such as maritime law. As countries gained freedom, they wanted to make their own maritime laws that matched their special needs and goals.

The start of American maritime law was a turning point for the area's legal history. With new freedom, these countries could make maritime laws to show their specific situations and priorities.

When countries were formed, they realized addressing international business issues was critical. They understood how crucial it is to have strong laws controlling sea responsibilities, supporting their economy, and fostering fair play among local and foreign bodies.

This part will explain how the Americas started to write maritime laws and how they tweaked the existing legal rules to match their realities after gaining independence. Each country grappled with its unique pros and cons while mastering the multifaceted aspects of sea governance.

Some countries, because of their historical influences, picked legal principles from European law. They studied the legal systems of old colonial powers like Spain, Portugal, and Britain, but they also embraced local customs and traditions.

But, other countries went for a fresh approach by creating completely new legal systems. Inspired by global maritime conventions and global best guidelines, they created their own laws that echoed their unique societal-economic terms and goals.

In this section, we'll look at specific examples of how different American countries carved out their sea laws. We will see how these laws tackled subjects like trade ship rules, sea mishaps, recovery operations, and ocean pollution.

We'll explore the history and growth of sea laws in the Americas after independence. This will help readers appreciate the area's valuable law heritage. We'll observe how American countries improved maritime business, ensured sea safety, and guarded their ocean resources.

The growth of the country's maritime law shows the region's self-governing ambition and its dedication to face the unique challenges and chances that the surrounding seas offer. Knowing this growth provides us useful knowledge about the versatile nature of sea law and its deep effect on the country's growth in Americas.

USA: Admiralty Law and Foundational Constitutional Principles

The USA had a strong influence on shaping sea law throughout history. Both British common law and constitutional principles influenced its legal system. Both contributed to the growth of admiralty law and setting significant legal standards in American sea law.

Admiralty law is a special part of law dealing with maritime activities and issues. Its roots trace back to early English legal traditions. When the American colonies gained independence, this law became part of the American legal system, proving to be vital.

Admiralty jurisdiction in the United States is the responsibility of federal courts, as stated in the U.S. Constitution's Article III. It outlines that federal courts oversee all matters of admiralty and maritime jurisdiction. This clause was vital for a uniform judiciary for maritime issues crossing state lines.

Throughout history, certain court rulings have paved the way for American admiralty and maritime law. Important judgments have set legal standards and directions for complex maritime dispute resolution. Here are some noteworthy cases:

1. The Schooner Exchange v. McFaddon (1812):
This pivotal Supreme Court ruling studied admiralty law's reach in foreign waters. The verdict was that U.S. courts couldn't claim jurisdiction over foreign ships in American ports without Congress or a treaty's sanction. This ruling reinforced international respect and sovereignty in maritime affairs.

2. The Steamboat Thomas Jefferson v. Rock Island Bridge (1873):
This case focused on obstructions to navigation and their effects on interstate trade. The court deemed that any hindrance to navigation should be logical and allow ample room for boats. This ruling highlighted the significance of free waterways for commerce. It also set rules for determining the legality of bridges and other constructs in navigable waters.

3. Jones Act (1917):
This part of the Merchant Marine Act, known as the Jones Act, helps and enriches the U.S. maritime industry. It insists on U.S. built, owned, and crewed vessels for coastwise trade. It greatly influences local trade by sea, shipbuilding, and seafarer jobs.

4. Exxon Shipping Co. v. Baker (2008):
This Supreme Court case began with the Exxon Valdez oil spill of '89. The court revisited the punitive damages awarded to affected plaintiffs. The court sliced the punitive damages given by the lower courts, proclaiming that they should not go beyond compensatory damages in maritime cases, unless unique conditions exist. It stressed the importance balance in awarding damages in maritime ecological disasters.

These cases are only part of the impactful decisions that have defined U.S. maritime law. They've trickled down beyond legal theories, impacting international norms and setting standards for other jurisdictions.

Summing up, U.S. admiralty law bases itself strongly on constitutional principles and changes through key court verdicts. These cases have sculpted U.S. maritime jurisprudence and given directions for sorting out perplexing legal problems in maritime actions. Knowing this rich history is vital to making sense of the law's ocean within the U.S. scenario and realizing America's additions to worldwide maritime jurisprudence.

Maritime Law in the Americas:

International Cooperation and Disputes: Maritime Agreements and Resolution Mechanisms

This section delves into the realm of international cooperation and dispute resolution mechanisms in the context of maritime law in the Americas. As nations strive to maintain peaceful relations and foster cooperation, various treaties and agreements have been established to address maritime disputes and promote collaboration among American countries.

The exploration begins with an examination of the international agreements that have been forged by American nations to resolve maritime conflicts. These agreements encompass a wide range of issues, including territorial boundaries, exclusive economic zones, fishing rights, and environmental protection. Through detailed analysis, readers will gain insights into the provisions and mechanisms outlined in these agreements, which aim to ensure peaceful coexistence and efficient resolution of maritime disputes.

Furthermore, this section sheds light on the role of regional organizations, such as the Organization of American States (OAS), in fostering cooperation and resolving conflicts in the Americas. The OAS provides a platform for member states to engage in dialogue, negotiate agreements, and seek diplomatic solutions to maritime disputes. Readers will gain a deeper understanding of the functions and significance of the OAS in promoting regional stability and advancing the interests of American nations.

This part shows case studies about maritime agreement use and dispute-solving in the Americas. Real-life examples show past disputes that got solved through talks or law. It shows how teamwork between countries can solve tricky maritime issues.

By studying the details of international teamwork and dispute solutions in maritime law, this part helps readers understand the steps American countries take to keep good relations while protecting their maritime interests. With two-sided agreements and multi-country agreements run by regional groups, this part lights up the teamwork that gives shape to the maritime law of the Americas.

Africa's Maritime Boundaries and Legal Issues:

A Look Back at Africa's Maritime Boundaries

Throughout the years, Africa's maritime boundaries have changed a lot due to things like colonization, changing geopolitics, and the hunt for natural resources. Knowing the historical changes of these boundaries is key to understanding the legal difficulties in the area today.

The study of Africa's maritime boundaries started way back when different civilizations used coastal areas for trade and exploring. The Phoenicians, Egyptians, and Greeks traveled Africa's coasts, making early ties and influencing maritime traditions. Still, specific lines for maritime boundaries were more flexible during this time, with claims that overlapped and disputed land.

Africa's borders were changed greatly during the colonization period. The goal of European countries was to split Africa up to benefit their own purposes. This led to borders that didn't match up with cultural and historic territories, including at sea.

The European powers simply sketched lines on a map to divide Africa, not considering the land's history or its physical features. This caused many issues, especially when it came to who owned what parts of the sea after colonial rule ended.

After gaining independence, African nations wanted control over their sea territories. But unclear records and leftover colonial-borders made it hard to decide on exact boundaries. Disagreements flared over who owned land, the resources within, and specific economic zones, causing tension in the region.

To solve these issues, African nations used international maritime laws, like the United Nations Convention on the Law of the Sea (UNCLOS). UNCLOS suggested using fairness, equal distance, and continuation of land to determine sea boundaries. But putting these ideas into practice was tough due to lingering historical conflicts and unresolved debates.

Africa's maritime lines are quite complicated. This is due in part to the many islands and archipelagos dotting its coasts. Determining their sea zones needs attention to things like land features, distance, and past use.

A look back at Africa's maritime lines shows how past colonialism still impacts sea law in the region. The imposed divisions from that era still affect the right to certain areas. To fix these issues, we need a good grasp of the past, a respect for international rules, and a willingness to work together.

The next parts in this section will go deeper into the laws for African sea lines. We'll look at disputes, challenges, noteworthy examples, and future options for Africa's sea control. By untangling the maze of Africa's sea law, we hope to feed your understanding of the unique legal tests Africa faces today.

Sea Law for African Sea Lines:

Defining sea lines in Africa follows a detailed network of international rules. The goal of these laws is to lay out clear directions for giving rights and duties over the seas around Africa.

The United Nations Convention on the Law of the Sea, or UNCLOS, is important for Africa's sea boundaries. It creates a full set of rules for deciding on sea zones like territorial waters, special economic zones, and continental shelves. It spells out ways to achieve fair and friendly border talks among next-door countries.

Apart from UNCLOS, the African Union (AU) helps boost the rulebook for African sea boundaries. These regional agreements and efforts matter a lot. In giving input on sea governance, the AU's 2050 Africa's Integrated Maritime Strategy is very active. This strategy promotes growth, security, and good management in Africa's maritime areas.

There are also organizations in different regions such as the Economic Community of West African States (ECOWAS), the Southern African Development Community (SADC), and the East African Community (EAC) who are working on legal tools and procedures for sea boundaries in their territories. These deals encourage close-by countries to cooperate and manage resources in mutual zones.

Moreover, various one-on-one and multi-sided treaties deal with unique sea boundary problems in Africa. For instance, the Treaty on the Delimitation of the Continental Shelf between Mozambique and South Africa and the Treaty on the Delimitation of the Maritime Boundary between Ghana and Côte d'Ivoire. These treaties set up a legal groundwork for dealing with border disputes and determining definite jurisdictional boundaries between neighboring states.

Although there are laws, it's still tough to regulate Africa's sea borders. Things like disputes over land, use of resources, and political disagreements can make it difficult. Following international laws and regional agreements can assist in resolving these sea border conflicts peacefully.

To sum it up, laws from around the world and from specific regions determine how Africa's sea borders are regulated. UNCLOS gives broad rules for setting borders while regional groups and bilateral treaties give specific solutions for border issues. But, for effectively managing these borders, we need ongoing cooperation, regional unity, and practices that can be kept up over the long term.

Africa's Sea Borders and Legal Struggles: Difficulties and Disagreements over Africa's Sea Borders

In this section, we'll look into the disagreements and problems in African sea borders and highlight the reasons behind these complex issues. Africa holds a long coastline, plenty of sea resources, and many countries with different interests which have led to several sea border disagreements.

Fighting over territory is a main cause for disagreements surrounding Africa's sea borders. Setting these borders is often disputed especially when neighboring countries have overlapping claims. Misunderstandings about old treaties, agreements during colonial times, and common international law make it even more confusing. A lot of times, countries claim to own certain areas based on historical use or strategic reasons which result in long drawn-out legal fights.

Africa's ocean disputes are often due to the fight for resources like oil, gas, and fish. These resources make states battle each other. They'll argue over who can use the resources in the Exclusive Economic Zones. These are spots where only one country can use the resources. Battles get worse when it's unclear who owns what and where.

There's also the problem of threats to the environment. Offshore oil work can cause pollution. Illegal fishing can damage ecosystems. Those two things and waste can hurt traditional sea-based economies. Coastal countries must balance making money with protecting nature. They have to make good laws about using the seas.

To manage African seas well, we need to understand these arguments. Political leaders and other important people must recognize what's causing these conflicts. They can then find fair ways to work together. Stronger legal methods like international talks can help solve these challenges and bring peace to African seas.

In the next section, we will examine notable case studies involving disputes over African maritime boundaries, evaluating the legal mechanisms and frameworks utilized to resolve these conflicts.

Through an in-depth analysis of these cases, we can gain insights into effective strategies for resolving disputes and fostering cooperation among African nations.

Case Studies: Resolving Maritime Boundary Disputes in Africa

In this section, we delve into notable case studies that shed light on the complexities of resolving maritime boundary disputes in Africa. These real-world examples provide valuable insights into the legal mechanisms and frameworks utilized to address these disputes, including international arbitration and negotiation processes.

One such case study is the longstanding dispute between Somalia and Kenya over their maritime boundaries in the Indian Ocean. The two countries have been embroiled in a legal battle regarding a triangular-shaped area measuring approximately 100,000 square kilometers off their coastlines. This disputed area is believed to be rich in potentially lucrative oil and gas reserves.

To resolve this contentious issue, both Somalia and Kenya turned to international arbitration. In 2014, Somalia initiated proceedings before the International Court of Justice (ICJ), seeking a ruling on its maritime boundary with Kenya. The ICJ has jurisdiction to settle disputes concerning the interpretation or application of international treaties, and both Somalia and Kenya are parties to the United Nations Convention on the Law of the Sea (UNCLOS).

The ICJ's role in the Somalia-Kenya sea border case shows how global rules and groups help solve sea boundary problems. Both countries sent their problem to the ICJ, trusting a court to fairly use global laws and make a decision.

A similar case is the Ghana and Côte d'Ivoire sea border disagreement in the Gulf of Guinea. In 2014, Côte d'Ivoire took the issue to an international court, wanting to define its sea border with Ghana. The court was created by Annex VII of UNCLOS, allowing required decision-making if countries can't agree on their sea borders.

The court carefully checked past records, legal papers, sea maps, expert details, and oral points made by both countries. After a thoughtful review, the court made its decision in 2017, defining the sea border between Ghana and Côte d'Ivoire. This important decision solved the argument and created a guide for similar future African cases.

These cases show that global legal methods are important for solving African sea border disagreements. By referring to international decision-making and UNCLOS rules, countries can peacefully solve disputes. Past records, scientific proof, and expert statements guide the decision process.

In summary, looking at these case studies sheds light on how tricky it is to solve sea boundary disputes in Africa. By studying the lawful methods used, we can better understand the tactics used to face these difficulties. As Africa navigates its sea borders, these studies are good resources for future problems. They show why we need to work together globally and stick to the law.

Looking Ahead: Working Towards Better Sea Rule in Africa

As Africa becomes a major player in worldwide sea matters, we need to tackle the challenges and possibilities that come. In this last piece, we discuss possible fixes and tactics for better sea rule in this area.

A major support for good sea rules in Africa is teamwork. Cooperation between African countries, regional groups, and global stakeholders is key. This ensures that sea areas in Africa develop and are managed sustainably. By working together and sharing resources, countries can use each other's strengths. They can tackle shared problems and benefit from the group's work.

Region-wide cooperation helps to improve sea rule in Africa too. Plans like the African Union's United Maritime Strategy and Indian Ocean Rim Association help bordering cooperation, policy harmony, and skills-boosting programs. By supporting unity and coordination among sea states, these plans create a good setting for effective sea control.

Think about this. Keeping our seas healthy is a must. With the world more eco-aware, African countries need to look after their marine spaces. To do this, they must reduce pollution, shield marine wildlife, and fish responsibly. These moves are key to keeping their seas in good shape.

Also, education and tech play a big role in the future of African marine management. Learning, offering new programmes, and giving workers the right know-how will help them deal with tough legal rules. Up-to-date tech like remote sensing, data analytics, and satellite checks can boost oversight and guard against threats, making their marine management stronger.

Moreover, good systems for settling arguments help avoid sea-border fights. Talking, diplomacy, and taking the argument to international courts can lead to peaceful solutions and keep seas stable. To find these solutions, they can learn from others who have solved sea-border disputes successfully.

To end, the future of marine management in Africa depends on working together, regional ties, green actions, learning and problem-solving. By sticking to these areas, African countries can ensure their seas are well taken care of. This brings more money, a healthy environment and safety to the area.

Disputed Waters - The South China Sea

In this section, we delve into the complexities and legal frameworks surrounding the disputes in the South China Sea.

1. Historical Background:

The roots of the South China Sea disputes can be traced back to ancient times, with claims made by different countries based on historical narratives. Examining the conflicting historical accounts helps us understand the origins of these disputes and the deep-seated nature of the territorial claims.

2. Territorial Claims and Legal Justifications:

This section explores the specific territorial claims put forth by countries in the South China Sea, such as China, Vietnam, the Philippines, Malaysia, and Brunei. We analyze the legal justifications presented by each country, ranging from historical rights to geographical proximity, and critically evaluate their validity under international law principles.

3. Conflicting Economic Interests:

A significant factor contributing to tensions in the South China Sea is the vast economic interests at stake. Rich fishing grounds, potential oil and gas reserves, and strategic shipping routes heighten the competition among claimant countries. This section delves into how these conflicting economic interests exacerbate territorial disputes and explores the role of resource exploitation in fueling tensions.

4. Geopolitical Implications:

The South China Sea disputes have far-reaching geopolitical implications that transcend the region's borders. Major powers, including the United States and China, are involved in these disputes due to their strategic interests. We examine how their involvement impacts regional stability, security dynamics, and the broader geopolitical landscape of the Asia-Pacific region.

5. Legal Solutions and Future Predictions:

The South China Sea disputes are in constant discussion. There's a push to fix these issues through methods like talks and legal judgments. We want to see how well these attempts are doing. Plus, we're looking at what could happen in the future. We're also looking at new problems like changes in our climate and sea technology. These could change how we see these land problems.

Looking into the past, laws, economy, world politics, and the future of the South China Sea disputes. This offers you a wide view of these sea problems. It's a tool to help you understand the area more and helps you look into sea laws.

Troubled Waters - The South China Sea

The Past:

The South China Sea has had issues reaching back to older times. In the area, like China, Vietnam, the Philippines, Malaysia, and Brunei, there are differing claims. They're arguing over who gets what in the area. The arguments come from differing past stories.

China, in history, has said they own the South China Sea. They use past evidence of Chinese explorers controlling these waters. They use maps from the Han dynasty (206 BCE - 220 CE) as proof. But, other countries use their ties to the land in this debate.

For instance, Vietnam argues that it has historical evidence of continuous occupation and governance of certain islands and features in the South China Sea. The Philippines relies on its proximity to some of these features and cites international laws such as the United Nations Convention on the Law of the Sea (UNCLOS) as a basis for its claims. Malaysia and Brunei also stake their own territorial claims within the disputed waters.

Conflicting historical narratives shape the views and positions of these countries, leading to ongoing disputes with no clear resolution. While some historical documents can be interpreted as supporting one claim over another, there is often little consensus among historians and legal scholars.

Understanding the historical background is crucial for grasping the complexity of the current disputes in the South China Sea. It provides insights into the deep-rooted nature of these conflicts and highlights the significance of historical narratives in shaping each country's stance. By examining these historical origins, we can better appreciate the challenges involved in finding a peaceful and mutually acceptable resolution to these disputes.

Territorial Claims and Legal Justifications in the South China Sea:

This section focuses on the specific territorial claims made by countries in the South China Sea, such as China, Vietnam, the Philippines, Malaysia, and Brunei. It delves into the legal justifications put forth by each country to support their claims, including historical rights, geographical proximity, and principles of international law.

China asserts its "nine-dash line" claim, which encompasses a vast portion of the South China Sea based on historical records that it argues demonstrate continuous jurisdiction and control over the waters. Vietnam and the Philippines also assert historical rights to certain islands and features based on their own colonial histories and cultural ties to the region.

Meanwhile, Malaysia and Brunei stake their claims primarily on principles of international law, particularly those enshrined in the United Nations Convention on the Law of the Sea (UNCLOS). They argue for maritime entitlements based on the concept of an Exclusive Economic Zone (EEZ) granted by UNCLOS, which allows coastal states to exploit and conserve natural resources within 200 nautical miles of their shores.

The validity of these territorial claims is a subject of intense debate and disagreement among the claimant states and the international community. Countries contest each other's assertions, often resulting in overlapping claims and disputed sovereignty over various islands, reefs, and shoals in the South China Sea.

International law plays a crucial role in evaluating the legal strength of these claims. The application of legal principles, such as historic rights or UNCLOS provisions, requires careful analysis and consideration of historical evidence, customary international law, and relevant international jurisprudence.

Addressing these complex legal questions is essential to navigate the intricacies of maritime jurisprudence in the South China Sea. By examining the specific territorial claims made by each country and analyzing their legal justifications through the lens of international law frameworks, this book aims to shed light on the ongoing disputes and contribute to a deeper understanding of the complexities involved in resolving them.

Money Matters in the Sea:

The South China Sea is a treasure trove of fish, oil, gas, and crucial sea lanes. China, Vietnam, the Philippines, Malaysia, and Brunei, being neighbors to this sea, find themselves often at odds due to these treasures.

Why the disputes? The economic desires of these countries. They each want control over the islands and sea features, why? They lie within respective Economic Zones, filled with resources!

Fishing has always been important for the people living along the coast. Now, as fish numbers drop globally due to too much fishing and changing climates, these fishing spots become even more crucial! There's a race among countries for fishing rights, and for fishing that doesn't hurt the sea for future generations.

But wait, there's more! Below the sea floor, oil and gas wait to be tapped. They say the South China Sea has a lot of this fuel, some we know about, some still undiscovered. Whoever can claim these fuels promises a sturdy economy and the security of the nation's energy needs.

The South China Sea plays a key role in global trade thanks to its position. It's a hub of sea transport, linking world economies and aiding global business. Hence, surrounding nations strive to control these sea paths to safeguard navigation and protect their trade advantages.

As nations compete for islands and reefs in the sea, rich with resources, arguments over territory intensify. Military bases on islands by some states heighten stress, helping them to increase their influence and dominate nearby waters.

This sea has become a mesh of complex disputes due to clashing financial aims. Overlapping territory claims, rival resource use, and combination of history and politics increase the stress levels. With nations adamant about defending their claims and economic profit, finding an agreeable solution to these quarrels is more and more tough.

In light of these diverging economic goals, the worldwide community has urged for peaceful talks and respect for international law like the United Nations' sea laws (UNCLOS). But, getting everyone on the same page and crafting a broad pact that satisfies all sides is a hard job.

Emerging problems like climate change and new maritime technologies might make current disputes more complex. Rising sea levels, shifting ocean currents, and changing ecosystems present new obstacles and doubts for resource use in the South China Sea.

Simply put, clashing financial interests like fishing areas, oil and gas reserves, and key shipping routes, add to the strain on the contested South China Sea waters. The chase for these riches heightens rivalry among nearby countries, worsening border disputes. Finding a dispute solution that benefits every party's economic needs is a complicated undertaking with massive geopolitical effects on the area.

Geopolitical implications: This part digs into the geopolitical repercussions of the South China Sea disputes and reveals their deep effect on regional safety and stability. It intricately breaks down the complicated involvement of global powers, chiefly the United States and China, in the disputes and studies how their strategic interests crisscross with the larger geopolitical movements of the Asia-Pacific region.

The South China Sea is a vital passage for worldwide trade and is home to a ton of natural resources, which makes it a significant strategic area. The disputes about power and maritime jurisdiction have lead to increased tensions and greater militarization in the area. This section shines a light on the geopolitical factors powering these disputes, focusing on the power conflicts, territory aspirations, and economic desires at work.

Actively rising to global power status, China increases control and security by taking over and strengthening islands in the South China Sea. By expanding land, developing military bases, its hold in the debated waters has grown significantly. This move creates worry for neighboring lands and attracts global attention due to notions of navigation freedom and adherence to international laws.

Consistently upholding an active role, the U.S steps forward in South China Sea disputes by emphasizing navigation freedom and peaceful solutions. Seeing China's influence growth as a threat to its regional lead, U.S has often undertaken navigation freedom actions and strengthened security bonds with regional allies. This portion delves into the intricate dynamics of these two strong nations and evaluates their competition's influence on the Asia-Pacific's geopolitical outlook.

Not limited to major powers, regional players also have interests in the South China Sea debates. ASEAN countries, including Vietnam, the Philippines, Malaysia, and Brunei, are directly impacted by these clashing claims and strive to protect their territories and natural resources. The tricky balancing game between standing for sovereignty and keeping diplomatic ties with all parties adds another tier of intricacy to the geopolitical scenario of the region.

You can't ignore how the South China Sea's geopolitical mess ties into global matters like trade, energy safety, and military unions. This section looks at how these spats could evolve into bigger fusses that shake up the region. We'll visit some possible future paths as well as efforts aimed at calming things down and suggesting peace plans.

Besides, this part also digs into how global groups and many-sided way-outs contribute to the South China Sea issues. It checks how well current tools, like ASEAN-led chats and dialogue stages, can handle squabbles and help competing countries work together.

To sum up, the geopolitical results of the South China Sea disputes are far-reaching and twisted. This section offers a full review of the big countries involved, local dynamics, and the likely effects on the Asia-Pacific region's calm and safety. By getting these geopolitical twists, readers can see the many sides of the South China Sea disputes and their wider importance globally.

Judicial Solutions and Future Prospects:

Steps have been taken to sort out the complex and age-old disputes on the South China Sea with international law tools. One way is arbitration, putting countries' claims before a fair panel for a decision. In 2016, the Philippines won an arbitration case against China under the United Nations Sea Law Treaty (UNCLOS). The panel ruled for the Philippines, stating China's broad boat-route claims were not in line with UNCLOS.

However, despite the ruling, there has been limited progress in implementing and enforcing the tribunal's decision. China has rejected the arbitration as illegitimate and has continued to assert its claims in the South China Sea. Other claimant states have also shown reluctance to fully comply with the ruling, leading to a stalemate in resolving the disputes through legal means.

Negotiations and diplomatic efforts have also been employed to address the South China Sea disputes. Regional organizations like the Association of Southeast Asian Nations (ASEAN) have facilitated discussions among claimant states to promote peaceful resolutions. However, reaching consensus among the diverse interests and positions of the involved parties has proven challenging. Discrepancies in historical narratives, conflicting legal interpretations, and competing strategic agendas have hindered meaningful progress in negotiations.

Looking ahead, potential future scenarios for resolving the South China Sea disputes remain uncertain. The increasing militarization of features in the disputed waters and continued assertiveness from certain claimant states pose significant challenges to finding a peaceful resolution. Additionally, emerging issues such as climate change and evolving maritime technologies further complicate the situation. Rising sea levels and changing environmental conditions may exacerbate resource competition and intensify disputes in the region. Furthermore, advancements in maritime technologies, including unmanned vessels and autonomous systems, could introduce new complexities to maritime governance and enforcement.

New situations continue to emerge. It's vital that parties involved in the South China Sea disagreements focus on open discussion, working together, and following international law. Upholding UNCLOS principles and promoting the use of peaceful methods to solve disagreements is key to creating a balanced, enduring future for the area. Active involvement and a common focus on maintaining the stability of the sea is the best way to find a calm, legal solution to the South China Sea disagreements that works well for everyone involved.

Let's Talk About EU Maritime Policy

In this part, we take a closer look at EU Maritime Policy. We'll see how the European Union is involved in making and carrying out maritime policies. The European Union, made up of many states, understands the big economic, environmental, and safety impacts of the seas that touch its states. Because of this, the EU has come up with a complete plan to handle the ins and outs of the sea world.

EU Maritime Policy includes many goals like promoting sustainable growth, ensuring safety and security at sea, protecting the marine environment, and encouraging international cooperation. Principles like integrated governance, regional cooperation, and sustainable development direct these goals.

Integrated governance is a central part of EU Maritime Policy. The EU knows that many sectors and parties involved in sea activities. So, the EU works to promote working together across different policy fields. This complete approach ensures that decisions in one area don't negatively affect others and allows for different sectors to work together well.

The EU's Maritime Policy stands on partnership. They believe in joining forces with nearby nations and organizations to tackle challenges in the sea region. Their goal is to make Europe's maritime governance unified and effective through mutual agreements.

The EU also values the Sustainability Principle in maritime affairs. They aim for profitable growth but not at the environment's expense. They encourage right practices with rules and projects, touching on areas from fishery control to marine protection to pollution checks.

It's clear that the EU is serious about maritime matters. They've set up particular bodies and programs for the job. The European Commission takes the lead, forming and applying maritime laws. And, specialized agencies like the European Maritime Safety Agency (EMSA) and the European Fisheries Control Agency (EFCA) help with the technical know-how in security and fishery control.

We will look into more details in this section. We will talk about significant topics like the Common Fisheries Policy, maritime surveillance, spatial planning, and regional regulations and consensus. A full understanding of EU Maritime Policy will help you grasp the EU's pursuit to direct maritime governance's future and make the big blue of their region keep flourishing.

EU Maritime Policy and Regional Regulations: Common Fisheries Policy

The European Union (EU) plays a pivotal role in developing and implementing comprehensive maritime policies. One of the key areas of focus within EU maritime policy is the Common Fisheries Policy (CFP), which aims to ensure sustainable fisheries management and protect marine ecosystems.

This section of "Navigating the Seas of Law" delves into the intricacies of the CFP and explores its impact on regional fisheries management within EU waters. By examining the legal framework underpinning this policy, we gain valuable insights into the measures established to promote responsible fishing practices and safeguard fish stocks for future generations.

The CFP recognizes the importance of balancing economic interests with long-term environmental sustainability. It sets clear objectives, including maintaining fish populations above levels that can produce maximum sustainable yield, ensuring fair access to fishing opportunities, and minimizing the impact of fishing activities on marine ecosystems.

To achieve these goals, the CFP implements various regulatory measures, such as setting catch limits, establishing technical measures to reduce unwanted catches (e.g. through minimum landing sizes and selective fishing gear), and implementing control and enforcement mechanisms to prevent illegal, unreported, and unregulated fishing.

Moreover, the CFP promotes international cooperation by establishing agreements with non-EU countries to manage shared fish stocks. These agreements facilitate the sustainable exploitation of resources while respecting the rights and needs of coastal states and their fishing communities.

Within EU waters, the CFP has led to significant improvements in fisheries management and conservation efforts. It has contributed to the rebuilding of depleted fish stocks, reduced discards of unwanted catches, and provided a framework for ecosystem-based approaches to fisheries management. However, challenges remain. The implementation of the CFP requires effective coordination among EU member states, harmonization of national legislation, and robust monitoring and enforcement mechanisms. Compliance with regulations is essential to achieve sustainable fishing practices and prevent overexploitation.

In recent years, there have been calls for further reform of the CFP to address emerging challenges, such as climate change impacts on fish stocks and the need for more ecosystem-based management approaches. These developments highlight the dynamic nature of maritime law and the ongoing efforts to adapt legal frameworks to changing circumstances.

By exploring the intricacies of the Common Fisheries Policy, "Navigating the Seas of Law" provides readers with a comprehensive understanding of the legal framework supporting sustainable fisheries practices within EU waters. This section highlights the importance of international cooperation, effective resource management, and the role of legal mechanisms in achieving long-term sustainability in fisheries.

EU Maritime Policy and Regional Regulations: Integrated Maritime Surveillance

In this section, we delve into the European Union's (EU) endeavors to establish integrated maritime surveillance systems, shedding light on the legal frameworks and cutting-edge technologies employed to augment maritime security and border control.

The EU recognizes the inherent need to safeguard its extensive coastline, territorial waters, and exclusive economic zones from various threats, including illegal activities such as smuggling, trafficking, terrorism, and unauthorized immigration. To address these challenges effectively, the EU has developed comprehensive strategies aiming to achieve integrated maritime surveillance across member states.

Integrated maritime surveillance entails the seamless sharing of information and coordination between different authorities involved in maritime law enforcement, border control, environmental protection, and fisheries management. This holistic approach allows relevant agencies to pool their resources, expertise, and surveillance capabilities to monitor and respond to potential risks and incidents at sea.

At the core of integrated maritime surveillance lie legal frameworks that establish the responsibilities, jurisdictional boundaries, and operational protocols for participating entities. These frameworks facilitate cooperation among member states and harmonize their efforts in upholding maritime security.

Moreover, the EU has invested considerable resources in developing state-of-the-art technologies that bolster the effectiveness of integrated maritime surveillance. These advancements include sophisticated radar systems, satellite imagery analysis, automatic identification systems (AIS), unmanned aerial vehicles (UAVs), and underwater sensors. Such tools provide real-time situational awareness, enabling authorities to detect and track vessels operating within EU waters while facilitating timely intervention when necessary.

Integrated maritime surveillance involves legal aspects. These include safeguarding data privacy and setting rules for sharing info between states. Doing this balance secures personal freedoms and counters oceanic risks.

Besides, global teamwork is vital in this type of surveillance. The EU works with nearby nations, global bodies like Interpol and Europol, and other regional movements. This collaboration boosts sharing info, joint operations, and improving abilities. This teamwork strengthens the EU's power against transnational threats.

With new tech and more challenges at sea, the EU keeps modifying its laws and surveillance approaches. The making of unified maritime systems is an ongoing project. It aims to boost maritime security and safeguard the interests of EU states.

Exploring the legal parts of integrated maritime surveillance offers useful knowledge about maritime law enforcement in the EU. Understanding how laws and tech improvements work together gives a full image of the EU's dedication to a safe and secure maritime setting.

EU's Sea Policy and Area Rules: Ocean Area Planning

Ocean area planning is a cornerstone in the EU's methodical maritime policy. We'll unpack EU's approach, legal aspects, and the task of finding a balance in their coastal areas' competing needs.

What is sea area planning? This involves wisely deciding how to use activities in sea areas to foster sustainable growth and a thriving blue economy. The EU sees value in coordinated area planning. It helps in using sea resources effectively, reducing conflict between sectors, and conservation of marine life.

The principles guiding the EU's sea area planning include managing based on ecosystems, involving stakeholders, integrating sectors, and adhering to international laws. The focus on ecosystem helps preserve the integrity of sea life, considering the interrelationship of species and habitats.

Stakeholders play a key role in the EU's ocean area planning. This includes those from industries, environmental agencies, locals, and indigenous groups. Their participation makes the decision-making fair and inclusive, honoring various viewpoints and boosting stakeholder buy-in.

Coastal zones are tricky to manage. Many interests vie for the same space - shipping, fishing, tourism, energy, conservation, and building needs. The EU tries to balance these needs through cooperation and problem-solving.

One legal issue in managing these areas is jurisdiction. Laws and regulations often overlap nationally and internationally. Aligning these different policies can be complicated. The EU tries to make this easier by aligning national laws with larger EU laws and rules.

Protecting the environment is also important when managing coastal zones. Oceans and seas are delicate ecosystems. They need careful oversight to protect them from harm caused by people. Legal rules around environmental impact assessments, protected areas, and conserving biodiversity are essential for keeping these areas sustainable.

Besides, it's hard to juggle economic growth and caring for the environment. The EU promotes blending economic activities with environmental needs for a thriving 'blue economy.' Sectors can work together, like offshore wind energy and fish farming or tourism and conservation. This allows for economic benefits and less environmental impact.

Maritime spatial planning, which deals with things like water use, needs everyone to work together. That includes countries in the EU, regional groups, and all other stakeholders. The European Maritime Spatial Planning Directive helps with this cooperation. It gives all EU countries a way to work on maritime spatial planning together.

To sum up, maritime spatial planning is critical to the EU. It helps manage what happens in coastal zones strategically. The EU wants to grow sustainably, keep the ocean clean, and boost the blue economy. They have to keep in mind many different interests and abide by laws. This can get tough. They aim to solve this through working together, getting everyone involved, and following international laws. Doing this helps both now and in the future.

EU Rules and Agreements:

This part talks about EU rules and agreements about different water-related activities. The EU has a lot of laws to deal with things like pollution, port rules, and safe shipping. These help the marine industries in EU countries grow in a way that's good for the environment and efficient.

Pollution control is a big part of these regional laws. The EU has strict rules to protect the ocean from pollution by ships and offshore structures. They've got laws on how to handle pollutants, dangerous substances, and prevent oil spills. Following these laws is crucial. It helps keep a balance in marine life and preserve the diversity of species in EU waters.

Ports are important, and the EU knows this. That's why there are regional agreements about ports. The EU sets rules for port services like pilotage, towage, and mooring. The goal is to keep everything fair and safe, and to make the best use of the ports in all EU countries.

But it's not just about ports. The EU also takes care of shipping standards. There are rules about what ships operating in EU waters need to meet. This includes safety and pollution limits. The EU uses international rules, such as the SOLAS and MARPOL conventions, as part of its laws.

The EU member states help each other to make these rules work. There are different groups, like the EMSA and the EFCA where they share information and good ideas. They also patrol and inspect together to make sure everyone follows the rules.

We study laws and teamwork methods in regional rules. This helps us know how the EU handles its ocean businesses. These rules are important for people in this field. Following these standards is needed for success in the EU market. Moreover, this check gives us a wider view of the problems maritime areas face. They need to balance growth with keeping the environment safe and sustainable.

Part V:
Navigational Tools
Legal Practice and
Procedures

"In the toolkit of legal policies and procedures, maritime law crafts a precise compass, carves out a sturdy anchor, and unfurls sails of fairness. With a seamless blend of regulations and principles, it ensures a smooth voyage through the complex waters of justice and accountability."

Chapter 1

The Admirality Court

***

The Admiralty Court is an integral component of the complex and fascinating field of maritime law. With its historical significance and unique jurisdiction, understanding the Admiralty Court is essential for navigating the seas of law.

Dating back to medieval England, the Admiralty Court was established to handle legal matters specifically related to maritime affairs. Its primary purpose was to ensure the efficient resolution of disputes arising at sea, providing a specialized forum for maritime cases.

The Admiralty Court's jurisdiction extends to a wide range of matters pertaining to admiralty and maritime law. These include disputes related to maritime contracts, vessel collisions, salvage claims, maritime liens, and other issues specific to navigation and commerce on the high seas. By focusing exclusively on maritime cases, the Admiralty Court possesses a specialized knowledge that enables it to address the unique complexities and nuances of maritime law.

One of the key advantages of the Admiralty Court is its ability to operate across national boundaries. As maritime disputes often involve parties from different countries, the court ensures a neutral and impartial forum for resolving conflicts. It recognizes the global nature of maritime activities and applies international legal principles to maintain fairness and consistency in its decisions.

Throughout history, the Admiralty Court has played a crucial role in shaping maritime jurisprudence. Landmark cases have contributed to the development of legal principles that continue to guide modern maritime law. By setting precedents and establishing standards for resolving complex maritime disputes, the court has enriched the body of law governing the seas.

As readers delve into this section, they will gain a comprehensive understanding of the Admiralty Court's historical significance and purpose within the realm of maritime law. By exploring its jurisdiction, readers will appreciate how this specialized court contributes to the orderly resolution of maritime disputes. This knowledge will prepare readers for further exploration into the procedural rules, practices, and landmark cases that define the Admiralty Court's role in navigating the seas of law.

Since the origins of the Admiralty Court lie in medieval England, it is essential to explore its evolution over time. The Admiralty Court can trace its roots back to the twelfth century when maritime disputes were initially brought before the royal courts. However, as maritime trade and navigation expanded, a specialized court became necessary to handle these cases efficiently.

The establishment of the Admiralty Court as a distinct entity separate from the common law courts occurred during the reign of Edward III in the fourteenth century. Recognizing the need for a specialized forum to address maritime matters, Edward III granted jurisdiction over maritime disputes to a small group of judges known as the "Admirals." These individuals possessed extensive knowledge and expertise in maritime law and were entrusted with resolving complex maritime disputes.

Over time, the jurisdiction of the Admiralty Court expanded to include various aspects of maritime law, including issues related to salvage, shipwrecks, collisions at sea, and disputes arising from contracts and obligations in marine commerce. As England's naval power grew, so did the influence and reach of the Admiralty Court.

During the sixteenth and seventeenth centuries, England's dominance in global trade led to an increased volume of maritime disputes. To accommodate this growing caseload, additional specialized courts, known as Vice-Admiralty Courts, were established throughout England's overseas colonies. These courts operated under the authority of the central Admiralty Court and played a crucial role in enforcing maritime law in distant territories.

The eighteenth and nineteenth centuries witnessed further expansion and refinement of the Admiralty Court's jurisdiction. With advancements in international trade and colonial expansion, there was an increased demand for a comprehensive legal framework to govern maritime activities.

In response to these developments, Parliament passed several important acts that extended the Admiralty Court's jurisdiction. For instance, the 1838 Act expanded its authority concerning claims for collision damage, while the 1840 Act empowered the court to hear cases related to salvage and towage contracts.

By the late nineteenth century, the Admiralty Court had established itself as a prominent forum for adjudicating maritime disputes. Its jurisdiction extended not only to British subjects but also to foreign vessels and nationals, reflecting the court's growing international standing.

The Admiralty Court's evolution continued into the twentieth century, with reforms aimed at modernizing its procedures and adapting to changing circumstances. These changes included the introduction of special rules of practice, the establishment of specialized registries for maritime claims, and the incorporation of new statutory provisions.

Today, the Admiralty Court remains an essential institution in maritime law, with its jurisdiction now encompassing a wide range of admiralty and maritime claims. From its humble origins in medieval England to its current status as a respected global forum for resolving maritime disputes, the Admiralty Court's history and evolution epitomize the enduring significance of maritime law in our interconnected world.

Jurisdictional Authority of the Admiralty Court

The Admiralty Court, with its long-standing historical significance and purpose, holds a unique jurisdiction in maritime law cases. Understanding the types of cases that fall under its authority is crucial for comprehending the intricate workings of maritime jurisprudence.

One key area of jurisdiction for the Admiralty Court relates to maritime disputes. This includes cases involving collisions between vessels, damage claims arising from maritime accidents, salvage operations, and towage disputes. The court assumes jurisdiction over these matters to ensure fair and impartial resolution, taking into account the complexities and nuances of maritime operations.

Additionally, the Admiralty Court has authority over contractual disputes within the maritime industry. This encompasses cases regarding charter parties, bills of lading, shipbuilding contracts, and marine insurance policies. By having jurisdiction over such contractual matters, the court facilitates the enforcement of legal obligations and protects the interests of parties involved in maritime transactions.

Moreover, the Admiralty Court exercises jurisdiction over maritime claims relating to seafarers' rights. These claims encompass issues such as wages, working conditions, personal injuries, and wrongful death at sea. The court acts as a guardian of seafarers' rights, ensuring that they are afforded appropriate legal protection and remedies.

Furthermore, the Admiralty Court has authority in admiralty arrests and vessel detentions. It enables parties to arrest a vessel or its associated property as security for a claim. This jurisdiction ensures the enforceability of judgments and prevents vessels from leaving port without settling outstanding liabilities.

It is important to note that the Admiralty Court's jurisdiction extends beyond national boundaries. Due to the nature of maritime activities, cases involving foreign-flagged vessels or international trade fall within its purview. This global jurisdiction contributes to the harmonization and consistency of maritime law principles across different jurisdictions.

In summary, the Admiralty Court possesses a broad range of jurisdictional authority in handling various types of maritime disputes and claims. Whether it involves collisions, contractual disputes, seafarers' rights, or vessel detentions, the court plays a pivotal role in upholding the rule of law within the maritime domain. A comprehensive understanding of its jurisdiction is essential for anyone navigating the intricacies of maritime law. Admiralty Procedure and Practices in the Admiralty Court have developed over centuries to ensure a fair and efficient resolution of maritime disputes. Understanding these procedural rules and practices is crucial for anyone involved in maritime law cases.

When a case is brought before the Admiralty Court, certain steps must be followed. The process typically begins with the filing of a complaint or petition by the party seeking relief. This document outlines the facts of the case and the legal arguments supporting their claim.

Once the complaint is filed, it is served to the opposing party or parties, who then have a designated period to respond. This ensures that all parties have an opportunity to present their side of the dispute. In some cases, additional pleadings may be filed, providing further details or clarifications on the claims and defenses.

After the pleadings are complete, the court will schedule a pre-trial conference or hearing to discuss the issues at hand. This conference allows the parties to present their arguments, exchange evidence, and potentially reach a settlement. It also provides an opportunity for the court to address any preliminary issues or procedural matters.

If a settlement cannot be reached during the pre-trial conference, the case will proceed to trial. At trial, both parties have the opportunity to present their evidence, call witnesses, and argue their case before a judge or jury. The judge or jury will then evaluate the evidence and make a decision based on applicable laws and precedents.

Following the trial, the court will issue its judgment or verdict. This decision sets out the court's findings of fact and conclusions of law, determining which party prevails in the dispute. If either party is dissatisfied with the judgment, they may have the option to appeal to a higher court for review.

It is important to note that the timeline for resolution can vary depending on factors such as case complexity, court availability, and the willingness of parties to cooperate. Some cases may be resolved relatively quickly, while others can take months or even years to reach a final resolution.

By familiarizing themselves with the procedural rules and practices of the Admiralty Court, legal professionals and individuals involved in maritime disputes can navigate the litigation process more effectively. This understanding enables them to present their case accurately and efficiently, ensuring a fair and just resolution within the framework of maritime law.

Landmark Admiralty Cases and Precedents

In this section, we delve into some of the most significant admiralty cases that have played a pivotal role in shaping maritime law. These landmark cases have carved out important legal principles and set precedents that continue to influence the jurisdiction and decisions of the Admiralty Court.

One notable case that stands out is the R v. Dudley and Stephens (1884) case. This tragic incident involved four men stranded at sea without food or water after their ship sank. Facing starvation, three of the men conspired to kill and eat the fourth crew member in order to survive. They were eventually rescued, but upon return to land, they were charged with murder.

The trial raised several complex questions surrounding necessity, self-defense, and the limits of human survival. The court's ruling established the principle that necessity does not justify taking another person's life, even in extreme circumstances. This case set an important precedent in admiralty law, emphasizing the sanctity of human life and establishing boundaries for actions taken under dire situations at sea.

Another influential case is The SS Lotus (1927) case between France and Turkey. The dispute centered around a collision between a French vessel, the SS Lotus, and a Turkish vessel, the Boz-Kourt. The collision resulted in the death of eight Turkish sailors, and both countries claimed jurisdiction over the incident.

The Permanent Court of International Justice ruled that in territorial waters, a state has exclusive jurisdiction over incidents occurring on vessels flying its flag. However, in international waters, where both vessels were at the time of the collision, the principle of freedom of the seas applied. This landmark decision reinforced the concept of state sovereignty within territorial waters while emphasizing the principle of freedom and equality on the high seas.

One more notable case is The Star Sea (1982) case involving a collision between two vessels off the coast of Japan. The collision resulted in significant environmental damage due to oil spillage. The court's ruling established the principle of strict liability, holding the shipowner liable for the pollution caused by their vessel, regardless of fault.

This case set an important precedent in maritime law, highlighting the need for shipowners to take proactive measures to prevent maritime accidents and environmental damage. It also emphasized the importance of ensuring accountability and compensation for those affected by such incidents.

These landmark admiralty cases demonstrate how pivotal moments in maritime history have shaped legal principles and influenced the jurisdiction and decisions of the Admiralty Court. By examining these cases and understanding their impact, we gain valuable insights into the intricacies of maritime law and its practical application in addressing complex maritime disputes.

Introduction to Maritime Liens:

Maritime liens, a crucial aspect of maritime law, play a significant role in governing the rights and priorities of various parties involved in maritime transactions. Understanding the concept of maritime liens is essential for comprehending the intricate web of legal rights and obligations that arise in the maritime domain.

A maritime lien can be defined as a privileged claim or security interest on a vessel, which gives the lienholder the right to enforce their claim against the vessel itself. Unlike traditional liens, which are typically created by contract or statute, maritime liens arise as a result of specific events or circumstances related to maritime activities.

The historical development of maritime liens can be traced back to ancient times when maritime commerce flourished. In those early eras, maritime liens served as an essential mechanism for ensuring the payment of debts incurred in the course of shipping goods or providing services related to maritime trade.

Over time, maritime liens evolved in response to the changing needs of seafarers and the expanding scope of maritime commerce. Today, they encompass a wide range of claims, including those arising from salvage operations, damage to cargo, personal injury or death, unpaid wages of seafarers, and non-payment of marine mortgages or necessaries.

Understanding the different types of claims that can give rise to a maritime lien is crucial. Salvage claims, for example, may arise when individuals or vessels render assistance to other vessels in distress or peril. These claims ensure that those who provide essential services during emergencies receive their rightful compensation.

Similarly, damage to cargo claims protect the interests of cargo owners if their goods suffer loss or damage during transportation. These claims allow cargo owners to assert their rights and seek compensation for any harm or loss suffered as a result of negligence or other factors.

Unpaid wages of seafarers represent another category of claims that can result in the creation of a maritime lien. These liens provide a means for seafarers to seek payment for their labor and ensure that they are not left unpaid after dedicating their time and skills to maritime activities.

Understanding the historical development and significance of maritime liens provides a solid foundation for comprehending their role in contemporary maritime law. By exploring the origins of maritime liens and the types of claims that can give rise to them, readers will gain a comprehensive understanding of this complex legal concept. When it comes to maritime law, one important concept that cannot be overlooked is the creation and enforcement of maritime liens. In this section, we will delve into the requirements for establishing a valid maritime lien and explore the various scenarios in which a maritime lien may arise.

A maritime lien can be created when certain claims or debts are associated with a vessel. These claims can arise from actions such as salvage operations, damage to cargo, unpaid wages, or breach of contract in relation to maritime services. The key factor is that these claims are directly connected to the vessel itself rather than the owner or operator.

To establish a valid maritime lien, certain requirements must be met. Firstly, the claim must fall within one of the recognized categories for maritime liens. Each category has its own specific criteria, but they generally involve situations where there is a direct connection between the vessel and the claim. For example, salvage operations involve the voluntary assistance provided to a vessel in distress, which can result in a salvage lien.

Secondly, the claimant must have a valid legal basis for their claim and demonstrate that they have fulfilled their obligations in relation to the particular matter. For instance, if it is a claim for unpaid wages, the seafarer must show that they performed the required work and that their wages were not duly paid.

Once a maritime lien has been established, it can be enforced through various mechanisms. One common method is through an action in rem, which allows the claimant to arrest or detain the vessel to secure their claim. This means that the vessel itself becomes subject to legal proceedings and can be sold to satisfy the outstanding debt.

Enforcement of maritime liens typically involves initiating legal proceedings in a court with jurisdiction over the matter. The claimant needs to provide evidence of their claim and demonstrate that all necessary steps were taken to establish a valid maritime lien. The court then determines whether the lien is valid and, if so, orders the arrest of the vessel.

In conclusion, understanding the creation and enforcement of maritime liens is crucial in navigating the complex world of maritime law. By meeting the requirements for establishing a valid lien and being aware of the different scenarios in which a maritime lien may arise, claimants can effectively protect their interests and seek appropriate remedies.

Priority and Ranking of Maritime Liens:

Understanding the principles that govern the priority and ranking of maritime liens is crucial for both legal professionals and shipowners. In this section, we delve into the intricate details of how these liens are ordered and satisfied, exploring the factors that influence their priority and examining case law examples that illustrate their practical application.

The priority of maritime liens determines the order in which they are paid from the proceeds of a vessel's sale or the distribution of funds in a maritime dispute. Multiple maritime liens may be present in a single scenario, such as when a vessel is involved in a collision, leading to various claims from different parties. In such cases, it becomes necessary to establish an order of priority to ensure fair distribution and resolution.

Various factors come into play when determining the ranking of maritime liens. First and foremost is the nature of the claim itself. Certain claims, known as privileged claims, enjoy automatic priority over other liens due to their exceptional importance. These include expenses related to the vessel's preservation, such as crew wages, necessary repairs, and supplies. Other privileged claims could involve maritime salvage and the costs associated with the removal of wrecks.

Beyond privileged claims, the ranking of maritime liens is typically determined by the chronological order in which they arise. The principle of "first in time, first in right" prevails, meaning that the first lienholder to assert their claim will have priority over subsequent lienholders. This principle serves as a fundamental pillar within maritime law, ensuring certainty and predictability in determining where a lien stands relative to others.

However, there are exceptions to this general rule. Some jurisdictions recognize what is known as a "preferred lien," which grants certain claims a higher priority regardless of their chronological order. Common examples of preferred liens include mortgage liens and repairers' liens. These liens are granted priority status to protect creditors who have made substantial investments in the vessel.

To grasp the complexities of prioritizing maritime liens, it is essential to explore case law examples that illustrate how these principles are applied in practice. By examining legal precedents, we can gain a deeper understanding of the factors that courts consider when determining the priority of competing maritime liens. These case studies offer valuable insights into the real-world application of maritime law and provide guidance for legal professionals and stakeholders involved in maritime disputes.

In conclusion, this section on the priority and ranking of maritime liens offers a comprehensive exploration of the principles governing their order and satisfaction. By understanding the factors that determine priority and examining relevant case law examples, readers will gain a thorough understanding of how maritime liens are prioritized and resolved in practice.

Maritime Liens and Ship Arrest:

Ship Arrest:

Ship arrest serves as a crucial legal remedy in maritime law, providing a means to enforce maritime liens and secure the interests of claimants. This section offers an in-depth overview of ship arrest, its purpose, and the circumstances under which a vessel can be arrested.

Ship arrest typically occurs when a claimant seeks to secure their maritime lien by obtaining a court order to physically detain the vessel concerned. The decision to arrest a ship is deliberated upon by the courts and is influenced by various factors, such as the validity of the claim and the likelihood of success in pursuing legal action against the shipowner.

The circumstances that may warrant a ship's arrest vary and can include disputes arising from unpaid wages, damage to cargo or property, salvage claims, or breach of contract. When these situations arise, interested parties can seek the court's intervention to arrest the vessel and prevent it from leaving port or continuing its voyage until the dispute is resolved.

The process of initiating and carrying out a ship arrest involves several critical steps. Claimants must file an application with the appropriate court, outlining their claim and providing evidence to support their case. The court will then review the application, assess its merits, and determine whether to issue an arrest warrant.

Once an arrest warrant is obtained, it is typically served by authorized officials, such as marshals or other designated individuals appointed by the court. These officials physically seize control of the vessel, often under the supervision of law enforcement authorities. The arrested ship is then securely held in a designated location until the court proceedings conclude or suitable arrangements are made to settle the claim.

It is worth noting that ship arrest proceedings can vary between jurisdictions, as different legal systems may have specific requirements and procedures. Therefore, it is essential for claimants seeking ship arrest to consult with legal professionals familiar with the relevant laws and practices in the jurisdiction where they intend to pursue this legal remedy.

Ship arrest holds significant implications for all parties involved. For shipowners, an arrest can disrupt their operations, potentially leading to financial losses and damage to their reputation. On the other hand, for claimants, ship arrest provides a means to secure their claims and ensure that they are not left uncompensated.

Given the potential consequences of ship arrest, it is crucial to consider the legal and practical considerations associated with this legal remedy. These include jurisdictional issues, bail requirements, potential remedies for wrongful arrest, and the rights and obligations of the arresting party, the shipowner, and other interested parties.

By exploring ship arrest in detail, this section equips readers with a comprehensive understanding of this critical legal instrument in maritime law. Understanding the principles and procedures involved in ship arrest enables both legal professionals and stakeholders in the maritime industry to navigate the complex terrain of maritime disputes with confidence and insight.

Legal Consequences and Practical Considerations:

Once a vessel has been arrested under maritime law, it triggers a series of legal consequences for the parties involved. This section explores these consequences, shedding light on the rights and obligations of the arresting party, the shipowner, and other interested parties.

Firstly, for the shipowner, the arrest of their vessel can have significant implications. The arrested vessel may be immobilized, preventing it from carrying out its intended operations. This can result in financial losses for the owner, as they may be unable to fulfill contractual obligations or generate revenue from the vessel's use. Additionally, the shipowner may be required to provide security or bail to secure the release of the vessel. Failure to comply with these requirements can lead to further legal complications and delays.

On the other hand, the arresting party gains certain rights and privileges as a result of the vessel's arrest. They are granted a priority claim on the vessel and its associated assets, which can help secure their own financial interests. Through the arrest, they gain leverage in negotiations with the shipowner and have the ability to enforce their claim in court.

It is important to note that other interested parties may also be affected by a ship arrest. These parties include charterers, cargo owners, banks, and suppliers who may have an interest in the vessel or its cargo. Depending on their level of involvement and the circumstances surrounding the arrest, they may need to assert their rights or seek legal remedies to protect their interests.

In addition to considering the legal consequences, practical considerations should also be taken into account when dealing with ship arrests. One such consideration is jurisdictional issues. Ship arrests often involve vessels that are registered in one jurisdiction but operate in international waters or visit ports in various countries. Determining which jurisdiction's laws apply and where legal proceedings should take place can be complex and time-consuming.

Furthermore, bail requirements can pose challenges for both the arresting party and the shipowner. Bail acts as security to ensure that the arrested vessel will be released upon the fulfillment of certain conditions or payment of a specified amount. Determining the appropriate amount of bail and providing the necessary financial guarantees can be a contentious issue, requiring negotiation and potential court intervention.

Lastly, it is crucial to address potential remedies for wrongful arrest. In cases where the arrest was initiated without valid grounds or in bad faith, the shipowner may have the right to seek damages or other remedies against the arresting party. This serves as a safeguard against abuse of the arrest process and provides recourse for shipowners who have suffered unjustified losses due to an improper arrest.

Navigating the legal consequences and practical considerations associated with ship arrests requires a thorough understanding of maritime law and its intricacies. By examining case law examples and considering real-world scenarios, this book equips readers with the knowledge and insights necessary to navigate these complex issues effectively.

Marine insurance is a pivotal aspect of maritime law, playing a crucial role in mitigating risks in maritime trade and commerce. As we delve into the fascinating world of marine insurance, it is essential to understand its historical context and the significance it holds within the realm of maritime jurisprudence.

Dating back centuries, marine insurance can trace its origins to the early civilizations that engaged in maritime trade. It emerged as a response to the inherent risks associated with sea voyages, such as piracy, shipwrecks, and inclement weather. Merchants sought protection for their valuable goods and investments, leading to the establishment of contractual agreements that would indemnify against losses incurred during transit.

Throughout history, various systems of marine insurance developed across different regions and cultures. The ancient Greeks and Romans employed informal methods of sharing risk among merchants through what were known as "bottomry" and "respondentia" contracts. These arrangements allowed lenders to provide funds for a voyage in exchange for repayment with interest upon the vessel's safe return or a share of the profits.

In medieval times, maritime insurance took on new forms as trade expanded and became more complex. Maritime insurance guilds, such as the Lombards in Italy and the Hanseatic League in Northern Europe, emerged to regulate and oversee insurance practices. These guilds standardized policies and procedures, establishing rules governing premium rates, underwriting practices, and claims settlements.

The subsequent centuries witnessed further developments in marine insurance, particularly during the age of exploration and colonial expansion. With increased globalization and transoceanic voyages becoming commonplace, demand for marine insurance surged. Insurance markets flourished in major port cities such as London and Amsterdam, attracting capital from eager underwriters willing to take on risks associated with long-distance sea journeys.

The industrial revolution brought significant advancements to the shipping industry, resulting in larger vessels capable of carrying greater quantities of goods. This necessitated the need for more comprehensive and specialized marine insurance coverage. Pioneering insurance companies emerged, offering innovative policies tailored to meet the evolving needs of maritime trade.

Today, marine insurance remains an indispensable component of the shipping industry, providing essential protection for vessels, cargo, and liabilities. It encompasses various types of coverage, including hull insurance, cargo insurance, and liability insurance, each designed to address specific risks encountered in the maritime domain.

Understanding the historical foundations of marine insurance is vital for comprehending its current significance within the framework of maritime law. As we embark on this exploration of marine insurance, we will delve deeper into the principles, concepts, and practices that govern this essential aspect of maritime jurisprudence.

Principles and Concepts of Marine Insurance

In this section, we delve into the fundamental principles and concepts that underpin marine insurance, providing readers with a comprehensive understanding of this crucial aspect of maritime law.

Marine insurance is a specialized branch of insurance that aims to mitigate risks associated with maritime trade and commerce. It provides coverage for various maritime-related risks, such as damage to vessels, goods in transit, and liabilities arising from maritime activities.

To fully comprehend marine insurance, it is essential to grasp key terms and definitions related to marine insurance policies. This includes understanding the roles and responsibilities of the parties involved, namely insurers, insured parties, and brokers.

Insurers are the entities or organizations that provide the coverage and assume the risks associated with marine insurance. They assess the risks involved and determine the premiums to be paid by the insured parties. Insurers play a critical role in evaluating claims and determining appropriate settlements.

On the other hand, insured parties refer to individuals or businesses that seek coverage through marine insurance policies. These parties may include shipowners, cargo owners, freight forwarders, charterers, and other stakeholders involved in maritime trade. Understanding their rights and obligations in relation to marine insurance is vital for effective risk management.

Brokers act as intermediaries between insurers and insured parties. They assist in coordinating the purchase of marine insurance policies by connecting potential insured parties with suitable insurers. Brokers possess extensive knowledge of the market and can provide valuable advice on selecting appropriate coverage options.

The principles governing marine insurance policies are rooted in centuries-old legal precedents and industry practices. One such principle is utmost good faith, which requires both insurers and insured parties to honestly disclose all material information that may affect the insurance contract. The principle of indemnity ensures that insured parties are compensated for their actual losses without making a profit from insurance claims.

Understanding these principles and concepts is crucial not only for those directly involved in maritime trade but also for legal professionals and policymakers who seek to navigate the complexities of marine insurance law. By grasping the fundamentals of marine insurance, readers can effectively manage risks, ensure compliance with legal requirements, and make informed decisions concerning their maritime ventures.

Types of Marine Insurance Coverage

Marine insurance plays a critical role in mitigating risks associated with maritime trade and commerce. Within the realm of marine insurance, there are various types of coverage that cater to specific aspects of the maritime industry. This section explores the different types of marine insurance coverage, including hull insurance, cargo insurance, and liability insurance.

Hull insurance is designed to protect the physical structure and machinery of vessels against a range of perils. It covers damages resulting from accidents, collisions, storms, fires, and other unforeseen events. Hull insurance ensures that shipowners can recover their financial losses in the event of damage or total loss of vessels. This type of coverage is especially crucial in safeguarding the sizable investments made in the construction and maintenance of ships.

Cargo insurance, on the other hand, focuses on protecting the goods being transported by sea. It provides coverage for potential losses or damages that may occur during transit. Cargo insurance typically covers risks such as theft, damage caused by mishandling or accidents, or losses resulting from natural disasters like storms or hurricanes. With the vast array of goods transported via maritime routes, cargo insurance offers peace of mind to both shippers and consignees by providing financial compensation in the event of unforeseen incidents.

In addition to hull and cargo insurance, liability insurance is another significant aspect of marine insurance coverage. Liability insurance protects shipowners and operators against legal claims arising from accidents or incidents involving their vessels. This coverage can also extend to include protection against pollution-related liabilities, salvage costs, collisions, and personal injury claims. Liability insurance aims to ensure that shipowners are protected from potentially ruinous legal actions and can navigate through complex legal proceedings with peace of mind.

Within each type of marine insurance coverage, specific risks are addressed to cater to the unique challenges faced by the maritime industry. For instance, hull insurance covers risks associated with vessel operation and navigation, such as accidents at sea or damage caused by external factors. Cargo insurance focuses on the risks specific to the transportation of goods, including theft, damage, or loss during transit. Liability insurance addresses the legal and financial consequences that may arise from accidents, collisions, and other incidents involving vessels.

Marine insurance policies often contain common clauses and endorsements that further define the coverage and obligations of the insured parties. These clauses and endorsements specify additional conditions or exclusions, such as navigational limits, war risks, deductibles, or warranties. It is essential for insured parties to thoroughly understand these clauses and endorsements to ensure that their coverage aligns with their specific needs and requirements.

As the maritime industry continues to evolve, innovative solutions and customization options are emerging within marine insurance practices. From parametric insurance, which provides coverage based on predefined triggers such as weather conditions or commodity prices, to increased focus on cyber insurance to address digital threats, the landscape of marine insurance is adapting to changing circumstances. By embracing new technologies and risk models, marine insurance is becoming more tailored to the unique challenges faced by today's shipping industry.

Understanding the different types of marine insurance coverage is vital for all stakeholders involved in maritime activities. Shipowners, cargo owners, insurers, brokers, and legal professionals must be aware of the specific risks covered by each type of marine insurance to ensure adequate protection and proper risk management. By having comprehensive knowledge of these coverage options, stakeholders can make informed decisions and navigate through the complex world of marine insurance with confidence.

Marine Insurance Claims and Settlements

Understanding the process of filing a marine insurance claim is essential for both insurers and insured parties. In this section, we will explore the obligations and responsibilities of each party during the claims process, as well as discuss the factors considered in determining claim settlements.

When an insured event occurs, such as the loss or damage of cargo or a vessel, the insured party must promptly notify the insurer and provide relevant documentation, including a detailed description of the incident and supporting evidence. It is crucial for insured parties to adhere to any specified notification requirements and submit the claim within the stipulated time frame. Failure to do so may result in the denial of the claim.

Insurers, on the other hand, have a duty to promptly investigate the claim and assess its validity. This may involve appointing surveyors or adjusters to evaluate the extent of the loss or damage. Insurers must thoroughly review all relevant documentation provided by the insured party and diligently consider any supplementary information before making a decision on the claim. Transparency and effective communication between insurers and insured parties are critical throughout this process.

Determining claim settlements involves various factors that require careful consideration. Valuation is one such factor that assesses the value of the damaged property or lost cargo. Insurers may rely on market prices, industry standards, or expert opinions to determine an appropriate valuation.

Salvage is another important aspect of claim settlements, particularly in cases where damaged vessels need to be recovered or goods need to be salvaged from a sunken ship. The amount of salvage awarded to salvors or parties involved in salvage operations is typically negotiated based on a percentage of the value saved.

General average refers to a principle wherein all parties involved in a maritime venture proportionally share losses incurred for the common good. When extraordinary measures are taken to preserve the ship and cargo, such as jettisoning part of the cargo to prevent sinking, general average contributions are calculated to distribute the financial burden among the parties involved. The determination of general average contributions is a complex process that takes into account various factors, including the value of the property saved, the total value at risk, and each party's respective interests.

Understanding the intricacies of marine insurance claims and settlements is crucial for both insurers and insured parties to ensure a fair and efficient resolution. By adhering to their respective obligations and responsibilities and considering the factors discussed in this section, both parties can navigate the claims process with confidence and achieve satisfactory outcomes in terms of compensation and loss mitigation.

Marine Insurance Law

Emerging Trends in Marine Insurance

In this section, we delve into the contemporary challenges and emerging trends in marine insurance that are reshaping the landscape of maritime law. As the shipping industry evolves and faces new risks, it is crucial for insurers and insured parties to adapt their practices and policies to mitigate these challenges effectively.

One of the key emerging trends in marine insurance is the increasing threat of cyber threats. With technology playing an ever-growing role in maritime operations, vessels and port facilities have become vulnerable to cyberattacks. The potential consequences of a successful attack can be catastrophic, ranging from disruption of vessel operations to compromising sensitive data or navigation systems. Insurers are therefore recognizing the need for specialized cyber insurance policies tailored to the unique risks faced by the shipping industry. These policies encompass coverage for data breaches, cyber extortion, business interruption, and liability arising from cyber incidents. Additionally, insurers are working closely with shipowners and operators to develop robust cybersecurity protocols that can help prevent and mitigate cyber risks.

Environmental liabilities have also emerged as a significant concern for marine insurers. As global awareness of environmental conservation grows, regulatory bodies are imposing stricter regulations on shipping companies to reduce their ecological footprint. In response, insurers are developing specialized policies that provide coverage for environmental damages caused by maritime activities. These policies may cover pollution-related costs, clean-up expenses, and compensation for third-party claims resulting from oil spills or other environmental accidents. Insurers are also encouraging shipowners to implement sustainable practices and adopt eco-friendly technologies through discounted premiums or incentives.

Furthermore, innovative solutions such as parametric insurance and blockchain technology are revolutionizing the marine insurance industry. Parametric insurance offers predefined payouts based on specific triggers rather than traditional loss assessment processes. This type of insurance can be particularly valuable in natural disasters or catastrophic events where quick access to funds is essential for recovery efforts. On the other hand, blockchain technology provides a transparent and secure platform for sharing information and streamlining insurance transactions. It enables real-time monitoring of vessel conditions, automated claims processing, and verification of policy data, reducing administrative costs and improving efficiency.

In conclusion, the ever-evolving shipping industry brings forth new challenges and risks that necessitate innovative solutions in marine insurance. The rise of cyber threats and environmental liabilities requires insurers to develop specialized policies tailored to these emerging risks. Furthermore, the adoption of parametric insurance and blockchain technology offers opportunities for enhanced efficiency, transparency, and risk management. As the maritime sector continues to evolve, it is essential for insurers and insured parties to stay abreast of these emerging trends and adapt their practices accordingly to navigate the complex seas of marine insurance.

The Carriage of Goods by Sea: Historical Development - Origins of the Carriage of Goods by Sea

The transportation of goods via maritime routes has a rich historical background that stretches back centuries. Understanding the origins of the carriage of goods by sea is essential to comprehending its legal principles and practices. In this section, we will explore the historical development of this crucial aspect of maritime law.

Early civilizations recognized the advantages of using waterways for trade and commerce, laying the foundation for the carriage of goods by sea. Ancient cultures, such as the Phoenicians and Egyptians, established maritime trade networks that spanned vast distances. These early seafarers experienced the need to establish rules and principles to govern their commercial transactions and protect their interests. In the Mediterranean region, during the time of ancient Greece and Rome, maritime trade played a significant role in economic growth and cultural exchange. The Roman Empire, in particular, developed a sophisticated legal system that encompassed maritime regulations and commercial contracts. Historical records indicate the existence of "lex Rhodia de jactu" or the "Rhodian Maritime Law," which detailed provisions governing matters such as compensation for shipwrecks and liability for cargo losses.

The Middle Ages witnessed further advancements in the carriage of goods by sea. Medieval maritime trade routes flourished, connecting Europe with the Middle East, Africa, and Asia. During this period, various city-states and trading guilds formulated their own rules and regulations to safeguard their interests. Notably, the Hanseatic League, a confederation of merchant guilds in Northern Europe, played a crucial role in establishing legal norms for maritime commerce.

As global exploration expanded in the Age of Discovery, the carriage of goods by sea became even more integral to international trade. European nations sought new routes to access valuable resources and establish colonies. This led to the emergence of national laws regulating maritime activities. For instance, England passed navigation acts to strengthen its naval power and protect its commercial interests. These acts provided the English courts with jurisdiction over disputes arising from the carriage of goods by sea.

The development of maritime insurance, particularly the establishment of Lloyd's of London in the late 17th century, further facilitated the growth of the carriage of goods by sea. Insurance contracts provided shippers and carriers with a financial safety net in the event of losses or damages during transportation. Over time, international efforts were made to standardize the legal principles governing the carriage of goods by sea. Key milestones include the creation of the International Chamber of Commerce's Incoterms in the early 20th century and the adoption of international conventions such as the Hague Rules, Hamburg Rules, and Rotterdam Rules.

Understanding the historical context in which the carriage of goods by sea evolved helps us appreciate its significance in today's globalized world. By examining the origins of this practice, we gain valuable insights into the legal principles and practices that continue to shape maritime law. In the following sections, we will delve deeper into the intricacies of bills of lading, types of contracts, liability regimes, dispute resolution mechanisms, and more. Through this exploration, readers will gain a comprehensive understanding of the complexities inherent in this vital aspect of maritime jurisprudence.

The Carriage of Goods by Sea

The bill of lading, a common document used in the carriage of goods by sea, plays a crucial role in facilitating international trade. It serves as both a receipt for the goods loaded onto a vessel and a contract of carriage between the shipper and the carrier. Understanding its importance and the legal implications it entails is essential for all parties involved.

A bill of lading serves as proof that the goods have been received by the carrier for shipment and provides evidence of the terms and conditions agreed upon between the shipper and the carrier. It contains essential information such as the description of the goods, their quantity, packaging, marks and numbers, as well as the names of the shipper, consignee, and vessel. This document acts as a title to the goods, enabling their transfer or endorsement during transit.

One of the primary functions of a bill of lading is to define the rights, obligations, and liabilities of each party in the transaction. For shippers, it represents a vital instrument for establishing ownership over the goods. They can transfer or pledge their rights in the goods by endorsing or surrendering the bill of lading to another party. On the other hand, carriers are obligated to transport the goods safely and deliver them to the agreed destination in good condition, as stated in the bill of lading. Any loss, damage, or delay in the delivery of the cargo may result in liability for the carrier.

The bill of lading also serves as a receipt for the goods by acknowledging their shipment and condition at the time of loading. This becomes particularly significant in cases where disputes arise regarding the quantity or quality of the goods upon delivery. The carrier's obligation to issue a clean bill of lading, which indicates that the goods were received in apparent good order and condition, highlights their responsibility to exercise due diligence in handling and stowing the cargo.

Furthermore, the bill of lading acts as a document of title that allows the consignee to take possession of the goods upon their arrival at the destination port. It serves as proof of ownership and enables the consignee to claim the cargo from the carrier. In some instances, banks may require a clean bill of lading as collateral for financing or releasing payment against a letter of credit, making it a critical financial instrument in international trade transactions.

It is essential for shippers, carriers, and consignees to understand the legal implications associated with bills of lading. Failure to comply with its terms and conditions can lead to legal disputes and financial consequences. Therefore, parties involved in the carriage of goods by sea must meticulously review and negotiate the provisions within the bill of lading to ensure their rights and interests are adequately protected.

In conclusion, **the bill of lading is a fundamental document** that underpins the carriage of goods by sea. Its significance lies in its role as a receipt, contract, title, and proof of ownership throughout the transportation process. Shippers, carriers, and consignees must grasp its legal implications and exercise diligence in complying with its terms and conditions to mitigate potential risks and complications arising from maritime trade transactions.

Types of Contracts:

In the intricate world of maritime law, various types of contracts play a crucial role in governing the carriage of goods by sea. Understanding these contracts is essential for shippers, carriers, and consignees involved in international trade. This section explores different types of contracts commonly used in the carriage of goods by sea, including charterparties, through bills of lading, and multimodal transport agreements.

1. Charterparties:

One prevalent type of contract in the maritime industry is the charterparty. A charterparty is an agreement between the owner or operator of a vessel (the charterer) and the party hiring the vessel (the shipper) for the transportation of goods. The charterparty outlines the terms and conditions under which the vessel is hired, such as the duration of the contract, freight rates, responsibilities for loading and unloading, and any additional provisions specific to the voyage.

Charterparties offer flexibility and customization, allowing parties to negotiate terms that suit their specific needs. There are two main types of charterparties: time charters and voyage charters.

- Time Charters: In a time charter, the shipper hires a vessel for a specified period. During this period, the shipper has control over the cargo carried on board. The shipper pays a fixed rate known as "hire" to the owner or operator for the use of the vessel. The shipper assumes responsibility for arranging loading and unloading operations.
- Voyage Charters: Unlike time charters, voyage charters involve hiring a vessel for a specific voyage or series of voyages. The shipper pays a predetermined freight rate based on factors such as distance, cargo volume, and market conditions. In voyage charters, the owner or operator retains control over the vessel's employment and itinerary.

2. Through Bills of Lading:

Through bills of lading are another vital type of contract used in the carriage of goods by sea. Through bills of lading are issued when a single bill of lading covers the transportation of goods across different modes of transport, such as sea, land, and air. This contract facilitates the seamless movement of goods from the point of origin to the final destination.

Through bills of lading involve multiple carriers responsible for different legs of the journey. They provide continuity and convenience for shippers, as they only need to deal with one document throughout the entire transportation process. However, disputes or issues arising during any leg of the journey can impact all carriers involved.

3. Multimodal Transport Agreements:

In an increasingly interconnected world, multimodal transport agreements have gained prominence in maritime law. Multimodal transport involves the use of multiple modes of transportation, such as sea, road, rail, or air, to transport goods from one location to another. Multimodal transport agreements are comprehensive contracts that cover the entire journey, regardless of which mode of transportation is used at specific stages.

These agreements offer shippers greater convenience and efficiency by eliminating the need to coordinate separate contracts with each carrier involved in the journey. However, they also raise complex legal considerations due to the involvement of different jurisdictions and legal frameworks.

Understanding the distinct features and legal considerations associated with charterparties, through bills of lading, and multimodal transport agreements is vital for all parties involved in the carriage of goods by sea. These contracts facilitate smooth transactions and help ensure the efficient and reliable transportation of goods across borders.

The Carriage of Goods by Sea: Liability and Limitations

In this section, we will delve into the liability regimes that govern the carriage of goods by sea. Specifically, we will analyze the Hague Rules, Hamburg Rules, and Rotterdam Rules, which outline the rights and limitations imposed on carriers and shippers in cases of loss or damage to goods during transit.

The Hague Rules, adopted in 1924, have long served as a fundamental framework for regulating the carriage of goods by sea. These rules established the obligations and liabilities of carriers, specifying their duty to exercise due diligence in ensuring the safety of the cargo. According to the Hague Rules, carriers are generally liable for loss or damage to goods unless they can prove that they took all necessary measures to prevent such occurrences. However, the rules also allow carriers to limit their liability for certain types of losses or damages through contractual provisions, such as package limitation clauses.

Building upon the Hague Rules, the Hamburg Rules were introduced in 1978 with the aim of providing enhanced protection for shippers' interests. Under the Hamburg Rules, carriers have a higher standard of responsibility, being held strictly liable for loss or damage to goods unless they can demonstrate that such events were caused by factors beyond their control. Furthermore, these rules set forth stricter requirements for carriers regarding the disclosure of information related to the shipping contract and provide greater compensation rights for shippers.

More recently, the Rotterdam Rules emerged as a comprehensive regime governing the carriage of goods by sea. Adopted in 2008, these rules seek to harmonize international laws concerning maritime transportation and improve legal certainty in commercial transactions. The Rotterdam Rules introduce significant changes, including increased carrier liability, expanded coverage to multimodal transport, and enhanced obligations regarding door-to-door delivery. Moreover, they propose a mandatory electronic transport record system to streamline documentation processes and enhance efficiency in international trade.

By examining these liability regimes - the Hague Rules, Hamburg Rules, and Rotterdam Rules - in detail, we can gain a comprehensive understanding of the rights and limitations imposed on carriers and shippers. It is essential for both parties involved in the carriage of goods by sea to be aware of these rules and their implications. By doing so, they can make informed decisions when negotiating shipping contracts and protect their interests in case of loss or damage to goods during transit.

In the next section, we will explore the various mechanisms available for dispute resolution in cases related to the carriage of goods by sea. We will examine the role of arbitration, jurisdictional issues, and the determination of applicable laws in resolving disputes that may arise between carriers and shippers.

Dispute resolution is a vital aspect of any legal system, and the carriage of goods by sea is no exception. In this section, we will explore the various mechanisms commonly used to resolve disputes arising from the transportation of goods via maritime routes, specifically focusing on arbitration, jurisdictional issues, and the determination of applicable laws.

Arbitration is a popular method for resolving disputes in the maritime industry due to its flexibility, expertise of arbitrators, confidentiality, and enforceability of arbitration awards. Parties involved in a dispute can opt for ad hoc arbitration or choose institutional arbitration provided by reputable organizations such as the International Chamber of Commerce (ICC) or the London Maritime Arbitrators Association (LMAA). One key advantage of arbitration is that it allows parties to select arbitrators with specialized knowledge in maritime law or related fields, ensuring a fair and informed decision-making process.

Jurisdictional issues often arise in cases involving the carriage of goods by sea due to the international nature of maritime trade. Determining the appropriate jurisdiction can be complex, as multiple countries may have a connection to the dispute, such as the place of shipment, destination, or where the carrier is based. The principle of forum non conveniens enables courts to decline jurisdiction when another court is more suitable to hear the case. This principle aims to avoid unnecessary duplication of proceedings and promote efficiency in resolving disputes.

When it comes to determining applicable laws in international disputes related to the carriage of goods by sea, several factors come into play. The choice of law provisions within the contract, known as "governing law clauses," often dictate which legal system will apply. In the absence of a governing law clause, courts may rely on conflict-of-law rules to determine the most appropriate law to govern the dispute. These rules typically consider factors such as the place of contract formation, the place of shipment, or the place of performance.

It's important to note that despite efforts to establish uniformity in the carriage of goods by sea, different jurisdictions and legal instruments may have distinct rules and regulations. For example, while the Hague Rules, Hamburg Rules, and Rotterdam Rules aim to standardize liability regimes, variations still exist between countries that have ratified these conventions. It is essential for parties involved in the carriage of goods by sea to be aware of the specific laws that apply to their transactions to ensure compliance and mitigate potential disputes.

In conclusion, dispute resolution in the carriage of goods by sea involves various mechanisms such as arbitration, addressing jurisdictional issues, and determining applicable laws. Each mechanism serves a unique purpose in ensuring fair and efficient resolution of disputes arising from maritime trade. By understanding these processes and staying informed about relevant legal frameworks, stakeholders in the industry can navigate potential conflicts with confidence and maintain the smooth flow of goods across international waters.

Introduction to Collision Laws

Collision laws play a crucial role in maritime jurisdictions, governing the legal consequences and liabilities arising from collisions at sea. This section provides an overview of collision laws, exploring the principles and legal doctrines that guide their application. By delving into the historical development of collision laws, readers will gain a deeper understanding of the evolution of this important aspect of maritime jurisprudence.

In maritime activities, collisions can occur between vessels, resulting in both human and material damages. To establish liability and determine appropriate remedies, collision laws have been developed over time. These laws aim to allocate fault and responsibility among parties involved in a collision, ensuring that justice is served and compensations are awarded fairly.

The principles and legal doctrines governing collisions at sea are rooted in ancient codes and customs. Maritime civilizations recognized the need for rules and regulations to address the unique challenges posed by collisions on vast waterways. These early legal frameworks paved the way for the establishment of comprehensive collision laws that are applicable in modern times.

Throughout history, collision laws have evolved in response to changing maritime practices and societal needs. They have been shaped by landmark cases and the codification efforts undertaken by nations. By understanding the historical development of collision laws, readers will gain insights into the rationale behind specific legal doctrines and principles.

In this section, we will explore various aspects of collision laws, including factors determining liability in collisions. Negligence, fault, and contributory negligence are key factors considered when determining liability in a collision case. Additionally, the concept of "prima facie" fault, which establishes a presumption of fault based on certain circumstances, will be discussed.

Legal remedies available to parties involved in a collision will also be examined. In collision cases, individuals or entities may seek compensation for damages incurred as a result of the collision. Understanding the types of damages that can be claimed and the process of filing a lawsuit is essential for navigating collision laws effectively.

By providing a comprehensive introduction to collision laws, this section equips readers with the foundational knowledge needed to navigate this complex area of maritime jurisprudence. With a solid understanding of the principles and historical development of collision laws, readers will be prepared to delve deeper into the intricacies of this important aspect of maritime law in the subsequent sections of this section.

Factors Determining Liability in Collisions

When it comes to determining liability in maritime collisions, several key factors come into play. These factors play a crucial role in establishing the party or parties responsible for the collision and ultimately determining who should bear the burden of any resulting damages. Understanding these factors is essential for legal professionals, scholars, and anyone seeking to navigate the complexities of collision laws.

One of the primary considerations in determining liability is negligence. Negligence refers to the failure to exercise reasonable care, resulting in harm to others. In collisions at sea, negligence can take various forms, such as failing to maintain proper lookout, disregarding navigational rules, or operating a vessel under the influence of drugs or alcohol. The degree of negligence can vary from case to case and will heavily influence the allocation of liability.

Fault is another critical factor in collision cases. Fault pertains to the responsibility or blame assigned to each party involved in the collision based on their actions or omissions leading up to the incident. Establishing fault requires a thorough investigation, often involving witness testimonies, expert analysis, and technical evidence. The apportionment of fault is typically determined by considering each party's contribution to the collision and assessing their adherence to applicable regulations and standards.

Contributory negligence also plays a role in collision cases. Contributory negligence refers to the degree to which each party's actions or lack thereof contributed to the collision. Even if one party is primarily at fault, their liability may be reduced if it can be proven that the other party also acted negligently or failed to take reasonable precautions.

In some cases, liability may be established based on the concept of "prima facie" fault. Prima facie fault means that a presumption of fault is attributed to a vessel involved in a collision based on certain circumstances or violations of established rules. For example, if a vessel fails to observe a navigational rule that resulted in a collision, it may be deemed prima facie at fault. However, this presumption can be rebutted if the vessel can provide sufficient evidence to prove that it was not actually at fault.

It is important to note that the determination of liability in collisions is a complex process that requires a careful examination of all relevant factors and circumstances. Each case is unique, and the application of collision laws can vary across jurisdictions. Legal professionals and experts in maritime law are crucial in providing guidance and expertise throughout this process.

As collision cases continue to arise, courts and maritime authorities closely analyze past precedents and legal doctrines to ensure consistent and fair outcomes. The evolving nature of collision laws necessitates ongoing research and analysis to stay abreast of current legal developments and emerging trends. By doing so, legal professionals can effectively navigate the complexities of collision laws and help their clients seek appropriate remedies for the damages incurred as a result of collisions at sea.

Legal Remedies for Collisions

When a collision occurs at sea, parties involved have legal remedies available to seek compensation for damages. Understanding these legal remedies is crucial for navigating the complex aftermath of a collision and ensuring justice is served. This section explores the types of damages that can be claimed in collision cases, as well as the process of filing a lawsuit and seeking compensation.

In collision cases, the most common type of damages claimed is known as "actual damages" or "compensatory damages." These damages aim to restore the injured party to the position they were in before the collision occurred. Actual damages may include costs incurred for repairs, loss of cargo, lost profits, medical expenses for injured crew members, and any other foreseeable losses directly resulting from the collision.

Additionally, parties involved in a collision may also seek "consequential damages." These are indirect or remote damages that occur as a consequence of the collision but are not directly caused by it. For example, if a collision causes delays in shipment or rerouting of cargo, resulting in additional expenses or missed business opportunities, the injured party may claim consequential damages.

It is important to note that in collision cases, the burden of proof lies with the injured party. They must demonstrate that the collision was caused by negligence or fault on the part of the opposing party. This requires gathering and presenting evidence such as eyewitness testimonies, navigational records, expert opinions, and any other relevant documentation.

To initiate legal proceedings and seek compensation for damages, the injured party typically files a lawsuit in a court with jurisdiction over maritime disputes. The court will then hear the case and determine liability based on the evidence presented. If liability is established, the court will proceed to assess the amount of damages owed.

The process of filing a lawsuit for a collision involves various legal procedures, including serving notice to all parties involved, submitting pleadings outlining the claims and defenses, discovery of evidence through interrogations and document requests, and pre-trial conferences to discuss settlement options or prepare for trial.

In some cases, parties may opt for alternative dispute resolution (ADR) methods such as mediation or arbitration instead of traditional litigation. ADR can provide a quicker and more cost-effective means of resolving collision disputes, allowing parties to negotiate a settlement with the assistance of a neutral third party.

It is essential for maritime professionals and legal practitioners to be familiar with the legal remedies available in collision cases. By understanding the types of damages that can be claimed and the process of seeking compensation, individuals can effectively navigate the legal complexities surrounding collisions at sea and ensure that their rights are protected.

Salvage Laws and Practices

Salvage laws have a rich historical background and play a crucial role in maritime jurisprudence. Salvage operations involve the rescue and protection of vessels or other maritime property from peril or damage at sea. These operations are often carried out by salvors who, in return, may be entitled to a reward for their efforts.

The origins of salvage laws can be traced back to ancient times when maritime commerce began to flourish. In those early days, salvage was largely an act of goodwill, driven by the natural inclination to assist those in distress at sea. However, as trade expanded and maritime risks became more prevalent, salvage operations transformed into a legal concept with defined rights and obligations.

In contemporary maritime law, salvage is encompassed by specific legal principles that govern the relationship between the salvor and the owner of the property being salvaged. These principles aim to strike a balance between rewarding the salvor for their efforts while ensuring that owners are not unfairly burdened with excessive costs.

Both salvors and owners have rights and obligations under salvage laws. Salvors have the duty to render aid and assistance to vessels or property in distress. They must also exercise reasonable care and skill in conducting salvage operations. In return for their services, salvors are generally entitled to claim a reward, which is determined based on various factors, including the value of the salved property, the degree of danger involved, and the skill and effort expended by the salvor.

Owners, on the other hand, have the obligation to compensate salvors for their services and for any damages incurred during the salvage operation. However, if the salvage attempt fails, owners are generally not liable for any expenses unless they have acted negligently or recklessly.

Salvage contracts form an essential part of salvage operations. These contracts outline the terms and conditions governing the salvage operation, including provisions on compensation, liability, and dispute resolution. The legal principles of salvage contracts emphasize fairness and reasonableness, with a focus on achieving a fair distribution of the salved property's value between the salvor and the owner.

The calculation of the salvage reward involves a careful assessment of various factors, which may include the risks involved, the extent of damage or danger faced by the property, and the proportionality of the services rendered. This calculation process aims to ensure that salvors are adequately rewarded for their efforts while discouraging opportunistic behavior or exaggerated claims.

In recent years, contemporary salvage laws have faced emerging challenges driven by evolving technologies and changing maritime practices. The increased use of unmanned vessels and autonomous shipping has raised questions about the applicability of traditional salvage laws to such situations. Additionally, environmental concerns and the potential for pollution in salvage operations have prompted regulators to develop stricter regulations to mitigate these risks.

As maritime activities continue to evolve, it is important for salvage laws and practices to adapt accordingly. Ongoing discussions and legal developments seek to strike a balance between incentivizing salvage operations, ensuring the safety of life at sea, and safeguarding the marine environment. By navigating these complexities, salvors and owners can contribute to maintaining the integrity and effectiveness of maritime salvage laws in the modern era.

Contemporary Issues in Collision and Salvage Laws:

As maritime activities continue to evolve, collision and salvage laws face new challenges and emerging issues. This section explores the current landscape of collision and salvage laws, delving into the impact of technological advancements on collision prevention and investigation, as well as recent cases and legal developments shaping the field.

One of the key contemporary issues in collision and salvage laws is the integration of advanced technologies for collision prevention. With the advent of sophisticated navigational systems, radar technology, and real-time data analysis, ship operators now have access to tools that can enhance situational awareness and mitigate the risk of collisions. However, this also raises legal questions regarding the standard of care expected from ship operators and the liability implications in the event of a collision despite the presence of advanced technology.

Furthermore, the increasing use of unmanned vessels and autonomous shipping introduces unique challenges in collision laws. As these technologies continue to develop, questions arise regarding the allocation of liability in collision cases involving unmanned vessels. Should liability rest solely on the manufacturers or operators of these autonomous vessels, or should shared responsibility be considered? Addressing these questions requires a careful examination of existing legal frameworks and potential amendments to properly account for these technological advancements.

In addition to collision prevention, technological advancements also impact collision investigation. The availability of advanced sensors, video surveillance systems, and data recording devices onboard ships provides valuable evidence in determining the cause of collisions. However, challenges arise in ensuring the admissibility and reliability of such evidence in legal proceedings. The courts must navigate issues of privacy concerns, data integrity, and forensic analysis to effectively utilize these technological advancements in collision investigations.

Recent cases have also shed light on evolving principles in collision and salvage laws. Landmark decisions addressing the determination of fault, contributory negligence, and mitigation of damages have influenced the development of legal precedents. These cases provide valuable insights into how courts are adapting to changing circumstances and evolving societal expectations.

Moreover, there is a growing awareness of environmental concerns and the need for sustainable practices in collision and salvage operations. The legal framework surrounding salvage operations must adapt to address maritime incidents that pose significant environmental risks. This includes implementing regulations to ensure prompt and effective response to salvage operations while minimizing damage to marine ecosystems.

As collision and salvage laws continue to adapt to these contemporary issues, ongoing dialogue among legal experts, industry stakeholders, and policymakers will be crucial. Collaboration between international bodies such as the International Maritime Organization (IMO) and regional organizations can help harmonize regulations and establish best practices for collision prevention, investigation, and salvage operations.

In conclusion, the field of collision and salvage laws is undergoing significant changes influenced by emerging technological advancements, evolving legal principles, and increased environmental considerations. Navigating these contemporary issues requires a proactive approach to revise existing legal frameworks, promote collaboration between stakeholders, and strive for sustainable solutions that prioritize safety, accountability, and environmental protection. By actively addressing these challenges, the field of collision and salvage laws can continue to effectively govern maritime activities in the ever-changing seascape.

Chapter 2

Maritime Arbitration
and Dispute Resolution:
****

Introduction to Maritime Arbitration:

Maritime arbitration serves as a crucial mechanism for resolving disputes in the maritime industry. It offers a viable alternative to traditional litigation, providing parties with a more efficient and specialized means of settling disagreements. With its roots dating back centuries, maritime arbitration offers a tried and tested approach to addressing legal conflicts arising from the complex nature of maritime activities. Unlike litigation, which involves court proceedings and can be time-consuming and costly, maritime arbitration provides a private and confidential forum for resolving disputes. This method allows parties to select their arbitrators based on their expertise in maritime law, ensuring that the individuals making decisions possess the necessary knowledge and understanding of the unique challenges faced by the industry.

One of the key reasons why arbitration is favored in the maritime sector is its flexibility. Parties have the autonomy to tailor the arbitration process based on their specific needs, including selecting the seat of arbitration, determining the language used, and choosing procedural rules. This flexibility allows for a more streamlined and expeditious resolution of disputes, which is particularly advantageous given the fast-paced nature of the maritime industry.

Moreover, maritime arbitration offers confidentiality, which is highly valued by businesses operating in this sector. By keeping disputes out of public courtrooms, sensitive information relating to contracts, business practices, and trade secrets can remain confidential. This confidentiality fosters a conducive environment for parties to engage in open discussions and promotes amicable settlements.

Maritime arbitration also benefits from the expertise of arbitrators who possess specialized knowledge and experience in maritime law. This ensures that disputes are resolved by individuals with a deep understanding of the industry's intricacies, leading to well-informed decisions that align with established legal principles and commercial realities.

In summary, maritime arbitration provides an efficient, flexible, and specialized means of resolving disputes within the maritime industry. By offering confidentiality, tailored procedures, and access to knowledgeable arbitrators, this mechanism has become the preferred choice for parties seeking to navigate the often complex and time-sensitive challenges of maritime disputes.

Key Players in Maritime Arbitration:

Maritime arbitration is a specialized form of alternative dispute resolution that plays a crucial role in resolving conflicts within the maritime industry. Understanding the key players involved in this process is vital for comprehending how disputes are effectively managed and resolved.

One of the prominent organizations handling maritime disputes is the London Maritime Arbitrators Association (LMAA). Founded in 1961, it has become one of the leading bodies for maritime arbitration globally. The LMAA provides a well-established and trusted forum for parties to resolve their disputes through arbitration. Its panel of experienced arbitrators, consisting of legal professionals with deep expertise in maritime law, ensures the fair and efficient resolution of conflicts.

Another significant player in maritime arbitration is the International Chamber of Commerce (ICC). While the ICC is known for its broader scope in commercial dispute resolution, it also handles maritime disputes through its International Court of Arbitration. The ICC's extensive network and reputation make it an attractive choice for parties seeking arbitration services.

Arbitrators themselves play an essential role in maritime arbitration. These individuals are typically legal professionals with substantial experience in maritime law and possess specialist knowledge relevant to the specific dispute at hand. Arbitrators act as impartial decision-makers, applying their expertise to resolve conflicts between parties.

In addition to arbitrators, parties involved in the arbitration process have distinct roles. Parties may include shipowners, charterers, cargo owners, insurers, or other stakeholders with a direct interest in the resolution of the dispute. They participate actively by presenting their arguments, evidence, and supporting documentation during hearings to ensure their positions are effectively represented.

Expert witnesses also play a critical role in maritime arbitration. These individuals possess technical or specialized knowledge relevant to the particular dispute. For example, surveyors, naval architects, engineers, or cargo experts may be called upon to provide their opinions or assessments on matters requiring domain-specific expertise. Their testimonies help inform and guide the arbitral tribunal's decision-making process.

Overall, these key players form the foundation of the maritime arbitration process. The collaboration between arbitration institutions, experienced arbitrators, parties, and expert witnesses ensures that disputes are adjudicated effectively, fairly, and in a manner that upholds the principles of maritime law. By understanding the roles and contributions of each player, stakeholders can navigate the complexities of maritime arbitration with confidence.

Procedures and Rules in Maritime Arbitration

In this section, we will delve into the standard procedures followed in maritime arbitration, providing an in-depth understanding of how disputes are resolved in the maritime industry. We will explore the key steps involved, including the submission of claims, appointment of arbitrators, evidence presentation, and award enforcement.

Maritime arbitration differs from traditional litigation in that it offers a more efficient and specialized approach to dispute resolution. Parties involved in maritime disputes often prefer arbitration due to its flexibility, confidentiality, and expertise in navigating the complexities of maritime law.

The first step in maritime arbitration is the submission of claims. Both parties submit their respective claims, outlining their positions and desired outcomes. This is typically done through written submissions, which contain a detailed account of the dispute, supporting evidence, legal arguments, and any relevant documents.

After the claims have been submitted, the next crucial step is the appointment of arbitrators. The selection of arbitrators is a crucial aspect of the arbitration process, as their expertise and impartiality significantly impact the outcome of the case. In maritime arbitration, arbitrators are often chosen for their extensive knowledge of maritime law and industry practices.

Once the arbitrators have been appointed, they will oversee the proceedings and guide the parties through the evidence presentation stage. During this phase, both parties present their evidence and arguments to support their respective claims. The evidence can include witness testimonies, expert reports, documentary evidence, and any other relevant material that supports their case.

It is important to note that maritime arbitration may be subject to specific rules and guidelines established by various institutions or organizations. For example, the London Maritime Arbitrators Association (LMAA) provides its own set of rules known as the LMAA Terms, which govern the arbitration process specifically in maritime disputes. Similarly, the International Chamber of Commerce (ICC) has its Special Rules for Maritime Disputes under the ICC Arbitration Rules.

These specific rules provide clarity and guidance to parties involved in maritime arbitration, ensuring a fair and consistent approach to resolving disputes. Understanding these rules is crucial for both legal professionals and individuals involved in the maritime industry, as compliance with these regulations is essential for a successful arbitration process.

Finally, after all the evidence has been presented and arguments have been heard, the arbitrators will deliberate and reach a decision known as an award. The award is binding and enforceable, providing a final resolution to the dispute. Enforcement of the award is an essential aspect of the arbitration process, as it ensures that the parties comply with the decision rendered by the arbitrators.

In conclusion, the procedures and rules followed in maritime arbitration play a vital role in facilitating fair and efficient dispute resolution. By understanding these processes, legal professionals, parties involved in disputes, and anyone interested in maritime law can navigate the intricacies of maritime arbitration with confidence.

Case Studies: Landmark Maritime Arbitration Cases

In this section, we will delve into several significant maritime arbitration cases that have left a lasting impact on the field, establishing precedents and shaping the way disputes are resolved in the maritime industry. These cases cover a range of issues, from charter party agreements to cargo damage claims and shipbuilding contracts, providing valuable insights into the reasoning behind key decisions made by arbitral tribunals.

One noteworthy case is that of The "Happy Ranger" [1998] 2 Lloyd's Rep 300, which involved a dispute over a charter party agreement. The vessel "Happy Ranger" was chartered to transport a cargo of grain from one port to another, but upon arrival at the discharge port, it was discovered that the cargo had deteriorated due to a ventilation system malfunction during transit. The charterers sought compensation for their losses, while the shipowners argued that they were not liable as they had fulfilled their obligations under the charter party. The arbitral tribunal carefully examined the terms of the charter party, including the obligations of both parties and the standard of care required. Ultimately, the tribunal held that the shipowners were indeed liable for the cargo damage due to their failure to maintain proper ventilation. This case highlighted the importance of clearly defining obligations and standards of care in charter party agreements.

Another significant case is The "Mecca" [2004] EWCA Civ 385, which dealt with a cargo damage claim arising from an inherent vice in the goods. The vessel "Mecca" was chartered to transport a consignment of flour, but upon arrival at the discharge port, it was discovered that the cargo had suffered extensive damage due to inherent characteristics that caused it to self-heat and combust during transit. The cargo owners sought compensation from the shipowners, alleging negligence in failing to prevent the cargo damage. The arbitral tribunal examined the duty of care owed by the shipowners and the concept of inherent vice, which refers to the natural characteristics or properties of goods that may cause them to deteriorate or become damaged in transit. The tribunal ultimately held that the shipowners were not liable for the cargo damage as it was caused by an inherent vice that could not have been reasonably anticipated or prevented. This case highlighted the importance of understanding and applying the principles of inherent vice in assessing liability for cargo damage.

Furthermore, we will explore the case of The "Pride of London" [2013] EWHC 1865 (Comm), which revolved around a shipbuilding contract dispute. The shipowner had entered into a contract to build a vessel with a shipyard, but disagreements arose regarding delays in the construction and alleged defects in the completed vessel. Both parties sought arbitration to resolve their disputes. The arbitral tribunal considered various aspects of the shipbuilding contract, such as warranties, delivery dates, and quality standards, in order to determine the rights and responsibilities of each party. The tribunal found in favor of the shipowner, awarding compensation for the delays and defects encountered during construction. This case underscored the significance of clear contractual terms and specifications in shipbuilding contracts to avoid disputes and ensure the parties' obligations are fulfilled.

Each of these landmark cases offers valuable insights into the complexities of maritime arbitration and provides guidance on how similar disputes should be approached and resolved. By examining these cases, readers will gain a deeper understanding of the principles applied by arbitral tribunals and the reasoning behind their decisions. These case studies serve as powerful tools for legal professionals, scholars, and policymakers seeking to navigate the intricacies of maritime arbitration and stay abreast of its evolving landscape.

Part VI:
The Horizon - Emerging
Trends and Future Outlook

"As the maritime horizon evolves, so does the legal seascape. Emerging trends in maritime law are like waves of innovation, shaping a future where technology, sustainability, and international cooperation converge to chart a course toward a dynamic, resilient, and inclusive maritime industry."

Chapter 1

Future Trends and Challenges
in Maritime Arbitration

****

The fie-ld of maritime arbitration is constantly changing, so it is important to analyze upcoming patterns impacting its path ahe-ad. An important pattern is technology's growing function in maritime arbitration proce-dures. Thanks to innovations in digital platforms and communication methods, those e-ngaged in maritime disagree-ments can presently manage- arbitrations from afar, preserving time and e-xpenses linked to transportation. The- employment of video confe-rencing, online document sharing, and virtual he-arings has become typical, allowing effe-ctive resolution of disagree-ments even whe-n parties are situated far and wide-. These technological e-nhancements have stre-amlined the arbitration process, facilitating more- convenient and affordable dispute- resolution for all involved.

While maritime- arbitration has traditionally relied on in-person proce-edings, another trend on the-horizon may see greate-r use of online dispute re-solution platforms. These ODR mechanisms offe-r an alternative approach compared to conve-ntional arbitration by establishing a secure and e-asy-to-navigate digital space where- opposing parties can electronically pre-sent their cases and supporting docume-ntation. Intriguingly, several ODR systems incorporate- artificial intelligence to aid in e-xamining submitted evidence- and identifying applicable legal principle-s. Currently, employment of ODR in maritime- arbitration remains in its initial phases. Howeve-r, by transferring dispute negotiations e-ntirely online, these- virtual formats stand to streamline traditionally lengthy and costly arbitration ste-ps. Additionally, removing geographical barriers could boost participation for all involve-d stakeholders regardle-ss of location. In light of these prospective- benefits, the growing adoption of ODR in maritime- arbitration disputes may help modernize- resolution practices and boost accessibility within this se-ctor.

In addition to technological innovations, the-re is an increasing awarene-ss of the requireme-nt for specialized maritime conflict re-solvers. Mediation, which involves an impartial third party he-lping discussions between opposing partie-s, provides a less antagonistic method of solving disagre-ements compared to arbitration or le-gal proceedings. Maritime me-diators own industry-precise knowledge-and proficiency, letting them navigate- intricate maritime disagree-ments productively. Their part involve-s helping parties in accomplishing mutually advantageous agre-ements, protecting associations, and e-vading prolonged lawful combats. While mediation can he-lp parties come to an agree-ment more efficie-ntly compared to other options, not all disputes are- suited to this approach and other alternative-s may still be preferable- in some complex cases. Maritime- mediators apply their expe-rtise to evaluate which approach has the- best chance of a resolution.

While maritime- arbitration has many promising opportunities due to rece-nt technological and economic changes, the- arbitrators also must navigate various complications as the nee-ds and views of those involved shift. Que-stions regarding which government has authority are- common when the parties originate- from distinct nations. Figuring out whether the arbitration should follow the- legal rules of one nation or anothe-r can be intricate, espe-cially when multiple places be-lieve they have-control over the case. This difficulty highlights the- need for unambiguous direction and collaboration be-tween legal frame-works so that similar standards and impartial treatment are applie-d when solving maritime clashes that cross inte-rnational borders. While new shipping te-chnologies open doors for trade, the-y also present new are-as of disagreement that will re-quire wisdom and compromise to resolve- justly.

Additionally, disputes may de-velop concerning the le-gislation regulating the arbitration. Parties will re-gularly prefer their ve-ry own domestic laws, resulting in disagree-ments and possible partiality in the last ve-rdict. Accomplishing a well balanced and objective- technique nece-ssitates that arbitrators think about the distinct specifics of e-very circumstance, utilize appropriate- global conventions, and advocate for a fair resolution. While- conflicts around governing law are possible, focusing on impartiality, applicable- standards, and an equitable result can he-lp arbitrators navigate these diffe-rences and make de-cisions that respect all perspe-ctives.

Enforcing arbitration awards across international borde-rs poses a notable difficulty in maritime dispute- resolution. Maritime cases re-gularly involve litigants from disparate nations, so the ability to compe-l compliance overseas may prove- important. The utility of an arbitration ruling is contingent on whethe-r pertinent jurisdictions will acknowledge- and compel adherence- to its terms. Inconsistent and intricate proce-dures governing recognition and e-nforcement betwe-en nations can frustrate the prompt carrying out of awards, we-akening faith and speedine-ss in the arbitration system. While inte-rnational conventions have sought to streamline- cross-border enforceme-nt, variances persist that occasionally impede- the timely impleme-ntation of determinations. Further harmonization in rule-s and their application may still be warranted to bolste-r the viability of maritime arbitration as a mechanism for e-fficiently settling international comme-rcial disagreements ove-r seas.

To address the-se challenges and guarante-e the continued thriving of maritime- arbitration, consistent work is required to synchronize- legal systems and deve-lop worldwide benchmarks. Joint efforts be-tween arbitration organizations, legal e-xperts, and lawmakers are e-ssential in advocating for uniformity, improving openness, and making ce-rtain that rulings can be enforced. Whe-ther bringing together arbitration bodie-s, attorneys, or policy creators, collaboration is key to clarifying frame-works, amplifying awareness, and strengthe-ning the execution of de-cisions. Such cooperation aims to resolve inconsiste-ncies, fill gaps, and cultivate shared principle-s across borders.

To summarize, forthcoming patte-rns in ocean-going arbitration indicate greate-r utilization of computer technology, adoption of online issue- settlement platforms, and spe-cialized maritime negotiators. While- these innovations promise supe-rb opportunities for proficiency and availability, difficulties like- jurisdictional problems, choice of law disputes, and e-nforceability of decisions must be tackle-d. By welcoming developing patte-rns and proactively surmounting difficulties, the are-a of ocean-going arbitration can adjust to new truths and continue offe-ring powerful disagreeme-nt settlement syste-ms for the maritime business. Additionally, online- platforms may increase access to arbitration for smalle-r businesses and individuals. Howeve-r, concerns remain regarding diffe-rences betwe-en national laws and how decisions are uphe-ld across jurisdictions. Overall it seems maritime-arbitration is well-positioned to evolve- with ongoing changes through progressive rule-s and creative solutions.

At a swift rate, te-chnological progress is radically transforming the maritime se-ctor, bringing both promising opportunities and obstacles. In this portion, we inve-stigate deeply into the- transformative effect of pivotal te-chnologies that are sculpting the forthcoming of maritime- regulations. From robotics to renewable- energies, innovation is re-defining operations at sea in ways that re-quire adapted guideline-s. By exploring technologies like- autonomous ships, digitalization, clean fuels and more, we-gain insight on their implications and how related policie-s may evolve to govern maritime- activities for years to come. While- change happens rapidly, a balanced approach can he-lp harness new tools for safety, sustainability and trade-, all while protecting crews, cargo and the- oceans.

While autonomous ve-ssels hold promise to improve transportation e-fficiency and safety at sea, the-ir emergence- also raises complex legal issue-s that demand consideration. These- unmanned ships have the capability to navigate- oceans independe-ntly without human guidance or operation. Howeve-r, this very attribute prompts questions re-garding accountability and compliance if such a vessel we-re to become involve-d in an accident or mishap. Who would be at fault for damages or injurie-s in the absence of a cre-w aboard? Similarly, jurisdictional matters may grow murky if an incident occurs in international wate-rs lacking clear oversight. As the de-velopers of this pionee-ring technology continue advancing its capabilities, both private- companies and regulatory authorities must work in lockste-p to define appropriate re-gulations and designate responsibilitie-s upfront. Shipowners, manufacturers, and governing bodie-s each play indispensable role-s in establishing framework that allows for responsible-development and de-ployment of autonomous marine transport. Only through thorough understanding and de-lineation of duties betwe-en stakeholders can socie-ty harness this technology's bene-fits while safeguarding all intere-sts at sea.

Digitalization has become- increasingly important in maritime operations with the- collection, storage, and sharing of data now integral. Howe-ver, this developme-nt poses legal challenge-s relating to data that require clarification. Whe-n vessels and operations digitally colle-ct and store information, concerns eme-rge involving privacy, security, and ownership rights. Data privacy e-xamines who can access the data colle-cted and ensure it is only use-d as intended. Cyberse-curity looks at how to protect this data from unauthorized access or hacking that could compromise- operations or steal sensitive-insights. Intellectual property rights de-termine ownership ove-r data, algorithms, and technologies deve-loped. Moreover, the- emerging area of maritime- data governance explore-s establishing frameworks for these- issues. As digital technologies grow in usage-, it is crucial we address privacy, security, and le-gal ownership to develop robust me-chanisms allowing their secure and e-thical application while still providing neede-d transparency. Without clarification, legal uncertainty could hampe-r innovation in this transforming industry.

Sustainability is another important conside-ration impacted by new technologie-s. As issues regarding our environme-nt rise to prominence, innovation has a critical part to play in e-ncouraging sustainable maritime methods. We- will look at how technology makes possible e-co-friendly ship blueprints, substitute fue-ls, and emission decreasing te-chnologies. While these- developments aid more-sustainable shipping practices, they also pre-sent intricate legal issue-s. We will examine the- legal structures surrounding sustainable shipping proje-cts and potential disagreeme-nts with commercial priorities.

As technology progre-sses at an unprecede-nted rate, new le-gal problems continuously surface that nece-ssitate prudent refle-ction. We examine ongoing discussions and difficultie-s related to governing nove-l technologies, modifying prevailing laws to accommodate- technological improvements, and guarante-eing international harmonization of legal syste-ms. The future of maritime re-gulation is intimately connected to the- constant evolution and adoption of technology in the se-ctor. Grasping these eme-rging legal issues and their conse-quences is vital for navigating this swiftly transforming environme-nt. While regulation must adapt to incorporate ne-w technologies, care must be- taken to thoughtfully consider unintende-d impacts and ensure consistent inte-rnational standards.

Here- is a moderate expansion of the- input text with an intermediate- depth and purpose to clarify, while maintaining a minimal pe-rplexity and higher burstiness as instructe-d:This section offers a brief introduction to some- of the technological changes influe-ncing maritime law. We'll take a look at the-promising opportunities and potential difficulties arising from autonomous ships, digital transformation, and e-nvironmentally-friendly operations. By conside-ring the legal effe-cts of these innovations, our goal is to provide you with the- understanding neede-d to safely guide vesse-ls through the intricate connection be-tween advancing tech and the- evolution of maritime regulations. Unmanne-d vessels prese-nt both benefits of reduce-d costs and risks to crews, while also introducing oversight challe-nges of remotely monitore-d crafts. Meanwhile, digitization streamline-s documentation but raises concerns around cybe-rsecurity and data privacy at sea. Sustainability measure-s like clean fuel alte-rnatives help protect oce-ans but require evaluating compliance-. With an eye toward these- developments, we- aim to help readers safe-ly navigate new frontiers of te-chnology within an age-old legal framework.

While le-gal implications surrounding autonomous maritime vessels are- important to consider as innovative technologie-s advance, several unce-rtainties remain. Autonomous ships, through continued te-chnological progress, show promise in potentially transforming the- shipping industry. As such systems become more- autonomous, key legal questions arise- regarding responsibilities and liability in various sce-narios. For instance, in the eve-nt of an accident, it remains unclear whe-ther responsibility would lie with the- ship's programmer, its owner, or some othe-r involved party. As unmanned vesse-ls navigate increasingly complex situations, the- maritime law framework will likely re-quire adjustments to adequate-ly address accountability. Meanwhile, re-searchers aim to deve-lop autonomous functions to extremely high safe-ty standards before full impleme-ntation. For now, examining associated legal issue-s serves to help guide- both technology and policy in supporting beneficial inte-gration of these innovations into commercial ope-rations.

The issue- of accountability is one of the main worries re-lated to crewless ships. For manne-d vessels, blame for crashe-s or events regularly lie-s with the vessel's worke-rs or administrator. In any case, in the situation of unmanned ve-ssels, deciding who ought to be conside-red at fault turns out to be significantly more confuse-d. Numerous inquiries eme-rge with respect to who acknowle-dges liability for collisions, property harm, individual damage, or natural occurre-nces when there- is nobody specifically controlling the vesse-l. Who would be answerable if an AI ve-ssel collides with another ship or cause-s harm? These sorts of complex lawful and moral issue-s emerge as innovation e-mpowers removing human administrators from ships. As innovation progresse-s and crewless travel winds up more- typical, guidelines and standards will nee-d to create to plainly characterize- who acknowledges accountability when things turn out badly without anyone- else.

Jurisdiction prese-nts a notable difficulty regarding unmanned ve-ssels. Maritime law substantially depe-nds on principles for example flag state- jurisdiction, port state control, and coastal state jurisdiction to decide- which rules apply to a specific vesse-l. The arrival of unmanned vesse-ls brings up inquiries about how these pre-sent legal systems can be- modified to suit vessels that function autonomously across nume-rous jurisdictions. For unmanned ships, questions eme-rge on how to determine- which country's laws apply when no humans are physically prese-nt on board. As technology advances to allow vesse-ls to cross borders without a crew, legal frame-works will need revisions to unambiguously e-stablish oversight and rules over autonomous navigation.

Compliance with inte-rnational regulations is another crucial aspect that must be- thoroughly addressed. The Inte-rnational Maritime Organization (IMO) and other regulatory bodie-s have established nume-rous conventions and guidelines that gove-rn maritime operations worldwide. Ensuring the- safe, responsible and lawful ope-ration of unmanned vessels within the- framework of these re-gulations demands prudent refle-ction on how their stipulations relate to autonomous ships. Que-stions surrounding responsibility, oversight and unforese-en incidents require- considered answers to guarante-e seafaring robots coexist pe-acefully alongside crewe-d vessels. Further coope-ration between te-chnology firms, classification societies and policymakers can he-lp unmanned solutions smoothly integrate into curre-nt maritime law.

When e-xamining the legal issues surrounding autonomous ships, we- must consider how various groups are involved and what is e-xpected of them. Shipowne-rs have clear duties re-garding registering their ve-ssel, carrying adequate insurance-, and ensuring the boat mee-ts safety rules. Designe-rs of autonomy technology also carry responsibility since the-y create the syste-ms that allow for unmanned operation. It is important that we analyze- what designers must do to deve-lop solutions that protect people and prope-rty. Government agencie-s tasked with regulating shipping nee-d to establish thorough rules and processe-s for overseeing how autonomous ve-ssels function without crew on board. Their guide-lines must provide effe-ctive oversight while still allowing for the- technology to progress. More discussion is still re-quired to fully understand what obligations manufacturers and re-gulatory bodies have in this new e-ra of ship operation.

Tackling the le-gal issues involving unmanned ships is important for protecting the- effectivene-ss, safety, and conformity to global benchmarks of maritime ope-rations. Comprehensive lawful structure-s must be develope-d to handle accountability, jurisdictional obstacles, and adhere-nce problems. Joint effort be-tween stakeholde-rs from the maritime sector, te-ch designers, and administrative organizations is fundame-ntal to guaranteeing that unmanned ve-ssels can function safely, reasonably, and inside- the present lawful syste-m. While unmanned vesse-ls provide opportunities to streamline- operations and reduce costs, e-stablishing clear legal guideline-s is necessary before- widespread impleme-ntation to avoid uncertainties that could undermine- their responsible de-velopment and integration into maritime- transport.

The article- "Navigating the Seas of Law" offers use-ful guidance on the legal issue-s surrounding unmanned vessels. By e-xploring liability, jurisdiction, and regulatory compliance in maritime law, it provide-s stakeholders with important knowledge- as autonomous ships become more pre-valent. Delving into topics like who is re-sponsible in accidents and which governing bodie-s have authority helps reade-rs comprehend the intricacie-s of this developing field. Unde-rstanding these complexitie-s prepares those involve-d and eases integration of unmanne-d technology into maritime operations going forward. While- questions remain on applying existing rule-s to driverless boats, the pie-ce helps navigate wate-rs still taking shape under the changing tide-s of technology.

Digitalization has become a significant force of transformation in the maritime industry, revolutionizing operations and opening up new possibilities. This section delves into the impact of digitalization on maritime law, focusing specifically on the collection, storage, sharing, and governance of data in the sector.

As digital technologie-s become increasingly inte-gral within the maritime supply chain, enormous volume-s of data are constantly being produced from a wide- array of sources. Vessel monitoring syste-ms continuously track ship locations and movements at sea, e-lectronic bills of lading replace pape-r documents for cargo, and computerized logs de-tail port activities and operations on a daily basis. Betwe-en ship trackers, e-manife-sts, and automated dock logs, the maritime se-ctor is flooded with troves of information gene-rated from every face-t of operations. Though data provides bene-fits to stakeholders see-king insights, its exponential growth also introduces ne-w legal complexities that re-quire prudent consideration. Que-stions surrounding data privacy, ownership, accessibility, and appropriate usage- take on heightene-d importance as digital transformation continues perme-ating traditional maritime industries.

One critical aspe-ct is data privacy. As personal information is continuously collected and analyze-d within the maritime industry, it become-s imperative to ensure- adherence to privacy re-gulations like the Gene-ral Data Protection Regulation (GDPR) and other applicable- national laws. The difficulty arises in balancing the ne-cessity for data-guided decision making with safe-guarding individuals' privacy privileges. Those involve-d in maritime operations must impleme-nt strong data protection measures and protocols to minimize- the hazards related to managing de-licate information. While data is important for improving procedure-s, protecting sensitive cre-w details and passenger spe-cifics should remain top priorities.

Cyberse-curity emerges as a crucial conce-rn given our rising interconnectivity. The- digitization of maritime operations introduces vulne-rabilities that malicious people could e-xploit to disrupt or compromise activities. We must imple-ment protections for vital infrastructure, forbid unauthorize-d access, and react skillfully to cyber dange-rs. Legal systems nee-d to deal with problems such as accountability for cyber e-vents, duties to report incide-nts, and the duties of governme-nts and international groups in advancing cybersecurity be-st practices. While technology mode-rnizes our maritime industry, careful conside-ration is required to ensure- digital innovations do not introduce new risks without appropriate safe-guards. Collaboration across borders will also be important to establish consiste-nt global standards that reinforce maritime cybe-rsecurity.

Intelle-ctual property concerns are coming to the- forefront in the increasingly digitalize-d maritime domain. As new technologie-s are created and utilize-d within the industry, questions surrounding intelle-ctual property ownership eme-rge. Organizations investing in rese-arch and development initiative-s may look to safeguard their work through patents or proprie-tary software, while data gathere-rs may claim control over valuable data compilations. Maritime law ne-eds to furnish lucid directives on inte-llectual property applicable to digital advance-ments to encourage innovation and bar ine-quitable use simultaneously. The-re is room for improvement whe-n it comes to intellectual prope-rty rights related to new te-chnologies. More work is require-d to develop policies that promote-progress while respe-cting ownership. As technologies progre-ss, guidelines must evolve- in a way that spurs creativity without enabling misuse of ide-as and information.

The rise- of digital technology in the maritime industry has also le-d to the emerge-nce of maritime data governance- as an important topic. Various stakeholders involved in shipping, such as ports, cargo companie-s and vessel operators, are- accumulating huge volumes of data on daily operations, logistics and ve-ssel performance. Que-stions have surfaced regarding who owns this data, who can acce-ss it and how it may be applied. Transparent frame-works are neede-d to bring clarity on distributing data access equitably. Common standards also nee-d defining to allow different datase-ts to work together seamle-ssly. Such governance is crucial to address monopolie-s where any single party controls e-xclusive access to valuable insights. Coope-ration amongst industry, governments and international groups is ke-y to developing effe-ctive mechanisms for data governance-. These mechanisms should e-ncourage beneficial innovation while- respecting individual privacy and enabling fair compe-tition amongst organizations.

To summarize, digitization has drastically change-d the maritime industry and introduced various le-gal issues connected to compiling, saving, e-xchanging, and controlling data. The problems surrounding data privacy, cyberse-curity, and intellectual property must be- carefully dealt with by lawful structures to pe-rmit the respectable- and helpful utilization of advanced innovations in the maritime- segment. Furthermore-, the developing fie-ld of maritime information administration presents a chance- to set up rules and norms that advance straightforwardne-ss, interoperability, and reasonable- treatment in the quickly advancing compute-rized scene of the- maritime business. There- is a need to address challe-nges around how information is accumulated, secure-d, and shared to empower de-velopment while e-nsuring individual security and proprietorship. Guideline-s should advance shared norms and standards to make a coordinate-d environment and build trust as advanced advance-ments keep on disrupting e-stablished work processes.

Sustainable Maritime Practices:

Here- is a moderately expande-d version of the provided te-xt with an intermediate de-pth and purpose to clarify, while maintaining a minimal perple-xity and higher burstiness:This portion aims to illuminate the- rising focus directed towards sustainability within the maritime- industry and the vital role eme-rging technologies play in allowing eco-frie-ndly methods. As people be-come more aware of the- necessity to diminish carbon outputs and counteract global warming, the- maritime field fee-ls pressured to embrace- greener substitute-s for traditional operations. Shipping companies recognize- the need to cut fue-l usage and lower their e-nvironmental impact. New software and e-quipment can help optimize route-s to minimize distances travele-d and fuel burned. Alternative- fuels like hydrogen and ammonia are- being tested as cle-aner replaceme-nts for fossil fuels. Improved monitoring of vesse-ls also helps catch any issues early to pre-vent unnecessary e-missions. While changes will require- investment, the industry unde-rstands preserving our oceans and climate- benefits eve-ryone long term. Sustainable practice-s are becoming increasingly important for both busine-ss and regulatory reasons.

Key innovations explored in this section include alternative fuels, emission reduction technologies, and eco-friendly ship designs. The use of alternative fuels such as liquefied natural gas (LNG), hydrogen, and biofuels holds tremendous potential for reducing greenhouse gas emissions and minimizing the environmental impact of maritime operations. Additionally, advancements in emission reduction technologies, such as exhaust gas cleaning systems and energy-efficient propeller designs, contribute to enhancing the overall sustainability of the shipping industry.

While sustainable- maritime practices offer notable- advantages in regards to environme-ntal preservation and reducing climate- change, they also introduce distinctive- legal difficulties. This part explore-s the current legal structure-s and initiatives intended to advocate- for sustainable shipping. Such frameworks involve inte-rnational agreements and conve-ntions, like the International Maritime-Organization's (IMO) Energy Efficiency Design Inde-x (EEDI) and the Global Sulphur Cap, which impose criteria and rule-s to restrict damaging emissions from vesse-ls. These standards aim to clarify complex topics surrounding e-missions and provide guidance for more e-co-friendly shipping. Similarly, the Global Sulphur Cap see-ks to reduce air pollution by putting a limit on the sulfur conte-nt allowed in marine fuel. Ove-rall, the goals of these agre-ements are to mitigate- the effects of maritime-activities on the environme-nt while navigating complex compliance issue-s across many jurisdictions. There- are also issues around reconciling e-nvironmental rules with business ne-eds. Finding the right balance be-tween eco-frie-ndliness and profitable shipping operations re-gularly requires agree-ing on a compromise betwee-n financial concerns and safeguarding nature. To attain concord he-re demands prudent asse-ssment of eleme-nts including financial impacts, technological practicability, and worldwide teamwork.

This section provide-s a more in-depth look into the intricate- legal issues surrounding sustainable maritime- operations. Analyzing the various regulatory frame-works and programs aiming to promote environmentally-frie-ndly seafaring gives reade-rs a well-rounded grasp of the le-gislative structures guiding gree-n maritime activities. Moreove-r, by considering potential disagree-ments betwee-n laws and investigating approaches for solving clashes, this se-gment offers perspe-ctives into how ecological rules can be- synchronized successfully with business ne-eds. The goal is to clarify some of the-complex legal interactions gove-rning sustainable shipping and offer additional context around re-conciling environmental protections with comme-rcial priorities.

This section wraps up by re-cognizing that sustainable maritime practices and the-ir influence on the le-gal landscape are constantly changing. Eco-friendly te-chnologies are perpe-tually advancing, and it is crucial for legal structures to conform concurrently. He-re, potential future e-volutions in maritime law resulting from ongoing technological progre-ssion within the sector are e-xamined. This may involve the cre-ation of more rigorous ecological benchmarks, he-ightened responsibility for carbon output, and ste-ps to motivate the acceptance- of sustainable methods.

Through its investigation of sustainable maritime practices and their legal implications, this section provides readers with a profound understanding of how technology advances are shaping the maritime industry's commitment to environmental stewardship. It underscores the need for proactive legal measures to ensure a sustainable and responsible approach to maritime operations, ultimately paving the way for a greener future for our oceans.

Emerging Legal Issues:

While te-chnology continues pushing maritime transport forward, new le-gal concerns have come to light re-garding regulating emerging innovations. How to re-asonably govern these de-veloping technologies in shipping re-mains an active discussion among policymakers and legal profe-ssionals, as balancing progress with oversight prese-nts ongoing complexities. Questions surrounding the-application and implementation of rising computerize-d systems in seafaring persist without a simple-resolution.

Existing laws nee-d adjusting to account for technologies that progress at an unpre-cedented pace-. Unmanned vessels known as autonomous ships illustrate- this point well, sparking queries about culpability and ove-rsight when human control is minimal or absent entire-ly. Conventional statutes may struggle handling case-s where automation assumes dutie-s people once he-ld. Assigning fault after mishaps or collisions involving autonomous ships poses intricate le-gal difficulties demanding prudent re-flection.

Achieving consiste-ncy in international maritime regulations is anothe-r important matter that demands attention. As diffe-rent nations implement dive-rse rules and protocols, achieving uniformity across borde-rs grows more vital to streamline global comme-rce and guarantee cohe-rent safety benchmarks. Attaining inte-rnational harmonization necessitates broad coope-ration and discussion between countrie-s, regulatory agencies, and industrial playe-rs. While regulations may vary somewhat be-tween regions due- to local needs and priorities, e-stablishing core standards of interoperability and a share-d framework can smooth cross-border operations. This allows all partie-s to navigate laws with clarity while still accounting for legitimate- regional distinctions. Moving in this direction nece-ssitates input from a range of voices to find balance-d solutions respecting both common intere-sts and particular circumstances.

Furthermore-, the future progression of maritime- law will be significantly impacted by continuous technological advance-ment in the field. As te-chnologies for example artificial inte-lligence, blockchain, and large data analytics ke-ep developing, nove-l lawful and ethical issues will surface. The- employment of such technologie-s in maritime procedures brings up matte-rs pertaining to data confidentiality, cyberse-curity, and intellectual property le-gal rights. Achieving a balance betwe-en innovation and set lawful guideline-s will be critical in molding the upcoming lawful panorama of the maritime- industry. While technology continues to e-volve at a rapid pace, establishing re-gulations that promote responsible de-velopment without stifling progress will be- an ongoing challenge. Privacy concerns around ve-ssel monitoring and big data collection must be addre-ssed proactively through open dialogue- between all stake-holders. Intellectual prope-rty regulations may also need re-visions to reflect new applications of e-merging technologies. Ove-rall, navigating legal uncertainties surrounding ne-w maritime technologies will re-quire flexibility and cooperation across inte-rnational jurisdictions. Furthermore-, guaranteeing sustainable practice-s in the maritime industry through technology introduce-s its own set of lawful difficulties. Environmental rule-s and efforts to advance maintainability sometime-s clash with business interests. Addre-ssing these clashes e-xpects cautious balancing of monetary feasibility, e-cological insurance, and public requests. While- innovation can encourage more e-co-accommodating procedures, its rece-ption presents lawful questions with re-gards to current directions and business activitie-s. Careful examination is expe-cted to distinguish potential clashes and discove-r reasonable arrangeme-nts that think about every single pe-rtinent viewpoint.

To briefly summarize-, the rise of technological progre-ssions within the maritime industry brings about seve-ral legal matters that must be de-alt with. Adapting current laws to control new technologie-s, accomplishing worldwide uniformity, and navigating opposing interests are- merely some of the-difficulties that necessity be- confronted. Moving forward, upcoming evolutions in maritime re-gulations will unquestionably be molded by continual te-chnological transformation, necessitating lawful structures to stay synchronize-d with development though guarante-eing the protection of privile-ges and advancing sustainable methods.

Climate change- poses serious risks, as rising sea le-vels threaten coastal re-gions worldwide. This introduction explores how climate- change may impact maritime law over time-. Coastlines are increasingly vulne-rable to flooding and erosion as melting glacie-rs and ice sheets raise- ocean levels. Maritime- boundaries that, As the Earth's warming climate- progresses, with tempe-ratures increasing and ice she-ets diminishing, the conseque-nces for our oceans and seas cannot be- understated. In this portion, let me- explain how climate change is intricate-ly connected to swelling se-a levels and the profound implications the-se alterations have for maritime- law. Rising seas don't just threaten coastal re-gions with flooding or erosion - they influence- international borders and territorial claims unde-r law. A moderate rise in se-a level could shift maritime boundarie-s and redraw legal maps governing issue-s from fisheries to oil drilling. Coastal nations may face dispute-s as the ocean cree-ps farther inland. This brings uncertainty for deve-lopment and security. As waters warm, spe-cies also migrate or perish, re-shaping entire marine e-cosystems and economies that de-pend on them. Adapting policies for alte-red coastlines and managing disruption to international wate-rs both present complex challe-nges. Though changes unfold gradually, effe-cts will mount and intensify if emissions continue unche-cked. Prudent planning is nee-ded to navigate a future of highe-r seas.

Firstly, it is essential to understand the connection between climate change and rising sea levels. The warming of our planet caused by greenhouse gas emissions leads to the melting of glaciers and ice sheets, contributing to the expansion of seawater volume. This phenomenon directly results in a rise in global sea levels, putting coastal areas and low-lying islands at risk of inundation.

Rising sea le-vels pose serious implications for maritime- law that span vast distances and have wide-ranging e-ffects. A profoundly impacted area involve-s establishing maritime boundaries and te-rritorial waters. Should sea leve-ls persist in climbing, coastal nations may discover their domains shrinking, pote-ntially triggering intricate legal disagre-ements regarding posse-ssion and control. As threats to coastal lands mount, the nece-ssity for well-defined le-gal structures to handle these- difficulties becomes more- pressing.

Furthermore-, the consequence-s of climbing sea levels go be-yond territorial problems. It additionally introduces major difficultie-s for maritime facilities, such as docks, harbors, and shipping lanes. Infrastructure- along the coast must adjust to shifting shorelines and incre-ased risks of flooding, requiring changes to e-xisting laws governing building norms and navigational security. These-facilities are crucial for trade but vulne-rable to environmental shifts. Adapting rule-s and reconstructing could help ensure- ongoing operation during an unstable climate.

Beyond this point, climate- change-associated happenings for instance- devastating storms, rising sea leve-ls, and more typical normal calamities modify danger appraisals for maritime- exercises. The-se progressing changes re-quest a reassessme-nt of obligation and remuneration structures in case-s where natural harm happens be-cause of maritime industry rehe-arses. Specifically, unpredictable- climate marvels like more- grounded typhoons and more rele-ntless downpours because of e-nvironmental change influence- waterway security and transportation. Additionally, the e-xpansion in sea levels brings about highe-r storm surges that presentation more- prominent dangers to ports and docks. Subseque-ntly, the maritime part nee-ds to rethink its hazard evaluations and protection approache-s to adapt to the progressively unstable- climate conditions brought about by environmental change-.

Addressing the- complex issues surrounding rising ocean le-vels within maritime law require-s worldwide teamwork and partnership. Curre-nt worldwide agreeme-nts and rules relating to environme-ntal change, like the Paris Arrange-ment, can offer a basis for dealing with the-se difficulties on a planetary scale-. Furthermore, associations like the- Global Maritime Organization (IMO) have a pivotal part in shaping guideline-s to reduce the impacts of e-nvironmental change on maritime ope-rations. The IMO must work with coastal and island nations to establish policies facilitating adaptation to se-a level rise while- continuing to enable global shipping and trade.

It is prudent to e-nvision creative lawful structures that e-nergize and advance maintainable- maritime practices heading into the- future. This could incorporate steps like- carbon evaluating or outflows exchanging plans custom-made particularly for the- maritime business. By coordinating financial motivators with natural objective-s, these systems can assist with adjusting and mitigation e-ndeavors expecte-d to react to expanding sea le-vels. Specifically, the utilization of carbon asse-ssing or emanation exchanging could encourage- lower discharges from ships and boats. By putting a cost on carbon outflows or permitting e-xchanging of outflows credits, these frame-works give monetary rewards for bringing down discharge-s. This encourages the maritime- industry move starting with one fuel source- then onto the next that produce-s less contamination. Along these line-s, innovative lawful structures, for example-, carbon evaluating can encourage the- maritime part's change to more maintainable- rehearses and add to global e-ndeavors to battle environme-ntal change.

In conclusion, the introduction of this section has highlighted the link between climate change and rising sea levels and discussed its implications for maritime law. The following sections will delve into specific legal challenges posed by rising sea levels, explore international agreements and regulations addressing climate change in the context of maritime law, examine liability and compensation issues, and propose potential future directions for adapting maritime law to address climate change effectively. By doing so, we aim to equip readers with a comprehensive understanding of how maritime law must adapt to the pressing challenges posed by climate change and rising sea levels.

Legal Challenges Posed by Rising Sea Levels

As our planet face-s the pressing effe-cts of climate change, one primary conce-rn involves the climbing ocean le-vels and the relate-d lawful difficulties. This part explores de-eply into the authorized issue-s emerging from this marvel, e-mphasizing its novel impacts on maritime outskirts, territorial wate-rs, and the necessity for fle-xible and mitigation techniques inside- the realm of maritime law. The- rising sea levels are- presenting new challe-nges associated with maritime boundarie-s and territorial waters. There- is a need to carefully e-xamine these issue-s and develop strategic solutions to adapt to the- changes being caused by the- climbing ocean levels. Furthe-r clarification on some of these le-gal matters could help address the- implications of this phenomenon.

Rising sea le-vels will have widespre-ad effects for coastal countries and the-ir control over adjacent waters. As the- shoreline moves backwards and pre-viously dry land gets covered by wate-r, defining maritime boundaries be-comes more complicated. The- changing nature of these boundarie-s presents substantial problems for nations wanting to maintain the-ir authority over neighboring seas. Ne-ighboring states may get into conflicts because- of opposing statements over re-gions that recently went unde-r water. Legal systems ne-ed to be deve-loped or changed to deal with the-se conflicts and make sure fair de-cisions. As coastlines recede- with rising sea levels, the- task of delineating maritime boundarie-s grows increasingly complex. Countries close- to one another could find themse-lves in disagreeme-nt regarding territories that now lie- underwater due to se-a level rise. To addre-ss potential disputes betwe-en nations and ensure e-quitable resolutions, laws must be e-stablished or revised to handle- boundaries as they shift with the changing coastline-s.

Additionally, the incre-asing sea levels carry de-ep consequence-s for territorial waters, which spread a nation's control ove-r neighboring waters. As coastlines de-grade, territorial waters may change- or decrease, pote-ntially impacting a country's power to practice oversight and powe-r in traditionally understood regions. This brings up inquiries about the- preservation of sovere-ign privileges, protection of normal asse-ts, and authorization of laws inside these transforme-d maritime locales. There- are questions around how nations will manage the-ir rights to the seas and resource-s if boundaries change over time- due to environmental factors outside- of their control. The stability of international agre-ements regarding use- of waters could also be impacted. Furthe-r discussion is needed on balancing sove-reign control with responsibilities to addre-ss the underlying causes and e-ffects of rising tides.

Adaptation and mitigation strategie-s play pivotal roles in addressing the le-gal issues posed by increasing se-a levels in maritime law. Countrie-s must take proactive steps to e-stablish measures safeguarding susce-ptible coastal communities, infrastructure, and natural e-nvironments from the ramifications of inundation and abrasion. Such initiatives involve- building coastal protections, executing sustainable- land use regulations, and formulating thorough calamity administration plans. Furthermore-, worldwide teamwork is critical in designing impactful re-sponses to mitigate the unfavorable- impacts of mounting sea levels on maritime- operations. While defe-nses, policies, and preparations can he-lp reduce vulnerability, the- progressive impacts of rising waters will like-ly present ongoing challenge-s requiring innovative legal and political solutions. Continue-d international dialogue on long-term adaptation and re-sponsibility may help establish equitable- frameworks for coastal resilience- and management of transboundary issues.

By exploring the legal issues arising from rising sea levels and examining their impact on maritime boundaries and territorial waters, this section sheds light on the urgent need for adaptation and mitigation strategies within maritime law. It underscores the importance of proactive measures to address the challenges brought about by climate change, safeguarding the interests of coastal nations, and ensuring the sustainable use of our oceans. As we navigate the uncharted waters of rising sea levels, a comprehensive understanding of these legal challenges is vital in shaping the future of maritime legislation.

International Agreements and Regulations Addressing Climate Change in Maritime Law

In this section, we will delve into the international agreements and regulations that specifically address climate change within the context of maritime law. As the effects of climate change become increasingly severe, it is essential for legal frameworks to adapt and provide solutions to mitigate its impact on maritime activities.

One of the most influential organizations in this regard is the International Maritime Organization (IMO). Established as a specialized agency of the United Nations, the IMO plays a vital role in developing and implementing regulations to address various environmental issues in the maritime industry. Specifically, the IMO has taken significant steps to tackle climate change through the adoption of international agreements and regulations.

The Inte-rnational Convention for the Preve-ntion of Pollution from Ships, also known as MARPOL, includes an important agreeme-nt concerning climate change mitigation. Anne-x VI of MARPOL specifically addresses air pollution and gre-enhouse gas emissions from oce-an-faring vessels. Entering into force- in 2005, Annex VI established limitations on the- amounts of sulfur oxides and nitrogen oxides that ships can discharge- from their smokestacks. These- restrictions aim to curb two significant air pollutants. Annex VI also introduced the- Energy Efficiency Design Inde-x and Ship Energy Efficiency Manageme-nt Plan, abbreviated as EEDI and SEEMP. The EEDI and SEEMP targe-t enhancing energy e-fficiency in ship design and operations. The-ir overarching goal is to gradually reduce the- volume of carbon dioxide emitte-d by ships over time.

The Ballast Wate-r Management Convention within the- International Maritime Organization framework is an important agre-ement. Though this convention doe-s not directly relate to climate-change, it holds great importance in safe-guarding marine biodiversity and ecosyste-m resilience - both of which are- closely connected to the- effects of climate alte-ration. The convention impleme-nts criteria and methods for handling ballast water, se-eking to stop the transmission of exotic aquatic spe-cies that can disturb delicate habitats. While- not aimed at climate change itse-lf, regulating ballast water helps fortify marine- environments against future climate- pressures by maintaining natural balances among local plants and cre-atures.

Furthermore-, numerous local and worldwide arrangeme-nts have been actualize-d to address atmospheric devation's impact on maritime- law. For instance, the Paris Arrangeme-nt, received unde-r the United Nations Structure Conve-ntion on Atmospheric Change (UNFCCC), expe-cts to limit worldwide warming to very far bene-ath 2 degrees Ce-lsius over pre-mechanical le-vels. While it doesn't particularly ze-ro in on maritime law, it underscores the- requirement for diminishing ozone- harming substance outflows, which in a roundabout way influences the- maritime business' tasks and directions. Ne-w standards have been pre-sented on a local and worldwide scale- to help the marine are-a in diminishing its ozone harming substance impression. The-se incorporate usage of cle-aner energize-s and advances to screen and re-port emanations. In any case, more note-worthy worldwide joint effort is require-d to actualize more sustainable arrange-ments and advance advanceme-nts that can empower marine transporte-rs to turn out to be more natural.

Furthermore-, regional agreeme-nts such as the European Union's Emission Trading Scheme- aim to regulate gree-nhouse gas emissions from ships operating within Europe-an waters. This agreeme-nt has introduced mechanisms to closely track, re-cord, and validate ship emissions, there-by promoting openness and responsibility for the-ir environmental impact. Similarly, other jurisdictions have- initiated comparable initiatives within the-ir respective wate-rs to reduce pollution and uphold accountability.

The role of these international agreements and regulations is crucial in addressing climate change challenges within the maritime sector. By promoting energy efficiency, reducing emissions, and preventing environmental harm, they contribute to a more sustainable and resilient future for maritime activities. However, it is important to note that continuous evaluation and adaptation of these agreements are necessary to keep pace with the evolving needs and realities of climate change.

In the following part, we- will investigate the le-gal responsibility and payment matters that e-merge from weathe-r change effects on maritime- activities, emphasizing the authorize-d structures intended to handle- natural harm brought about by the business. A portion of the significant lawful issue-s remember-d for the conversation will include de-ciding obligation and deciding remuneration sums for climate- influenced business activitie-s, for example, ocean shipping and angling. Othe-r legitimate points will incorporate transboundary air contamination and worldwide- organization on shared environmental issue-s identified with marine natural life- and coastlines. While lawful instruments pre-sently exist to manage ce-rtain kinds of natural harm from maritime exercise-s, the developing se-riousness of climate change will like-ly require more broad coordinate-d worldwide activity to

While climate- change and rising sea leve-ls present serious risks, addre-ssing issues of liability and compensation can help communitie-s prepare. As global tempe-ratures increase due- to greenhouse gas e-missions, sea levels will like-ly continue rising, threatening coastal re-gions with greater flood risks and storm surges. Evaluating ways to e-quitably

One of the- most pressing issues stemming from climate- change involves the incre-asing sea levels, which carry substantial ramifications for maritime- law. Since oceans continue to swe-ll due to climate change, those- who make their living from maritime industrie-s must now grapple with emerging que-stions of accountability and compensation that warrant prudent examination. As our se-as rise at the behe-st of climate change, people- working in fields tied to the wate-rs face novel problems of fault and payme-nt when damages occur that require- judicious analysis to resolve fairly.

To begin with, taking a close-r look at the legal responsibilitie-s stemming from the effe-cts of climate change on maritime ope-rations is important. As ocean levels incre-ase, coastal structures, such as docks, ship repair yards, and te-rminals, are at risk of harm. This brings up queries about who must pay to fix or re-position these installations. Moreove-r, maritime businesses may de-al with liability accusations for ecological harm brought on by their activities. For instance-, oil leaks and other hazardous substance discharge-s can have far-reaching impacts, nece-ssitating suitable authorized structures to manage- these matters. The-re are questions around who pays for damage- to ports from rising seas. What legal frameworks addre-ss oil spills or other pollution that has wide effe-cts? Further consideration of these- important issues is clearly warranted.

Careful analysis of pre-vailing legal structures become-s essential in tackling ecological harms brought on by maritime- industries. International agree-ments like the Inte-rnational Convention on Civil Liability for Oil Pollution Damage (CLC) and the Inte-rnational Convention on Liability and Compensation for Damage in Conne-ction with the Carriage of Hazardous and Noxious Substances by

Se-a (HNS) offer direction for reimburse-ment in the case of pollution e-vents. Nonethele-ss, these systems may ne-ed revision or broadening to manage- the distinct difficulties prese-nted by damage connecte-d to climate change. Climate change- is producing new types of environme-ntal damages through rising sea leve-ls, stronger storms, and other impacts. These- frameworks provide a starting point but require- updates to fully address the scale- and unique nature of climate change--related pollution incidents from maritime- shipping. Further clarification and modifications may be warranted to e-stablish responsibility and facilitate compensation for the- various kinds of damages now occurring. There- are a few factors to take into account to e-nsure appropriate payment for impacte-d groups. One possibility worth investigating involves cre-ating a global pool of money specifically focused on coping with climate- change harms in the shipping industry. This fund might collect donations from gove-rnments, maritime companies, and othe-r invested parties. Such a syste-m would offer not just economic assistance for injure-d communities but also motivate environme-ntally-friendly and long-lasting behaviors within the fie-ld. While more options require- exploration, a dedicated inte-rnational fund shows potential for addressing damages in a fair manne-r and encouraging positive change.

Furthermore, collaboration among nations and organizations will play a vital role in addressing liability and compensation issues related to climate change in maritime activities. Sharing best practices, harmonizing regulations, and fostering international cooperation will lead to more effective responses to climate change challenges. Platforms like the International Maritime Organization (IMO) can facilitate these discussions and help establish global standards for liability and compensation.

As our planet continue-s to experience- the harmful impacts of climate change, with global warming causing se-a levels to rise at an alarming rate-, it has become crucial that we adapt the- laws governing maritime activities to de-al with the liability and compensation issues re-sulting from higher ocean water le-vels. By investigating creative- legal solutions and reinforcing collaboration betwe-en nations, those involved in oce-an transportation can effectively handle- the difficulties prese-nted by climate change. Putting in place- suitable systems of responsibility and payme-nt for damages will guarantee that pe-ople negatively affe-cted by the conseque-nces of climate change re-ceive proper re-imbursement while also e-ncouraging environmentally-friendly me-thods that aid in reducing prospective dange-rs. Though the challenges are- vast, with coordination and compassion we can craft policies to both assist victims and incentivize- reductions in greenhouse- gas emissions, giving vulnerable coastal re-gions a fighting chance at a sustainable future de-spite the unprece-dented changes alre-ady set in motion.

Future Directions: Adapting Maritime Law to Address Climate Change

As the global climate- continues to transform and ocean leve-ls climb, the area of maritime law ne-cessitates adjustment to ade-quately address the difficultie-s introduced by these e-nvironmental alterations. This portion examine-s potential future progressions in maritime- law and presents creative-lawful systems planned to ene-rgize maintainable maritime practice-s. The effects of e-nvironmental change on oceans and se-as are already being se-en and felt, with rising sea le-vels submerging some low-lying coastal are-as and increasing the intensity of hurricane-s and typhoons. Maritime law will need to conside-r these impacts and potentially support re-location efforts for communities now threate-ned. New policies may also focus on ince-ntivizing more fuel-efficie-nt and environmentally-friendly te-chnologies and operations among shipping flee-ts. While maritime trade will re-main economically important, ensuring it deve-lops sustainably will be crucial to mitigate climate impacts and adapt to ongoing change-s.

There- are a few areas within the- maritime industry that could benefit from close-r scrutiny to help curb environmental damage-. As ocean levels climb due- to climate change, more coastline-s are wearing away and natural areas are- disappearing. To counter this, we must e-stablish strong guidelines covering construction ne-ar shorelines and vesse-l transportation. Tougher limits regarding exhaust, trash re-moval, and ballast water handling within maritime law may aid in lesse-ning the sector's environme-ntal impact. One specifically important region is e-nsuring activities related to shipping and coastal de-velopment do not exce-ssively contribute to further e-rosion or habitat destruction. As seas cree-p higher, certain areas will be-come more vulnerable-, making prudent oversight critical. Carefully crafte-d policies have the pote-ntial to benefit both ecological and e-conomic interests through a balanced approach.

Additional progressions in maritime- law could involve the application of financial motivators to advance sustainable- practices. For instance, carbon pricing systems may be- incorporated into international shipping procedure-s, giving financial rewards for vessels that e-mploy cleaner fuels or e-mbrace energy-e-fficient technologies. Such marke-t-based approaches have the- capacity to stimulate invention and promote industry-wide- acceptance of sustainable practice-s. Economical rewards could inspire shipping companies to inve-stigate novel ene-rgy-efficient technologie-s or cleaner-burning fuels. If adopte-d widely, these innovations may significantly re-duce the carbon emissions from inte-rnational shipping operations. While more re-search and developme-nt is still needed, using e-conomic incentives holds promise to transform the- sector into a more environme-ntally friendly industry.

To properly de-al with climate change and increasing se-a levels, worldwide te-amwork will play an essential part. Maritime law ne-eds to keep on advancing union among countrie-s, associations, and partners to devise e-xhaustive methodologies to battle- environmental change. This incorporate-s synchronizing guidelines crosswise ove-r purviews, sharing successful practices, and coordinating e-ndeavors to eliminate unlawful angling, contamination, and diffe-rent destructive e-xercises. While worldwide- cooperation is basic, individual nations additionally need to guarante-e that nearby arrangeme-nt and activities address nearby qualitie-s and difficulties. Regular assets administration should be- a joint effort betwee-n public and private partners. Neighborhood local are-a inclusion can likewise guarantee- that arrangements think about nearby ne-eds and conditions. As the effe-cts of environmental change incre-ment, more collaboration and shared obligation at all le-vels will be fundamental.

The de-veloping area of environme-nt equity may likewise shape- the future of maritime le-gislation. As powerless networks confront re-moval because of ascending se-a levels, it turns out to be fundame-ntal for maritime law to give instruments for re-asonable remuneration and re-location. This may include building up worldwide assets to he-lp adjustment and mitigation endeavors in influe-nced districts, guaranteeing that those- generally influence-d by environmental change ge-t satisfactory help. The field of atmosphe-re equity addresse-s the moral part of environmental change-. Rising ocean levels as brought about by e-nvironmental change prese-ntly displace networks from their home-s. It is subsequently basic that maritime law give-s lawful arrangements, for example-, relocation offices and pay rese-rves. This guarantees ne-tworks influenced the most ge-t the help they have- to adapt. Worldwide reserve-s could fill in as a wellspring of subsidizing for adjustment and mitigation tasks in districts confronting the most notice-ably awful impacts. This assistance guarantees a re-asonable result for the ge-neral population living in regions most powerle-ss against environmental change.

While te-chnology will certainly hold significant influence in guiding how maritime- law evolves to address climate- change going forward, certain technological de-velopments promise to he-lp transport goods by sea in a more environme-ntally-friendly manner. For instance, autonomous ships could transport cargo with re-duced carbon emissions through more optimize-d routing. Similarly, renewable e-nergy solutions and sophisticated tracking systems may allow ve-ssels to travel in a gree-ner fashion. As such innovations start to transform maritime operations, the- associated laws and policies should be update-d to both encourage these- technologies and handle any nove-l situations they bring about. By thoughtfully integrating promising advances like- renewable powe-r sources and self-driving capabilities, e-xisting legal frameworks can be adapte-d to support more sustainable and efficie-nt ocean transportation for years to come.

In conclusion, the future of maritime law lies in adapting to the impacts of climate change and rising sea levels. By implementing stricter regulations, incentivizing sustainable practices, promoting international cooperation, and embracing technological innovations, maritime law can effectively address these challenges. The time to act is now, and through forward-thinking approaches, the seas can be navigated in harmony with the environment.

Chapter **2**

The Future of
Autonomous Shipping
****

Introduction to Autonomous Shipping:

Autonomous shipping, a revolutionary concept in maritime transportation, is poised to transform the seascape of the future. In this section, we delve into the intricacies of autonomous shipping, exploring its definition, key components, and the groundbreaking technological advancements that have paved the way for this paradigm shift.

At its core, autonomous shipping involve-s vessels operating without imme-diate human guidance or command. Instead of re-lying on people to navigate and make- choices, these ships e-mploy innovative technologies like- artificial intelligence, machine- learning, robotics, and sophisticated sensing e-quipment to independe-ntly travel, decide course-s of action, and carry out duties. By utilizing these le-ading-edge instruments, ve-ssels have potential to maximize- productivity, elevate pre-cautions, and perhaps fundamentally change global shipping. Autonomous ope-rations allow for continuous monitoring of conditions to aid safe passage and optimize route-s according to real-time updates.

While the- development of se-lf-driving ships has progressed due to impre-ssive innovations across multiple domains, some conside-rations remain. Breakthroughs in artificial intellige-nce and machine learning have- allowed vessels to proce-ss huge volumes of information instantly, helping the-m make informed judgments and re-act rapidly to shifting scenarios. Moreover, incorporating pre-cise navigation, remote ove-rsight functions, and sophisticated communication into vessels has guarante-ed smooth connectivity and heighte-ned contextual understanding for autonomous crafts. Howe-ver, further refining the-se emerging te-chnologies could help address re-maining safety questions to fully realize- the promise of autonomous shipping.

While the- potential advantages of autonomous shipping are quite- appealing, it is important to consider all perspe-ctives on this complex issue. Supporte-rs believe autonomous ve-ssels could enhance productivity and pe-rformance by removing human constraints intrinsic to traditional shipping methods. For instance-, without human operators aboard, autonomous ships may be capable of optimizing route-s to minimize fuel usage and carbon footprints, the-reby lowering expe-nses and reducing environme-ntal impact. The capacity for precise navigation in busy shipping lane-s through automated decision-making also raises the- prospect of avoiding accidents at sea. Howe-ver, replacing human seafare-rs with autonomous technology introduces new unce-rtainties that require care-ful consideration. Overall, both the be-nefits of enhanced logistics and the- challenges of transitioning to new marine- infrastructure deserve- balanced discussion as the shipping industry explore-s modernization through emerging innovations.

While autonomous shipping pre-sents promising opportunities, we must also conside-r various complications. Transforming the entire maritime- industry to operate without humans introduces intricate- legal and governance challe-nges that demand resolution for se-amless incorporation. Issues involving accountability in unforese-en incidents or technical malfunctions, conforming to global standards, pre-venting digital vulnerabilities, and re-solving ethical queries pe-rtaining to automated choice-making are just some- of the issues warranting prudent inspe-ction. Additionally, establishing specialized guide-lines for autonomous navigation through crowded sea route-s and unpredictable conditions require-s judicious planning to safeguard crew and cargo. Though exciting advance-s are on the horizon, gradually impleme-nting self-driving changes after addre-ssing these complex matte-rs ensures continuing progress re-sponsibly.

Furthermore-, the effective- execution and endorse-ment of self-governing shipping re-lies not just on innovative headways ye-t in addition on broad partner involvement, worldwide- coordination, and agreement building. Ne-arby collaboration among industry partners, maritime specialists, and lawful spe-cialists is basic for establishing a strong lawful and administrative structure that advance-s sheltered, de-pendable, and good autonomous shipping practices. It is vital for all gathe-rings to cooperate to guarantee- the most noteworthy wellbe-ing guidelines are se-t up and that innovation is created and actualized se-curely. Worldwide cooperation will guarante-e guidelines are- uniform over all maritime areas. Care-ful thought regarding lawful issues and security will support the- trust in and selection of these- new advances.

While autonomous shipping may re-shape the maritime industry, se-veral factors require conside-ration as this technology advances. Legally and from a re-gulatory standpoint, autonomous vessels prese-nt challenges that will nee-d addressed. We must analyze- how maritime law and legal prece-dents may require updating to account for re-duced or eliminated onboard cre-ws. Environmental impacts also warrant examination to ensure- autonomous tech helps shipping progress sustainably. Though autonomous shipping's pote-ntial seems vast, steady work is e-ssential to develop principle-s guiding its integration safely and for the be-nefit of all. The following sections e-xplore these important le-gal, regulatory, environmental and pre-dictive aspects so we may navigate- both challenges and opportunities wise-ly as this field continues rapidly evolving.

While autonomous shipping te-chnology holds promise for increased e-fficiency and safety at sea, e-stablishing an appropriate legal framework will be- crucial for allowing this future to unfold responsibly. Some ke-y issues that will need clarification include- liability in various accident scenarios While te-chnological developments push the- maritime industry toward autonomous operations, transitioning to fully autonomous shipping brings both promise and proble-ms that warrant careful consideration. Currently, le-gal structures and international rules do not fully addre-ss unmanned vessels, ne-cessitating scrutiny of existing conventions and guide-lines to comprehend autonomous ships' place- within the regulatory framework. He-re, we look at laws covering autonomous shipping today, conve-ntions and standards from organizations addressing robot-driven boats, and the ne-cessity of consistent, harmonized policie-s for guaranteeing autonomous vesse-ls' secure and ethical navigation. While the- existing legal structure gove-rning self-governing ships is still in its earlie-st stages, as the innovation progresse-s at a quick rate, various worldwide traditions and rules have- been set up to addre-ss particular parts of self-governing vesse-ls. For example, the Global Maritime- Organization (IMO) has discharged rules on maritime se-lf-governing surface ships (MASS) tasks, concentrating on we-llbeing, security, and natural contemplations. The-se early standards give fundame-ntal direction, yet further advance-ment is expecte-d to completely address the- specialized and legitimate-ramifications of self-governing shipping as innovation propels. For the- time being, controllers and strate-gy creators are chipping away at building up more particular rule-s identifying with the outline, de-velopment, and activities of robotize-d ships to guarantee they work se-curely and as expecte-d.

While e-xisting maritime regulations cente-r around crew and navigation, autonomous vessels pre-sent novel issues. A standardize-d legal framework is urgently ne-eded addressing the-ir distinct challenges. Current rule-s focus on human aspects like staffing and maneuve-rs that may conflict with autonomous ship operations. Therefore-, policymakers and attorneys must cooperate- to craft consistent, synchronized statutes tailore-d for autonomous shipping. This will provide much-neede-d clarification handling its peculiar characteristics.

One ke-y area of concern regarding autonomous ships is liability. De-termining responsibility become-s more intricate as control transitions from human operators to artificial inte-lligence algorithms and systems. Traditional le-gal principles like neglige-nce and fault-based liability may nee-d reassessment to accommodate- autonomous vessels' novel qualitie-s. Additionally, establishing jurisdiction in incidents involving unmanned ships functioning across inte-rnational borders presents furthe-r difficulties demanding prudent re-flection.

Environmental sustainability factors significantly influe-nce the legal structure- governing self-driving ships. Autonomous vesse-ls potentially lower emissions through e-fficient voyage planning and fuel use-, yet pose hazards like pollution and e-cosystem effects ne-eding addressed. Crucial re-gulations should encourage eco-frie-ndly operations and harness autonomy's upsides, all while- ensuring maritime transport progresse-s sustainably. Lawmakers face ensuring re-gulations both maximize benefits like- decreased e-missions and minimize issues such as pollution rele-ases. Doing so involves promoting optimized route-s that lessen environme-ntal impacts. Simultaneously, oversight maintains protections for marine- life and habitats. Navigating these nuance-s proves important to charting autonomous shipping's course and marine transport's future- health.

While te-chnological developments in autonomous shipping show pote-ntial, uncertainties remain. Advance-s like unmanned cargo ships and drone de-livery may transform shipping but also necessitate-updated laws and regulations to handle ne-w situations. As self-driving vessels and automate-d package transport progress, maritime guide-lines will likely require- clarification to successfully manage eme-rging issues and prospects. Progress in are-as like robot-operated oce-an freight carriers or airborne de-livery drones will probably demand adjuste-d legal standards and protocols to appropriately govern unfamiliar conditions. It is important that statute-s and protocols evolve in step with te-chnological shifts to successfully address unexpe-cted complications and openings create-d through continued innovations.

While the- legal and regulatory structures gove-rning autonomous shipping continue developing, se-veral issues demand thoughtful conside-ration going forward. Establishing regulations that are consistent and standardize-d across jurisdictions will be important, as will addressing open que-stions around liability in accidents involving autonomous vessels. As this te-chnology progresses, ensuring e-nvironmental sustainability remains a priority, and adapting agilely to innovations will be- key to unlocking autonomous shipping's possibilities. Howeve-r, safety must come before- all else in this quickly changing field. Care-ful handling of these pertine-nt topics can help autonomous shipping serve comme-rcial needs responsibly as re-gulations evolve with the te-chnology.

The Future of Autonomous Shipping: Implications for Maritime Law and Jurisprudence

While te-chnological progress in the maritime se-ctor brings exciting opportunities through autonomous vesse-ls, certain legal questions arise- that require examination. This se-gment investigates how se-lf-driving ships impact typical lawful frameworks and standards, takes a dee-per look into accountability issues from any crashes involving autonomous crafts, and analyze-s the difficulties in allocating responsibility and de-ciding appropriate jurisdiction in situations concerning these- innovative transports. There is a ne-ed for intermediate- clarification on some key topics to help facilitate-continued responsible de-velopment and operation of such advance-d marine technology.

The introduction of autonomous ve-ssels brings up many new legal issue-s that need to be addre-ssed as existing frameworks have- long relied on humans to operate- ships. With self-driving ships operating without people- directly in control, important questions eme-rge about who should be liable if accide-nts or collisions occur. For example, if an autonomous ship causes harm, who is re-sponsible - the owner of the- vessel, the company that de-veloped the autonomous te-chnology, or some other involved party? The-re are no straightforward answers as comple-tely driverless ve-ssels break new ground. Lawmake-rs will need to carefully conside-r how liability can be fairly assigned to properly prote-ct all stakeholders while still allowing innovation in autonomous maritime- transport to progress.

Dete-rmining accountability becomes espe-cially intricate when taking into account the nume-rous bodies engaged with the- functioning of self-governing watercraft. With an assortme-nt of interested partie-s, such as vessel proprietors, te-chnological enterprises, and manufacture-rs, ascertaining fault can demonstrate pe-rplexing. Furthermore, the- potential absence of human mistake- may complexify the designation of blame-, as incidents may be connecte-d not to carelessness but inste-ad to mechanical defect or programming flaws. The- allocation of responsibility amongst owners, creators, and te-chnicians requires cautious consideration of the-ir particular roles and duties to guarantee- passenger and worker prote-ction. While technology continues advancing navigation, safe-guards must be established to rightly assign accountability whe-n things do not go as planned.

Establishing jurisdiction poses another significant challenge when it comes to autonomous shipping. Traditional legal systems rely on well-defined geographical boundaries and registries to determine which country's laws apply to a particular incident at sea. However, with autonomous vessels capable of traversing multiple jurisdictions in a single voyage, determining the appropriate legal jurisdiction becomes a complex task. The issue is further complicated by the fact that different countries may have varying regulations and standards for autonomous shipping.

There- are several issue-s that need to be addre-ssed regarding autonomous shipping. Deve-loping international regulations for safe and re-sponsible autonomous operations on the wate-r is key. Close cooperation be-tween global maritime groups, gove-rnments, and companies involved is re-quired to generate- comprehensive le-gal structures dealing with responsibility worrie-s and set consistent guideline-s across all authorities. Such regulatory work must think about a variety of e-lements, like how re-liable the technology is, what safe-ty protocols are in place, how information is protecte-d, and security against hackers. Ultimately, cle-ar rules from collaboration betwee-n those stakeholders can he-lp autonomous shipping navigate new waters while- protecting all sailors.

While autonomous shipping te-chnology advances and its use spreads, que-stions relating to accountability and applicable laws demand prude-nt reflection and a future-orie-nted mindset. It is imperative- that legal experts, those- who shape policy, and intereste-d parties in the field active-ly debate these- issues and endeavor to e-stablish adaptable legal structures guarante-eing responsibility, safeguarding against prospe-ctive dangers, and facilitating secure- and eco-friendly autonomous shipping operations. As autonomous ve-ssels gradually transport more cargo across oceans, the-re must be clear rule-s in place regarding who may be he-ld liable in different sce-narios, such as equipment malfunctions, communication breakdowns, or collisions at se-a. Conversations are warranted to de-termine which jurisdictions automatic ships will fall under as the-y cross international waters. With open discussion and coope-rative work, suitable solutions can be found that allow this promising ne-w means of marine transport to progress re-sponsibly.

In the following portion, we- will investigate the e-cological and sustainability perspectives conne-cted with self-governing de-livery, inspecting both its possible advantage-s and the difficulties it offers as far as marine- contamination and biological community effect. The future- of self-governing delive-ry holds immense capacity not just for innovative he-adways however additionally for advancing maintainable maritime- practices. This area takes a gande-r at how self-governing delive-ry can add to a more ecologically mindful and gree-ner maritime business. We- will take a brief look at how robotization could diminish human errors and accordingly fore-stall mishaps, spills, and other natural issues. Additionally, we will talk about how the- utilization of savvy sensors and keen programming could stre-amline courses and limit non-important vitality utilize and ozone- harming substance outflows. Then again, the de-ficiency of human insight brings up worries with regards to how se-lf-governing boats may respond in unpredictable- circumstances and how protection might be guarante-ed. General, autonomous shipping holds guarante-e however additionally difficultie-s that must be tended to as the- innovation creates.

Autonomous vesse-ls may potentially lower emissions in me-aningful ways. When outfitted with sophisticated te-chnologies, unmanned ships can judiciously sele-ct their precise course-s, travel speeds, and fre-ight amounts to curtail fuel usage. By removing human mistake-s and inefficiencies from transport ope-rations, autonomous shipping presents opportunities to gre-atly diminish the discharge of gree-nhouse gases. Sizeable- carbon reductions could make self-piloting boats an appe-aling choice for corporations aiming to shrink their environme-ntal impact.

Additionally, self-gove-rning shipping can permit enhanced route- planning and navigation, resulting in more eco-frie-ndly habits. By making the most of real-time data on we-ather, traffic blockage, and ocean curre-nts, self-governing vesse-ls can opt for the most fuel-proficient paths, de-creasing both travel time and e-missions. This optimization of routes can also help decre-ase the probability of accidents and spills, thus shie-lding marine habitats from possible contamination. While autonomous ve-ssels certainly offer be-nefits, ensuring their safe- operation will require care-ful testing and oversight.

Autonomous vesse-ls hold promise for greater e-fficiencies and reduce-d costs compared to manned ships. Howeve-r, we must thoughtfully consider the e-nvironmental challenges. While- autonomous technology aims to prevent accide-nts, human error can never be- fully eliminated. A technical malfunction or unfore-seen eve-nt could potentially lead to pollution. Regulators and industry le-aders must establish stringent safe-ty standards to minimize such risks. Continuous testing and operator ove-rsight can help ensure autonomous syste-ms function properly under all conditions. Emerge-ncy response procedure-s and backup control measures are also vital. With proactive- safeguards and contingency planning, we may re-alize benefits while- still protecting sensitive e-cosystems. Progress require-s balancing innovative advances with sound precautions.

Furthermore-, bringing self-governing ships into the curre-nt maritime framework demands prude-nt reflection on their e-ffect on marine biological systems. The- utilization of robotically controlled vessels ought to be- joined by extensive- natural appraisals to guarantee that they don't disturb de-licate natural surroundings or touchy regions. Advances in hull outline-s, drive frameworks, and vitality wells should like-wise coordinate with supportability objective-s to limit contrary impacts on marine assorted variety and wate-r quality. While innovation progresses, e-nsuring the security of our seas stays a top ne-ed.

While autonomous shipping brings opportunitie-s to increase efficie-ncy and reduce environme-ntal impacts, developing this technology re-sponsibly is imperative. Careful re-search and testing will be ke-y to understanding how autonomous vessels can safe-ly and sustainably operate within existing re-gulations. International organizations should facilitate discussions betwe-en stakeholders to e-stablish comprehensive standards. With ope-n cooperation betwee-n technologists, policymakers, and mariners, guide-lines can balance innovation with protecting natural re-sources and crew safety. Autonomous ships hold promise- for lowering emissions if designe-rs address relevant conce-rns and prove capabilities through gradual, regulate-d implementation. A measure-d approach integrating perspective-s from engineers, re-gulators, and environmental advocates may he-lp autonomous shipping aid the maritime sector's transition to cle-aner operations over the- long run.

The Future of Autonomous Shipping:

In this final section of "Navigating the Seas of Law: Unraveling the Depths of Maritime Jurisprudence," we delve into the future trends and predictions for autonomous shipping. As technology continues to advance at an unprecedented pace, the maritime industry is on the brink of a paradigm shift with the emergence of autonomous vessels.

A cursory analysis of continuous technological advance-s in the domain of self-governing shipping uncove-rs a bounty of intriguing opportunities. Breakthroughs in artificial intellige-nce, machine learning, and se-nsor technologies are cle-aring a path for completely autonomous cargo ships compete-nt of navigating the expansive oce-ans without human involvement. State-of-the--art mechanization systems paired with re-fined algorithms empower the-se vessels to make- real-time judgeme-nts, optimize courses, and productively ove-rsee their tasks. While- innovations progress, examination of automated navigation re-mains ongoing.

A moderate- examination of possible future use-s and developments highlights the- broad-ranging effect that self-gove-rning transport may have on different ve-ntures. Unmanned freight ships offe-r the capability for brought down costs, more prominent proficie-ncy, and enhanced wellbe-ing by wiping out human mix-ups and exhaustion related e-vents. Furthermore, se-lf-ruling conveyance frameworks may upse-t the marine stockpile busine-ss by empowering proficient and we-ll-timed conveyances to far off te-rritories and diminishing reliance on conve-ntional transportation strategies. While se-lf-ruling transport promises various advantages, its advantages and disadvantage-s merit additional investigation as advanceme-nt proceeds. Additional rese-arch could likewise give more- understanding into how best to actualize and ove-rsee such innovations as they start to be- embraced all the more- extensively.

A discussion on how self-driving ships could mold se-afaring guidelines later highlights the- necessity for change and progre-ss in lawful structures. The prese-ntation of self-governing vesse-ls requires astute thought of obligation issue-s, mishap examination strategies, and the- arrangement of worldwide norms for we-llbeing and security. As the duty for ve-ssel operation moves from human cre-ws to progressed advances, de-ciding liability in case of collisions or occurrences turns into a critical te-st that maritime purviews should manage. Additional conside-ration is expected to guarante-e responsibility is clearly characte-rized and that exploration strategie-s can recognize how advances may have- added to any occasions, while as yet pe-rmitting development.

Furthermore-, ecological and sustainability issues are e-xtremely important as the maritime- sector aims to decrease- its effect on the e-nvironment. Autonomous shipping possesses huge- prospective for lowering e-missions by way of optimized voyage scheduling, e-fficient vessel handling, and progre-ssed energy administration syste-ms. But it additionally raises issues about marine contamination and possible- ecosystem influence-s if not adequately controlled and tracke-d.

While wrapping up our e-xamination into the forthcoming destiny of self-gove-rning transporting, it is evident that this deve-loping innovation conveys immense guarante-e and capacity. In any case, it additionally prese-nts novel lawful, administrative, and natural difficulties that must be- painstakingly sorted out. The maritime busine-ss, policymakers, and lawful experts should coope-rate to create ste-ady and uniform regulations that guarantee the- protected, liable, and supportable- joining of self-ruling vessels into our worldwide- maritime systems. As new advance-s are receive-d, we should guarantee we-llbeing stays the nee-d while encouraging deve-lopment. Together, through joint e-ffort and shared comprehension, we- can make a future where- machine and people coope-rate securely on the- high seas.

With this final section, "Navigating the Seas of Law: Unraveling the Depths of Maritime Jurisprudence" equips readers with a comprehensive understanding of the historical foundations, current practices, and future developments in maritime law. We hope this book serves as an indispensable resource for legal professionals, scholars, policymakers, and anyone intrigued by the intricacies of law and its profound connection to the vast blue expanse that has shaped human history - the seas.

An introduction to the conce-pt of space law and its connection to maritime law. Space- law emerged as ne-w frontiers opened be-yond Earth's atmosphere. Just as the oce-ans were once unre-gulated, early space e-xploration lacked oversight and clear principle-s. With more nations, The vast expanse of outer space has captivated humanity's imagination for centuries. As technology advanced, our understanding of space expanded, leading to the emergence of space law as a specialized branch of international law. This section explores the concept of space law and its intriguing relationship with maritime law, shedding light on the parallels between these two fascinating domains.

Space law involve-s a diverse collection of le-gal guidelines and protocols that overse-e human actions beyond our planet's atmosphe-re. It covers topics such as satellite- communications, space exploration missions, potential e-xploitation of resources found in outer space-, and how countries may peacefully coe-xist and cooperate in space. Much like- maritime law administrates occurrence-s on the oceans, space law de-velops the authorized structure- for activities beyond Earth's environme-nt. Some key aspects space- law addresses are de-signing international space stations, disposing of space de-bris, broadcasting signals via satellites, and publishing scientific data from probe-s investigating other cele-stial bodies. It clarifies ownership of ite-ms retrieved from space-, like rocks from the Moon, and protects astronauts and e-quipment involved with discovery e-ndeavors. Overall, the purpose- of space law is to promote safe, productive-, and lawful utilization of the cosmos through established inte-rnational space treaties and national space- legislation.

While jurisdiction ove-r space and seas pose similaritie-s in their borderless nature-, some key distinctions exist be-tween the le-gal frameworks governing each domain. Like- the high seas, outer space- exists outside any singular nation's control and belongs to all of humanity. Howe-ver, the vastness of space- introduces even gre-ater challenges to ove-rsight and governance than that afforded by Earth's oce-ans. Whereas ships traverse- defined routes across inte-rnational waters, spacecraft navigate the- limitless expanse above- our atmosphere. Further, human pre-sence remains sparse- in space compared to routine maritime- traffic. These differe-nces informed modifications to principles originally de-veloped for the se-as when applied to this new frontie-r. Still, certain parallels remain - both re-alms uphold freedom of access and ope-rations therein, on the condition that all activitie-s proceed peace-fully for the benefit of all.

While both domains must addre-ss establishing regulatory frameworks to e-nsure safety and preve-nt harmful interference-, their approaches differ in important ways. Maritime- law has a long history of establishing rules and conventions ce-ntered around safeguarding navigation, avoiding collisions be-tween vesse-ls, and protecting the seas. Re-gulations have evolved ove-r centuries to achieve- these crucial aims as shipping traffic expande-d exponentially. Meanwhile-, the fledgling field of space- law also focuses on regulating satellite- launches and managing orbital debris, but nece-ssarily tackles entirely ne-w challenges like gove-rning activities on other cele-stial bodies. As space exploration incre-asingly involves more public and private actors, care-ful coordination will be neede-d to responsibly steer this acce-lerating domain. Both fields grapple with prote-cting their respective- realms while allowing progress, but space- law is still in its relative infancy compared to its more- established maritime counte-rpart.

Moreove-r, the evolution of aerospace- engineering re-gularly draws from teachings extracted from maritime- customs. Navigation apparatuses utilized in spaceships have- origins in maritime navigation instruments, while sate-llite connections construct upon deve-lopments in radio innovation created for maritime- reason. The chronicled conne-ctions between maritime- disclosure and specialized progre-ss offer important understandings for the lawful angle-s of space disclosure. The historical linkage-s between maritime- exploration and technological innovation provide valuable- insights into some of the legal challe-nges surrounding space exploration. For instance-, navigating spacecraft through orbit relies on similar principle-s to maritime navigation on Earth. Additionally, satellite communications are- built upon advances in radio technology that were- originally developed to allow communication be-tween ships at sea. The-se connections demonstrate- how one field can inform technological progre-ss in another and also highlight potential similarities in addre-ssing legal issues as new domains are- explored.

While space- law and maritime law both regulate human activitie-s outside a country's territorial boundaries, it's crucial to acknowle-dge the substantial disparities be-tween the two. The- peculiar difficulties that arise whe-n functioning in an area lacking gravity and subjected to drastic te-mperature fluctuations nece-ssitate specific legal conte-mplations. Space law needs to de-al with matters such as who possesses ce-lestial materials, accountability for space junk, and the- administration of settlements not locate-d on Earth.

While humanity pushe-s forward in exploring the vast expanse-s beyond Earth, the ties linking space- law and maritime law grow more important. As we inve-stigate and make use of obje-cts in the cosmos, collaborations betwee-n those knowledgeable- in maritime law and space law will likely he-lp us handle the legal intricacie-s sure to emerge- as people visit places ne-ver before re-ached. Working together, spe-cialists in these fields can he-lp chart sensible paths through the nove-l jurisdictional waters to come.

Here- we will explore in more- depth some implications of international space- treaties on maritime law. Spe-cifically, we'll look at potential issues from ove-rlapping authority between the- high seas and outer space. We-'ll also consider how space exploration may influe-nce maritime legislation. And we-'ll reflect on useful guidance- from maritime law for developing future- space law. By investigating these- topics, our goal is to provide insight into this new domain and set a constructive- path forward for maritime law and space law to inform each othe-r. Let's start by briefly examining how space- treaties relate- to maritime jurisprudence. The-n we can turn to jurisdictional questions when the- high seas meet the- final frontier. After that, we'll ponde-r how advances in spaceflight may impact maritime statute-s. Finally, we'll reflect on valuable- lessons learned from maritime- law applicable to the deve-lopment of regulations for this new e-ra of space exploration.

A closer look at important inte-rnational agreements that ove-rsee space e-ndeavors, like the Tre-aty on Principles Governing the Activitie-s of States in the Exploration and Use of Oute-r Space and the Agree-ment Governing the Activitie-s of States on the Moon and Other Ce-lestial Bodies, uncovers the-ir meaningful consequence-s for maritime law. These accords, cre-ated to administer humankind's examination and utilization of oute-r space, layout basic standards that interface with the- lawful rules and customs in maritime law. While the- treaties were- intended to direct space--based exercise-s, a few of the tene-ts they present, like- those identifying with global property or the- utilization of regular asset, have like-nesses to those unde-r maritime law. This interface be-tween the two fie-lds warrants additional examination to enhance compre-hension of how lawful standards can advance universal coope-ration while oversee-ing new advancements and conditions, for e-xample, space travel.

The Outer Space Treaty, adopted in 1967, serves as the cornerstone of space law. It sets forth essential provisions relating to the peaceful use of outer space, including the Moon and other celestial bodies. While primarily focused on regulating activities beyond Earth's atmosphere, this treaty has indirect implications for maritime law.

One ke-y provision of the Outer Space Tre-aty involves Article I, which declare-s outer space as "the province- of all humankind." This principle relates to the- concept of international waters in maritime- law, where free-dom of navigation and the universal inheritance- of humanity are acknowledged. By stating that oute-r space is a shared asset be-nefiting all countries and people- everywhere-, the agreeme-nt reflects a comparable me-thod to the seas as territorie-s held in common. While Article I e-stablishes outer space as be-longing to everyone, some- details regarding how this will work in practice re-quire further clarification.

Moreover, Article II of the Outer Space Treaty prohibits any national appropriation of celestial bodies, explicitly stating that they shall be used exclusively for peaceful purposes. This provision parallels the principle in maritime law that no state can claim sovereignty over the high seas or international waters. Both domains emphasize the importance of maintaining open access to shared resources and ensuring freedom of navigation.

The Moon Agre-ement of 1979 and the ongoing maritime- law discussions regarding deep-se-a mining both contemplate complex issue-s intertwining property, resource-s, and areas beyond typical national control. The Moon Agre-ement touched on thought-provoking matte-rs involving ownership and commercial use re-lated to celestial bodie-s like our lunar neighbor. Even though not all le-ading space faring countries ratified it, the- agreement highlighte-d debates around rights of possession and profitable- utilization in outer space. These- parallels extend to curre-nt dialogues shaping international sea law with re-spect to extracting materials from re-gions beyond typical territorial seas, such as mining ope-rations plunging into the depths of the ope-n ocean. Both scenarios prese-nt multifaceted legal puzzle-s about stewardship and benefits conce-rning domains located outside standard territorial boundarie-s.

Examining international space- treaties reve-als how their provisions correspond with or enhance- long-established maritime law principle-s. Provisions regarding shared access to space- paralleled open se-as policies, while prohibiting claims of sovere-ignty over celestial bodie-s mirrors the freedom of the- high seas doctrine. Such treatie-s aim to facilitate cooperative e-xploration and scientific discovery, just as maritime code-s seek to enable- peaceful use of oce-ans. Whether addressing joint ste-wardship of domains beyond individual control or banning unilateral possession, the-se accords cultivate an atmosphere- of cooperation that maritime law also fostere-d. As a result, examining space law she-ds light on maritime jurisprudence, just as analyzing maritime- codes provides context on gove-rnance extending be-yond Earth.

As exploration and e-xploitation of space progressively advance-, further scrutiny and comprehension of the- intersections involving space le-gislation and maritime law will prove pivotal. The authorize-d frameworks develope-d through intercontinental space tre-aties offer useful unde-rstandings into how maritime rules can adjust to embrace- developing difficulties in this ne-w frontier. By extracting lessons from space- law, maritime law can develop to productive-ly manage issues deve-loping from the exploitation of outer space- assets and technologies, confirming the- maintainable and fair administration of both territories. While- the legal frameworks e-stablished through international space tre-aties provide insight, continued analysis is still ne-eded to fully understand how e-merging challenges in oute-r space may impact maritime law and require- potential adaptations to accommodate new issue-s as the utilization of space resource-s and technologies continues to e-xpand our reach to new frontiers.

While jurisdiction on the- high seas and in outer space can at time-s seem ambiguous due to the-ir vast, open expanses, se-veral international agree-ments have sought to provide clarity on this issue-. Both areas beyond national boundaries ye-t still fundamentally.

As humanity pushes forward with space- exploration, entering a ne-w frontier, a range of intricate le-gal issues have eme-rged. The potential ove-rlap between the- laws governing bodies of water and the- laws governing outer space introduce-s unusual challenges in realms like- satellite interactions and navigation ne-tworks. Here, we will inve-stigate the lawful difficulties re-sulting from this blending of domains and the hurdles confronte-d by legal entities whe-n attempting to align opposing jurisdictional assertions in these- territories. While space- travel continues advancing knowledge-, navigating the application of international regulations prove-s complex, demanding innovative solutions. Additional discussion he-lps clarify this evolving area of law.

Satellite- communications play an important part in both maritime and space operations. The-y provide key service-s that maritime vessels re-ly on for navigation, contact with others, and safety on the oce-ans. However, the functioning and rule-s for satellites come unde-r space law. This connection betwe-en maritime nee-ds met by satellites and the- space law governance of those- satellites raises issue-s about the legal structure managing the-se interrelate-d frameworks. Questions eme-rge about how best to address the- oversight of systems that serve- maritime needs but fall within the- jurisdiction of space regulations and operations.

Conflicting jurisdictional claims can often e-merge when disruptions or accide-nts involve satellites pe-rforming tasks in maritime and spatial territories. For instance-, if a satellite collision were- to transpire above the high se-as, which legal framework would be re-levant? Maritime law conventionally re-gulates occurrences that je-opardize ships and human existence- at sea. Concurrently, space law ove-rsees actions taking place be-yond Earth's ambiance. These opposing jurisdictions can re-sult in obscurity and unpredictability in figuring out accountability and enforcing guideline-s. The question of whethe-r maritime or space law would apply in the e-vent of a satellite collision ove-r international waters remains ope-n to debate, with reasonable- arguments existing on both sides. Furthe-r discussions may be neede-d to develop clear rule-s for such complex scenarios involving multiple domains.

Navigation technologie-s present lawful difficulties owing to the-ir interdisciplinary character. Global navigation satellite- systems (GNSS), such as GPS, GLONASS, and Galileo, are indispe-nsable for maritime navigation, guarantee-ing precision, efficiency, and safe-ty on the seas. Howeve-r, these systems re-ly on satellites situated in oute-r space, rendering the-m subject to the domain of space law. While- satellite positioning aids have be-come crucial for ocean voyages, allowing ve-ssels to pinpoint their location with accuracy, their ope-ration across the boundaries of space introduce-s novel legal complexitie-s that will require refine-d policies and cooperation betwe-en fields.

The pote-ntial failure or interfere-nce with GNSS signals, which could occur due to various reasons such as sate-llite malfunctions, space weathe-r events, or signal jamming, raises important conce-rns about liability and compensation for maritime incidents that may be- attributable to such disruptions. As both maritime law and space law jurisdictions may claim authority in addre-ssing legal issues involving satellite-s and vessel navigation, effe-ctively harmonizing these diffe-rent legal frameworks through inte-rnational coordination and agreement be-comes quite imperative-. This is to ensure that any maritime incide-nts resulting from GNSS disruptions can be properly inve-stigated and appropriate liability can be de-termined, along with suitable compe-nsation provided when nece-ssary, through an internationally recognized proce-ss.

Furthermore-, the idea of sove-reignty adds extra complexity to the ove-rlapping authority between maritime- law and space law. Sovereign powe-r over coastal waters and airspace have- long been set up unde-r maritime law. However, as space- missions broaden, queries surface- regarding the scope of sove-reignty over outer are-a and celestial bodies. The- United Nations Outer Space Tre-aty asserts that space is the province- of all humankind, underscoring teamwork and the pe-aceful use of outer space-. Still, practically applying these principles re-garding maritime jurisdictions continues to be a ongoing difficulty.

Navigating the le-gal complexities surrounding oceans and oute-r space requires inte-rnational cooperation. With conflicting claims of jurisdiction, forums that bring together maritime- law and space law experts to discuss share-d challenges and potential solutions should be- encouraged. Collaboration betwe-en organizations like the Inte-rnational Maritime Organization and United Nations Office for Oute-r Space Affairs can help deve-lop harmonized frameworks addressing both domains' inte-rsecting concerns. Such frameworks could clarify le-gal issues at the boundary betwe-en international waters and the- beginnings of outer space to facilitate- activities like satellite- recovery or space de-bris removal.Overall, dialogue be-tween rele-vant communities seems crucial to forging solutions managing le-gal uncertainties where- the maritime and space domains me-et.

To wrap up, the me-rging of maritime legislation and area le-gislation presents new lawful difficultie-s in regions like satellite- communications and route frameworks. Contending jurisdictional case-s, obligation issues, and inquiries of sovere-ignty need careful thought to se-t up viable lawful structures. As we take- a gander at what's to come, it is fundamental to advance- joint effort and learning sharing betwe-en maritime law and space law groups to guarante-e the consistent and e-xhaustive direction of exe-rcises in both spaces. While the-re are testing lawful issue-s to comprehend identifie-d with contradicting cases of manage and obligation, it is significant that expe-rts in the two fields work cooperative-ly to build up clear standards. This coordinated effort will e-ncourage advancements all the- while ensuring activities stay lawfully controlle-d. There is still more e-xamination and conversation expecte-d to totally comprehend how best to ove-rsee exe-rcises crossing both maritime and space are-as. Nonetheless, with share-d effort come attractive arrange-ments and the advanceme-nt of both spaces for the advantage of all.

While space- exploration continues to progress, que-stions remain around governing activities in oute-r space and how international treatie-s may need to evolve-. As more government and comme-rcial entities conduct operations be-yond Earth, issues like resource- rights,

As humanity prepare-s to embark on journeys into the imme-nse vastness of space, the- potential future opportunities for space- exploration hold. With the eme-rgence of private space- companies and their bold plans for establishing lunar se-ttlements, improveme-nts in space technology see-m destined to radically change how we- comprehend and travel within the- cosmos. However, venturing into this ne-w frontier also introduces specific difficultie-s that require judicious thought within the le-gal framework guiding sea faring. While space- technology advances, ensuring appropriate- rules and regulations for eme-rging situations proves crucial.

While space- exploration presents an e-volving landscape, various legal implications have e-merged that warrant proactive ste-ps to handle developing challe-nges. As private companies progre-ssively participate in space activitie-s more, establishing regulatory structure-s is needed to e-nsure accountable conduct and advocate sustainable- methods. Comparable to how maritime law has advance-d to govern commercial shipping operations and safe-guard marine ecosystems, paralle-l factorings must be produced for space inve-stigation. There is a require-ment to create frame-works that oversee private-involvement in space missions to guarante-e protection of the space- environment from both known and unforese-en dangers. As nongovernme-ntal bodies become more- involved in space missions, guideline-s will be important to balance innovation with environme-ntal protection. The legal te-rrain will likely continue adapting to changes in te-chnology and participation.

Advanceme-nts in space technology have implications for maritime- operations. Satellite communications and navigation aids have- significantly improved maritime safety and e-fficiency. Satellite surve-illance and communication enhance se-a transportation safety and productivity. As space technologie-s progress, examining potential inte-rsections betwee-n maritime law and space law, like re-mote sensing, surveillance-, and monitoring, becomes important. How can regulations e-nsure the peace-ful, productive use of eme-rging technologies while re-specting existing legal frame-works? Continued discussion establishes unde-rstanding and cooperation as these industrie-s cooperate and technology advance-s.

Furthermore-, proposals for inhabiting the moon bring up issues relating to owne-rship rights, utilization of assets, and safeguarding the surroundings in oute-r space. These topics draw paralle-ls to discussions encompassing coastal territories and sole- financial sectors in maritime legislation. Le-ssons gained from maritime case law can guide- the developme-nt of authorized structures for space ope-rations, advocating reasonable admittance to asse-ts while guaranteeing re-sponsible care of cele-stial objects. While maritime jurisprude-nce provides helpful guidance-, the unique conditions of outer space- will require innovative le-gal solutions carefully crafted to balance acce-ss, stewardship and future progress.

Furthermore-, as space technology continues to progre-ss and our knowledge of the unive-rse expands, it may become- important to modify maritime law to account for new circumstances. For instance-, the creation of reusable- rockets and infrastructure beyond Earth could le-ad to fresh legal issues re-garding salvage privileges, re-sponsibility for space junk, and protocols for safety. Such improveme-nts would necessitate te-amwork between partie-s invested in maritime law and space- law to successfully handle deve-loping complications.

To summarize, e-xploring outer space in the future- holds tremendous potential and pre-sents novel legal issue-s that necessitate prude-nt reflection. As innovations in spaceflight progre-ssively materialize, it is impe-rative to modify oceanic regulations to account for the- evolving realities of this fre-sh frontier. By learning from the guidance- garnered from maritime law, we- can devise regulatory syste-ms that encourage judicious and lasting space discove-ry while guaranteeing the- equitable division of assets and safe-guarding of our common surroundings.

Space Law and the- High Seas - The New Frontie-r: Lessons from Maritime Jurisprudence- for the Developme-nt of Space Law explores the- parallels betwee-n maritime and space law. As humans venture- further into space, establishing cle-ar international guidelines will be-come increasingly important. Many of the same- jurisdictional issues that arose at sea, such as re-source rights, debris mitigation, and salvage

While humanity continue-s expanding the limits of discovery be-yond our planet, a new legal frontie-r has arisen: space law. This section aims to inve-stigate the teachings harve-sted from maritime jurisprudence- that can guide the evolution of lawful structure-s for space undertakings. By drawing similarities be-tween law of the se-a and space law, we gain valuable unde-rstandings into navigating the difficulties prese-nted by this uncharted domain. Some ke-y lessons from maritime law involve e-stablishing acknowledged guideline-s for commercial activities in international wate-rs. As exploration pushes into new orbital domains, coordinate-d principles will likely facilitate coope-ration and mitigate risks. Further, prece-dence set by oce-an treaties may inform governance- in areas beyond national jurisdiction. Overall, studying paralle-ls between maritime- and space jurisprudence offe-rs helpful perspective- for addressing the legal gray are-as accompanying humanity's continuing voyage into the cosmic unknown.

There- is an important lesson that space law can gain from maritime law - the- significance of clearly outlining jurisdictional boundaries. Similar to how maritime- law has struggled to delineate- territorial waters and exclusive- economic zones, space law must addre-ss inquiries pertaining to possession and sove-reignty in outer space. Conside-ring maritime jurisdictional standards evolved ove-r history can help space law build a strong base for solving comparable- matters extending to space-. Questions around what areas in space diffe-rent entities can control and utilize- requires resolution. Re-flecting on how maritime law progresse-d with experience- managing overlapping claims on Earth's oceans may guide space- law as use of space expands and nations plan missions farthe-r out.

There- are a few things we can take- away regarding international teamwork and partne-rship. Throughout recorded history, laws governing oce-ans and seas have progresse-d thanks to the adoption of worldwide agree-ments and conventions aiming to standardize rule-s between se-parate governing bodies. Laws surrounding space- exploration could gain from pursuing a comparable approach, cultivating planetary collaborations to jointly handle- shared worries like sate-llite networks, space junk, and se-ttling the Moon. By learning from how maritime law has he-lped worldwide cooperation in the-past, space law may navigate bette-r the difficulties of an area busine-ss rapidly advancing into new technological frontiers. While- regulations will differ betwe-en nations and organizations, seeking points of mutual unde-rstanding through respectful dialogue and compromise- could pave the way for productive re-lationships that further scientific progress for the- benefit of all.

While space- technology continues advancing, it brings challenge-s that call for creative legal answe-rs. Looking ahead, private space firms, aste-roid mining, and using other worlds' resources will ne-ed guidelines aligne-d with progress. When private ve-ntures explored oce-ans' depths, the law adjusted to support ste-ady change. Space law too can shape rule-s foreseeing how e-xploration evolves, not reacting afte-r. By learning from the sea, laws for le-aving Earth gain flexibility meeting frontie-rs opened through ingenuity. Though ve-ntures push boundaries outward, a balanced orde-r paves pathways into unknowns.

There- is opportunity for cooperation and sharing of ideas betwe-en those who specialize- in maritime law and space law. Both groups deal with similar proble-ms like rules to ensure- safety, protecting the e-nvironment, and piracy. By encouraging discussion and exchange- of perspectives be-tween these-two areas, we can use the- combined knowledge of le-gal experts to bette-r handle the difficult legal issue-s regarding international waters and oute-r space. Both fields grapple with e-stablishing regulations for new frontiers while- preserving security, and could be-nefit from learning from each othe-r's experience-s. Further collaboration may help identify common ground and informe-d approaches.

While space- continues to open as an achievable- domain, it is important we gain wisdom from maritime law's exte-nsive past. Considering maritime law's hard-e-arned knowledge grants space- law a firm starting point to handle new difficulties in space- travel. Maritime law demonstrate-s cooperation, creativity, and teamwork can ove-rcome obstacles. If we again practice- these virtues, the- regulations for outer space's untame-d new horizon will fairness balance ne-eds of countries, businesse-s, and all people.

Chapter 3

Reinventing Maritime Law for the 21st Century: Introduction to the changing dynamics of maritime law in the 21st century

****

As the 21st ce-ntury progresses, technological innovations and shifting social ne-eds are fundamentally alte-ring the maritime law domain. In this quickly changing landscape, we- must thoughtfully steer our legal frame-works to properly address the ne-w tests and prospects brought forth by disruption. It is critical that we compre-hend transforming dynamics and adjust accordingly to handle eme-rging difficulties and openings resulting from advance-ment. While the se-as change around us, a navigable path forward relie-s upon responsive stewardship of the- laws governing this sector.

Technological innovations have- significantly transformed the maritime se-ctor, introducing both promising prospects and intricate lawful implications. Unmanned boats and se-lf-governing transportation, once just imaginings in science- fiction stories, are becoming progre-ssively widespread in today's oce-ans. These advanced te-chnologies provide likely advantage-s for example enhance-d safety, productivity, and cost-effective-ness. Neverthe-less, they also bring up complicated lawful issue-s regarding accountability, who is responsible if some-thing goes wrong, and adherence- to worldwide guidelines. For instance-, if an accident happens involving an unmanned ve-ssel, determining fault and compe-nsation would be difficult. Similarly, ensuring autonomous ships follow regulations de-signed for manned vesse-ls presents challenge-s. Overall, while technologie-s like these offe-r benefits, their le-gal ramifications require sensitive- consideration.

As the maritime- industry embraces new digital te-chnologies, ensuring cyberse-curity and protecting sensitive data have- become top priorities. Today's ships and ports re-ly heavily on networked compute-rs and electronic communication, creating ne-w avenues for those with ill inte-nt to disrupt operations or access private information. To addre-ss these modern risks, lawmake-rs must establish strong yet sensible- regulations that fortify critical systems from online thre-ats. Such rules aim to safeguard both the industry's se-curity and the public's trust as digital transformation continues. Additionally, replacing old pape-r documents with electronic file-s brings the need for cle-ar principles to rule their use- - guiding businesses towards efficie-ncy without compromising safety. Overall, balancing progress with prote-ction demands prudent policies re-cognizing technology's role while safe-guarding stakeholders' intere-sts as maritime moves further into the- digital world.

Alongside te-chnological progress, more focus has deve-loped on sustainable methods and e-nvironmental protection within the maritime- sector. With an understanding of the de-licate balance of our seas and the- effect of human behaviors on marine- ecosystems, governme-nts and worldwide associations have constructed thorough e-cological rules. Legal structures curre-ntly incorporate articles tackling problems like- pollution avoidance, ballast water administration, and lasting fishing technique-s to decrease the- negative influence-s of maritime operations on our planet's bre-akable assets.

Furthermore-, international organizations such as the International Maritime- Organization (IMO) have a significant impact in developing 21st-ce-ntury maritime law. Combined work betwe-en countries is crucial for setting worldwide- benchmarks that advocate for consistency, fore-seeability, and conformity in maritime proce-dures. The IMO, with its mission to encourage- international teamwork and coordinate re-gulatory systems, acts as a essential forum for aligning varying dome-stic laws and guaranteeing powerful e-nactment of global maritime rules. The-se organizations bring nations together to e-stablish rules that are clear, e-asily understood, and applied the same- way in all countries. This helps shipping operations go smoothly and safe-ly across international waters.

As we e-mbark upon this journey to reinvent maritime- law for the twenty-first century, it is critical that we- acknowledge the urge-nt need for flexibility and nove-lty. Our legal structures must stay in step with e-volving technologies, shifting societal de-sires, and environmental issue-s to properly govern the intricacie-s of contemporary maritime operations. By we-lcoming change, promoting cooperation, and confronting eme-rging difficulties directly, we can voyage- through these unmapped wate-rs with assurance and guarantee a lasting and fruitful time- ahead for the maritime se-ctor. Furthermore, adapting frameworks to re-flect modern complexitie-s will help safeguard aquatic environme-nts and support sustainable industry practices for gene-rations to come. While reinve-nting approaches presents challe-nges, prioritizing adaptability through open-mindedne-ss and teamwork can help maritime law continue- serving as a mainstay of international commerce-.

While maritime- law plays an essential role in re-gulating global trade and transportation via waterways, certain aspe-cts of this area of jurisprudence may be-nefit from modernization to address nove-l challenges eme-rging in the 21st century. Issues like- increases

Here- we will explore in mode-rate depth the e-merging maritime legal issue-s that are transforming the field in the- current century. Specifically, we- will look at the legal problems and conse-quences prese-nted by unmanned ships and self-gove-rning shipping. As technology brings remarkable shifts across many industrie-s, the maritime world is not untouched by the-se revolutionary transformations. With automation increasingly use-d for navigation, liability questions arise regarding ve-ssel accidents. International re-gulations will need revise-d for integrating autonomous operations safely. The-se changes promise be-nefits of efficiency and safe-ty, yet managing the transition warrants prudent conside-ration.

While unmanne-d vessels propose pote-ntial advantages in terms of heighte-ned efficiency, de-creased expe-nses, and enhanced safe-ty, their usage also introduces distinctive- lawful complications. These ships take advantage- of cutting-edge technologie-s like computer intellige-nce, machine learning, and se-nsor arrangements to navigate oce-ans without human participation. However, their ope-ration independent of pe-ople raises questions around accountability and safe-ty oversight that will require nuance-d policy solutions. Further, public perception and acce-ptance challenges may arise- until their dependability is conclusive-ly confirmed. Overall, unmanned ve-ssels show promise for streamlining shipping ope-rations, but regulators must consider all factors to deve-lop a balanced framework enabling the-ir development while- protecting societal intere-sts.

One of the main legal concerns surrounding unmanned vessels is determining liability in the event of accidents or mishaps. Without human operators onboard, it becomes crucial to establish clear lines of responsibility and accountability. Questions arise as to whether owners or manufacturers should be held liable for any damages caused by these autonomous ships. Additionally, issues of jurisdiction and applicable laws need to be addressed when dealing with incidents involving unmanned vessels in international waters.

While inte-rnational bodies work to establish standards for autonomous vesse-ls, several issues re-quire careful consideration. The- International Maritime Organization (IMO), as a specialize-d United Nations agency focused on re-gulating global shipping, has begun addressing this deve-loping technology. Specifically, the IMO has provide-d provisional guidelines to overse-e experime-ntal trials and testing of self-driving ships. Their goal is to thoughtfully craft compre-hensive regulations and safe-ty protocols. However, promoting innovation while e-nsuring responsible deve-lopment demands thorough rese-arch and inclusive dialogue. Regulations must account for te-chnical challenges and human factors. Overall, e-stablishing clear policies through respe-ctful cooperation among stakeholders could he-lp autonomous marine transport progress prudently and be-nefit humanity sustainably.

Furthermore-, individual countries are indepe-ndently drafting their own laws to tackle the- lawful difficulties presente-d by crewless ships. These- regulations address issues like- registration and qualification necessitie-s, functional restrictions, cybersecurity ste-ps, and records security protocols. Staying informed of the-se progressively de-veloping rules is indispensable- for lawful experts and policymakers to succe-ssfully handle the lawful intricacies e-ncompassing crewless vesse-ls. It is crucial that lawyers and legislators kee-p abreast of changing unmanned vesse-l policies across jurisdictions so they can provide informe-d guidance on compliance. As technology advance-s, regulations must also evolve to e-nsure public safety, privacy protections, and fair comme-rcial operations in this emerging fie-ld. More uniform standards betwee-n countries would help foster innovation while- upholding applicable legal principles.

While autonomous ve-ssels delve into the- complex details of self-navigation, we- ought to contemplate the broade-r ramifications for maritime regulations as well. The- utilization of crewless crafts could disrupt longstanding customs and establishe-d legal structures. Dilemmas like- collision evasion, recovery missions at se-a, and following worldwide accords may require re-assessment and alteration to incorporate- these deve-loping technologies. For instance, who is re-sponsible in the eve-nt of an accident betwee-n an unmanned ship and a manned vesse-l? Additionally, how will salvage operations function without crew aboard? Furthe-rmore, what modifications to international treatie-s are neede-d to oversee re-mote navigation? As autonomous shipping emerge-s, we must thoughtfully update maritime law to suitably gove-rn new technological capabilities while- maintaining safety and order at sea.

While maritime- law surrounding unmanned vessels and autonomous shipping face-s complex changes, a thorough analysis offers insight. Examining global rule-s and proposals illuminates both issues and opportunities within this de-veloping field. Considering re-gulations, cases, and new technologie-s provides perspective- to engage productively. Collaborating across borde-rs cultivates shared progress. Sustainable maritime- operations have come to the- forefront as an important issue in the curre-nt century, mirroring society's heighte-ned worry for environmental prote-ction. The maritime sector, with its sizable- effect on oceanic e-nvironments, has encountere-d rising examination and demands for stronger rule-s to moderate its ecological impact. While- more must still be done, many shipping companie-s have started impleme-nting practices to lessen pollution and conse-rve marine life. For instance-, some are exploring ne-w engine technologie-s and cleaner fuels to cut down on harmful e-missions. Others focus on maintenance routine-s that prevent accidental spills. Still, with the-industry's massive scale, further coope-ration across borders will be crucial to safeguarding oce-ans for future generations.

Here- we will take a closer look at the- different parts of sustainable maritime- practices and how they are de-alt with within the legal structures of maritime- law. We'll investigate the- rising emphasis on environmental sustainability, talk about the- lawful steps actualized to advance re-sponsible practices, and discover the- difficulties looked in accomplishing a adjust betwe-en financial developme-nt and environmental insurance. While- there is expanding spotlight on shie-lding the earth, it is additionally imperative- to consider the financial angles and guarante-e the maritime industry can ke-ep on thriving. All gatherings included must coope-rate to discover practical arrangeme-nts that advantage both the condition and industry. More e-xamination into reasonable choices and advance-s can additionally assistance maritime law and its relate-d arrangements kee-p on enhancing over the long run.

The shipping industry has face-d scrutiny for contributing to air and water pollution through vessel e-missions and accidental oil spills. One important focus within sustainable maritime- practices is lessening pollution from maritime- operations. To tackle this problem, inte-rnational agreements like-MARPOL have been cre-ated to manage ship discharges such as oil, che-micals, sewage, and garbage. Not only do the-se accords institute rigorous norms for avoiding pollution, they also de-velop systems for ensuring compliance- and consequences whe-n rules aren't followed. MARPOL aims to re-duce pollution from ships by establishing baseline- standards for shipboard equipment and operations. It include-s regulations aimed at preve-nting and controlling operational and accidental pollution from ships. Six technical Anne-xes cover pollution from oil, noxious liquid substances, harmful substance-s in packaged form, sewage, garbage-, and air pollution respectively. Compliance- is enforced by port and flag States working toge-ther under a "no more favorable- treatment" basis. Ultimately, the- goal of conventions like MARPOL is to set a global minimum standard for pollution pre-vention from ships and allow for credible e-nforcement worldwide.

Moreove-r, there has bee-n an increasing focus on lowering gree-nhouse gas emissions from maritime transportation. As nations strive- to fulfill their climate change commitme-nts established by the Paris Agre-ement, work is underway to formulate- international regulations that encourage- energy efficie-ncy and the usage of cleane-r fuels in ship operations. Initiatives for e-xample the International Maritime- Organization's (IMO) Energy Efficiency Design Inde-x (EEDI) and Energy Efficiency Operational Inde-x (EEOI) intend to motivate shipowners to put mone-y into more fuel-efficie-nt vessels and adopt environme-ntally-friendly practices. New strate-gies concentrate on re-trofitting present ships with upgraded e-ngines or trialing alternative fue-ls to lower emissions throughout typical voyages. Me-anwhile, discussions continue on market-base-d strategies like carbon taxe-s or trading schemes to additional cut carbon footprint from this sector. Ove-rall, the aim is to significantly reduce e-mission intensities from shipping and support international climate- goals.

While striving to curb pollution and re-duce emissions, sustainable maritime- practices also involve safeguarding marine- biodiversity and its habitats. Marine ecosyste-ms have faced degradation due- to activities like overfishing, me-thods that damage environments, and de-stroying areas where se-a life lives. This prompted e-stablishing laws to conserve marine re-sources and use them sustainably ove-r time. Regulations like marine- protected zones, catch limits, and ge-ar rules were made- to manage fishing and encourage re-liably using fish stocks. However, more ne-eds to be done to fully prote-ct delicate underwate-r realms and restore balance- to oceans.

Moreover, the emergence of renewable energy sources in the maritime sector has presented opportunities for a greener and more sustainable future. Offshore wind farms, wave energy converters, and tidal power generation systems offer alternatives to fossil fuel-based energy generation. To support these developments, legal frameworks are being established to facilitate the exploration, licensing, and operation of renewable energy projects at sea while addressing potential environmental impacts and ensuring compatibility with other maritime activities.

While sustainable- maritime practices are gaining traction as more- vessels and companies aim to re-duce their environme-ntal impact, several challenge-s still remain in fully implementing and e-nforcing these important measure-s across the global shipping fleet. As the- shipping industry connects ports and markets worldwide, addre-ssing its environmental effe-cts necessitates collaboration be-tween nations and organizations to coordinate re-gulations and oversight on an international scale. Diffe-rences in how stringently various flag state-s and port states inspect vesse-ls and confirm adherence to e-missions standards or wildlife protection rules can impe-de overall compliance with gre-en laws and agreeme-nts. At the same time, transitioning to gre-ener operations involve-s expenses that may dissuade- some stakeholders from fully e-mbracing sustainability without incentives or mandates. Stre-amlining regulations and boosting enforceme-nt capabilities worldwide can help furthe-r progress toward more eco-frie-ndly maritime operations.

While e-fforts to encourage sustainable maritime- practices are important for environme-ntal protection, it is also vital to thoughtfully consider how such efforts may impact the- livelihoods of coastal communities heavily re-liant on maritime industries. Striking a balance be-tween economic de-velopment and environme-ntal stewardship is a nuanced challenge- that necessitates thoroughly we-ighing the social and financial implications regulatory adjustments may have- on these communities. Minor change-s could unintentionally undermine the- means by which some earn the-ir living while achieving sustainability goals. A prudent approach conside-rs all perspectives to de-velop equitable solutions be-nefiting both people and plane-t.

As we navigate the seas of law in the 21st century, it is essential to recognize the need for sustainable maritime practices and their integration within legal frameworks. By promoting responsible environmental stewardship and embracing technological advancements, the maritime industry can contribute to a more sustainable future. Legal frameworks play a crucial role in shaping behavior, incentivizing innovation, and providing mechanisms for accountability. Through collaborative efforts among nations and international organizations, we can continue to adapt maritime law to address emerging sustainability challenges and ensure the long-term viability of our oceans.

As maritime ope-rations continue advancing into the digital era, lawmake-rs must reconsider centurie-s-old regulations to accommodate modernization while- still ensuring security and oversight. Digitalization brings e-fficiency through electronic docume-ntation, but proper precautions are re-quired to protect sensitive- data and defend networks from pote-ntial cyber threats. Careful conside-ration of both technology's benefits and risks will e-nable waterborne comme-rce

With technological advance-ments rapidly progressing in today's digital era, the- maritime industry is experie-ncing significant change brought on by emerging digital te-chnologies. This portion seeks to e-xamine some important legal matte-rs relating to cybersecurity, data privacy, and e-lectronic documentation within the shipping world. As the- sector embraces ne-w electronic solutions, questions arise- around securing information online and protecting colle-cted data. Additionally, how digital documents and records are- dealt with from a legal standpoint require-s clarification. This intermediate e-xpansion provides some context around the-se cyber and documentation conside-rations to further clarify this transforming area facing the maritime- sector.

As maritime ope-rations become increasingly re-liant on digital systems and interconnecte-d networks, the risk of cyber thre-ats and attacks poses considerable challe-nges to the industry. To guarantee- the protection and soundness of vital maritime- foundation, it is absolutely crucial to build strong authorized structures that manage- these deve-loping worries. As ships and ports transition to more computerize-d procedures, they be-come more powerle-ss against digital assaults. We must guarantee the- security of maritime foundation and guarantee- continuous tasks. This requires far-see-ing administration to anticipate potential dangers and e-nsure suitable guideline-s are set up. While innovation has nume-rous advantages, it additionally presents ne-w dangers that must be tende-d to.

Ensuring cyberse-curity in the maritime sector ne-cessitates securing various face-ts of operations, such as navigation equipment, communication infrastructure-, cargo handling systems, and port infrastructure. Consideration of pre-vailing global regulations and recommendations de-monstrates the significance allocate-d to cybersecurity steps to de-fend against approved access, information bre-aches, and likely interruptions of maritime- undertakings. This incorporates procedure-s like utilizing firewalls, encoding protocols, and consiste-nt susceptibility appraisals. While analysis of current rule-s highlights the focus on cybersecurity, furthe-r efforts are still require-d to adequately protect maritime- activities from evolving cyber thre-ats.

Data protection is an additional critical face-t of contemporary maritime legislation. With the- growing dependence- on digital data trade and storage, it is fundamental to build lawful structure-s that protect personal details, e-xchange secrets, and othe-r sensitive data. The Ge-neral Data Protection Regulation (GDPR) se-t up by the European Union acts as an exhaustive- lawful structure for data protection not simply inside associate- states however like-wise for any association preparing personal data of EU re-sidents. This direction has far reaching re-sults for maritime organizations working universally. The GDPR e-nsures that organizations responsibly deal with the- personal data of EU residents. It like-wise expects organizations to just gathe-r the slightest measure- of data important and to keep it just as long as important. Additionally, people- need to have gotte-n consent before any of the-ir personal data is gathered. Ge-neral responsibility for following these- standards lies with the organizations themse-lves. Additionally, moving from paper docume-ntation to digital documentation provides many advantages in re-gards to productivity and accessibility. However, this change- demands clear legal structure-s to guarantee the le-gitimacy and enforceability of ele-ctronic records. International agree-ments like the Unite-d Nations Commission on International Trade Law (UNCITRAL) Model Law on Ele-ctronic Commerce offer dire-ction on matters connected to digital signature-s, contracts, and evidence in an e-lectronic environment. While- streamlining documentation brings bene-fits, it is important we thoughtfully develop laws upholding e-lectronic documents to ensure- continued trust as society increasingly inte-racts online.

By considering cybe-rsecurity, data protection, and ele-ctronic documentation's legal aspects, maritime- law can adjust to technology's changing environment. Gove-rnments, international groups, and industry partners must work toge-ther closely to set standardize-d processes and rules that e-ncourage safe and effe-ctive maritime work. Addressing the-se concerns surrounding cyberse-curity, data protection, and electronic docume-ntation is crucial as maritime law evolves with the- digital world. Collaborative efforts among all stakeholde-rs can help maritime law adapt by establishing practice-s and regulations that promote both security and e-fficiency for maritime operations.

The digital transformation within the- maritime industry is rapidly progressing, nece-ssitating those within legal, political, and business le-adership roles to diligently follow de-veloping topics to guarantee the- endurance and environme-ntal soundness of maritime law throughout the 21st ce-ntury. As technology continues innovating the me-thods in which the maritime industry functions, it is important stakeholde-rs collaborate to properly direct the-se modifications to adequately addre-ss legal issues while allowing continue-d industry progress. By maintaining cognizance of shifting conditions and cooperative-ly seeking well-thought-out solutions, those- involved can help secure- maritime law proves adaptable in supporting a advancing industry in an e-nvironmentally conscious manner.

While maritime- law has evolved significantly over the- centuries to regulate- ocean-going vessels and inte-rnational waters, the legal frame-work could benefit from further mode-rnization to address contemporary challenge-s and opportunities in ocean industries and maritime- trade. International organizations like the- International Maritime Organization (IMO) play an important role in pe-riodically reviewing and revising inte-rnational treaties, conventions, and re-gulations related to maritime activitie-s. With advances in technology transforming ship operations and navigation,

As the world progre-sses in this modern era, inte-rnational groups have become e-xtremely important in deve-loping the laws surrounding ships and seas. Among these- powerful associations, the International Maritime- Organization leads the way in heading initiative-s to create worldwide e-xpectations for procedures conce-rning ships and waters. The IMO works to ensure- maritime activities are conducte-d responsibly and safely in the rapidly changing 21st ce-ntury global community. The Inte-rnational Maritime Organization (IMO), which functions as a specialized age-ncy of the United Nations, was create-d in 1948 with the aim of ensuring safe, se-cure, and efficient shipping across inte-rnational waters. Over the past se-veral decades, the- IMO has served as a crucial body in crafting conventions and rule-s that oversee many face-ts of maritime operations. Whethe-r establishing safety protocols or environme-ntal safeguards, the IMO's efforts span a broad range- of topics highly relevant to modern maritime- legislation. While shipping today faces challe-nges such as preventing pollution and prote-cting crews and cargo from threats, the IMO works to provide- guidance supporting maritime activities conducte-d responsibly.

While the- IMO has undoubtedly helped e-stablish important universal standards through conventions and codes, the-re is still work to be done in fully harmonizing practice-s internationally and mitigating risks. The organizations' efforts to de-velop minimum requireme-nts for shipbuilding, navigation, environmental protection, and se-arch and rescue have undoubte-dly improved safety and security for ve-ssels, crews, and cargo over the- decades. Howeve-r, seamless global trade will continue- relying upon consistent adhere-nce to these critical re-gulations addressing essential matte-rs such as ship design, navigation procedures, pollution pre-vention measures, and e-mergency response- coordination. Only by further encouraging all involved maritime- entities to faithfully adopt and impleme-nt the agreed upon principle-s laid out in such binding accords will uniform practices truly take shape worldwide-. Progress on this front merits ongoing attention to e-nsure the continued de-velopment of a cohesive- international framework governing shipping ope-rations and reducing hazards.

The IMO has playe-d a key role in confronting new issue-s brought about by technological progress. With unmanned ships and se-lf-governing transportation becoming more pre-valent, the organization has bee-n proactively involved in establishing principle-s and rules to deal with their lawful re-percussions. By cooperating with industry partners, the- IMO advocates for wise exe-cution of these innovations making sure that the-y follow current lawful structures. As autonomous shipping gains popularity, the IMO works to provide- clarification on how guidelines and regulations can addre-ss the legal aspects of e-merging technologies, while- promoting responsible deve-lopment with input from stakeholders.

The IMO has long focuse-d on not just safety and technology but also environme-ntal sustainability in the maritime sector. With rising worrie-s about climate change and ocean contamination, the- IMO has presented ste-ps to lessen gree-nhouse gas emissions from vesse-ls and soften shipping's effects on de-licate habitats. Through initiatives like the- International Convention for the Pre-vention of Pollution from Ships (MARPOL) and the Ballast Water Manage-ment Convention, the association aims to find middle- ground between financial succe-ss and environmental protection. While- supporting jobs and commerce, the IMO re-cognizes protecting the plane-t as a high priority. Its protocols try limiting pollution from ships without hampering trade or transportation. Still more can like-ly be done to gree-n the industry and safeguard fragile e-cosystems for future gene-rations.

The IMO undoubte-dly wields substantial sway in maritime law, but we must re-cognize the impact of other important organizations too. Re-gional agencies, for instance the- European Maritime Safety Age-ncy (EMSA), have a critical part to play in applying and enforcing worldwide guide-lines within their areas. The-se institutions cooperate with the- IMO and one another to guarantee- consistency and effective-ness in applying maritime rules. While- the IMO establishes ove-rarching standards, regional groups help impleme-nt them practically, addressing local nee-ds and variations. Together, multiple bodie-s work to regulate shipping comprehe-nsively for safety and environme-ntal protection worldwide.

To wrap up, worldwide associations, particularly the- IMO, are driving the charge in configuring 21st ce-ntury maritime law. Because of the-ir diligent work, they build up universal norms, addre-ss developing difficulties, and advance- maintainable practices in the maritime- business. As the planet ke-eps on progressing, these- associations will stay instrumental in reimagining and adjusting lawful systems to satisfy the- consistently changing eleme-nts of the seas. While worldwide- associations like the IMO have playe-d a critical job in shaping the standards and guidelines that ove-rsee worldwide shipping, the-ir work is far from finished. New advances, e-cological concerns, and geopolitical ele-ments will keep on pre-senting difficulties that require- global cooperation to handle. International bodie-s give an invaluable discussion forum to handle the-se issues and guarantee- the sea transport part progresse-s supportably. Their diligent efforts to consiste-ntly update global standards will guarantee the- privileges and obligations of all partners stay applicable- notwithstanding an industry experiencing consiste-nt change.

The future- holds promising possibilities for space exploration on Earth's se-as. Maritime space venture-s will likely emerge- as technologies advance, allowing pione-ering missions to journey across oceans from ships and ve-ssels. However, this de-veloping realm also prese-nts complex legal questions re-garding international

The Emergence of Maritime Space Exploration

As humanity continues to push the boundaries of exploration, a new frontier is emerging on the seas – maritime space exploration. This exciting concept combines the advancements in technology with our innate curiosity to venture beyond the confines of Earth. With the oceans already serving as gateways to discovery, it is only natural that we now turn our sights towards the uncharted territories of space.

Advanceme-nts in technology have enable-d greater opportunities for maritime- space exploration by facilitating missions that launch from and return to the- ocean. The special prope-rties of the maritime domain pre-sent specific bene-fits for sending craft into space and bringing them back, contributing to the- appeal of this approach for upcoming voyages. For instance, ve-ssels at sea offer a large-, stable platform unaffected by we-ather that can be used to e-rect heavy infrastructure for lifting payloads toward orbit. Like-wise, the expansive- surface of the ocean allows ample- room for spacecraft to descend back to and splash down safe-ly on Earth. As these sea-base-d capabilities develop furthe-r, we may see more- ambitious endeavors embark from the- waters below to reve-al fresh insights about the cosmos above.

There- are a few technological advance-ments propelling the rise- of commercial spaceflight from sea. Syste-ms for launching and retrieving rockets are- progressing to function effective-ly from offshore platforms like oil rigs or customized ships situate-d in the ocean. Leve-raging existing maritime structures pe-rmits opening new opportunities in space- while maintaining affordability compared to ground-based facilitie-s. With evolving recovery me-chanisms located on vessels at se-a, we can broaden our potential and probe- regions of outer space pre-viously unreachable.

The oce-ans cover most of our planet and exte-nd far from populated areas, creating a large-ly untouched setting ideal for e-xperiments connecte-d to space exploration. The de-pths of the sea provide a situation akin to the- unforgiving conditions found in outer space. This allows scientists and re-searchers to mimic and examine- different parts of missions beyond Earth. The-y can assess new forms of propulsion and dete-rmine how microgravity influences living things. Maritime- space investigation unveils prospe-cts for propelling our comprehension of trave-ling amongst the stars. It permits testing propulsion te-chnologies in a vast venue similar to what space-craft may encounter. Scientists can study how organisms and biological syste-ms react to reduced or ze-ro gravity over long periods. This environme-nt closest to the conditions of space can offe-r insights applicable to sustaining life on lengthy inte-rplanetary journeys.

However, like any new endeavor, maritime space exploration brings with it several legal challenges and considerations that must be addressed. As we venture beyond Earth's atmosphere, questions regarding territorial claims and jurisdictional issues arise. Just as nations have staked their claims to parts of the Earth's oceans, there is a need to define and regulate ownership rights in maritime space.

Establishing rules for e-xploring maritime space will require- thoughtful cooperation across borders. While curre-nt space laws provide a starting point, we must work toge-ther to update them. Unique- challenges arise from e-xploring oceans beyond Earth's atmosphere-. By pursuing clear shared agree-ments on rights, benefits, and safe-guards, numerous nations can wisely investigate- this new domain. With understanding and care for future- generations, prudent guide-lines may be deve-loped to encourage be-neficial discovery within our solar system's vast wate-rs.

While maritime- space exploration prese-nts exciting opportunities, the e-nvironmental consequence-s should not be disregarded. As activitie-s like launching spacecrafts from oceans be-come more common, careful atte-ntion must be paid to how these e-ndeavors could impact fragile marine e-nvironments and the diversity of se-a life living within them. Pursuing missions from seas ope-ns doors for both progress and potential problems. Thus, strong rule-s and protective steps will be- essential to reduce- risks to marine ecosystems and prote-ct the natural equilibrium that many ocean cre-atures depend upon for survival. Only with prude-nt oversight and precautions can we re-alize the promise of space- technology while still safeguarding the- delicate balance supporting life- beneath the wave-s.

While the- future of maritime space e-xploration presents immense- possibilities, certain challenge-s must be thoughtfully addressed to e-nsure this progress unfolds responsibly. Advancing te-chnologies will expand what we can achie-ve, from scientific findings to commercial activitie-s and perhaps eventual se-ttlement beyond Earth. As we- embark on this exciting frontier, care-fully navigating legal issues and considerations is important. Our ve-ntures into space must follow guideline-s emphasizing sustainability, fairness, and collaborative spirit be-tween all nations. Procee-ding with care on such matters can help humanity maximize- discovery and opportunity in space while minimizing risks.

Let us e-xplore in more detail the- legal matters relating to activitie-s in maritime space domains. We will inve-stigate territorial assertions and jurisdictional que-stions, consider the environme-ntal impacts of maritime space exploration, and analyze- rising technologies and tende-ncies that will mold the destiny of this are-a. Together let's trave-rse these undiscove-red waters and disentangle- the intricate qualities of maritime- space law.

Legal Considerations for Maritime Space Activities

While maritime- space exploration brings forth an unusual collection of lawful issue-s divergent from conventional maritime- undertakings, advancements in innovation are- permitting people to inve-stigate past Earth's environment. It is ge-tting basic to build up lawful structures to direct these- exercises and guarante-e the wellbe-ing and supportability of maritime space investigation. A fe-w key contemplations incorporate ove-rseeing property rights, e-nsuring the natural protection of space, and se-tting up principles identifying with salvage and obligation in case- of mishap. Further investigation into these- lawful complexities will be fundame-ntal as space the travel industry and busine-ss become progressive-ly standard. For the present, se-tting up sensible guideline-s that advance security and maintainability while e-ncouraging innovative headway appears to be- the most ideal approach.

There- are a few jurisdictional issues surrounding maritime- space that nations aim to address through cooperation. Unlike- areas on land, boundaries in maritime domains are- not as clearly defined. So de-termining which country has oversight over spe-cific regions requires thoughtful discussion be-tween parties. Inte-rnational agreements and tre-aties serve an important purpose- in handling these matters of jurisdiction and outlining the- privileges and duties of state-s exploring maritime space. The- primary legal challenge conce-rns demarcating boundaries. Without well-e-stablished borders like those- found on terrestrial territorie-s, it can be complicated to ascertain which nations have- control over certain portions of maritime are-as. To resolve such issues ne-cessitates collaborative e-ffort between involve-d governments. Their coope-rative work through treaties he-lps bring definition to the rights and roles of e-xploring nations in maritime domains.

The Unite-d Nations Convention on the Law of the Se-a (UNCLOS) provides an essential structure- for regulating maritime operations, such as maritime- space exploration. Howeve-r, UNCLOS mainly centers around actions within Earth's seas and coastal wate-rs. Therefore, supple-mentary legal documents are- required to handle the- distinctive difficulties prese-nted by activities relate-d to spacefaring in maritime regions. While- UNCLOS establishes a starting point, evolving te-chnologies may lead to situations not fully addresse-d. Further cooperation can help clarify re-sponsibilities to safely support exploration.

Cooperation be-tween nations is crucial for creating lawful structure-s for investigating maritime areas be-yond Earth. Joint efforts amongst countries can result in e-stablishing distinct compacts and protocols customized to tackle these- new difficulties. Nations must collaborate to formulate- principles and rules that guarantee- reasonable admission to assets in oce-anic areas outside our world, while also guarante-eing ecological safeguarding and saving oute-r space for future progenie-s. Additional clarification around specific issues like comme-rcial mineral mining or long-term dee-p space missions could help form the basis for inte-rnational agreements that facilitate- progressive utilization of extrate-rrestrial domains.

Moreove-r, private sector participation in ocean space- exploration introduces additional legal factors to conside-r. Business organizations engaged in the-se pursuits need to follow dome-stic legislation and rules while also honoring inte-rnational accords. Governments have a critical part to play in building a supportive- legal framework that encourage-s innovation, funding, and accountable behavior in maritime space- discovery. Such a framework should provide cle-ar guidelines for both public and private e-ntities to safely explore- new frontiers in accordance with inte-rnational standards. As commercial interests be-come more involved in oce-anic research and resource- development, nations must work toge-ther to develop compre-hensive yet adaptable- regulations addressing issues like- territorial claims, environmental prote-ction, and the use and sharing of collecte-d data. Only through open cooperation on the de-velopment and impleme-ntation of a sensible regulatory syste-m can emerging industries ade-quately balance progress with re-sponsibility when pushing the boundaries of maritime- exploration.

While te-chnological progress marches forward at a swift pace, our le-gal systems must evolve quickly in ste-p. The swiftly shifting frontiers in maritime and space- travel demand consistent re-assessment and refining of pre-vailing statutes to ensure applicable- guidelines remain up-to-date-. Adaptability is important to incorporate developing innovations and tackle- impending issues that groundbreaking discove-ries may bring. As inventions eme-rge at an unprecede-nted rate, so too must our frameworks of gove-rnance to maintain relevance- and functionality governing exploration's new horizons.

To wrap up, legitimate- thought for oceanic space exe-rcises are fundamentally crucial in guarante-eing the protecte-d, liable, and maintainable investigation of oute-r space. Setting up unmistakable authoritative- outskirts, teaming up globally, and adjusting lawful systems to coordinate with me-chanical headways are central stride-s toward tending to the novel difficultie-s introduced by maritime space inve-stigation. By deftly handling these lawful convolutions, humankind can ope-n the immense pote-ntial offered by the oce-ans of space while supporting the standards of re-asonable play, joint effort, and natural stewardship. The- assorted difficulties prese-nted by maritime space inve-stigation require global coordinated e-ffort and adjustment of current lawful structures. Clarifying authoritative- outskirts and guaranteeing consistence- with standards of reasonable play when inve-stigating undiscovered marine re-gions will encourage further advance-ment. Concentrating on maintainable othe-rworldly investigation and ensuring natural insurance of space- will open its potential while e-nsuring its preservation for future e-ras.

Territorial Claims and Jurisdictional Issues

Territorial claims in maritime- areas have taken on adde-d importance as the investigation and utilization of asse-ts in these spaces picks up force-. This area investigates the- multifaceted nature e-ncompassing territorial cases in maritime zone-s and the lawful structures set up to addre-ss authoritative discussions. While jurisdictional issues can e-merge as coastal states se-arch for control of expanding zones of the se-a and ocean floor, worldwide law as set up by the- United Nations Convention on the Law of the- Sea attempts to adjust state sove-reignty with the maintenance- of seas as worldwide goods. The Conve-ntion characterizes differe-nt maritime zones like inland wate-rs, territorial seas, extraordinary financial zone-s and common heritage zones, and allocate-s rights and obligations of states inside eve-ry one. In any case, some comple-x issues can emerge- identified with fringe zone-s or unsolved cases. Additionally, new advance-ments

The imme-nse scale of maritime domains, spanning oce-ans, seas, and other aqueous e-xpanses, introduces distinctive difficultie-s when delineating te-rritorial ownership. Dissimilar to land territories with we-ll-established borders, the- margins enclosing aqueous spaces are- not invariably distinctly defined, potentially instigating dispute-s between countrie-s aiming to assert sole stewardship ove-r particular locales. This lack of unambiguous demarcation surrounding maritime claims can ge-nerate confusion regarding jurisdiction ove-r waters, natural resources, navigation route-s, and more. With their intangible nature- rendering boundaries in se-as and oceans more indistinct than upon terre-strial surfaces, coastal nations may interpret de-limitations divergently, at times disputing control of ove-rlapping zones. Further complicating maritime de-limitation includes considerations like a re-gion's geological formations beneath wate-rs, prevailing currents, and ecological inte-rconnectedness transce-nding perceived limits. The- vastness of maritime territory pre-sents ongoing questions about shared utilization and how be-st to avoid tensions amid neighboring states within this le-ss clearly partitioned domain.

One of the primary sources of conflict is the overlapping claims over exclusive economic zones (EEZs) and extended continental shelves. The United Nations Convention on the Law of the Sea (UNCLOS) provides a framework for the delimitation of maritime boundaries and the establishment of EEZs. However, the interpretation and application of UNCLOS can still give rise to disputes, particularly in regions with competing interests.

For instance, the- South China Sea has long been a conte-ntious zone for territorial conflicts, with seve-ral nations laying claim to assorted isles and their surrounding wate-rs. These disagree-ments regularly pivot on diverging analyse-s of UNCLOS stipulations and antiquated assertions grounded in pre-historic civilizations' happenings in the vicinity. Conseque-ntly, pressures have inte-nsified, resulting in amplified militarization and diplomatic impasse-s. While UNCLOS attempts to provide a frame-work for reasonably resolving maritime jurisdictional issue-s, conflicting interpretations of history and international law have- hindered effe-ctive cooperation. Continued discussion e-mphasizing shared interests in re-gional stability may help de-escalate- tensions and facilitate mutually agree-able solutions.

Untangling territorial dispute-s necessitates astute-ly picking a path through the lawful structures set up by worldwide- arrangements. One re-gular methodology includes two-sided or multilate-ral talks among worried gatherings. Through diplomatic efforts and discussion, nations can work towards mutually agre-eable characterizations of outskirts that re-gard each other's privilege-s and accomplish a reasonable circulation of marine space-. These sensitive- conversations require tole-rance, cooperation and a longing to comprehe-nd diverse perspe-ctives to achieve arrange-ments that all sides can acknowledge-.

Where- discussions between partie-s reach an impasse or drag on inconclusively, the-y may turn to the dispute settle-ment avenues pre-sented in UNCLOS. Potential choice-s involve compulsory arbitration or judgment by the Inte-rnational Court of Justice or specialized judicial bodie-s. These forums prese-nt an unbiased setting for solving border disagre-ements, furthering pe-aceful decisions and pree-mpting possible clashes. While ne-gotiations can sometimes become- protracted, going to third party arbitration or courts ensures the- dispute can still be handled fairly and lawfully according to UNCLOS inste-ad of potentially escalating.

There- are a couple key points to ke-ep in mind regarding the e-nforcement of territorial rights and control ove-r maritime regions. Primarily, the ability for nations to uphold the-ir claimed territories at se-a relies heavily on willingne-ss to abide by international regulations and participate- in cooperative partnerships. Whe-n situations arise where countrie-s do not obey global laws or remove the-mselves from agree-d upon frameworks, it complicates the proce-ss of working through disputes further. Non-compliance or le-aving collaborative accords can make finding resolutions quite- difficult and heighten the pote-ntial for tensions to intensify betwe-en involved parties. Ove-rall, maintaining compliance with international standards and involveme-nt in cooperative networks se-ems crucial for reasonably enforcing te-rritorial control over maritime spaces.

Technology continue-s to progress rapidly, enabling exploration of oce-ans and seas in new innovative ways. As humanity pushe-s farther into maritime domains previously une-xplored, differing perspe-ctives on territorial ownership and le-gal control may potentially cause issues. The- frameworks of law currently in place for se-ttling disagreements and assigning authority will ne-ed to adapt and adjust to these change-s in a timely manner, establishing unambiguous rule-s for sharing maritime spaces cooperative-ly and maintaining sustainable stewardship of marine re-sources. Progress into uncharted wate-rs is sure to bring undiscovered complications; inte-rnational cooperation on clarifying legal matters will smooth future- navigation.

To wrap up, territorial claims in oce-an areas and the legal issue-s surrounding jurisdiction in those spaces stay intricate and controve-rsial subjects. As countries carry on investigating and taking advantage- of maritime resources, it is e-xtremely important to handle the-se difficulties through diplomatic discussions, worldwide te-amwork, and following recognized lawful structures. By acting in this manne-r, we can safeguard tranquility, advance maintainable- advancement, and guarantee- reasonable access to the- immense ranges of maritime- space. There are- numerous perspective- to consider identified with the-se issues and working togethe-r can assist us with understanding every one- of them all the more comple-tely while discovering re-asonable arrangements.

Environmental Implications of Maritime Space Exploration

Venturing into uncharte-d waters brings both opportunities and responsibilitie-s. As we expand our horizons into maritime domains, we- must thoughtfully consider the repe-rcussions for Earth's fragile environments and the- life within them. The conse-quences on planetary e-cosystems and biodiversity should not be dismisse-d or downplayed. Here, we- will deeply investigate- the environmental e-ffects of maritime space inve-stigation and analyze the legal structure-s and guidelines intende-d to alleviate possible damage-s. While exploration broadens our unde-rstanding, care for delicate balance-s sustains our shared home.

While space- exploration in and of itself prese-nts opportunities for discovery, we must e-nsure precautions are take-n to protect precious ecosyste-ms. Activities conducted in maritime zone-s as well as newly accessible- regions like the oce-ans and celestial bodies introduce- risks of releasing foreign substance-s that could disrupt fragile environments. Just as thoughtfulne-ss regarding pollution has helped safe-guard land and traditional maritime areas, a similar mindfulness will be- needed to avoid harming se-nsitive oceanic or extrate-rrestrial places through the discharge- of noxious fluids, refuse, or contaminants. With care and fore-sight, we can work to minimize detrime-ntal impacts to nature from the expansion of human e-xploration.

Spacecraft propulsion syste-ms frequently depe-nd on an array of fuels and propellants that may incorporate unsafe- materials. Unintentional drips or cracks amid lift off, maneuve-ring, and re-passage stages can taint e-ncompassing waters and influence marine- life. Moreover, the- discarding of used rocket stages and diffe-rent debris can additionally add to contamination in maritime space-. It is important that space agencies take- necessary precautions to minimize- any potential risks to the environme-nt from leaks or disposal of rocket parts. By adopting gree-ner fuels and impleme-nting stringent safety protocols, we can he-lp ensure space e-xploration does not endanger the- delicate ecological balance- in our oceans.

Furthermore-, gaining useful materials from heave-nly objects proposes an important ecological difficulty. Though e-xtracting efforts in maritime area might contain tre-mendous possibilities for financial deve-lopment and scientific progress, the-y similarly present dangers of habitat harm, e-cosystem interfere-nce, and the deple-tion of priceless minerals and substance-s from celestial bodies. We- must consider both the prospective- advantages in addition to the environme-ntal costs of space mining and discover approaches to le-ssen its unfavorable impacts on delicate- celestial ecosyste-ms. Even a minimally invasive operation risks long-lasting contamination if not carrie-d out with utmost care and oversight. As our reach e-xtends past Earth, it is crucial we safeguard the- untouched wonder of the wide-r cosmos.

To address these concerns, international organizations and treaties have sought to establish legal frameworks for responsible maritime space exploration. The United Nations Office for Outer Space Affairs (UNOOSA) plays a crucial role in promoting international cooperation in space activities while emphasizing sustainable development principles.

The Oute-r Space Treaty of 1967 plays an important role in e-stablishing rules for exploring outer space-, specifically barring the placeme-nt of nuclear weapons on planets and moons and holding e-ntities accountable for any damages cause-d by objects launched into space. This founding agre-ement lays the groundwork for a re-sponsible way forward in maritime space e-xploration that considers our environmental re-sponsibilities.

Furthermore-, considerable work has gone into crafting dire-ctives and benchmarks particularly aimed at maritime- space discovery. For example-, the International Astronautical Fede-ration and the International Institute of Space- Law have cooperated on de-veloping advisories for sustainable space-mining methods that balance environme-ntal protection with long-term access to re-sources. Their guideline-s stress preserving the- surroundings in space while tapping into deposits to fue-l further exploration. Some ke-y principles call for carefully monitoring mining sites, re-stricting how much is taken at a time, and leaving e-nough behind for future nee-ds.

Furthermore-, continuous studies are cente-red around creating gree-ner propulsion innovations and more productive waste- administration frameworks for spacecraft. As innovations kee-p on advancing, it is basic to give first need to natural arrange-ments that lessen harm to the- delicate biological systems of both Earth's se-as and spaceborne zones. Scie-ntists are investigating propulsion strategie-s, for example, plasma propulsion and sun oriente-d sails that utilization less or non-dangerous ene-rgies. They are additionally cre-ating improved frameworks to overse-e solid and fluid waste create-d on board spacecraft and guarantee it doe-sn't taint the Earth or space. As space trave-l turns out to be progressively we-ll known, it is urgent that we ensure- the security of our regular surroundings both on Earth and past it for pre-sent and future eras.

To wrap up, the implications of maritime- space exploration on the e-nvironment cannot be ignored. Though this are-a possesses terrific pote-ntial for scientific progress and financial deve-lopment, it necessitate-s being pursued with a robust dedication to safe-guarding nature. Achieving equilibrium be-tween investigation and conse-rvation necessitates tough authorize-d structures, intercontinental te-amwork, and embracing sustainable methods in the- sphere of maritime space- investigation. Only through uniting all these e-ndeavors can we make ce-rtain our discovery of the oceans above- does not arrive at the e-xpenditure of irreve-rsible damage to the se-tting.

A thoughtful investigation into arising te-chnologies and patterns in maritime space- revelation unveils an inte-rnational of boundless opportunities and capabilities. Te-chnological progress keeps on shifting the- restrictions of disclosure in exciting ways, ope-ning the entrance to many ne-w discoveries and understandings about the- oceans and areas past. As innovations kee-p enhancing, the long run potential for maritime- space examination looks really promising. While- there is still much more to find out, e-very new discovery brings us close-r to completely understanding our plane-t and its relationship to the vast universe- beyond.

The fie-ld of unmanned and autonomous vessels is gaining conside-rable attention as innovators see-k to transform ocean transportation. These e-merging technologies could mode-rnize maritime operations through highe-r productivity, lower expense-s, and boosted safety. Yet bringing such autonomous ships to the- seas also introduces fresh le-gal issues that require addre-ssing. The deployment of cre-wless craft prompts inquiries about accountability and adhere-nce to global rules. Without people- aboard, issues arise around responding rapidly to difficultie-s and confirming judicious choices are made. Additionally, que-stions emerge re-garding who may be found at fault should any incidents occur. As with introducing other advance-d systems, ensuring appropriate safe-guards and oversight can help society harne-ss promising technologies while minimizing uninte-nded risks.

As maritime space- exploration continues advancing, creating unambiguous le-gal structures becomes e-xtremely important. This involves e-stablishing the rights and duties of countries participating in e-ndeavors in maritime space, along with addre-ssing territorial assertions and jurisdictional matters. Without a thorough le-gal arrangement governing maritime- space, it could result in clashes and disagre-ements betwe-en nations looking to take advantage of its re-sources or conduct study.

While e-xploring outer space can further scie-ntific discovery, we must thoughtfully consider impacts to fragile- environments. As intere-st grows in space mining and resource e-xtraction from celestial objects, maintaining re-sponsible and sustainable approaches is incre-asingly important. Developing new re-gulations and legal guidelines can he-lp balance advancement with e-nvironmental protection. Careful policie-s will be key to safeguarding de-licate celestial e-cosystems while allowing rese-arch to continue aiding our understanding. More re-mains to be learned about pote-ntial effects, so taking preve-ntative steps now through prudent planning se-ems wise.

While maritime- space exploration will undoubtedly face- obstacles going forward, the future also pre-sents promising possibilities if we apply our growing knowle-dge resourcefully. Te-chnological progress is steadily enhancing our abilitie-s and deepening our insights into the- unknown frontiers outside Earth's atmosphere-. Unlocking the secrets of the- cosmos will depend on maintaining the collaborative- spirit of open-minded teamwork among countrie-s, cooperative networks, and scholarly communitie-s that have already brought so many discoverie-s. With a shared dedication to cooperative- progress over competitive- priorities, the mysterie-s of the maritime realm and be-yond can continue yielding bene-fits for all.

As we move- forward into this new frontier, it is extre-mely important that we consider the- legal difficulties that may deve-lop. This involves dealing with problems such as inte-llectual property laws, data sharing understandings, safe-ty rules, and moral concerns surrounding human attendance- or disruption with heavenly objects. By active-ly addressing these difficultie-s ahead of time, we can e-mbrace the limitless capability of maritime- area investigation while making ce-rtain its maintainability and following to worldwide lawful norms. There are- many new legal areas that will ne-ed addressed to he-lp protect investment and safe-ty as we explore the- vast opportunities of space.

The future- holds great potential for discovery and progre-ss. With prudent consideration of what's ahead, coope-ration across borders, and a dedication to sustainability, we can safe-ly traverse undiscovere-d maritime territories. As our voyage- begins, upholding guidelines grounde-d in worldwide participation and protection of shared conce-rns is crucial. Let our course be ste-ered by balanced policie-s enabling all to experie-nce maritime space's marve-ls while shielding humanity's collective- well-being.

Introduction to Biotechnology in the Maritime Context

Here- we delve into the- intriguing crossover betwee-n biotechnology and the seas to a mode-rate degree-, illuminating certain legal aspects re-garding maritime genetic mate-rials. Biotechnology in the marine se-tting involves researching and manipulating the- genes and biological substances obtaine-d from ocean creatures. The-se genetic re-sources possess huge possibilitie-s for scientific progress, medical discove-ries, and commercial uses. The-y may lead to improved medicine-s, new materials and a dee-per understanding of life. Howe-ver, access and use of the-se resources raise-s important legal questions around ownership, be-nefit-sharing and protection that require- careful consideration.

Maritime genetic resources refer to the diverse array of genetic material found in marine organisms, including bacteria, algae, plants, and animals. These resources are considered a treasure trove of biological diversity, harboring unique genes and compounds that can be harnessed for various purposes. From finding new drugs and therapies to developing innovative biofuels and sustainable materials, the applications of maritime genetic resources are vast and promising.

Comprehe-nding the lawful aspects encompassing biote-chnology in the maritime setting is indispe-nsable because of nume-rous factors. Initially, admittance to these he-reditary assets raises inquirie-s about proprietorship, control, and advantage sharing understandings be-tween nations and partners include-d. Given the worldwide e-xtent of the seas and the- assorted actors engaged with marine- examination and improvement, e-stablishing a sensible and fair system is fundame-ntal. Questions emerge- about how genetic material e-xtracted from international waters can be- used and protected. Additionally, many stake-holders from different countrie-s may lay claim to discoveries involving marine ge-netic resources, so coope-ration will be neede-d to develop equitable- solutions. Further consideration of ownership and inte-llectual property issues can he-lp clarify responsibilities and promote ope-n access to knowledge gaine-d from studying our oceans.

Furthermore-, tapping into the potential of maritime ge-netic resources de-mands consideration of biodiversity protection and e-nvironmental preservation. As scie-ntific progress marches on, finding equilibrium be-tween utilizing these- assets to enhance human we-ll-being now and safeguarding them for ge-nerations to come grows increasingly important. Harne-ssing opportunities offered by organisms inhabiting the- seas must be handled judiciously so the-ir habitats remain intact and diversity is maintained to sustain both e-cological balance and future discoverie-s.

Lastly, the comme-rcialization of biotechnological inventions derive-d from maritime genetic re-sources presents inte-llectual property rights (IPRs) challenge-s. Patenting discoveries obtaine-d from marine organisms raises important questions about owne-rship of such inventions. It brings up discussions on who has the legal right to pate-nt biological material and discoveries de-rived from marine life. Such pate-nts also prompt debates on how exclusive- rights might impact continued scientific progress, availability of ne-w technologies to the public, and e-quitable distribution of benefits be-tween originating nations and commercial e-ntities. Further clarity on these- complex issues can help balance- innovation with equitable sharing of resource-s and knowledge gained from the- genetics of ocean life-.

This section se-eks to illuminate the quickly changing fie-ld surrounding marine genetic re-sources through examining international accords and initiative-s governing these asse-ts, access and benefit sharing syste-ms, intellectual property rights matte-rs, emerging lawful difficulties, and prospe-ctive directions in biotech and maritime- law. By diving deeper into the- legal measureme-nts encompassing ocean gene-tic resources, we aim to offe-r a more nuanced grasp of the intricate- nature and possibilities located at the- meeting point of biotechnology and the- worlds oceans. This field is transforming at a swift pace, so unpacking the- agreements, frame-works, and unsolved legal issues re-garding access, innovation and equity involving marine sample-s and derivatives can impart helpful insight. Exploring e-merging topics like bene-fit sharing for traditional knowledge or coastal community participation in blue biote-ch ventures may also provide pe-rspective on balancing ecological ste-wardship, scientific progress and local community intere-sts.

International Agreements and Initiatives on Marine Genetic Resources

The use and conservation of marine genetic resources have become increasingly important in the context of biotechnology and maritime law. As such, numerous international agreements and initiatives have been established to govern the utilization and protection of these resources. This section provides an overview of these agreements and explores the key organizations and conventions involved in regulating biotechnology in the maritime context.

One prominent agreement is the United Nations Convention on the Law of the Sea (UNCLOS), which recognizes the importance of marine genetic resources beyond national jurisdiction. UNCLOS establishes a legal framework for their conservation and sustainable use, emphasizing the principle of equitable sharing of benefits derived from these resources. Additionally, UNCLOS seeks to promote scientific research and international cooperation in the field of marine biotechnology.

The Nagoya Protocol on Acce-ss to Genetic Resource-s and the Fair and Equitable Sharing of Bene-fits Arising from their Utilization, also known as the ABS Protocol, is another note-worthy international agreeme-nt. Mainly centered around te-rrestrial genetic re-sources located within national borders, the- ABS Protocol also considers access to gene-tic resources situated in are-as that no single nation has jurisdiction over, such as the high se-as. It prompts member countries to collaborate- to ensure that obtaining marine ge-netic resources is done- through a transparent and equitable approach. Additionally, the- ABS Protocol advocates for establishing bene-fit-sharing agreements whe-re the rewards of marine- genetic resource- use are distributed fairly among providing and utilizing nations.

Additionally, international bodie-s like the International Maritime- Organization (IMO) have an important part to play in dealing with biotechnology-re-lated matters in the shipping industry. The- IMO has created direction and be-nchmarks to stop possible unfavorable outcomes e-merging from the utilization of oceanic he-reditary assets. These- guidelines incorporate re-gions, for example, natural effe-ct appraisals, hazard examinations, and forestalling contamination from biotechnology e-xercises. Howeve-r, there is still work to be done- to fully clarify and strengthen the IMO's position, as ne-w innovations may produce unforesee-n effects.

Additionally, several conventions specifically target the conservation and management of marine biodiversity and genetic resources. The Convention on Biological Diversity (CBD) aims to promote conservation, sustainable use, and equitable sharing of benefits derived from genetic resources. The CBD's Protocols, including the Cartagena Protocol on Biosafety and the Nagoya-Kuala Lumpur Supplementary Protocol on Liability and Redress, further contribute to the regulation of biotechnology activities and the protection of marine genetic resources.

While othe-r initiatives focus on conserving plant gene-tic resources, they may also impact marine- life. The International Tre-aty on Plant Genetic Resource-s for Food and Agriculture addresses prote-cting plant varieties for food and farming. This relate-s to genetic material found in the- ocean. Collaborations betwee-n groups seek to sustainably use marine- genetics. For instance, the- Intergovernmental Oce-anographic Commission and Convention for the Protection of the- Marine Environment of the

North-East Atlantic work toge-ther to oversee- ocean genetics. The-y aim to manage and safeguard marine life-'s building blocks.

To briefly wrap up, nume-rous worldwide understandings and activities are- currently set up to administer the- utilization and protection of marine here-ditary assets in the setting of biote-chnology and maritime law. These unde-rstandings concentrate on reasonable- sharing of advantages, advance maintainable hone-s, and urge worldwide joint effort. By pe-rceiving the significance of the-se assets and setting up administrative- structures, these unde-rstandings and associations contribute to in charge and moral utilization of maritime he-reditary assets for future e-ras. While there is as ye-t work to be done, the curre-nt frameworks give expe-ctation that these important assets will be- tended to sustainably.

Access and Benefit Sharing (ABS) Frameworks for Marine Genetic Resources

Marine genetic resources hold immense potential for biotechnological advancements and scientific discoveries. As such, it is crucial to establish effective frameworks that govern the access to and sharing of benefits derived from these valuable resources. This section explores the concept of Access and Benefit Sharing (ABS) in the context of maritime genetic resources, shedding light on the legal obligations and mechanisms that ensure fair and equitable sharing of benefits.

Access to marine genetic resources refers to the acquisition of biological material for scientific research or commercial purposes. It involves activities such as bioprospecting, where scientists collect samples from marine organisms to study their genetic makeup and potential applications in biotechnology. However, due to the inherent value of these resources, concerns arise regarding the need for equitable distribution of benefits derived from their use.

To address these concerns, ABS frameworks have been developed at both the international and national levels. These frameworks aim to balance the interests of resource-rich countries and those seeking access to marine genetic resources. The Convention on Biological Diversity (CBD) serves as a primary international instrument governing ABS in the context of genetic resources, including those found in marine environments.

While countrie-s are urged to devise- domestic rules over gaining acce-ss to their genetic asse-ts under the CBD, such a framework ne-cessitates obtaining consent from the- supplying nation before tapping into its biological diversity. This prior informe-d assent, often called PIC, is ce-ntral to the arrangement. Furthe-rmore, the provider country has le-eway to delineate- conditions for entry and later profit participation, typically refe-rred to as mutually agreed te-rms or MAT. Together, PIC and MAT establish the- ground rules for collaborating on genetic re-source utilization betwee-n partnering governments, with e-quity and fairness as guiding principles.

ABS frameworks highlight the- importance of reasonably and fairly dividing the advantage-s acquired from marine here-ditary assets. This includes guarantee-ing that both money related incre-ases just as non-money relate-d advantages, for example, innovation e-xchange and limit structure, are share-d among all applicable stakeholders. The- Nagoya Protocol, a supplemental understanding to the- CBD, gives extra direction on ABS as far as he-reditary assets, including those re-moved from marine conditions. The Nagoya Protocol stre-sses that stakeholders ought to coope-rate to ensure re-asonable and equivalent sharing of the- advantages from the utilization of marine organic asse-ts. This agreement unde-rlines that innovation exchange and limit structure- among nations can encourage maintainable utilization of oce-an assets and safeguard marine biodive-rsity.

Impleme-ntation mechanisms for ABS frameworks usually require- forming national contact centers, qualified dome-stic administrators, and specialized digital databases to facilitate- the sharing of data and guarantee conformity. The-se frameworks play an extre-mely important role in enabling ope-nness, responsibility, and efficie-nt tracking of access and advantage sharing efforts. National contact ce-nters work as the primary points of contact betwe-en governments on ABS issue-s, allowing requests and notifications to be- prope-rly directed. Compete-nt national authorities are designate-d to take management re-sponsibility for overseeing dome-stic ABS activity and ensuring users comply with contractual terms and dome-stic regulatory requireme-nts. Specialized databases the-n help national authorities and providers e-ffectively coordinate by allowing mutually agre-ed terms like utilization contributions and monitoring plans to be- recorded and refe-renced. Togethe-r these ele-ments of national infrastructure help build confide-nce betwee-n providers and users engaging in ABS by promoting a transpare-nt process that confirms obligations are being appropriate-ly addressed.

While ABS frame-works for marine genetic re-sources could offer potential be-nefits, effective-ly applying them poses various difficulties. One- important hurdle involves the ambiguity surrounding gove-rnmental control in international waters. Since- marine genetic re-sources do not restrict themse-lves to a single nation's borders, e-stablishing which country holds power over these- assets becomes intricate-. The continuing discussions under the Unite-d Nations Convention on the Law of the Se-a (UNCLOS) concerning the protection and long-te-rm application of marine biological diversity outside national boundarie-s seek to tackle such difficultie-s. However, jurisdictional boundaries for marine- resources in international wate-rs remains a complex challenge-.

To summarize, frame-works for access and benefit-sharing se-rve a crucial role in guarantee-ing that advantages gotten from marine natural asse-ts are shared reasonably and re-asonably. By setting up clear lawful commitments and instrume-nts, these structures improve- straightforwardness, encourage joint e-ffort, and advance maintainable utilization of oceanic he-reditary assets. Be that as it may, tackling difficultie-s identified with jurisdictional limits and synchronizing current administrative-systems stays a continuous need to viably actualize- access to advantages sharing in the se-tting of marine biotechnology. Addressing issue-s identified with debatable- maritime fringes and coordinating existing administrative- systems stays a continuing need.

Intellectual Property Rights (IPRs) and Patents related to Maritime Biotechnology

Biotechnology's utilization of maritime- genetic resource-s has brought various legal issues, espe-cially regarding intellectual prope-rty rights (IPRs) and patents. Researche-rs exploring the abundant biological diversity within our se-as are finding new prospects for me-dical progress, environmental answe-rs, and industrial uses. However, the- legal surroundings encompassing IPRs and patents involving maritime- biotechnology stays intricate and multi-facete-d. As scientists delve furthe-r into the substantial biological diversity uncovere-d underneath the se-as, they are discovering promising opportunitie-s for healthcare deve-lopments, ecological solutions to problems impacting our plane-t, and innovative applications that could advantage our lives. While- their discoveries raise- hopes, determining owne-rship and access to these discove-ries raises difficult legal que-stions without easy answers. As the possibilitie-s from our seas increasingly impact people-'s lives, navigating the relate-d intellectual property issue-s will remain an ongoing challenge.

At the heart of the issue lies the question of ownership and access to marine genetic resources. While some argue that these resources should be considered as part of the common heritage of humanity, others advocate for exclusive rights and control over their usage. This debate is further intensified when it comes to patenting biotechnological inventions derived from maritime genetic resources.

The challe-nges stemming from patenting marine- genetic resource-s come in two parts. First, it can be quite hard to pin down and de-scribe specific gene-tic sequences or compounds that come- from sea creatures. The- immense size and intricacy of oce-an environments make it difficult to trace- a particular genetic resource- back to its exact source, bringing up doubts about the nove-lty and obviousness neede-d for a patent. The vast oceans contain an e-normous diversity of life, from the tinie-st microbes to the largest whale-s. Within this incredible diversity are- untold numbers of genetic mate-rials with potential medical or industrial uses. Howe-ver, the complex inte-rconnectedness of marine- ecosystems and the minute- scale of genes and mole-cules pose difficulties for satisfying pate-nt requirements of ide-ntifying unique inventions.

While comme-rcialization of nature's bounty raises profitable prospe-cts, certain concerns eme-rge on further refle-ction. Some argue patents on marine- genes may spawn monopolies hinde-ring scientific progress and innovation. Moreove-r, implications for indigenous and developing pe-oples frequently holding oce-an biodiversity in trust require prude-nt consideration. Equitable arrangeme-nts ensuring fair benefits for all partie-s utilizing such resources demand atte-ntive safeguards be installe-d.

To navigate these complex issues, various international agreements and initiatives have sought to establish guidelines for IPRs and patents related to maritime biotechnology. The Nagoya Protocol on Access to Genetic Resources and the Fair and Equitable Sharing of Benefits Arising from Their Utilization under the Convention on Biological Diversity provides a framework for access and benefit-sharing (ABS) for genetic resources, including those from the seas. However, the application of this protocol to maritime genetic resources remains a subject of ongoing debate and interpretation.

As we move forward, it is crucial to address the challenges posed by patenting marine genetic resources in a manner that promotes scientific progress while safeguarding environmental conservation and ensuring fair access and benefit-sharing. Collaborative efforts between scientists, policymakers, legal experts, and indigenous communities are necessary to strike the delicate balance between private rights and public interests.

In conclusion, intelle-ctual property rights (IPRs) and patents relate-d to maritime biotechnology prese-nt intricate and multifaceted le-gal issues that warrant deepe-r inspection. Identifying gene-tic resources found in oceans, addre-ssing ethical concerns surrounding their comme-rcialization, and guaranteeing fair access and be-nefit-sharing for all involved parties are- crucial matters requiring judicious assessme-nt. As biotechnology persists in progression, it is absolute-ly essential that the le-gal structure encompassing IPRs and patents stays consiste-nt with evolving investigation and progress te-chniques, confirming equitable outcome-s for every person impacte-d.

While e-merging biotechnologies and maritime- industries present opportunitie-s for innovation, they also introduce novel le-gal considerations that require thoughtful e-xamination and clarification. As new scientific discoverie-s progress and technologies advance-, applying established laws may require- As biotechnology progre-sses, the connection be-tween biotechnology and maritime- law brings up many upcoming lawful difficulties. One such test is the- institutional issues encompassing bioprospecting in unive-rsal waters. With huge zones of the- world's oceans falling outside of national purviews, inquirie-s emerge with re-spect to the lawful system for ge-tting to and exploiting maritime here-ditary assets. While bioprospecting could yie-ld advantageous new medications and diffe-rent items, there- are worries about ecological we-llbeing and the reasonable- sharing of advantages. Furthermore, without worldwide- assent on institutional issues, there- is potential for clash. All gatherings hope to coope-rate to build up reasonable and practical arrange-ments as innovation keeps on advancing.

Currently, there is no universally accepted legal regime governing bioprospecting in international waters. This lack of clarity creates uncertainties and potential conflicts among countries seeking to exploit the untapped potential of marine genetic resources. Jurisdictional disputes can arise when different countries claim ownership over genetic resources found in areas beyond their national boundaries.

Resolving the-se jurisdictional challenges ne-cessitates enhance-d international teamwork and partnership. De-veloping an impactful governance structure- for the sustainable utilization of maritime ge-netic resources de-mands the involvement of all appropriate- stakeholders, such as coastal nations, flag states, industry e-xperts, researche-rs, and indigenous communities. The e-stablishment of clear guideline-s regarding the sustainable use- of ocean resources found be-yond national jurisdiction requires open communication and compromise- between all inte-rested parties. Only through re-spectful, multifaceted discussions can we- determine an e-quitable path forward that considers the varie-d interests and protects the- diversity of life in our oceans.

To address this issue, a collaborative approach involving international organizations such as the International Seabed Authority (ISA) and the Convention on Biological Diversity (CBD) is essential. These organizations play a crucial role in facilitating discussions, negotiations, and the establishment of mechanisms that balance the interests of different stakeholders while ensuring the conservation and sustainable use of marine genetic resources.

There- are important ethical issues to think about whe-n considering where biote-chnology and maritime law related to oce-ans may be heading. As more is e-xplored and discovered from the- sea, it is essential that we- protect marine environme-nts and indigenous groups from being abused or use-d in unsafe ways. All people and organizations doing bioprospe-cting must make sure not to damage de-licate ocean ecosyste-ms or disrespect the traditions of native- communities that live near the- water. We nee-d good rules and shared agree-ments about how to responsibly learn from the- sea, value the wise- lessons of local tribes, and set up fair syste-ms so everyone he-lps and gains from new discoveries. This will he-lp progress happen while also ke-eping important values like prote-cting nature and culture.

While biote-chnology holds promise to address issues in the- maritime sector, its unique characte-ristics warrant tailored oversight. With technological progre-ss outpacing changes to laws and regulations, existing frame-works may fail to accommodate evolving applications. To ensure- biotechnology's benefits are- realized while risks are- mitigated, legislators and policymakers must partne-r closely to craft agile legal structure-s. Such adaptive approaches see-k to encourage innovation but also protect e-nvironmental and communal priorities. By pursuing a balanced solution through collaborative- work, all interests can be se-rved as this consequential fie-ld continues its rapid advancement.

In conclusion, the emerging legal challenges in biotechnology and maritime law, particularly in relation to jurisdictional issues and ethical considerations surrounding bioprospecting in international waters, require comprehensive and collaborative solutions. The future directions of this field depend on improved regulation, increased international cooperation, and the establishment of ethical guidelines. By addressing these challenges head-on, the legal framework governing biotechnology in the maritime context can adapt to ensure sustainable and responsible exploitation of maritime genetic resources for the benefit of all stakeholders involved.

**Importance of Navigation Freedom: **

Navigation free-dom has immense importance as a core- principle in maritime law, significantly impacting worldwide trade- and business. For centuries, the- liberty to traverse oce-ans has served a pivotal function in enabling financial growth and promoting inte-rcontinental teamwork. While navigation fre-edom allows unrestricted transit on wate-rways connecting nations and markets, its roots exte-nd deeper into facilitating comme-rce flows and relations betwe-en lands separated by se-as. By preserving open acce-ss to maritime domains, nations worldwide can more e-asily exchange goods and ideas to mutual be-nefit.

The concept of navigation freedom can be traced back to ancient civilizations, where seafaring nations recognized the inherent value of open seas for trade and exploration. The Phoenicians, for example, established a network of trade routes spanning the Mediterranean Sea, promoting cultural exchange and economic growth among various societies. Similarly, the Hanseatic League in medieval Europe relied heavily on navigation freedom to expand their trade networks and establish prosperous merchant cities. In more recent times, navigation freedom has been enshrined in various international conventions and treaties. One of the earliest examples is the Treaty of Utrecht in 1713, which upheld the principle of free navigation on international rivers as a means to promote peaceful relations between states. This principle was further reinforced by the Paris Declaration Respecting Maritime Law in 1856, which emphasized the right of ships to navigate freely on the high seas.

While navigation fre-edom holds significant economic bene-fits, allowing transport between nations, its value- transcends monetary concerns. The- ability for vessels of diverse- origins to traverse the oce-ans connecting countries without unreasonable- limitations is profoundly important for encouraging diplomatic ties and sustaining tranquility among states. Whe-n ships can traverse international wate-rs with minimal impediments, dete-rmined by their flag rather than the-ir cargo or destination, pathways open for discussion, comprehe-nsion, and teamwork betwee-n governments. Navigation free-dom forms the basis for constructing robust associations grounded in mutual regard and common obje-ctives. By permitting flow of trade be-tween borders, re-lationships have potential to blossom beyond mone-tary exchange alone.

Moreover, navigation freedom enables nations to access vital resources and engage in international trade, thereby promoting economic growth and prosperity. It facilitates the movement of goods, fuels innovation, creates employment opportunities, and contributes to the overall development of both coastal and landlocked states. Without navigation freedom, economies would be stifled, and nations would be deprived of the benefits arising from global trade networks.

While navigation fre-edom remains crucially significant, it unfortunately confronts issue-s in today's maritime environment. Acts of piracy, te-rrorism, unlawful behavior, and jurisdictional disagreeme-nts endanger the libe-rating movement of vesse-ls and products across worldwide seas. In the re-cent past, cases of piracy in the Gulf of Ade-n and the Strait of Malacca have interrupte-d commerce paths and heighte-ned worries concerning maritime- protection. Moreover, prote-cting the freedom of move-ment across oceans while also addre-ssing modern security threats prove-s increasingly complex, requiring improve-d international cooperation to safeguard ope-n seas for all.

Addressing global challe-nges like piracy require-s coordinated international cooperation and strong le-gal structures. When nations work togethe-r through shared patrols and military drills, they can bette-r discourage harmful acts and safeguard ships on the oce-an. Additionally, the United Nations Convention on the- Law of the Sea establishe-s a united rulebook for maritime law that acknowle-dges free navigation while- providing guidelines. By outlining navigation rights and responsibilitie-s, it gives a framework to facilitate pe-aceful and lawful use of the se-as. Overall, collaborative multinational efforts and global agre-ements help e-nable safe and secure- passage for all vessels trave-rsing the waters.

As we look toward the- future, guaranteeing unre-stricted navigation necessitate-s sustained vigilance and aptitude to adapt. Te-chnology continues progressing and new worldwide- power eleme-nts arise, consequently it is crucial to e-ncourage worldwide conversation and te-amwork to successfully address evolving difficultie-s. By protecting the free-dom of navigation, governments, worldwide associations, and lawful e-xperts can add to enduring worldwide e-xchange developme-nt, guaranteeing sea route-, and general wealth of countrie-s everywhere- on the planet. Ensuring unhindere-d movement over the- oceans is fundamental on the grounds that worldwide- exchange relie-s upon it. Numerous nations around the globe re-ly upon import and fare by ocean. On the off chance- that there is any limitation or disturbance to oce-anic exchange courses, it could have- genuine budgetary e-ffects. Furthermore, guarante-eing the opportunity to explore- universally significant waterways is basic to kee-ping away from geopolitical pressures. With consiste-nt correspondence and coope-ration between associate-d gatherings, these difficultie-s can be tended to in a tranquil manne-r.

Ensuring Maritime Security:

In this section, we delve into the critical issue of maritime security and the challenges it poses in the modern era. With emerging threats such as terrorism, piracy, and illegal activities at sea, safeguarding maritime interests has become a top priority for nations across the globe.

While analyzing the- contemporary condition of maritime security, we- carry out an extensive e-valuation of the prevailing legal structure-s and projects that have bee-n applied to confront these difficultie-s. We assess their e-fficacy and pinpoint possible territories for progre-ss to reinforce maritime se-curity on a worldwide scale. There- are several inte-rnational agreements and national laws that gove-rn maritime security. It is important we care-fully study these existing frame-works to understand their strengths and limitations. This would he-lp identify targeted e-fforts to address existing loopholes. For instance-, assessing information sharing protocols betwee-n countries could help protect se-a routes. Overall, only by thoroughly investigating curre-nt measures and see-king diverse perspe-ctives, can we recomme-nd principled improvements to maritime- security worldwide.

Strengthe-ning international cooperation and collaboration is vital for enhancing maritime- security. Bilateral agree-ments betwee-n nations help foster joint efforts to addre-ss maritime threats. Multilateral conve-ntions also facilitate coordinated response-s through legal frameworks that multiple countrie-s support. International organizations further promote coope-ration by bringing various stakeholders togethe-r. Examining the work of groups like the Inte-rnational Maritime Organization provides insight into successful mode-ls of collaboration. Coordination between naval force-s, coast guards, and law enforcement age-ncies from different jurisdictions is like-wise important. When these- entities share information and coordinate- patrols, they can more effe-ctively monitor maritime activity and interdict thre-ats. While jurisdictional boundaries may exist be-tween forces, prioritizing coope-ration improves overall security. Looking close-r at how coordination currently functions and where it could be- strengthened offe-rs a path forward for tackling shared maritime security challe-nges.

To address the issue of piracy, which has resurfaced as a significant concern in recent years, we examine the legal frameworks and measures that have been put in place to combat piracy in high-risk regions such as the Gulf of Aden. We critically analyze their effectiveness and propose potential strategies for countering pirate activities more comprehensively.

Furthermore, we also highlight the need for robust surveillance systems and intelligence sharing among maritime nations to detect and prevent illegal activities at sea. This includes addressing issues such as drug trafficking, arms smuggling, and human trafficking. We discuss how advancements in technology can be leveraged to bolster maritime security efforts, including enhanced monitoring systems and satellite imagery.

By fully understanding the challenges posed by emerging threats at sea and carefully evaluating the effectiveness of current legal frameworks, we can identify gaps and propose innovative solutions to ensure maritime security. In doing so, we aim to provide policymakers, legal professionals, and scholars with valuable insights into shaping future policies and regulations that can effectively safeguard our seas.

Part VII:
Safe Harbor
Concluding Reflections

"Safe harbors in maritime law are not just sheltered bays; they are sanctuaries of justice, where the storms of legal uncertainty find calm, and the vessels of fairness find refuge. In the embrace of safe harbors, the beacon of the law guides all mariners to a sanctuary of equity and resolution."

Chapter 1

The Future of
Maritime Governance
*****

This segme-nt investigates the part of worldwide- associations, for example, the Inte-rnational Maritime Organization (IMO), in forming and implementing maritime- directions. It analyzes conceivable-advancements in innovation and their re-sults for future maritime administration. The IMO works with maritime- nations to set up universally acknowledge-d security, wellbeing and natural se-curity rules for global exchange. As ne-w innovations are receive-d, for example, computerize-d navigation and sensor frameworks, the IMO will probably adjust curre-nt standards or make new ones to ove-rsee their utilization. Innovation can possibly upgrade- security on ships however additionally pre-sents new difficulties to guide-line. Coastlines are additionally advancing to de-al with the administrative parts of new advance-s,

Maritime gove-rnance holds significant importance in guarantee-ing the proper guideline-s and administration of the oceans. The pre-sent condition of maritime administration confronts differe-nt difficulties and requires consiste-nt assessment to adjust to deve-loping needs and rising issues. The-re are various parts included in guarante-eing the seas are- overseen productive-ly, including approach making, guidelines, oversight, and coope-ration between various maritime- organizations and nations. Continuous audits of current approaches and strategie-s can recognize territory for improve-ment to more readily te-nd to new difficulties, for example-, environmental change, ove-r-utilization of marine assets, or illicit fishing. Collaboration is fundamental as oce-anic issues don't acknowledge political outskirts. Gove-rnance should adjust and advance as comprehe-nsion of oceanic frameworks and the e-ffect of human exercise-s

International organizations like- the IMO have bee-n extremely impactful in e-stablishing and promoting worldwide benchmarks and rules for maritime- activities. The IMO has assumed a crucial part in tackling issue-s like safety, security, natural prote-ction, and work standards in the maritime business. It has e-ncouraged joint effort among countries through the- endorsement of unde-rstandings, codes, and rules that direct diffe-rent parts of maritime tasks. The IMO works dilige-ntly to guarantee maritime activitie-s run easily and viably while ensuring the- security of sailors and the earth. Through worldwide- cooperation, it advances guideline-s that upgrade wellbeing on ships, fore-stall contamination, and ensure fair treatme-nt of shippers. Its conventions give dire-ction on issues like building and gear ne-cessities, discharge controls, and transporte-r obligations. This worldwide administration and direction have significantly improve-d conditions over the globe's se-as.

Let us care-fully consider the prese-nt circumstances regarding maritime rule-s and regulations, and pinpoint where progre-ss can still be made. A primary focus ought to be boosting the- means by which existing guideline-s are upheld. Tighter coope-ration across port authorities, flag-bearing nations, and coastal governme-nts is absolutely critical to guarantee laws are- properly execute-d and penalties are impose-d when necessary. Furthe-rmore, cultivating higher leve-ls of openness and responsibility within the- shipping sector could assist in enhancing how the industry is ove-rseen. For instance, more-frequent information sharing betwe-en the various parties inve-sted in maritime affairs may streamline-oversight efforts. Ultimately, what matte-rs most is finding practical, mutually agreeable ways to stre-ngthen governance in a manne-r respecting all stakeholde-rs.

Technological progre-ss at sea opens doors while posing difficultie-s for upcoming ocean stewardship. Automated syste-ms, digital conversions, and robot boat creations are slate-d to transform maritime commerce. Such shifts promise- optimization through lessened human faults and e-nhanced protection. Yet que-stions emerge too re-garding legal blame, cyber risks, and re-quirements for refre-shed rules addressing arising te-ch fittingly. Advancements in areas like- computerized operations, online- records, and autonomous crafts may streamline shipping. But the-y could complicate liability in incidents and weake-n security versus hackers. As old principle-s meet new tools, laws re-quire revision acknowledging innovations thoroughly to safe-guard equity and safety alike going forward.

In order to stay curre-nt with technological progress, maritime gove-rnance in the future will ne-ed to adopt novel technique-s. Decision makers will nee-d to actively engage with inte-rested parties from both public and private- industries to craft flexible re-gulatory structures that can adjust to the evolving nature- of maritime work. Bringing together policy cre-ators, professionals in the field, and scholars can he-lp pinpoint effective me-thods and handle pending legal issue-s quickly as new circumstances arise. The-re is a changing tide in maritime ope-rations, so connecting experts from a range- of backgrounds can help uncover solutions and navigational changes that mode-rnize rules of transit while pre-serving safety at sea. By we-lcoming input from all vessels in this conversation, le-aders may chart a course for smart regulation that smoothly inte-grates advances while ke-eping passengers and cargo prote-cted.

Moreove-r, sustainable maritime practices will play a pivotal role- in upcoming maritime administration. The shipping business gre-atly influences the e-nvironment, adding to contamination, climate transformation, and loss of biodiversity. As worldwide- initiatives strengthen to fight climate-transformation and accomplish sustainable progress aims, the maritime- industry must synchronize its operations with these- targets. Potential maritime administration should e-mphasize incorporating environmental issue-s into rules and advocate sustainable te-chnologies and methods that decre-ase the sector's e-cological impact. The shipping industry currently has a considerable- environmental effe-ct through pollution, global warming, and harm to various ecosystems. While ships transport ove-r 80% of globally traded goods and support a significant portion of the world's economy, the-ir operations also produce large amounts of gre-enhouse gas emissions and discharge- waste into the oceans. As conce-rns about protecting the planet incre-ase globally, maritime authorities ne-ed to prioritize 'gree-ning' the sector by promoting cleane-r fuel use, waste manage-ment systems, and other e-co-friendly solutions on vessels to he-lp lower their environme-ntal footprint. Reducing pollution from ships will aid international efforts to curb climate- change and make progress on sustainability goals, be-nefiting both the maritime industry and global community.

To summarize, the- future direction of maritime manage-ment necessitate-s prudent inspection, creative- thinking, and proactive involvement. Inte-rnational organizations like the IMO will continue playing a pivotal part in de-signing and enforcing maritime rules. Adapting to te-chnological improvements and addressing e-merging lawful issues will be critical. More-over, encouraging sustainable me-thods within the maritime sector is e-ssential for guaranteeing a balance-d relationship betwee-n economic progress and environme-ntal stewardship. By contemplating on the pre-sent circumstance of maritime manage-ment and embracing these- viewpoints for tomorrow, we can guide towards a more- strong and effective structure- for directing the oceans. The- role of international cooperation on issue-s like regulating shipping, preve-nting pollution, and safeguarding seafarers will be- important. New technologies bring opportunitie-s but also challenges around issues such as automation, cybe-rsecurity and the collection and use- of data. Continued multilateral efforts can he-lp harness innovation and build consensus on an equitable- path forward.

Sustainable Maritime Practices:

As awarene-ss around the globe increase-s regarding the environme-ntal effects caused by human actions, the- maritime industry faces pressure- to embrace sustainable me-thods. Here, we de-lve into the increasing significance- of sustainable practices within the maritime- industry and their incorporation into maritime law. The maritime- industry must recognize the ne-ed to minimize environme-ntal damage from ships. Adopting greene-r technologies and operating proce-dures can help reduce- pollution in oceans and emissions. Sustainable practice-s, if integrated properly into law and re-gulations, may establish guidelines for e-co-friendly shipping. This could involve using cleane-r fuels, implementing e-nergy-efficient ship de-signs, and establishing protected marine- areas. As concern for the plane-t grows, the industry will need to de-monstrate responsible ste-wardship of marine environments to maintain trust.

The shipping industry has a sizable- environmental footprint through the e-missions it releases and pollution it cre-ates. A major focus for boosting sustainability has involved diminishing shipping's effe-ct on the environment. As a substantial source- of greenhouse gase-s, air pollutants, and marine contamination, the sector has sought strate-gies to tackle these- issues. Initiatives to address the-se problems have won growing acce-ptance in recent time-s. One of the key re-gions sustainability has gained importance involves de-creasing the industry's environme-ntal repercussions from transportation activities. Be-ing a significant contributor to greenhouse gas e-missions, air pollution, and ocean pollution, such plans aimed at dealing with the-se matters have picke-d up momentum in the past few ye-ars.

The Inte-rnational Maritime Organization (IMO) has launched an important initiative to lowe-r greenhouse gas e-missions from shipping. The IMO has established ve-ry ambitious goals to cut pollution from vessels and has enacte-d rules such as the Energy Efficie-ncy Design Index and the Ship

Ene-rgy Efficiency Management Plan. The-se regulations see-k to promote energy e-fficiency in ship architecture and ope-ration. By focusing on energy efficie-ncy, fuel usage and harmful emissions can both de-cline. The Energy Efficie-ncy Design Index evaluate-s how efficiently new ships transfe-r fuel energy into motion e-nergy. Meanwhile, the- Ship Energy Efficiency Manageme-nt Plan is a management tool for shipowners and ope-rators. It helps them monitor their ve-ssels' energy usage- and identify methods to slash consumption. Togethe-r, these IMO regulations aim to spur e-nergy-smart ship architecture and ope-rations. The goal is reducing the quantity of fue-l required and the quantity of e-missions discharged into the atmosphere-.

Sustainable maritime- operations involve more than just curbing gre-enhouse gas emissions. The-y also center around forestalling and addre-ssing marine contamination. Rigorous rules overse-e the rele-ase of pollutants into the ocean, such as oil, che-micals, wastewater, and trash. International agre-ements and protocols like the- International Convention for the Pre-vention of Pollution from Ships, often called MARPOL, e-stablish baselines and nece-ssities for dealing with refuse- and forestalling pollution. For example, MARPOL se-ts strict limits on the quantities and types of che-micals, oil, sewage, and garbage that ships can discharge- into sea waters, helping to re-duce pollution from ocean-faring vesse-ls. It aims to protect the marine e-nvironment by minimizing these type-s of ship-generated pollution. Toge-ther, such conventions play a key role- in preserving marine e-cosystems and safeguarding coastal communities that re-ly on ocean resources.

Moreove-r, tackling climate change within the frame-work of maritime law is another pivotal facet of sustainable- maritime practices. As sea le-vels progressively asce-nd, weather patterns unpre-dictably fluctuate, and storms intensify in ferocity, the-se phenomena pre-sent formidable difficulties for the- maritime industry. Integrating accommodations for climate change- into maritime legislation can aid guarantee- the endurance of coastal towns, ports, and shipping proce-dures opposite these- difficulties. Coastal communities, ports, and shipping operations face- considerable threats from rising se-a levels, changing weathe-r patterns with greater variations be-tween sente-nces, and intensified storms. Maritime- law needs to incorporate adaptations to climate- change in order to help e-nsure that coastal communities, ports, and shipping operations re-main resilient in the face- of challenges posed by a changing climate-.

There- are several othe-r crucial factors involved in sustainable maritime practice-s aside from merely e-nvironmental concerns. Social sustainability issues involving fair and humane- working conditions for seafarers, gende-r equality, and diversity are re-ceiving increased scrutiny within the- maritime industry. New proposals focused on e-nhancing labor protections, welfare standards, and re-presentation across differe-nces are currently unde-r review and application to cultivate a more- sustainable maritime labor force. Initiative-s promoting workers' rights, well-being, and inclusion are- in development and practice- to generate a maritime- sector defined as much by e-quitable treatment of its pe-ople as by responsible ste-wardship of oceans and waterways.

As concern for sustainability incre-ases in both international and domestic age-ndas, it is imperative for maritime law to adapt to the-se evolving priorities. By incorporating e-nvironmentally-sound principles into the le-gal structure, lawmakers can help assure- the maritime sector contribute-s constructively towards attaining worldwide sustainability targets. This industry, so vital to inte-rnational trade and travel, must transition towards operations that conside-r both present and future impacts if global sustainability ambitions are- to be realized. Practical policie-s can guide the maritime fie-ld in tackling pertinent issues like- pollution reduction and resource ste-wardship, harnessing its immense capabilitie-s to transport people and goods in a manner that safe-guards ecosystems and communities for ge-nerations to come.

To wrap up, this portion examine-s the progressively critical nature- of maintainable practices in the maritime- business and their incorporation into maritime law. Proje-cts focused on diminishing ecological effe-ct, advancing vitality proficiency, and tending to environme-ntal change inside the syste-m of maritime enactment are- pivotal in building up a more maintainable future for the- maritime business and the se-as it travels. These activitie-s are critical on the grounds that they can assist with e-nsuring the sea biological systems and asse-ts are secured for future- ages. Endeavors cente-red around diminishing ozone harming substance e-manations and expanding vitality effective-ness will likewise assist ve-ssels with lessening working costs. While- change won't happen quickly, by prese-nting green advances ste-p by step and changing directions, the maritime- part can turn out to be progressively maintainable- over the long haul.

Emerging Legal Issues:

In this final section, we- will delve dee-per into some of the burge-oning legal matters that are we-ll-positioned to define the- future landscape of maritime law. As the- maritime industry continues its evolution and adapts promising ne-w technologies, it is imperative- that we recognize pote-ntial prickly points and problems stemming from these- advancements. A moderate- level of analysis can help uncove-r issues that demand clarity to safely guide- further progress. Some e-merging topics may require more- nuanced consideration, while othe-rs might benefit from suppleme-ntary context or explanations. Togethe-r, a comprehensive ye-t accessible evaluation can he-lp all parties navigate changes ahe-ad and ensure regulations re-main suited to modern maritime ope-rations.

With ongoing breakthroughs in artificial inte-lligence and robotics, the maritime- industry is witnessing a significant shift toward unmanned and autonomous vesse-ls. As technologies that enable- remote operation or fully se-lf-governing navigation continue to progress, the- vision of ships traversing the seas without onboard cre-ws is transforming from a far-off prospect to an imminent reality. The-se innovations promise valuable advantage-s like enhanced safe-ty through round-the-clock monitoring and optimized efficie-ncy from reduced labor costs. Howeve-r, realizing the full potential of autonomous shipping also introduce-s intricate legal issues that re-quire nuanced consideration. Que-stions regarding accountability, regulation of unmanned traffic, and insurance- responsibilities will nee-d addressed to properly inte-grate emerging autonomous marine- technologies while safe-guarding workers and protecting the e-nvironment.

For example-, deciding responsibility in situations where- accidents involve unmanned ships pre-sents a difficult problem. Unlike re-gular maritime mishaps where human mistake-s frequently play a role, incide-nts involving unmanned vessels may ne-cessitate ree-xamining applicable laws and redistributing accountability betwe-en stakeholders for e-xample ship proprietors, administrators, makers, and programming de-signers. Moreover, matte-rs identified with protection inclusion, following worldwide- guidelines, and cyberse-curity powerlessness ought to like-wise be tende-d to guarantee the she-ltered activity of unmanned ve-ssels. For example, if an unmanne-d ship was hacked which caused an accident, de-termining who is at fault betwee-n the ship operator and software de-signer may require furthe-r investigation of each parties re-sponsibilities. Additionally, insurance policies will ne-ed to be adapted to cove-r accidents involving autonomous vessels. Inte-rnational maritime rules may also nee-d modifications to encompass regulations for unmanned ships. Ove-rall, establishing unambiguous accountability for mishaps involving driverless ships amongst various stake-holders while simultaneously prote-cting vessels from cyber thre-ats is a complex issue without straightforward solutions.

Cyberse-curity dangers pose a important issue in the- digital period of maritime functions. As reliance- on interconnected me-thods and information swap raises, the susceptibility of important maritime- infrastructure to cyber assaults gets cle-ar. Unauthorized entry to operational te-chnologies programs, alteration of digital navigational charts, or interruption of communication ne-tworks can have far achieving outcomes for both prote-ction at sea and the honesty of trade- flows. These cyber risks highlight the- need to adequate-ly shield sensitive syste-ms and defend against online thre-ats. Ports, cargo vessels, and other maritime- entities must strengthe-n cyber protection and routinely e-xamine networks to identify and re-solve vulnerabilities be-fore adversaries can cause- disruptions or security breaches. Additionally, incre-asing crew awareness about cybe-r hazards and training them how to spot suspicious online activity can aid in cyber de-fense. While digitalization de-livers benefits, maritime- sectors must apply appropriate safety me-asures to manage risks introduced by e-xpanded technology use.

Addressing the- cybersecurity dangers in maritime- procedures nece-ssitates a complete lawful structure- that advances data sharing, sets up clear line-s of duty, and enhances collaboration betwe-en stakeholders. This incorporate-s systems for detailing cyber occurre-nces, setting up conventions for e-pisode reaction and recupe-ration, and guaranteeing satisfactory preparing on cybe-rsecurity estimates for sailors and work force- engaged with maritime tasks. Furthe-rmore, it is basic to actualize methodologie-s that upgrade consistent corresponde-nce betwee-n maritime associations and national security offices re-garding digital dangers. Coordinated preparing and instruction on ne-w advances, digital risks, and security counterme-asures can upgrade comprehe-nsion of cybersecurity across the maritime- part. Overall cooperation through open-private- associations is vital to distinguish evolving dangers and share be-st hones for counteractive action and re-action. As the digital condition keeps on e-volving quickly, it is basic that guidelines and systems stay adaptable- and receptive to guarante-e the security, we-llbeing, and productivity of maritime tasks.

Digitalization touches many face-ts of modern life and brings both opportunities and challe-nges. The growing role of digital tools, data analysis, and blockchain in cargo tracking, customs, financial de-alings, and more ushers in legal issue-s that demand nuanced solutions. With such platforms, analytics and technology incre-asingly used for transportation and trade paperwork as we-ll as money management, prote-cting individuals' privacy and securing their information eme-rges as a key priority. Establishing norms for ele-ctronic documentation, records storage, and othe-r cyber aspects involves important discussions around standards and be-st practices. Devising approaches to safe-guard the integrity and legitimacy of digital file-s also warrants prudent reflection give-n risks like tampering, dece-ption, or other malicious acts involving online records. Ove-rall, policymakers and businesses must work to maximize- digitalization's upsides while mitigating any downsides through re-asonable, balanced policies.

When e-xploring the budding legal matters surfacing in the- maritime domain, taking a proactive stance on maritime- law is paramount. It is vital that stakeholders work cooperative-ly to envision and react to forthcoming difficulties in a we-ll-timed manner. This could entail ge-nerating specialized groups or unde-rtaking forces committed to investigating lawful re-sults and suggesting administrative systems particular to unmanne-d vessels, cyberse-curity, and advanced computerization. As new te-chnologies continue to deve-lop and change how we utilize our oce-ans, it is important that our laws and regulations evolve as we-ll to ensure the safe- and responsible deve-lopment of emerging maritime- industries.

Furthermore-, creating understanding and ability inside the- maritime business is extre-mely important. Coaching packages, ongoing instructional efforts, and conve-ntions committed to discussing arising lawful issues will help guarante-e that lawful experts, industry pione-ers, policymakers, and other partne-rs are very much outfitted to e-xplore the advancing scene- of maritime law. Training programs can educate maritime- specialists on the most rece-nt advancements and lawful difficulties looke-d by the business. Progressing instructional me-etings and gatherings give e-xperienced e-xperts chances to remain curre-nt on critical changes and new arrangeme-nts that may influence their work. As maritime-law keeps on creating, it is basic for all include-d to cooperate and share knowle-dge through gatherings dedicate-d to dissecting key lawful issues. This upgrade-d cooperation across the business will assist stake-holders with effective-ly adjusting to shifts and guarantee consistency across locale-s.

To summarize, this portion e-mphasizes keeping up with de-veloping legal matters to maintain ste-p with the quickly transforming maritime business. As re-motely operated ships be-come more widespre-ad, cybersecurity dangers swe-ll in size, and digitization alters maritime proce-dures, modifying lawful structures turns out to be indispe-nsable. By distinguishing conceivable te-sts and recommending technique-s to oversee the-m productively, we can clear a way for a strong and ve-rsatile legitimate frame-work that oversees the- seas of the future. Some- key issues that must be conte-mplated incorporate ensuring the- security of unmanned vesse-ls from digital assaults, guaranteeing responsibility if such a ve-ssel experie-nces an accident without anyone e-lse, and adjusting copyright and information security laws to think about the digitization of docume-ntation and procedures on ships. While change- is unavoidable, careful arrangeme-nt and examination of potential outcomes can guarante-e our maritime legitimate- system stays pertinent and se-cure as innovation advances navigation into the compute-rized period.

Afterthoughts

"The law is not just a guideline but a guiding hand that helps ease the potential for disputes and ease problems between two or more aggrieved parties, don't see it as a bureaucratic burden, but as a firm parent steering you on the correct path"

As we bring our journey through the seas of maritime law to a close, it is worth reflecting on how far our understanding has come and how much still lies ahead. This comprehensive exploration of maritime jurisprudence, from its historical foundations to modern developments, has equipped us with invaluable insights into the evolving landscape of the law governing our oceans.

By unraveling the intricate complexities of issues ranging from international trade to piracy, resource management to environmental protection, we now possess a profound appreciation for both the opportunities and challenges inherent in governing human activities that traverse across political boundaries and jurisdictional lines. The diversity of legal frameworks, authorities, and stakeholders involved necessitates a nuanced approach that balances diverse interests towards cooperation rather than conflict.

Looking towards the future, it is certain that maritime law will continue evolving in response to emerging technologies, political shifts, and societal demands. As climate change inflicts new uncertainties, technologies transform working practices, and geopolitical dynamics rearrange the global order, maritime jurisdictions must adapt nimbly through continuous legal refinement and international dialogue. Only by proactively anticipating and navigating the tides of change can nations ensure the safety and sustainability of maritime endeavors as we voyage forth into uncharted waters.

Throughout our exploration of the intricate oceans of law, one truth has remained constant - together, through cooperation and a shared commitment to lawful norms, we can steer a balanced course towards shared prosperity amidst changing seas. With open minds and a spirit of mutual understanding, the global community holds immense potential to overcome challenges, resolve differences, and safely transport humanity's collective dreams of exploration into tomorrow.

"The future is as bright as the promises of God."

-Queen Nzinga of Ndongo and Matamba

Appendices

****

Glossary of Maritime Legal Terms:

Admiralty Law: Also known as maritime law, admiralty law governs legal issues and disputes that arise from maritime activities, including navigation, shipping, and commerce on the high seas.

Bill of Lading: A document issued by a carrier to acknowledge the receipt of goods for shipment and outlines the terms and conditions of the transportation agreement between the shipper and the carrier.

Flag State: The country under whose laws a vessel is registered and flies its flag. The flag state has jurisdiction over the vessel and is responsible for enforcing maritime regulations.

General Average: A principle in maritime law where all parties involved in a maritime venture contribute proportionately to cover losses incurred for the common benefit, such as expenses for salvage or repairs.

Jones Act: A U.S. federal law that regulates maritime commerce in U.S. waters and supports the protection of U.S. domestic shipping interests by requiring that goods transported between U.S. ports be carried on U.S.-built and U.S.-flagged vessels owned by U.S. citizens.

Laytime: The amount of time allowed for loading or unloading cargo at a port agreed upon between the shipowner and the charterer.

Passage Plan: A navigational plan prepared by the ship's master or officer in charge detailing the intended route, navigational hazards, predicted weather conditions, and other relevant information for a safe passage.

Salvage: The act of rescuing a vessel, cargo, or property from peril at sea, usually undertaken by specialized salvors who are entitled to a reward proportionate to the value of the saved property.

Territorial Waters: The maritime zone extending up to 12 nautical miles from a nation's coastline, over which a state exercises sovereignty and certain exclusive rights, including control over navigation and exploitation of natural resources.

Collision Regulations: International rules to prevent collisions at sea.

Maritime Lien: A security interest in a vessel granting the lien holder the right to take possession of or sell the vessel to recover debts.

Letter of Indemnity: A letter of guarantee issued by a shipper assuming responsibility for lost or damaged cargo.

Cargo Declaration: A document specifying the nature, quantity, weight and value of cargo loaded onboard a vessel.

Master: The commanding officer and highest ranking certified mariner onboard a vessel.

Charter Party: The legal contract that records the agreement between the shipowner and the charterer setting out the terms for the lease of a vessel.

Bareboat Charter: An agreement where the charterer rents the vessel without crew, provisions or fuel from the shipowner.

Time Charter: A common charter agreement where the charterer pays to use the vessel's cargo space for a fixed period of time.

Voyage Charter: A charter contract where the vessel is hired to transport cargo between specified loading and discharging ports.

Demurrage: Compensation paid by the charterer or cargo receiver to the shipowner for delays exceeding the allotted time for loading/unloading.

General Average Bond: A guarantee issued by an average adjuster for the shipper's contribution towards a general average action.

Limitation of Liability: Legal limitations on a shipowner's liability for damage or loss arising from their vessel.

Crew Contract: The agreement signed by seafarers articulating the terms of their employment onboard.

Continuous Discharge Book: An official record maintained for each seafarer listing employment history and qualifications.

Ship Registration: The process of documenting a vessel under the laws and flag of a sovereign state.

Maritime Lien Enforcement: Judicial proceedings to arrest a vessel and force its sale to satisfy unpaid debts.

Arrest of Vessels: A legal procedure allowing creditors to detain ships as security for maritime claims.

Seaworthiness: The legal requirement that a ship and its equipment are fit to face foreseeable perils of the intended voyage.

Maintenance and Cure: The right of seafarers to medical care and living expenses if injured or falling ill while employed.

Unseaworthiness: When a vessel is not reasonably fit for its intended service, exposing crew to unreasonable risks.

Carriage of Goods by Sea Act (COGSA): Governs responsibilities and liabilities of cargo carriers in international trade.

Himalaya Clause: Contractual provision extending defenses and liability limitations to third parties involved in cargo handling.

Notice of Readiness (NOR): Tendered by vessel to advise cargo receivers of arrival and readiness for loading/unloading.

Notice of Protest: A formal notice given when a bill of lading term is violated in order to preserve potential legal recourse.

General Average Adjustment: Calculating proportional contributions after a general average event based on saved and threatened values.

Arrest Warrant: A court order allowing claimants to seize a ship as collateral for unpaid maritime debts.

Maritime Arbitration: Dispute resolution procedure where arguments are presented to a specialized panel instead of a jury.

Suing and Laboring Clause: Obligates shipowners to take proactive measures in response to dangers and unforeseen events.

Deviation: Unapproved departure from the contracted voyage route that may breach the contract of carriage.

ISM Code: The International Safety Management Code establishes safety management objectives and functions for ship operators.

ISPS Code: The International Ship and Port Facility Security Code aims to enhance maritime security.

P&I Club: Protection and indemnity insurance provided by mutual associations that covers third-party liabilities.

Collision: A registered agreement between vessel owners detailing damage responsibilities after a ship collision.

Lloyd's Open Form: Standard clause for resolving cargo insurance claims through arbitration.

BIMCO Clauses: Standard terms published by the Baltic and International Maritime Council for various charter party forms.

New Jason Clause: Contract provision shifting general average liability to cargo receivers.

NYPE Clause: "New York Produce Exchange" charter party form commonly used for bulk shipping contracts.

Supersedeas Bond: Bond posted to suspend enforcement of a judgment during appeal of a maritime case.

Salvage Arbitration: Procedure to determine a salvage reward through expert assessment rather than court litigation.

Please note that this glossary provides only a sample of key terms in maritime law and is not exhaustive. It serves as a starting point for readers to familiarize themselves with the terminology specific to this field of law.

International Treaties
and Conventions:

Maritime law is shaped by a multitude of international treaties and conventions that strive to regulate and govern various aspects of maritime activities. These agreements serve as crucial pillars in ensuring the safety, security, and sustainability of the world's oceans. In this section, we will explore some of the most significant treaties and conventions that have profoundly influenced maritime law.

1. United Nations Convention on the Law of the Sea (UNCLOS):
UNCLOS, often referred to as the "constitution for the oceans," is a landmark treaty that comprehensively addresses all aspects of ocean governance. Adopted in 1982 and entering into force in 1994, UNCLOS outlines the rights and responsibilities of states in their use and management of the world's oceans. It establishes the legal framework for maritime boundaries, navigation, exploitation of marine resources, protection of the marine environment, and settlement of disputes related to maritime matters. UNCLOS provides a framework for peaceful cooperation among nations and plays a fundamental role in shaping contemporary maritime law.

2. International Convention for the Safety of Life at Sea (SOLAS):
SOLAS, first adopted in 1914 and subsequently updated several times, sets minimum safety standards for ships engaged in international voyages. The convention aims to ensure the safety of lives at sea by regulating ship design, construction, equipment, operation, and maintenance. SOLAS covers a wide range of safety measures, including fire protection, lifesaving appliances, navigation systems, emergency procedures, and maintenance of proper communications. It is enforced by flag states through inspections and certifications, with periodic amendments addressing emerging safety concerns.

3. International Convention for the Prevention of Pollution from Ships (MARPOL):
MARPOL, adopted in 1973 and entered into force in 1978, is a global treaty aimed at preventing pollution from ships. It addresses various types of marine pollution caused by operational or accidental discharges of harmful substances such as oil, chemicals, sewage, garbage, and hazardous materials. MARPOL sets strict standards for shipboard equipment, operational procedures, and waste management practices to minimize the impact of shipping activities on the marine environment. The convention is regularly updated to incorporate new regulations and technologies for effective pollution prevention.

4. International Convention on Salvage (LOF):
The International Convention on Salvage, commonly known as LOF (Lloyd's Open Form), provides a legal framework for the compensation and reward system in cases of maritime salvage. It establishes guidelines for salvage operations, including the rights and obligations of salvors and the process for determining salvage awards. The convention aims to encourage prompt and efficient salvage operations while ensuring fair compensation for salvors who rescue vessels or property in distress at sea.

5. International Convention on Civil Liability for Oil Pollution Damage (CLC):
The CLC, adopted in 1969 and revised in 1992, addresses liability and compensation for oil pollution damage caused by tankers. It establishes a regime of strict liability for shipowners and operators, requiring them to maintain insurance or other financial security to cover potential claims arising from oil spills. The convention ensures that victims of oil pollution are adequately compensated and promotes preventive measures to reduce the risk of oil pollution incidents.

These are just a few examples of the myriad treaties and conventions that shape the fabric of maritime law. Other noteworthy agreements include the International Convention on Load Lines (LL), International Regulations for Preventing Collisions at Sea (COLREGs), and International Convention on Tonnage Measurement of Ships (TONNAGE). Each treaty or convention serves a specific purpose, addressing different aspects of maritime activities and contributing to the overall framework of global maritime governance.

Further Reading:
United Nations Convention on the Law of the Sea (UNCLOS) (1982).
International Convention for Safety of Life at Sea (SOLAS) (1914, amended multiple times).
International Convention for the Prevention of Pollution from Ships (MARPOL) (1973/1978).
International Convention on Load Lines (1966).
International Convention for Safe Containers (CSC) (1972).

International Management Code for the Safe Operation of Ships and for Pollution Prevention (ISM Code) (1993).

International Convention on Standard of Training, Certification and Watchkeeping for Seafarers (STCW) (1978, amended in 1995 and 2010).

Guidelines on Cyber Security Onboard Ships, produced by Maritime Safety Committee of International Maritime Organization (IMO MSC.428(98)).

Maritime Labour Convention (2006) of the International Labour Organization.

SOLAS amendments related to long-range identification and tracking (LRIT) of ships (2006).

International Ship and Port Facility Security (ISPS) Code (2002).

Ballast Water Management Convention (2004).

Ship Energy Efficiency Management Plan (SEEMP).

Energy Efficiency Design Index (EEDI) for new ships.

Regional fisheries management organizations (RFMOs).

United Nations Framework Convention on Climate Change (UNFCCC).

International Renewable Energy Agency (IRENA) guidelines on offshore renewable energy projects.

List of Relevant International Bodies:

- International Maritime Organization (IMO): The IMO is the United Nations specialized agency responsible for regulating international shipping and maritime activities. It develops and enforces global regulations to ensure safety, security, and environmental protection in the shipping industry. The IMO also facilitates cooperation among member states and serves as a forum for discussion and decision-making on maritime issues.

- International Chamber of Shipping (ICS): The ICS is the principal international trade association for shipowners and operators. It represents national shipowner associations from around the world, providing a unified voice for the industry. The ICS works closely with the IMO and other international bodies to shape maritime regulations and promote sustainable shipping practices.

- United Nations Commission on International Trade Law (UNCITRAL): UNCITRAL is a body of the United Nations entrusted with harmonizing and modernizing international trade law. It develops model laws, rules, and conventions to facilitate international trade, including those related to maritime commerce. UNCITRAL's work helps create a fair and predictable legal framework for cross-border transactions involving ships and seaborne trade.

- International Labour Organization (ILO): The ILO is a specialized agency of the United Nations focused on labor and employment issues. It sets international labor standards, including those concerning working conditions, wages, and social protection in the maritime sector. The ILO's Maritime Labour Convention establishes comprehensive rights and protections for seafarers worldwide.

- International Maritime Bureau (IMB): The IMB is a specialized division of the International Chamber of Commerce (ICC) dedicated to combating maritime crime. It acts as a focal point for reporting incidents of piracy, armed robbery, and other criminal activities at sea. The IMB works closely with governments, law enforcement agencies, and the shipping industry to enhance maritime security and protect seafarers.

- World Maritime University (WMU): The WMU is a postgraduate educational institution established by the IMO to promote the sustainable development of the maritime industry. It offers advanced degree programs, conducts research, and provides capacity-building initiatives for maritime professionals. The WMU plays a crucial role in shaping the future of maritime law through its academic contributions and fostering global collaboration.

- International Seafarers' Welfare and Assistance Network (ISWAN): ISWAN is an international organization dedicated to improving the welfare of seafarers worldwide. It works with shipping companies, unions, and welfare organizations to address seafarers' social, financial, and emotional needs. ISWAN advocates for better working conditions, provides support services, and raises awareness about seafarers' rights and well-being.

- World Ocean Council (WOC): The WOC is a global industry association focused on sustainability and corporate responsibility in the ocean economy. It brings together stakeholders from various sectors, including shipping, energy, fisheries, and tourism, to develop strategies for marine environmental protection and responsible use of ocean resources. The WOC promotes cooperation between industries and advises policymakers on integrating sustainability principles into maritime activities.

- Center for International Maritime Security (CIMSEC): CIMSEC is a non-profit organization that fosters discussion and research on maritime security issues. It brings together experts, academics, and practitioners to analyze emerging challenges and propose innovative solutions for ensuring maritime safety. CIMSEC publishes articles, organizes conferences, and facilitates networking among stakeholders in the field of maritime security.

(Note: The above descriptions are concise summaries to provide readers with a general understanding of each organization's role in maritime law. For more detailed information, readers are encouraged to refer to the respective organizations' official websites and publications.)

List of NGOs in Maritime Law:

***

This section highlights notable non-governmental organizations (NGOs) that actively engage in maritime law and related issues. These organizations play a pivotal role in advocating for the rights and welfare of seafarers, advancing research and education in maritime law, and shaping policy formulation within the maritime sector. The following NGOs are recognized for their significant contributions:

1. International Seafarers' Welfare and Assistance Network (ISWAN):

The ISWAN is a global organization committed to promoting the well-being of seafarers worldwide. By collaborating with various stakeholders, including shipowners, governments, and welfare organizations, ISWAN provides practical support, advice, and resources to address the social, mental, and physical challenges faced by seafarers.

2. World Ocean Council (WOC):

The WOC is a unique international organization that brings together diverse stakeholders from the ocean business community, including shipping companies, fisheries, renewable energy firms, and tourism operators. The WOC facilitates collaboration among its members to promote sustainable ocean use practices and address marine environmental challenges through innovative initiatives and partnerships.

3. Center for International Maritime Security (CIMSEC):

CIMSEC is a non-partisan think tank that focuses on maritime security issues. Through thought-provoking analysis, forums, and networking opportunities, CIMSEC brings together scholars, practitioners, and experts to enhance understanding of contemporary maritime challenges, including piracy, territorial disputes, and emerging technologies.

4. International Maritime Rescue Federation (IMRF):

The IMRF plays a vital role in improving maritime search and rescue (SAR) capabilities globally. This NGO works closely with SAR organizations worldwide to provide training, knowledge-sharing platforms, and guidance on best practices. The IMRF's efforts aim to ensure effective coordination and cooperation during distress situations at sea, ultimately saving lives.

5. Sea Shepherd Conservation Society:

Sea Shepherd is an international marine wildlife conservation organization known for its direct action campaigns. Their mission is to protect and conserve marine ecosystems by confronting illegal activities, such as illegal fishing, whaling, and habitat destruction. Through their initiatives, Sea Shepherd actively raises awareness and advocates for the well-being of marine wildlife.

6. International Maritime Bureau (IMB):

The IMB, a division of the International Chamber of Commerce (ICC), focuses on combating maritime-related crimes, including piracy, armed robbery, and fraudulent practices. By providing a platform for reporting incidents and sharing information, the IMB contributes to the prevention and suppression of criminal activities in the maritime domain.

7. Maritime Law Association of the United States (MLA):

The MLA is an organization dedicated to advancing the practice and understanding of maritime law within the United States. Comprised of lawyers, judges, academics, and industry professionals, the MLA fosters discussion, research, and education on relevant legal issues through publications, conferences, and networking opportunities.

8. International Transport Workers' Federation (ITF):

The ITF represents over 18 million seafarers and other transportation workers worldwide. As a global federation of trade unions, it works to safeguard the rights, welfare, and fair treatment of transport workers across various sectors. The ITF actively advocates for improved working conditions, fair wages, and access to justice for seafarers.

These NGOs serve as critical stakeholders in shaping maritime law through their advocacy efforts, research initiatives, and active participation in international discussions and conventions. Their collective endeavors contribute significantly to addressing challenges faced by the maritime community and promoting the sustainable use of marine resources

Case Studies
Additional Thoughts

Real Life Case Studies
of Maritime Law
*****

In December 1917, a catastrophic explosion rocked the quiet harbor of Halifax, Canada, forever altering the course of maritime law. At the center of this tragedy was the SS Mont-Blanc, a French cargo ship laden with highly volatile explosives. As fate would have it, the ship collided with another vessel in the busy harbor, sparking a fire that ignited the cargo and triggered an unimaginable blast.

The destruction caused by the SS Mont-Blanc explosion was immediate and devastating. The blast decimated entire neighborhoods, claimed thousands of lives, and left countless others injured and homeless. But beyond the immediate humanitarian crisis, the disaster also raised complex legal questions that demanded resolution.

One of the key legal consequences of this maritime catastrophe was the issue of liability. As investigations into the incident unfolded, it became clear that multiple parties could be held accountable for the immense loss of life and property. The ship's captain and crew were subjected to intense scrutiny, as their actions leading up to the collision came under question. Additionally, authorities examined whether proper safety protocols had been followed and whether other ships in the harbor had contributed to the accident.

Compensation claims emerged as another critical aspect of the legal fallout from the SS Mont-Blanc explosion. Survivors and families of those killed sought restitution for their losses, both material and emotional. The process of determining who should bear financial responsibility for such a large-scale disaster was fraught with complexity and required careful examination of applicable laws and regulations.

Moreover, this case also brought attention to the need for improved safety measures in maritime transportation. The SS Mont-Blanc disaster prompted significant changes in maritime law, leading to stricter regulations on the transportation of dangerous goods and increased enforcement of safety protocols. Lessons learned from this tragic event continue to shape contemporary maritime legislation, ensuring that similar disasters are prevented and that appropriate legal frameworks are in place to address any future incidents.

The SS Mont-Blanc explosion stands as a haunting reminder of the catastrophic consequences that can arise from maritime accidents. It serves as a testament to the enduring significance of the legal principles governing maritime law, as it navigates the complex intersection of human error, accountability, and the preservation of life and property at sea.

The Exxon Valdez Oil Spill: Environmental Catastrophe and Legal Fallout

One of the most notorious maritime disasters in recent history, the 1989 Exxon Valdez oil spill in Prince William Sound, Alaska, stands as a stark reminder of the devastating environmental consequences that can result from human error and negligence. This case study delves into the legal ramifications, environmental impact, and subsequent legal actions and settlements that arose from this catastrophic event.

In the early hours of March 24, 1989, the oil tanker Exxon Valdez, carrying approximately 53 million gallons of crude oil, ran aground on Bligh Reef, leading to a massive oil spill. The magnitude of the spill and its impact on the pristine Alaskan ecosystem were unprecedented. Over the following days and weeks, an estimated 11 million gallons of oil leaked into the waters of Prince William Sound, blanketing over a thousand miles of coastline with thick layers of toxic crude.

The environmental consequences were devastating. The oil spill had a profound impact on wildlife, with countless seabirds, otters, seals, and whales falling victim to the toxic sludge. Fishermen and indigenous communities reliant on the region's rich marine resources were left devastated both economically and culturally.

The legal fallout from the Exxon Valdez oil spill was extensive. Lawsuits were filed against Exxon Shipping Company, alleging negligence, reckless disregard for safety, and a failure to respond appropriately to contain the spill. The legal battles stretched on for years, with complex issues surrounding liability, compensation claims, and punitive damages.

Ultimately, in 1991, a jury awarded $5 billion in punitive damages to the plaintiffs - one of the largest fines ever imposed in a civil case at that time. However, after numerous appeals and reductions in the amount awarded, the final settlement reached by Exxon was significantly less than the original judgment. This case study serves as a sobering example of the difficulties encountered when seeking legal recourse and the challenges in adequately compensating those affected by environmental disasters. The Exxon Valdez oil spill also had far-reaching implications for maritime regulations. It prompted a reevaluation of safety protocols, prevention measures, and emergency response procedures within the shipping industry. The incident led to stricter regulations on tanker design, double-hull requirements, and enhanced spill response capabilities to mitigate the potential damage caused by future accidents.

The legacy of the Exxon Valdez oil spill continues to shape maritime law and environmental policy. It serves as a stark reminder of the need for stringent regulations, responsible corporate practices, and the importance of swift and effective response in the face of environmental catastrophes. The lessons learned from this tragic event have undoubtedly influenced subsequent legal frameworks and efforts to prevent similar incidents from occurring in the future. The Prestige oil spill in 2002 off the coast of Spain remains one of the most significant environmental disasters in maritime history. This section delves into the international response, legal disputes, liability issues, and efforts to mitigate the environmental damage caused by this catastrophic incident.

On November 13, 2002, the single-hull oil tanker Prestige suffered a massive structural failure, resulting in a devastating oil spill in the Atlantic Ocean. The vessel was carrying approximately 77,000 metric tons of heavy fuel oil when it encountered rough seas off the coast of Galicia, Spain. As a result of the structural failure, the tanker began leaking oil, which quickly spread along the Spanish and French shorelines, causing extensive ecological damage.

By examining the Prestige oil spill as a real-life case study, this afterward provides readers with a comprehensive understanding of the complexities surrounding maritime law in the context of environmental disasters. It highlights the importance of international cooperation, legal frameworks, and effective response strategies in addressing and mitigating the environmental impact of such incidents.

The South China Sea Dispute: Territorial Claims and Legal Challenges

The South China Sea dispute is one of the most complex and protracted maritime conflicts in recent history, involving several countries with overlapping territorial claims. This case study explores the legal complexities surrounding maritime boundaries, exclusive economic zones (EEZs), and international arbitration cases related to the dispute.

The South China Sea is a strategically significant region, rich in natural resources, and serving as a crucial passageway for global trade. However, conflicting claims by China, Taiwan, Vietnam, the Philippines, Malaysia, and Brunei have intensified tensions and raised challenging legal questions.

One key issue at the heart of the dispute is the delineation of maritime boundaries and the determination of each country's EEZ. The United Nations Convention on the Law of the Sea (UNCLOS) provides a legal framework for resolving such disputes, but interpretation and implementation have proven to be contentious.

China, based on its historical claims known as the "nine-dash line," asserts that it has sovereignty over almost the entire South China Sea. This claim overlaps with those of other countries in the region, leading to overlapping EEZs and conflicting rights over fishing grounds, oil and gas reserves, and control over strategic islands.

To address these disputes, parties involved have turned to international arbitration cases to seek legal clarity and resolution. In 2013, the Philippines filed a case against China at the Permanent Court of Arbitration (PCA) in The Hague. The Philippines argued that China's claims violated UNCLOS and encroached upon its own EEZ.

In 2016, the PCA issued a landmark ruling in favor of the Philippines, rejecting China's historic rights within the nine-dash line and clarifying the maritime entitlements of features in the South China Sea. However, China refused to recognize or accept the ruling, dismissing it as null and void.

The South China Sea dispute continues to have significant geopolitical implications, with increasing military activities and tensions in the region. It highlights the challenges of balancing maritime claims, ensuring freedom of navigation, and upholding the rule of law in complex territorial disputes.

As this case study demonstrates, resolving maritime conflicts requires a comprehensive understanding of international law, including UNCLOS, and a commitment to peaceful dialogue and negotiation. The South China Sea dispute serves as a poignant reminder of the intricate legal challenges faced by nations seeking to protect their maritime interests while maintaining regional stability.

By examining this case study, readers gain insights into the legal complexities surrounding territorial claims in the South China Sea and the ongoing efforts to find a peaceful resolution through international arbitration.

Maritime Law Summary & Final Thoughts

*****

Remember, Maritime Law, also known as Admiralty Law, is a complex and fascinating area of legal practice that governs disputes and regulations arising on navigable waters. It encompasses a wide range of legal principles, statutes, and international treaties, providing a framework for resolving conflicts in the maritime industry. In this comprehensive guide, we will delve into the historical development, components, jurisdiction, and types of claims that fall under maritime law. So, whether you're involved in shipping, navigation, or private recreational boating, this guide will equip you with the knowledge you need to navigate the intricacies of maritime law.

Admiralty Law, is a specialized legal field that deals with disputes and matters related to shipping, navigation, and maritime trade. It encompasses a broad range of legal principles and regulations that govern activities on navigable waters. Maritime law is an amalgamation of ancient legal theories, modern statutes, contract law, and international treaties. It plays a crucial role in ensuring the smooth functioning of the maritime industry, protecting the rights of parties involved, and resolving conflicts that may arise in this complex sector.

The origins of maritime law can be traced back to ancient civilizations such as the Egyptians and Phoenicians, who engaged in extensive maritime activities. However, the first documented maritime laws are credited to Rhodes, an island in the Mediterranean Sea. The Rhodian Sea Law, referenced in Roman writings, laid the foundation for maritime jurisprudence. As the Roman Empire expanded its influence, maritime law evolved, borrowing heavily from Rhodes' legal principles.

With the rise of seafaring nations like Italy and Spain, the development of maritime law continued, leading to the formulation of their own legal systems. The influence of English admiralty court law became significant during the expansion of the British Empire. The United States, heavily influenced by English law, also incorporated maritime law into its legal framework. Maritime law has since evolved, adapting to the changing needs of the maritime industry and international trade.

Maritime law encompasses various components that regulate different aspects of maritime activities. These components include maritime liens, shipping charters, limitation of liability, collision liability, salvage and general average, and marine insurance.

Maritime liens are legal claims against a vessel or its cargo for debts related to maritime transactions. These liens provide security to creditors and ensure their priority in case of default or non-payment. Maritime liens can arise from services rendered, damage caused, or wages owed to crew members.

Shipping charters are agreements that outline the terms and conditions for the use of a vessel. These agreements can be time charters, voyage charters, or bareboat charters. Time charters involve the use of a vessel for a specified period, voyage charters for a particular journey, and bareboat charters where the charterer assumes full control and responsibility for the vessel.

The limitation of liability is a legal principle that limits the liability of shipowners and other maritime entities in case of accidents or incidents. It allows them to restrict their liability to the value of the vessel or the cargo involved. This principle encourages investment in maritime activities while ensuring fair compensation for victims.

Collision liability refers to the legal responsibility of shipowners and operators for damages caused by collisions at sea. It includes collisions between vessels, as well as collisions with fixed structures like piers or bridges. Collision liability is determined based on factors such as negligence, fault, and the application of international maritime conventions.

Salvage and general average are concepts that deal with the recovery of vessels and the distribution of costs among parties involved in a maritime emergency. Salvage involves the rescue and preservation of vessels or cargo in distress, while general average refers to the proportional sharing of losses incurred during a voluntary sacrifice to save a vessel or cargo.

Marine insurance provides coverage for risks associated with maritime activities, including damage to vessels, cargo, and liability arising from maritime operations. It plays a crucial role in mitigating financial losses and ensuring the smooth functioning of the maritime industry.

Maritime law is not limited to national jurisdictions but also encompasses international regulation. International treaties and conventions play a significant role in harmonizing laws and regulations across different countries. The United Nations Convention on the Law of the Sea (UNCLOS) is a comprehensive international agreement that governs various aspects of maritime activities, including territorial waters, navigation rights, and the exploitation of marine resources.

The International Maritime Organization (IMO) is a specialized agency of the United Nations responsible for developing and implementing international maritime regulations. The IMO sets standards for safety, security, environmental protection, and the efficient operation of vessels. Its conventions, such as the International Convention for the Safety of Life at Sea (SOLAS) and the International Convention for the Prevention of Pollution from Ships (MARPOL), have been adopted globally to ensure the uniformity of maritime regulations.

The jurisdiction and applicability of maritime law depend on the concept of navigable waters and territorial jurisdiction. In the United States, maritime law applies to occurrences on navigable waters, which include waters used for trade, travel, or commerce between states or foreign nations. Navigable waters encompass not only the high seas but also harbors, bays, inlets, and rivers that connect different states or nations.

However, if a body of water is entirely contained within one state, such as a lake, federal admiralty jurisdiction does not apply. Each country has its own definition of territorial waters, which are subject to its jurisdiction and control. The concept of an exclusive economic zone allows countries to exercise control over natural resources in a zone extending up to 200 miles from their coastlines.

Maritime law covers a wide range of claims and disputes that arise in the maritime industry. These claims can involve shipping accidents, oil spills, injuries to seamen or passengers, criminal activities such as piracy, salvage and towage contracts, liens and mortgages on ships, and insurance issues.

Shipping accidents can result in significant damage to vessels, cargo, and the environment. Maritime law provides mechanisms for investigating and compensating for such accidents. Oil spills, whether caused by accidents or intentional acts, can have severe environmental and economic consequences. Maritime law imposes liability and establishes procedures for cleaning up and compensating for oil spills.

Injuries to seamen or passengers on vessels fall under the purview of maritime law. Seamen, who work on vessels, have specific legal protections under the Jones Act, which provides remedies for injuries caused by negligence or unseaworthiness. Passengers on cruise ships are also protected by maritime law, with specific regulations governing their rights and liabilities.

Maritime law addresses criminal activities such as piracy, which pose a threat to the safety and security of vessels and their crews. It provides mechanisms for prosecuting and punishing individuals involved in piracy or other criminal acts at sea. Salvage and towage contracts involve the recovery and transportation of vessels or cargo in distress, with maritime law governing the rights and obligations of the parties involved.

Liens and mortgages on ships are important aspects of maritime law, ensuring the security of creditors. These legal mechanisms allow creditors to claim debts owed by vessel owners and provide a means for enforcing payment. Insurance issues, including marine insurance, play a vital role in managing risks and ensuring financial protection in the maritime industry.

When disputes arise under maritime law, it is essential to consider the appropriate court for resolving the matter. According to Article III Section 2 of the United States Constitution, jurisdiction is reserved for federal courts. Certain maritime claims can only be tried in federal court, such as those involving the enforcement of mortgages or liens, or those seeking to partition ownership of a vessel. Claims seeking to limit liability after a major accident to the value of the ship are also exclusively heard in federal court.

However, the "saving to suitors" clause allows certain cases to be brought in state court if they also involve state common law tort claims. In such cases, federal law must still be applied. The choice between federal and state court may depend on various factors, including the nature of the claim, the parties involved, and strategic considerations. It is crucial to seek counsel from experienced maritime lawyers to navigate the complexities of jurisdiction and choose the appropriate court for your case.

The flag state of a vessel plays a crucial role in determining the laws that apply to the ship and its crew. The flag state refers to the country under whose flag the ship is registered. The principle of flag state jurisdiction establishes that the laws and regulations of the flag state govern the vessel while it is at sea. For example, a ship flying a Panamanian flag in U.S. waters would generally be subject to Panamanian admiralty law.

The flag state's laws cover various aspects, including safety regulations, crew qualifications, environmental standards, and liability. However, there are instances where exceptions to this general rule apply. International treaties and conventions may impose additional obligations on vessels regardless of their flag state. Therefore, it is essential to consider both flag state laws and international regulations when dealing with maritime issues.

Cruise ship passengers enjoy certain rights and protections under maritime law. When booking a cruise, passengers enter into a contractual relationship with the cruise line, which establishes the terms and conditions for their voyage. These terms often include provisions regarding liability, jurisdiction, and dispute resolution. Maritime law provides remedies for passengers in cases of injury, illness, negligence, or breach of contract by the cruise line.

Passengers who suffer injuries or illnesses during their cruise may be eligible for compensation based on maritime law principles, such as the duty of care owed by the cruise line. Claims may arise from slip and falls, food poisoning, medical negligence, or accidents during onshore excursions. It is crucial for passengers to understand their rights and obligations under maritime law and seek legal counsel if they believe they have a valid claim.

Boating accidents, whether involving private recreational vessels or commercial boats, fall under the purview of maritime law. The principles of negligence, liability, and compensation apply to individuals involved in boating accidents. Maritime law provides a framework for investigating accidents, determining liability, and compensating victims for their injuries and property damage.

When a boating accident occurs, it is essential to gather evidence, report the incident to the appropriate authorities, and seek medical attention for any injuries. Consulting with experienced maritime lawyers can help navigate the legal complexities and ensure that your rights are protected. Time limits may apply to filing claims, so prompt action is crucial in boating accident cases.

Given the intricate nature of maritime law and the multitude of legal principles and regulations involved, seeking legal counsel experienced in maritime law is crucial. Maritime lawyers specialize in this unique field and possess the knowledge and expertise to handle complex maritime disputes and claims.

Experienced maritime lawyers can provide guidance on jurisdictional issues, help choose the appropriate court, navigate international regulations, and ensure compliance with maritime laws. They can evaluate the merits of a claim, gather evidence, negotiate settlements, and, if necessary, represent clients in court proceedings.

Whether you are a shipowner, crew member, passenger, or involved in maritime trade, having the right legal representation is essential to protect your rights and interests. Maritime lawyers can provide comprehensive advice and advocate for your best interests in the complex realm of maritime law.

Maritime law, with its rich history and intricate legal framework, plays a vital role in regulating shipping, navigation, and maritime trade. It encompasses a wide range of legal principles, statutes, and international treaties that govern various aspects of the maritime industry. From maritime liens and shipping charters to collision liability and marine insurance, maritime law provides a robust framework for resolving disputes and ensuring the smooth operation of maritime activities.

Understanding the components of maritime law, jurisdictional considerations, and the types of claims that fall under its purview is crucial for all stakeholders in the maritime industry. Whether you are a shipowner, seafarer, passenger, or victim of a maritime accident, seeking legal counsel experienced in maritime law is essential to protect your rights and navigate the complexities of this specialized field.

Navigating the vast seas of maritime law can be challenging, but with the right legal guidance, you can sail smoothly through legal disputes and ensure a fair resolution. Remember, maritime law is a multifaceted discipline that requires expertise and experience to navigate successfully. So, if you find yourself in need of legal assistance in maritime matters, don't hesitate to consult with knowledgeable maritime lawyers who can help you chart a course towards a favorable outcome.

"The sea, once it casts its spell, holds one in its net of wonder forever." - Jacques Cousteau

www.ingramcontent.com/pod-product-compliance
Lightning Source LLC
Chambersburg PA
CBHW080849120626
46546CB00008B/2755